SAP PRESS e-books

Print or e-book, Kindle or iPad, workplace or airplane: Choose where and how to read your SAP PRESS books! You can now get all our titles as e-books, too:

- By download and online access
- For all popular devices
- And, of course, DRM-free

Convinced? Then go to www.sap-press.com and get your e-book today.

SAP° Sales Cloud

SAP PRESS is a joint initiative of SAP and Rheinwerk Publishing. The know-how offered by SAP specialists combined with the expertise of Rheinwerk Publishing offers the reader expert books in the field. SAP PRESS features first-hand information and expert advice, and provides useful skills for professional decision-making.

SAP PRESS offers a variety of books on technical and business-related topics for the SAP user. For further information, please visit our website: *www.sap-press.com*.

Singh, Feurer, Ruebsam
SAP Hybris: Commerce, Marketing, Sales, Service, and Revenue with SAP
2017, 329 pages, hardcover and e-book
www.sap-press.com/4394

Chudy, Castedo, Lopez
Sales and Distribution in SAP ERP: Business User Guide (3rd Edition)
2018, 518 pages, hardcover and e-book
www.sap-press.com/4526

Ricardo Lopez, Ashish Mohapatra
Configuring Sales and Distribution in SAP ERP (2nd Edition)
2016, 526 pages, hardcover and e-book
www.sap-press.com/3903

Chandrakant Agarwal
SAP CRM: Business Processes and Configuration
2015, 737 pages, hardcover and e-book
www.sap-press.com/3648

Sanjjeev K. Singh, Karan Sood

SAP® Sales Cloud

Sales Force Automation with SAP C/4HANA®

Rheinwerk
Publishing

Editor Meagan White

Acquisitions Editor Emily Nicholls

Copyeditor Julie McNamee

Cover Design Graham Geary

Photo Credit Shutterstock.com/273427379/© Olivier Le Moal

Layout Design Vera Brauner

Production Hannah Lane

Typesetting III-Satz, Husby (Germany)

Printed and bound in the United States of America, on paper from sustainable sources

ISBN 978-1-4932-1528-7

© 2018 by Rheinwerk Publishing, Inc., Boston (MA)

1st edition 2018

Library of Congress Cataloging-in-Publication Data

Names: Singh, Sanjjeev K., author. | Sood, Karan, 1979- author.

Title: SAP Sales Cloud : Sales Force Automation with SAP C/4HANA /
   Sanjjeev K. Singh, Karan Sood.

Description: 1st edition. | Bonn ; Boston : SAP Press ; Rheinwerk Publishing, 2018. | Includes index.

Identifiers: LCCN 2018001347 (print) | LCCN 2018026724 (ebook) | ISBN 9781493215294 (ebook) |
   ISBN 9781493215287 (alk. paper)

Subjects: LCSH: SAP ERP. | Selling--Data processing. | Sales management--Computer programs.

Classification: LCC HF5438.35 (ebook) | LCC HF5438.35 .S554 2018 (print) |
   DDC 658.8/100028553--dc23

LC record available at https://lccn.loc.gov/2018001347

Contents at a Glance

Dear Reader,

Most of us have some experience with sales, whether it was selling cookies as a Girl Scout, showing off catalogs of flower bulbs or wrapping paper to fund a field trip, or getting businesses to advertise in the playbill for a high-school theatre performance. Though the scale was small, we had to think about all the same things as a sales-based company:

- *Where are my opportunities and leads going to come from?* I recall that Calvin in my mom's office was always a good bet for Thin Mints, year after year.
- *What's my territory?* Has another student on my block already filled my neighbors' wrapping paper needs?
- *How do I give them a quote for cost?* Don't forget the discount for a full page ad in the playbill vs. a half-page ad!

On a larger scale, you need a system to help you manage your sales processes. Enter SAP Sales Cloud, and our guide to it! Expert authors Sanjjeev K. Singh and Karan Sood have provided you with the step-by-step instructions, screenshots, and detailed explanations you need to get your system up and running.

What did you think about *SAP Sales Cloud: Sales Force Automation with SAP C/4HANA*? Your comments and suggestions are the most useful tools to help us make our books the best they can be. Please feel free to contact me and share any praise or criticism you may have.

Thank you for purchasing a book from SAP PRESS!

Meagan White
Editor, SAP PRESS

meaganw@rheinwerk-publishing.com
www.sap-press.com
Rheinwerk Publishing · Boston, MA

Contents

3   Organization Management   59

4   Account and Contact Management   75

8   Activity Management

9   Partner Channel Management

10   Quotation Management

271

14   Account 360 and Sales Intelligence   371

15   Sales Reports and Dashboards   387

16   Integration   407

17 Data Migration and Replication

18 Personalization and Extensions   469

Appendices   497

Foreword

Customer relationship management (CRM) has evolved and developed into a multilevel application that drives sales force automation. Next-generation CRM is changing the priority of application development to an integrated ecosystem of applications that drive internal and external customer experience.

Internet of Things initiatives are rapidly changing business models. Driven by machine learning and artificial intelligence built on next-generation databases, these initiatives allow for organizations to be more agile and aggressive with their go-to-market strategies. The term *digital transformation* has multiple definitions, depending on the organization or the individual. While we have given attention and priority to the digital conversation, the questions we face now include:

- How will organizations execute their commercial objectives and what is the role of digital transformation?
- Are these goals conceptual or physical?
- Are they provocative in terms of augmenting and disrupting commercial strategy or are they applications that enable fundamental commercial sales and service processes (such as blockchain)?

The introduction of SAP C/4HANA demonstrates a digital transformation that continues today. The portfolio, back when it was SAP Hybris, originally consisted of just e-commerce processes. Later, SAP added traditional sales and service CRM processes from the SAP Cloud for Customer portfolio. The SAP Hybris suite of sales, service, marketing, and commerce enabled fundamental sales, service, and marketing processes. However, that alone was not sufficient. The SAP C/4HANA ecosystem provides an integrated suite of applications that drives the next level of sales force automation (SFA) with SAP S/4HANA and SAP HANA, accelerating and enhancing processes that enable next-generation selling.

SAP's acquisition of Recast AI and Callidus Cloud will not only strengthen but deliver a more complete SFA ecosystem, bringing in RPA, CPQ, SPM, and mature offline/online service capabilities. There is no doubt that these applications deliver more enhanced sales, service, and marketing use cases. The SAP C/4HANA suite promises to deliver even more unique use cases. Customers today consider disruptive enablement to augment go-to-market strategies in an agile fashion. Their expectation of the application layer is to provide agile and nimble characteristics while maintaining steady, stable, and seamless governance in the application ecosystem.

As SAP C/4HANA continues transform into a next-level SFA platform, SAP is driving the acceleration of functional application technology capabilities in HR, supply chain, and more, which will converge and enable agility throughout your organization to drive commercial value realization.

The authors of this book, Sanjjeev K. Singh (managing partner at ASAR America, Inc.) and Karan Sood (global vice president of product development at SAP) are true veterans and pioneers in the SAP C/4HANA domain, with contributions that drove significant change and evolution to the portfolio. This book contains the concise and succinct content that will enable readers to understand the portfolio in a seamless and fundamental way, synonymous with the internal and external customer experience delivered by the SAP C/4HANA portfolio.

Naveen Kandasami
Executive Director, SealedAir

Preface

Welcome to the first edition of *SAP Sales Cloud: Sales Force Automation with SAP C/4HANA*. Although there are five district solution areas within SAP C/4HANA (SAP Sales Cloud, SAP Marketing, SAP Commerce Cloud, SAP Service Cloud, and SAP Customer Data Cloud), here we focus on SAP Sales Cloud.

In this book, we'll provide insights on the key capabilities of SAP Sales Cloud, business process, and (most importantly) the configuration steps for these processes. SAP Sales Cloud is a sales solution offered by SAP in the public cloud. SAP adds new capabilities to the SAP Sales Cloud application every quarter, and the release cycles follow the YYMM naming convention (two digits for year and two digits for month, i.e., 1709). This book is based on SAP Sales Cloud release 1805, the latest available release at the time of publication. With each new release, SAP adds new features and capabilities to keep this product at the forefront of cloud-based sales solutions available in the market. This book will provide the foundational knowledge and ready reference needed to implement SAP Sales Cloud for any organization, regardless of size or industry. This book can serve as your first source of information for sales processes and configuration details for SAP Sales Cloud solution.

Who Is This Book For?

This book is for anyone interested in learning about the sales solutions available within the SAP C/4HANA portfolio. SAP partners, consultants, business subject matter experts, business analysts, and application administrators will find this book extremely helpful as they prepare to implement SAP Sales Cloud in their organizations. You don't need any prerequisite knowledge to read this book, as all the technical details included in this book are limited to configuring and setting up SAP Sales Cloud. We have not included any programming or enhancement details in this book.

How This Book Is Organized

This book is organized around sales business functions and how SAP Sales Cloud solution is aligned with each of these functions. We start with how to get started and scope SAP Sales Cloud, with chapters covering each key capability, such as organization management, account and contact management, territory management, lead, activity, opportunity, quotation, orders, and more. We then explore reporting and dashboards, integration, data migration, and replication to help readers understand the tools available in SAP Sales Cloud so you may get the most out of your system. Finally, we'll provide the details on personalization and extensions capabilities available in SAP Sales Cloud.

If you are familiar with SAP Cloud for Customer, then you can jump into any chapter and easily follow the instructions. If you're new to SAP Cloud for Customer or SAP Sales Cloud, then it's recommended that you begin with Chapter 1. Let's preview each chapter here:

- **Chapter 1:** This chapter provides a glance at getting started with SAP Sales Cloud. Here we review the CRM story; past, present, and future trends; and an introduction to SAP Sales Cloud. When you plan to implement any software solution, it's important to take the technical and project considerations into account. Here, we'll provide an overview of licensing, system requirements, user management, project planning, scoping, data management, training and change management, go-live, and administration.

- **Chapter 2:** This chapter focuses on scoping SAP Sales Cloud per your business requirements. SAP Sales Cloud provides a guided process to scope your solution. In this chapter, we provide step-by-step instructions on how to scope your solution for various sales processes in SAP Sales Cloud: account and activity management, products, opportunities, sales quotes and sales orders, lead management, sales planning, master data, and analytics.

- **Chapter 3:** In this chapter, we'll explore organization management in SAP Sales Cloud. Along with explaining the organization management process, we'll walk through the steps to setup organization structure and assign employees to organization units.

- **Chapter 4:** This chapter is focused on account and contact management. In this chapter, we'll introduce account and contract management in SAP Sales Cloud. We'll provide step-by-step instructions on how to create accounts and contacts in SAP Sales Cloud. We'll walk you through information you can maintain for accounts and contacts and how they influence other sales processes. Finally, we'll go over the configuration steps for accounts and contacts.

- **Chapter 5:** In this chapter, we'll cover territory management. Starting with that territory management process in SAP Sales Cloud, we'll provide details on how territories are created and processed, setting up territory hierarchy, using territory rules, and how territory data is used in transactions.

- **Chapter 6:** This chapter is dedicated to lead management, one of the foundational sales functionalities. Here, we'll cover the lead management process and provide you step-by-steps instructions on how leads are created and processed. We'll also provide configuration related details on lead management in SAP Sales Cloud.

- **Chapter 7:** In this chapter, we'll cover another foundational sales process: opportunity management. We'll provide an overview of opportunity management process in SAP Sales Cloud and walk you through the steps to create and process opportunities, including their key capabilities. Finally, we'll provide configuration options available in SAP Sales Cloud for opportunity management to achieve unique processes and business requirements.

- **Chapter 8:** In this chapter, we outline the activity management process and provide steps to create and process various types of activities, like appointments, phone calls, emails, and tasks. We'll also provide details on follow-up processes from activities and step-by-step instructions on how activities are configured in SAP Sales Cloud.

- **Chapter 9:** In this chapter on partner channel management, we'll provide details on the partner registration process and the partner portal, including the partner program, partner marketing, partner sales, and partner activities. We also cover deal registration, deal processing, and the deal follow-up processes.

- **Chapter 10:** This chapter on quotation management provides an overview of the quotation management process in SAP Sales Cloud. We provide step-by-step instructions on how to create and process quotations and the follow-up processes from quotations. Along with the details on configuring quotations in SAP Sales Cloud, we also provide details on integrating quotes with SAP ERP and options to price quotes natively within SAP Sales Cloud or from SAP ERP.

- **Chapter 11:** Similar to quotations in previous chapter, in Chapter 11 we provide details on the order management capabilities of SAP Sales Cloud. We'll walk you through key capabilities of sales orders and how they are created and processed. We'll also provide configuration details, integration to SAP ERP, and pricing options for sales orders in SAP Sales Cloud.

- **Chapter 12:** In this chapter on visit planning and execution, we'll review the visit planning and execution capabilities available in SAP Sales Cloud. Along with configuration steps for visits, we'll also introduce retail execution capability available in SAP Sales Cloud.

- **Chapter 13:** This chapter focuses on sales planning and forecasting capabilities in SAP Sales Cloud. Here, we'll walk you through the sales planning process and the step-by-step instructions on how sales plans and sales forecasts are created, along with configuration steps.

- **Chapter 14:** This chapter on account 360 and sales intelligence includes details on account 360, the account SAP ERP customer cockpit, the customer factsheet, and their configuration steps.

- **Chapter 15:** In this chapter on sales reports and dashboards, we'll introduce you to the standard and custom reports available in SAP Sales Cloud and how to configure reports and dashboards as per your business requirements.

- **Chapter 16:** This chapter is dedicated to integration. Here, we'll cover key integrations between SAP Sales Cloud and external systems along with their configuration steps. These integrations include SAP ERP, SAP CRM, Microsoft Outlook, Lotus Notes, and third-party cloud solutions. We also briefly cover the technologies available for integration such as SAP Cloud Platform Integration and SAP Process Integration.

- **Chapter 17:** In this chapter on data migration and replication, we'll provide you steps for configuring data integration and maintenance, including data upload, mass data maintenance, employee data migration, migrating products, migrating account hierarchies, and uploading territories.

- **Chapter 18:** This last chapter is dedicated to personalization and extensions. Here, we'll cover adapting user interface, extension fields, page layout, code list restrictions, custom forms, master template maintenance, smart phone layout, and how to adjust sections within item details.

Conclusion

Reading this book will provide you with the knowledge and technical details of SAP Sales Cloud that you need to take on any SAP Sales Cloud implementation. This book will serve as your guiding source for SAP Sales Cloud, and you can build upon your knowledge with SAP C/4HANA training and additional resources available from SAP. With that, let's begin with our first chapter: getting started with SAP Sales Cloud.

Chapter 1
Getting Started with SAP Sales Cloud

To take full advantage of your SAP Cloud for Customer system, it's extremely important that you understand the overall SAP C/4HANA product family, what is included in your SAP Sales Cloud license, and how to approach your implementation.

Welcome to this book on SAP Sales Cloud. Before we start explaining the unique capabilities of SAP Sales Cloud and how it can benefit your organization, we'll review a brief history of the customer relationship management (CRM) story, where it started, and where it's headed. In that backdrop, we introduce you to the SAP C/4HANA portfolio of products and especially SAP Sales Cloud. Next, we'll introduce you to the technical considerations of SAP Sales Cloud, such as licensing, system landscape and software requirements, and user management.

As you prepare to embark on the journey to migrate your sales team to SAP Sales Cloud, it's extremely important that you take into consideration some of the success factors related to project planning and scoping exercises. In this chapter, we review some of the critical components of successful project planning, including project scoping, teamwork, business workshops, data hygiene, training or change management, go-live, and administration.

1.1 Customer Relationship Management: Past, Present, and Future

The term "customer relationship management" (CRM) was coined in 1995 has evolved since then in its meaning and dimensions. You can get as many definitions of CRM as the number of CRM vendors, but the fact remains that the CRM market has been constantly evolving. A long cherished goal of those in CRM is to provide salespeople with the information they need about the customer from different sources and platforms to close deals faster. One recent survey found that there are more than

400 million people whose jobs are to talk to customers in business, and fewer than 30 million commercial seats (i.e., computers) of CRM have been sold so far. This clearly shows the potential the industry holds as CRM adoption is less than 10% of the overall size of the market. This will only fuel the evolution of CRM software beyond imagination.

CRM systems have evolved from merely data entry systems to artificially intelligent pieces of software. When a formal CRM system hit the market in late 1990s, it was focused on automating sales processes. During this time, collaboration between organizations began to take place as CRM became mobile enabled. By the year 2000, CRM systems evolved to become a tool for organizations to manage all customer relationships and analyze customer interactions and data throughout the customer lifecycle. Then came the cloud-based CRM systems, which offer a ready-to-use system for organizations of all sizes to get up and running. Although functional capabilities available within CRM applications are more or less the same from most of the leading providers, the key differentiator is the capability to integrate with internal and external systems through standard interfaces.

Let's look at some of the latest trends in the CRM marketplace. First, artificial intelligence (AI) technology is the most prominent enhancement to CRM applications. The personalized workflow automation through AI will define new dimensions for CRM applications and the value it derives for sales reps and sales managers. AI (also called machine learning) will enable CRM systems to learn from every customer interaction through data, help you find answers to your questions, predict customer needs, and, most importantly, take care of mundane and forgotten tasks so that you can focus on important tasks. AI will also reduce manual work by creating automatic actions to better suit your usage patterns. Using an AI-powered CRM system, you can collect information on a lead or an existing customer, analyze the data, predict trends, and make critical decisions that will reduce the number of cold calls for sales reps.

Secondly, social media is transitioning into social CRM. Interactions through service bots in social networking sites will keep customers engaged with brands and companies because they can influence a company's image and perception. Social CRM will not only engage and interact with existing and potential customers but also give organizations access to information about customer behavior and opinions. Social media integration with CRM systems allows businesses to better anticipate and respond to their customers' needs, as well as monitor, track, and manage conversations.

The capability for CRM to integrate with external tools and services is no longer optional but is now a necessity. Representational State Transfer (REST)-based application programming interfaces (APIs) are the key to successful collaboration by allowing systems to easily communicate with one another securely. The future CRM systems need to use information from various internal and external tightly integrated sources, including social media, communication frequency, and customer analytics, to generate meaningful and insightful intelligence.

Lastly, future CRM will drive personalization and individualized customer experiences. CRM is still crucial for reaching customers through messaging, but it has to enable businesses to reach the right audience exactly where and when they need to receive the message. Through social media integrations, organizations already know the demographics and other valuable user information, so they can identify potential market segments, as well as track traffic and sales patterns to personalize messages to customers based on this information.

With all these latest trends in CRM, one thing is for sure: use cases for new CRM applications are only limited by your imagination.

SAP's journey with CRM started with the on-premise version of SAP Customer Relationship Management (SAP CRM) in the late nineties. SAP CRM provided very robust capabilities around sales, service, and marketing and across all three channels of field (mobile), interaction center, and e-commerce. However, SAP CRM lacked user experience compared to contemporary cloud-based CRM applications with modern user interfaces (UIs). Most importantly, SAP CRM didn't allow changes to be made to the UI and end-user personalization without programmatically altering the codes. Realizing the bottlenecks in the on-premise SAP CRM application, SAP released its modern CRM application called SAP Cloud for Customer.

Since the launch of SAP Cloud for Customer, SAP has been bringing new releases to the market every quarter with broader and deeper functionalities, business processes, and industry best practices. SAP Cloud for Customer is marketed as SAP Sales Cloud and SAP Service Cloud. With SAP Cloud for Customer, SAP has again established itself as a leader in the CRM marketplace. With the recent acquisition of Callidus and inclusion of machine learning in SAP Cloud for Customer, SAP Cloud for Customer has emerged as the best CRM software on the market by far at the time of this writing.

In the next section, you'll learn about SAP Sales Cloud, which is the most comprehensive and futuristic CRM solution available today.

1.2   Introducing SAP C/4HANA and SAP Sales Cloud

SAP C/4HANA is a portfolio of products to help you engage with your customers like never before. The SAP C/4HANA portfolio includes solutions for five lines of business: SAP Sales Cloud, SAP Service Cloud, SAP Commerce Cloud, SAP Marketing Cloud, and SAP Customer Data Cloud (see Figure 1.1).

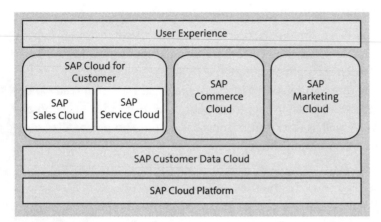

Figure 1.1 SAP Portfolio of Products

Although all of these solutions except SAP Sales Cloud are outside the scope of this book, we want to briefly introduce you to these components of the SAP C/4HANA solution as follows:

- **SAP Service Cloud**
  SAP Service Cloud offers cloud-based customer service and field service solutions. It enables a consistent experience across all channels, access to complete and contextual customer information, and real-time insight into call center performance and field service management.

- **SAP Marketing Cloud**
  SAP Marketing Cloud allows marketers to gain customer insights by using advanced analytics such as machine learning algorithms to understand real-time customer intent and interests. It's designed to deliver an in-the-moment customer experience to increase customer satisfaction and loyalty. It offers out-of-the-box integration with SAP Sales Cloud and SAP Service Cloud.

- **SAP Commerce Cloud**
  SAP Commerce Cloud drives digital transformation and enables you to become an omni-channel business, delivering contextual customer experiences and unifying

customer processes. SAP Commerce Cloud provides support from the SAP operations staff to ensure that your commerce site is up and running, optimized for the
best customer experience, and functioning properly 24/7.

- **SAP Customer Data Cloud**
  SAP Customer Data Cloud helps you securely identify consumers across devices
  and channels to drive registrations and engagement, manage permissions and
  consent, and transform data into unified customer profiles that are governed,
  orchestrated and analyzed from a central and secure environment.

This book is dedicated to the sales force automation functionality within SAP Sales
Cloud. Throughout the book, when we refer to SAP Cloud for Customer, you can
assume that statement applies to SAP Sales Cloud.

SAP Sales Cloud is a public cloud solution that is constantly enriched by SAP through
quarterly releases. This ready-to-use CRM system is built on the SAP Cloud Platform,
and, most importantly, it offers out-of-the-box integration with SAP CRM, SAP ERP,
and productivity tools such as Microsoft Outlook, Microsoft Excel, and Lotus Notes.
The modern SAP Fiori-based responsive user interface (RUI), as shown in Figure 1.2,
allows you to use SAP Sales Cloud applications from desktops as well as mobile devices
with a similar user experience.

Figure 1.2 SAP Fiori-Based RUI

You can choose from hundreds of standard reports and dashboards delivered with SAP Cloud for Customer to meet your business reporting requirements. Although we'll cover all the features of SAP Cloud for Customer later in this book, following are its key capabilities:

- Account and contact management
- Organization management
- Territory management
- Activity management
- Lead management
- Opportunity management
- Quotation management
- Sales order management
- Standard integration with SAP backend and other cloud solutions
- Reports and dashboards

1.3   Technical Considerations

While implementing SAP Cloud for Customer, you need to take into account the technical considerations for integrating with external systems either on premise or in the cloud. If you're running SAP ERP as your backend application, you might want to integrate your SAP Cloud for Customer instance with the backend SAP ERP system. Integration of SAP Cloud for Customer with SAP ERP using SAP middleware is used to exchange both master data and transactional data. Most of the communication is bidirectional, and automated replication that is mediated by the SAP middleware system is particularly for mapping purposes. You can control what master data and transaction data is replicated between the two systems.

SAP offers SAP Cloud Platform Integration as a cloud-based middleware platform to integrate your SAP Cloud for Customer system with SAP and non-SAP external systems.

In addition to integration with your backend SAP ERP system, you also might want to evaluate integration with other legacy applications. With RESTful APIs, it's much easier to implement SAP Cloud for Customer with most of the latest on-premise and cloud applications.

With this background on the technical considerations for SAP Sales Cloud, we'll next review the licensing options for SAP Sales Cloud, system landscape and software requirements, and user management.

1.3.1   Licensing

SAP offers three options for licensing SAP Sales Cloud, as follows:

- Standard edition
- Professional edition
- Enterprise edition

Be sure to pay close attention to which components are included in these editions so that you can determine which edition to license. You should visit *www.sap.com* or talk to your SAP rep or SAP Partner for more details on SAP Cloud for Customer licensing options. Table 1.1 compares the functionality available with the different editions of SAP Sales Cloud, however, you should check with SAP before licensing SAP Sales Cloud.

Sales Capability	Standard Edition	Professional Edition	Enterprise Edition
Account and contacts, persons	Yes	Yes	Yes
Lead management and opportunity management	Yes	Yes	Yes
Activity management and visit management	Yes	Yes	Yes
Collaboration and feeds	Yes	Yes	Yes
Sales analytics	Yes	Yes	Yes
Groupware integration (client side)	Yes	Yes	Yes
Mobility	Yes	Yes	Yes
Surveys	Yes	Yes	Yes
Sales target planning	Yes	Yes	Yes
Price and discount lists	Yes	Yes	Yes
Quotation management	Yes	Yes	Yes
Integration APIs	Yes	Yes	Yes
Territory management	Yes	Yes	Yes

Table 1.1 SAP Sales Cloud Licensing Options

Sales Capability	Standard Edition	Professional Edition	Enterprise Edition
Sales forecasting	Yes	Yes	Yes
Service tickets		Yes	Yes
Buying center		Yes	Yes
Route planning and execution		Yes	Yes
SAP Cloud Applications Studio (SDK)		Yes	Yes
Order capture		Yes	Yes
SAP Jam Collaboration		Yes	Yes
Offline		Yes	Yes
Groupware integration (server)			Yes
Deal finder			Yes
Influencer map			Yes
Contracts			Yes
Installed base view			Yes
Industry option			Yes

Table 1.1 SAP Sales Cloud Licensing Options (Cont.)

1.3.2   System Landscape and Software Requirements

For each SAP Cloud for Customer production tenant you purchase, one test tenant is permitted at any given time. Each tenant has a unique URL. If needed, you can purchase additional permanent test tenant subscriptions from SAP. SAP Hosting Services has three data centers in which tenants are established on systems. By default, a system houses many tenants for multiple customers. However, you can purchase private edition subscriptions, which entitle you to a system with no other customer tenants on it. For SAP Cloud for Customer, test and production tenants are always on separate systems.

Following are the SAP Cloud for Customer solution's minimum system and software requirements for web applications, mobile applications, language settings, and integration add-ins:

- **Web applications**
  The minimum desktop and laptop requirements for SAP Cloud for Customer are as follows:
  - Processor: Intel Core 2 Duo or better
  - Memory: Minimum 6 GB or more
  - Minimum bandwidth and network latency requirements: 2 Mbps for upstream, 2 Mbps for downstream, and 200 ms or better latency.
  - Screen resolution: Best display at 1280 × 768.

  Because the SAP Cloud for Customer solution can export files to your local device, you should enable your browser to download files. The popup blocker in your browser should either be disabled or the system URL should be registered as an exception site for the popup blocker. The **Trusted Sites** security zone settings listed in the **Downloads** section applies to popups as well. The recommended browsers for running SAP Cloud for Customer are Google Chrome (for Windows) and Apple Safari (for Mac); however, Microsoft Internet Explorer and Mozilla Firefox are supported as well.

- **Mobile devices**
  Minimum bandwidth requirements for mobile devices using SAP Cloud for Customer apps are 2 Mbps for upstream, 2 Mbps for downstream, and 200 ms or better for latency. A Wi-Fi or cellular network connection is required on your mobile devices to communicate with SAP Cloud for Customer servers. For Wi-Fi, the same minimum bandwidth requirements as just mentioned apply. For cellular connections, a 3G network or faster is required. For the best performance, we recommend using Wi-Fi or LTE. SAP tests the supported and recommended devices. Recommended devices provide better performance and usability. Devices with similar or better specifications than the recommended devices (octane score of 6500 or higher) should be compatible but aren't tested by SAP. For the supported and recommended devices, Intel Core M microprocessors aren't recommended because sufficient performance can't be guaranteed.

- **Language settings**
  To ensure that SAP Cloud for Customer texts appear consistently in the same logon language, review the language settings in the preferred language, and choose the preferred language from the **Language** dropdown list. Under **Personalization**, define your preferred language.

- **Integration and add-ins**
  SAP Cloud for Customer delivers additional functionality through integration to external systems and software that can be installed for specific business purposes and end users. To increase sales efficiency, large enterprises can integrate existing SAP ERP systems with SAP Cloud for Customer. Existing installations of SAP CRM can also be integrated with SAP Cloud for Customer, where desired.

1.3.3 User Management

When you license the SAP Cloud for Customer solution from SAP, the initial tenant information is sent to the email address on your customer account (with SAP) as the IT contact setup. The information to log in to the initial tenant will come in two separate emails: the first email includes a URL for the test tenant and initial user ID, and the second email includes the password. After receiving the initial user information, the initial user (usually the project manager) should log in and define the administrators of the system. The administrators are initially setup as service agents. After setting up the service agents, the initial user ID should be locked.

Through a combination of employee records, business users, business roles, and access restrictions, you can customize and control users' access to your SAP Sales Cloud solution. You can grant and restrict authorizations for most work center views. Typically, this is done at the business role level so that you can set the restrictions once and apply them to multiple users. Authorizations for certain views can be restricted to employees or territories associated with the specific item in a view or via assignment of the employee to an organizational unit.

Access contexts bundle context-specific restriction rules that are assigned to various work center views, and you can choose on the business role level which restriction rule will be used for which view, as shown in Figure 1.3.

You can create employee records manually or upload employee data via the migration tool in the implementation project activity. To facilitate the exchange of information, members of your organization can communicate within the solution with partner contacts, that is, individuals who are associated with the resellers, brokers, service providers, distributors, or other entities with which your organization collaborates. To simplify maintenance and assignment of access rights to users, SAP recommends that you define business roles to which you assign work centers and views. You can then assign one or more roles to each employee who has a user in the system.

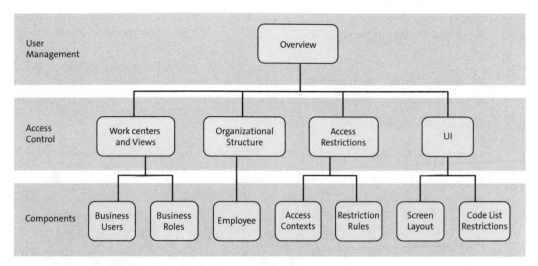

Figure 1.3 Access Restrictions to SAP Sales Cloud Application

1.4   Project Considerations

The SAP Cloud for Customer solution is different from the traditional SAP ERP solution, so project considerations are different for these cloud-based applications compared to the on-premise applications. In this section, we introduce the SAP Launch methodology to help you with your implementation along with other project considerations.

1.4.1   Project Implementation Methodology

SAP has developed SAP Launch, an implementation methodology that is based on best practices, to help you successfully implement SAP Cloud for Customer. It's strongly recommended that you follow this methodology to successfully deploy the SAP Sales Cloud solution for your organization. The methodology is the road map for the implementation project. Key activities, deliverables, and checkpoints, also known as quality gates (Q-gates) are defined during the project. Toolkits and accelerators are supplied to provide a standardized and prescriptive delivery of the project scope.

The methodology also supports cases where integration between SAP Cloud for Customer and an on-premise system is required. Implementation activities are spread across four phases of the implementation methodology and at the end of each phase there is a corresponding Q-gate:

- Prepare → Project Verification
- Realize → Solution Acceptance
- Verify → Readiness Acceptance
- Launch → Go-Live

Figure 1.4 shows the four phases of the SAP Launch implementation methodology.

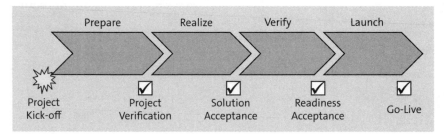

Figure 1.4 Four Phases of the SAP Launch Methodology

At the **Project Verification** Q-gate, all the stakeholders agree to the scope to be delivered during the implementation of the SAP Sales Cloud solution. During the **Solution Acceptance** Q-gate, all the stakeholders agree that the business scenarios demonstrated in the solution meet the requirements to be delivered by the project and that all configuration questions have been addressed. At the **Readiness Acceptance** Q-gate, all stakeholders agree that the systems, data, and people are ready to execute the cutover from the legacy system to the new SAP Sales Cloud system. Finally, at the **Go-Live** Q-gate, all stakeholders agree that the cutover is complete, and the organization is prepared to use and support the new solution.

1.4.2   Initial Setup of the SAP Cloud for Customer System

When you receive the initial tenant of SAP Cloud for Customer from SAP after signing the licensing agreement, you need to do an initial setup of the system before you start implementing the solution. There are five distinct milestones with clearly defined activities (different from the project methodology) that you need to carry to ensure that the initial setup is completed in SAP Cloud for Customer, as shown in Figure 1.5.

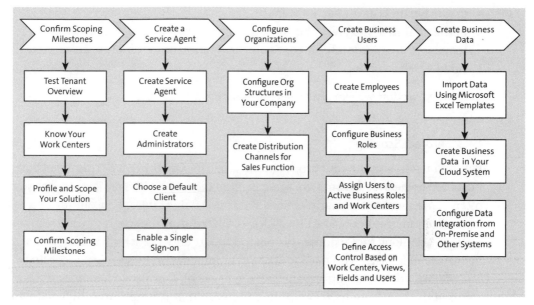

Figure 1.5 Steps for Initial Setup of SAP Cloud for Customer

Let's review these milestones related to the initial setup of SAP Cloud for Customer:

- **Confirm scoping milestones**
  In this step, you review the SAP Sales Cloud test tenant provided by SAP and become familiar with the work centers. After that, you profile and scope your solution.

- **Create a service agent**
  When you log in to your SAP Sales Cloud test tenant with initial credentials provided by SAP, you first create a service agent and then create administrator user IDs. After that, you can enable a default client for logging in to SAP Sales Cloud, that is, HTML5 or RUI (SAP Fiori). You can also enable single sign-on (SSO) for the users to log in to system.

- **Configure organizations**
  In this step, you configure your company's organizational structure (details are provided in Chapter 3).

- **Create business users**
  For users who will be using your SAP Sales Cloud system, you need to create business users, employees, and business roles. After that, you assign users to active business roles and work centers. Finally, you define access control based on work centers, views, fields, and users.

- **Create business data**
  In the final step, you create business data and import data using Microsoft Excel templates. In addition, you configure integration with on-premise and other cloud-based solutions.

In the next section, we explain project scoping in SAP Sales Cloud.

1.4.3   Project Scoping

Before you start scoping your project in SAP Cloud for Customer, it's critical that business stakeholders are in complete agreement on the scope of the project. Projects are often started without a clearly defined scope and deliverables. You can turn on or turn off certain features of SAP Cloud for Customer during the scoping process. To set up your SAP Cloud for Customer system to support only the sales features included in SAP Cloud for Sales, you need to scope your implementation project accordingly. The options you choose during the scoping phase of your implementation project are used by the system to generate an activity list that you need to complete to go live. In the next chapter, we'll cover scoping your sales solution in detail.

1.4.4   Teamwork

We've all heard that if everyone is moving forward together, then success takes care of itself. Like any successful project, teamwork is one of the critical components for successful deployment of the SAP Sales Cloud solution. Committed team members from business and IT, decision makers, sponsors, and consulting partners must work in harmony toward delivering the project scope as defined and agreed upon. A functional team has the risk of quickly becoming dysfunctional if the roles and responsibilities of each and every team members aren't clearly defined and understood.

Defining a Responsible, Accountable, Consulted, and Informed (RACI) matrix for all parties and project team members before starting the project can help avoid team differences. To move in one direction, people need to clearly understand the destination. Research evidence shows very consistently that performance is improved in situations where there are clear targets to aim at.

1.4.5   Business Workshops

During projects, workshops needs to be diligently scheduled and conducted based on the solution and the scope of the project. A workshop is an information-sharing session focused on knowledge transfer to key users about the project and the solution. Although workshops can be conducted remotely, it's strongly recommended that you conduct these workshops with all the stakeholders meeting in person. The workshop materials are contained within the Delivery Toolkit delivered as part of the implementation methodology. The topics covered in the business workshops are project kick-off, business scenarios, integration, system administration, functional topics, data migration, test planning, cutover planning, and incident management.

1.4.6   Data, Data, Data

We can't emphasis enough the importance of data for a successful adoption of any SAP CRM application. Many SAP CRM projects have failed primarily due to poor and inconsistent data quality. Data quality doesn't mean only the initial load of data in your SAP Cloud for Customer system. You can easily ensure that you load pristine customer and contact data as part of the initial data load and cutover activities. The key is ensure that you keep customer and contact data clean, complete, and without any duplicates.

SAP Cloud for Customer has an out-of-the-box duplicate check functionality to help you avoid adding duplicate records to your system. The system alone can only do so much, so it's important that you define consistent naming conventions for customers, contacts, and transactions. There is a trade-off between data policing and end-user freedom. Less-restrictive practices for creating data in your cloud for customers might appeal to your business users; however, the price you pay for duplicate/incomplete data is extreme. Investments made in ensuring the data consistency and accuracy has the highest rate of return as compared to any other investment made in your SAP Cloud for Customer solution.

1.4.7   Training and Change Management

User adoption has been a constant struggle for all of SAP's CRM applications since their inception. If you don't want your SAP Cloud for Customer initiative to meet the same fate as your previous SAP CRM initiatives, you must take into account the training and change management methods before you embark on your implementation journey. Whenever you implement any SAP CRM solution, the biggest question on the minds of your sales reps is "what's in it for me?"—SAP Cloud for Customer is no exception.

Organizational and business goals for implementing SAP Cloud for Customer must be clearly communicated to all the stakeholders and end users before starting the implementation. Key end users must be involved in the requirements-gathering workshops and end-user testing. End-user training shouldn't be treated as an afterthought. When it comes to end-user training, organizations often resort to virtual meetings and recorded videos to save on travel costs. After making hundreds of thousands of investments in software and services, saving a few thousand on training-related travel costs might not be a good idea.

1.4.8   Go Live and Administration

Before you go live with your new SAP Cloud for Customer system, you need to perform readiness acceptance to make sure that people and data are ready to proceed with the cutover into the production tenant. It's important that you've developed a transition and communication plan so that roles and organizations impacted by the go-live are prepared for the change. During go-live, all stakeholders agree to begin productive use of the solution, and support for users is available. After the project is live, your support team takes over the application administration and day-to-day operations.

1.5   Summary

In this chapter, we introduced you to the history of CRM and some of the emerging trends in SAP's CRM capabilities, such as AI (machine learning), social media, and integration. We described SAP Cloud for Customer and SAP Sales Cloud in detail, and introduced you to the SAP Launch methodology for successfully deploying your SAP Sales Cloud solution. We also included the preliminary steps you need to perform when you receive your test tenant from SAP. You also learned about the critical project considerations of scoping, data quality, training and change management, go-live, and administration. With this background on getting started with SAP Sales Cloud, the rest of the chapters will cover each and every function of SAP Sales Cloud in detail.

Chapter 2
Scoping SAP Sales Cloud

The scoping exercise in an SAP Sales Cloud implementation involves defining the business solutions you want to enable as part of your SAP Sales Cloud solution.

When you start your SAP Sales Cloud implementation, you start with a project scoping exercise through a guided process available in SAP Cloud for Customer. You can turn on or turn off certain features of SAP Cloud for Customer during the scoping process. To set up your SAP Sales Cloud system to support only the sales features included in SAP Sales Cloud, you need to scope your implementation project accordingly. The options you choose during the scoping phase of your implementation project are used by the system to generate an activity list that you need to complete to go live.

In this chapter, we'll review the scoping elements related to sales processes and how to select and deselect questionnaires to include solutions in your scope per business requirements. The scoping for sales processes are organized into the following scoping area options: **Account and Activity Management**, **Product and Service Portfolio for Sales**, **New Business**, and **Lead Management**. In this chapter, we follow the logical sequence available in applications to cover these scoping elements. Finally, we close the chapter by summarizing the key areas covered here.

2.1 SAP Sales Cloud Solution Overview

Before we introduce the scoping sales solution within SAP Sales Cloud, let's review the high-level steps in the sales process. Figure 2.1 shows the high-level graphic and description of the steps in the sales process and gives you a bird's-eye view of how the SAP solution can help your sales team.

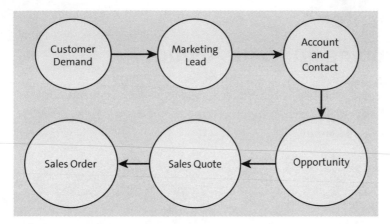

Figure 2.1 High Level Sales Process

Your sales team needs the agility and power to find answers, engage in meaningful customer conversations, and deliver the right impact every time. Going beyond the traditional approach to sales software, SAP Sales Cloud is easy to use and equips your sales team to close more deals faster in today's complex selling environment. The steps in the sales process are as follows:

- **Customer demand**
  Customer demand helps you recognize the demand for your product in the marketplace through multiple channels.

- **Leads**
  Through leads, you can capture information from prospects and customers that can eventually result in a sale.

- **Account and contact**
  With integrated account and contact management, you can make fast account updates, get complete customer intelligence, and keep everyone in the loop so that you and your team are delivering the right impact in every customer conversation.

- **Opportunity**
  The opportunity management process lets you accelerate sales wins by rapidly tracking activities; collaborating with internal teams, customers, and partners; keeping tabs on the competition; and obtaining guided selling materials for each deal.

- **Sales quotes**
  You can create and submit quotes to align with your internal approval process.

- **Sales orders**
  Utilizing the robust integration features available on the backend, you can also create sales orders as a follow-up from opportunities or quotes.

2.2   Scoping a Sales Solution

To scope a sales solution in SAP Cloud for Customer, you log in to your SAP-provided test tenant for SAP Cloud for Customer under HTML5 UI as an administrator and choose **Business Configuration • Implementation Projects,** as shown in Figure 2.2. Here you see the first project already created by SAP when you get your first tenant as part of the licensing agreement. To add scope to your project, you select the **First Implementation** project and then click **Edit Project Scope**.

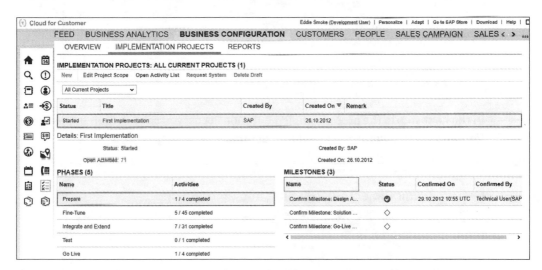

Figure 2.2 First Implementation Project in SAP Cloud for Customer

When you edit the project scope, SAP Cloud for Customer provides a guided process to complete the project scoping process. You need to go through a six-step process (**Country, Implementation Focus, Scoping, Questions, Review**, and **Confirmation**) before finalizing the scope of your implementation, as shown in Figure 2.3.

In the first step, you add the countries you want to roll out your SAP Sales Cloud solution to. For multiple country deployments, you'll add all those countries here so that country-specific settings for languages and currencies can be enabled.

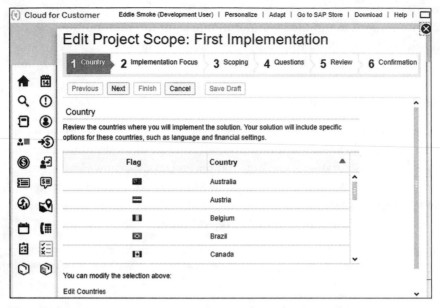

Figure 2.3 Six-Step Process to Edit the Scope of a Project

In the next step in the process, **Implementation Focus**, you see a default implementation focus selection for **SAP Cloud for Customer** (Figure 2.4).

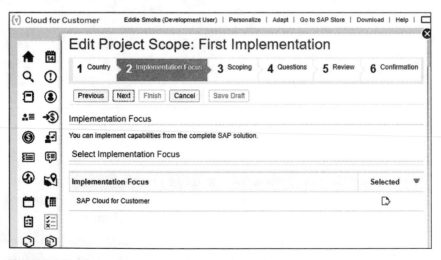

Figure 2.4 Implementation Focus in Project Scoping

Here you don't need to make any additional settings. Next, select the **Scoping** step, and you're taken to the **View Project Scope** screen shown in Figure 2.5.

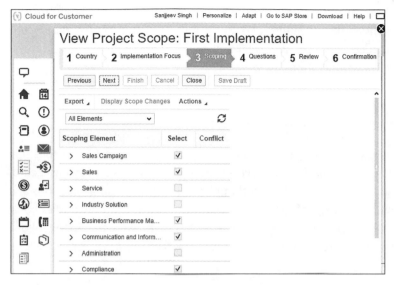

Figure 2.5 Scoping Elements for Selection

Here you can select the scoping elements based on the scope of your project. For a SAP Sales Cloud implementation, you select the **Sales** checkbox and also expand the **Sales** structure to select additional options such as **Account and Activity Management**, **Product and Service Portfolio for Sales**, **New Business**, and **Lead Management**, as shown in Figure 2.6.

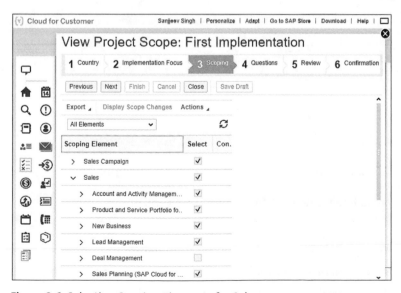

Figure 2.6 Selecting Scoping Elements for Sales

Here you can select all the elements under **Sales Campaign**, **Sales**, **General Business Data**, **Partner Channel Management**, and so on depending on the scope of your implementation. In the next section, we'll review the scoping elements and questions related to sales scoping items.

2.3   Account and Activity Management

The next step in the scoping process, **Questions**, as shown in Figure 2.7, provides specific questions you need to select for each of these elements. We'll review each of these elements in subsequent sections. Although we'll review scoping questions and fine-tuning activities for each of these functionalities in later chapters in this book, we're providing the list of questions for each of these scoping elements in the following sections for your easy reference.

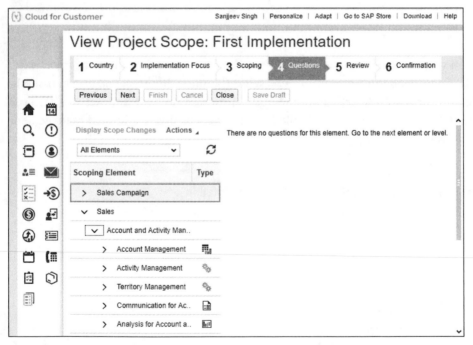

Figure 2.7 Questions Related to Account and Contact Management

2.3.1   Account Management

Select **Account Management** to see the list of questions as business options that define the scope of your solution related to that area, as shown in Figure 2.8.

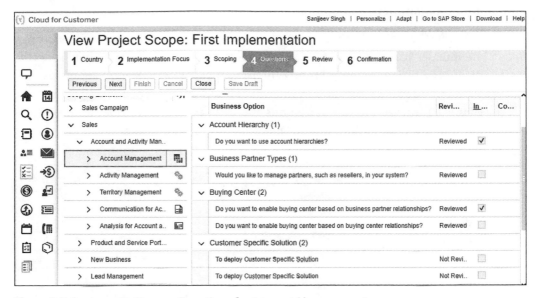

Figure 2.8 Business Options or Questions for Account Management

As part of your project scoping exercise, you review these business options or questions with business requirement owners and select the checkbox if they answer yes to these questions. For example, if you plan to use account hierarchies in your SAP Sales Cloud solution, then the answer to the first question—**Do you want to use account hierarchies?**—is yes, so you enable the checkbox. Similarly, there are questions for **Business Partner Types**, **Buying Center**, **Customer Specific Solution**, and **Distribution Channel**. These questions are self-explanatory. You can review these with your business process owners or key business requirement owners and check or uncheck them as needed. This will define the standard out-of-the-box scope for **Account Management** in your SAP Sales Cloud solution. Let's review the standard scoping questions available for **Account Management** as follows:

- **Do you want to use account hierarchies?**
- **Would you like to manage partners, such as resellers, in your system?**
- **Do you want to enable buying center based on business partner relationships?**
- **Do you want to enable buying center based on buying center relationships?**
- **Do you sell products and services using multiple distribution channels?**

2.3.2   Activity Management

To define the scope of activity management in your project, click on **Activity Management** under **Scoping Element** to see the questions for activity management for **Activities**, **Activity List**, **Activity Planner**, **Activity Types**, **E-Mail Blast**, **Summaries**, and **Surveys**, and then enable the checkboxes as needed per the scope of your project (see Figure 2.9). Answers to these questions also determine what capabilities you're able to configure within activity management as explained in Chapter 8.

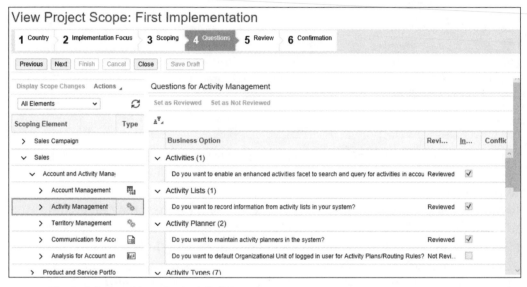

Figure 2.9 Questions for Activity Management

Let's review the scoping questions related to activity management as follows:

- Do you want to enable an enhanced activities facet to search and query for activities in account, contact, and individual customer work centers?
- Do you want to record information from activity lists in your system?
- Do you want to maintain activity planners in the system?
- Do you want to default Organizational Unit of logged in user for Activity Plans/ Routing Rules?
- Do you record appointments with your accounts?
- Do you record tasks?
- Do you use e-mail to communicate with your accounts?
- Do you record phone calls?

- Do you record chat activities?
- Do you want to track changes made to activities and visits?
- Do you want to record messaging activity?
- Do you want to send personalized mass e-mails to many accounts at the same time?
- You would be able to execute e-mail blasts for employees added in the target groups.
- You can synchronize activities in your SAP Cloud Solution with your users' local e-mail application (Microsoft Outlook or IBM Lotus Notes).
- Do you want to use route templates to schedule periodic creation of routes?
- Do you want to enable users to specify, per activity, a predetermined combination of sales organization, distribution channel, and division?
- Do you want to default the sales organization, distribution channel, and division based on the account and employee sales data?
- Do you want to use summaries as meeting minutes for appointments, phone calls, and visits in the system?
- Do you want to prevent summaries from being sent to external parties?
- Do you want to maintain surveys in the system?
- For Survey Execution In Extended Edition, do you want to display the product image along with the ID and Description?
- For Survey Execution in Extended Edition, do you want to hide Product ID?
- For Survey Execution in Extended Edition, do you want to hide Product description?
- For Survey Execution in Extended Edition, do you want to enable adding products from past orders?
- Do you want to execute tasks and surveys during phone calls?
- Instead of the sender's name "on behalf of" the system's e-mail address, do you want to use only the employee's e-mail address as the sender?
- You go to your customers' physical locations periodically. Do you want to record information from these visits in your system?
- Do you want to deactivate the check-in/check-out buttons for visits?
- Do you want to ensure that sales and service reps complete mandatory tasks and surveys before allowing them to close visits?
- Do you want to disable execution actions before check-in?

- Upon checking into a visit, do you want to update the visit status to "In Process"?
- Do you want to disable the "Do you want to create a new visit?" prompt when users check out from a visit?
- Do you want to prevent the deletion of completed visits?
- Do you want to prevent users from checking into multiple visits?
- Do you want to enable image recognition (planogram) for visits?
- Do you want to deactivate the business partner visiting information feature?

2.3.3 Territory Management

To enable territory management in your project and see the related business options in terms of questions, select **Territory Management**, as shown in Figure 2.9. Here you review questions with business users such as **Account - Territory Association**, **Determine Territory of Transaction Owner**, **Realignment Runs and Account – Territory Associations**, **Territory Management**, and **Transaction Documents Territory Change**, as shown in Figure 2.10.

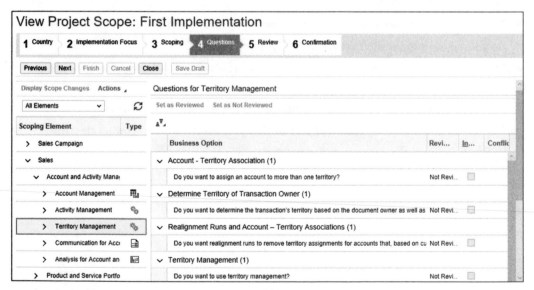

Figure 2.10 Territory Management Scoping Questions

Let's review the scoping questions for territory management:

- Do you want to assign an account to more than one territory?

- Do you want to determine the transaction's territory based on the document owner as well as the account?
- Do you want realignment runs to remove territory assignments for accounts that, based on current rules, qualify for no territories?
- Do you want to use territory management?
- Do you want to use account filters to create realignment runs?
- Do you want the territory changes you make to an account to be automatically updated in the open documents associated with the account?
- Include closed documents as part of realignment run and if update of open documents is enabled, also include closed documents in that update?

2.3.4   Communication for Account and Activity Management and Analysis for Account and Activity Management

There are no scoping questions related to these two scoping elements under **Account and Activity Management**, as shown in Figure 2.11.

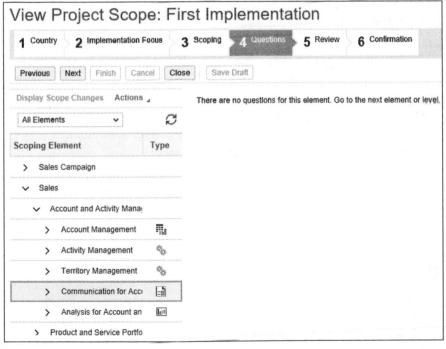

Figure 2.11 No Scoping Questions for Communication for Accounts and Activity Management

2.4   Products and Service Portfolio for Sales

Under **Products and Service Portfolio for Sales**, you have the **Sell Standard Products** option to sell products from stock. If you plan to sell products from stock and want to create sales orders in SAP Sales Cloud, then you enable this question to include the solution in the scope of your implementation, as shown in Figure 2.12.

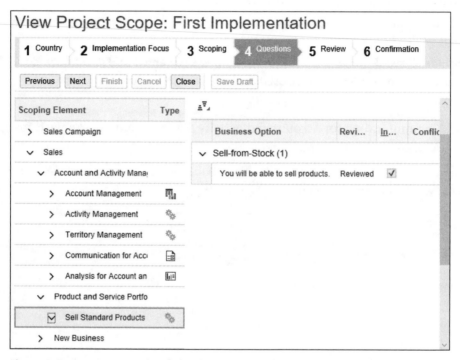

Figure 2.12 Scoping Question for Selling Products from Stock

The only scoping question related to products is for selling stock products as follows:

- **You will be able to sell products.**

2.5   New Business

Under the **New Business** scoping element, you can make selections for including sales-related solutions such as opportunities, sales quotes, communication for new business, sales orders, and sales contracts, as covered in the next sections.

2.5.1   Opportunities

Scoping-related questions related to opportunities control capabilities such as **Approval for Opportunities, Influencer Map,** and **Opportunity History**, as shown in Figure 2.13. Like previous sections, you review these questions with your business requirements owner and enable as needed to include in or exclude from your project scope.

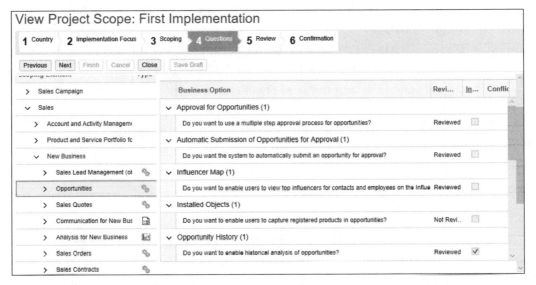

Figure 2.13 Scoping-Related Questions for Opportunities

The scoping questions related to opportunity management to enable standard functionality are as follows:

- **Do you want to use a multiple step approval process for opportunities?**
- **Do you want the system to automatically submit an opportunity for approval?**
- **Do you want to enable users to view top influencers for contacts and employees on the Influencer Map?**
- **Do you want to enable users to capture registered products in opportunities?**
- **Do you want to enable historical analysis of opportunities?**
- **Do you want to enable users to see earlier versions of opportunity notes?**
- **Do you want to enable users to edit or delete notes in the note history?**
- **Do you want to automatically redetermine opportunity parties based on changes to the account team of the associated account?**
- **Do you want to enable sales phase progress for opportunities?**
- **Do you want to add products during opportunity creation?**

- Do you want to enable quantity scheduling for opportunities on a monthly, quarterly, or yearly basis?
- Do you want an automatic update of the product revenue schedule based on the quantity schedule?
- Do you want to split revenue per opportunity among sales team members?
- Do you want to enable revenue scheduling for opportunities on a monthly, quarterly, or yearly basis?
- Do you want to enable users to specify, per opportunity, a predetermined combination of sales organization, distribution channel, and division?
- Do you want to default the sales organization, distribution channel, and division based on the account and employee sales data?
- You can assign sales cycles and phases to your opportunity.
- Would you like to use a sales assistant that proposes activities that you have to do in a certain phase of your opportunity?

2.5.2   Sales Quotes

The questions for sales quotes control the scoping elements such as **Approvals for Sales Quotes**, **Graphical Signature for Sales Quotes**, and **Sales Area Determination for Sales Quotes**, as shown in Figure 2.14.

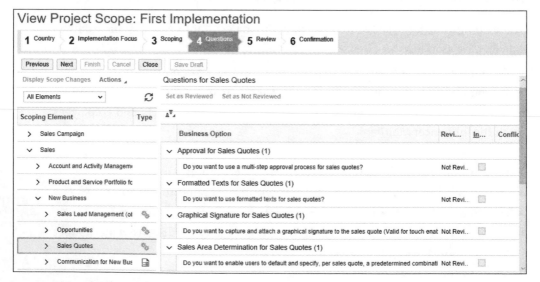

Figure 2.14 Sales Quotes Scoping Element Questions

The scoping questions related to sales quotes in SAP Sales Cloud are as follows:

- Do you want to use a multi-step approval process for sales quotes?
- Do you want to use formatted texts for sales quotes?
- Do you want to capture and attach a graphical signature to the sales quote (Valid for touch enabled devices only)?
- Do you want to enable users to default and specify, per sales quote, a predetermined combination of sale org., distribution channel, and division?
- Do you want to control the reset of the approval status and output status via workflow rules?
- Do you want to submit sales quotes without items?

2.5.3   Communication for New Business

Questions related to business collaboration enable you to use external applications to search, create, or edit quotes. You can also use templates to send quotes and sales orders to your customers by enabling relevant questions under this business option, as shown in Figure 2.15.

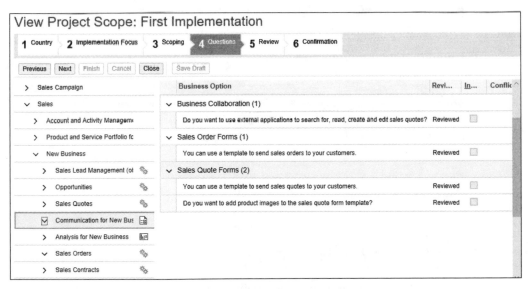

Figure 2.15 Scoping Questions for Communication for New Business

Let's review the scoping questions related to communication for new business as follows:

- **Do you want to use external applications to search for, read, create, and edit sales quotes?**
- **You can use a template to send sales orders to your customers.**
- **You can use a template to send sales quotes to your customers.**
- **Do you want to add product images to the sales quote form template?**

2.5.4   Sales Orders

Similar to sales quotes, the scoping questions for sales orders allow you to enable approval process for sales orders, text items for sales orders, capturing graphical signatures in sales orders, and so on. Figure 2.16 shows the scoping questions related to sales orders.

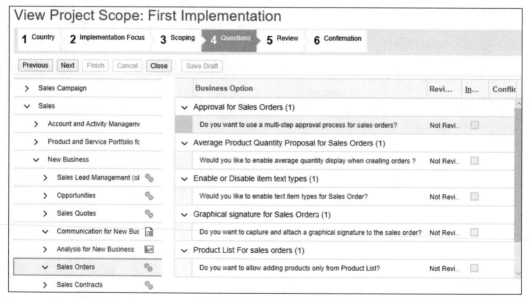

Figure 2.16 Business Options and Scoping Questions for Sales Orders

On similar lines with sales quotes, the scoping questions for sales orders are as follows:

- **Do you want to use a multi-step approval process for sales orders?**
- **Would you like to enable average quantity display when creating orders?**

- Would you like to enable text item types for Sales Order?
- Do you want to capture and attach a graphical signature to the sales order?
- Do you want to allow adding products only from Product List?
- Do you want to enable users to default and specify, per sales order, a predetermined combination of sales org., distribution channel, and division?

2.5.5   Sales Contracts

The last scoping element in the **New Business** section is related to sales contracts. As shown in Figure 2.17, we have only one scoping question related to enabling the multistep approval process for sales contracts:

- Do you want to use a multistep approval for sales contracts?

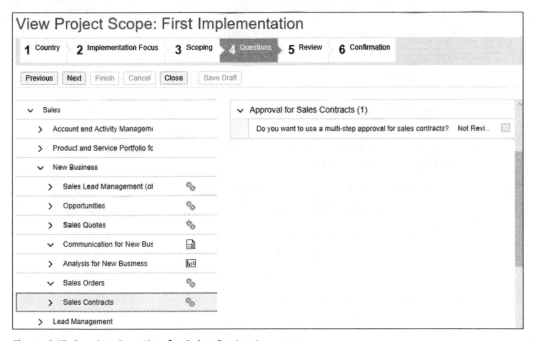

Figure 2.17 Scoping Question for Sales Contracts

2.6   Lead Management

As one of the key areas in SAP Sales Cloud, lead management has many more scoping options as compared to other scoping elements. Some of the questions for the **Leads** business option are approvals for leads, automatic submission of leads for approvals, ability to make contacts as optional fields for leads, lead duplicate check, lead aging, and so on, as shown in Figure 2.18.

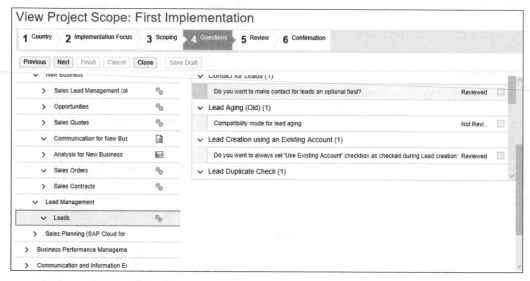

Figure 2.18 Questions Related to Leads

Let's review the scoping questions related to lead management to enable the standard functionality in SAP Sales Cloud as follows:

- Do you want to use a multiple step approval process for leads?
- Do you want the system to automatically submit a lead for approval?
- Do you want to enable integration with Avention?
- Do you want to make contact for leads an optional field?
- Do you want to disable historical analysis of leads?
- Do you wish to trigger lead aging notifications only when relevant, for better performance?
- Compatibility mode for lead aging.
- Do you want to always set 'Use Existing Account' checkbox as checked during Lead creation?
- Do you want to enable duplicate check for lead?
- Do you want to enable users to see earlier versions of lead notes?
- Do you want to enable users to edit or delete notes in the note history?

- Do you want to keep your Lead's Sales Area Data (Sales Org, Distribution Channel, Division, etc.) when converting a lead to a customer?
- Do you want to enable users to specify, per lead, a predetermined combination of sales organization, distribution channel, and division?
- Do you want to enable users to reopen accepted or declined leads?
- Do you want to enable integration with SAP InfiniteInsight?
- Would you like to assign leads to territories using lead routing rules?

After reviewing and selecting all the scoping-related questions, you select the next steps—**Review** and finally **Confirmation**—to update your scope.

2.7   Summary

In this chapter, we've reviewed the standard sales process and how you can use the guided process for defining the scope of your SAP Sales Cloud implementation. Under **Business Configuration** and **Implementation Project**, you edit the scope of the project and review the scoping elements and associated scoping questions. We reviewed scoping-related questions for all the sales-related functions such as account and contact management, activity management, lead management, opportunity management, sales orders, and sales contracts. After you define the scope of your project, you can do the actual configuration through the fine-tuning exercises as covered in subsequent chapters in this book.

In the next chapter, we'll cover organization management, which is one of the fundamental parts of master data setup for your SAP Cloud for Customer solution.

Chapter 3

Organization Management

Organization management enables you to map your sales organization to SAP Sales Cloud and assign employees and managers to specific organization units so that responsible individuals and teams are accounted for in business transactions.

Organization management is the central source of organizational information in the SAP Sales Cloud solution. It helps you model your organizational structure and provides a graphical representation via an organizational chart that reflects the legal, operational, and functional entities and aspects of your enterprise.

In this chapter, we'll start by providing an overview of the organization management process followed by how organizations are created and processed. We also review the process for setting up an organizational structure and assigning employees to it. We'll also cover how organization data can be linked to the transactions along with some related settings in SAP Sales Cloud.

3.1 Organization Management Process

SAP Sales Cloud accesses the organization management information whenever business processes require information on an enterprise's organization, such as which sales team and organization an employee belongs to, what sales team an employee manages, and who the direct reports are.

Although actual organizational structures may vary from company to company, most companies follow an organizational structure defined in their backend SAP ERP systems. Before we dive into the details of the organization management process in SAP Sales Cloud, it will be helpful to review an example organizational structure for a typical sales organization, as shown in Figure 3.1. Under the company, you can create and assign all the sales organizations. For each sales organization, you create and assign sales offices, and then finally you assign sales reps and sales managers to the sales offices.

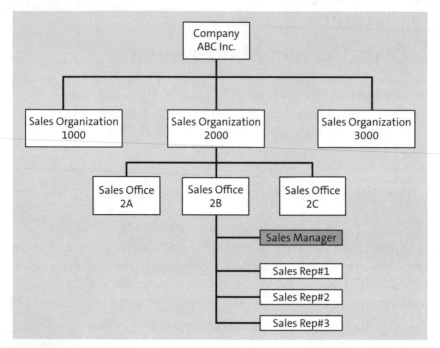

Figure 3.1 Sample Organizational Structure

In the organization management process, you can manage the organizational structure; create organizational units; assign employees, managers, and functions to organizational units (sales or service); and define organization-specific attributes such as postal code, city, region, country, sales area, and so on. Organization management is foundational in SAP Sales Cloud for work distribution and workflows. In the organizational structure, you can model organizational units and hierarchies according to different dimensions such as companies, sales organizations, sales units, and reporting lines.

Following are two key concepts in the organization management process:

- **Time dependency**
  All information maintained in organization management is time dependent with validity from and to dates. This allows easy handling of changes to organizational units and employee assignment in SAP Sales Cloud per your actual organizational changes.

- **Consistency check**
  The embedded organization management checks in SAP Sales Cloud ensure consis-

tency at each point in time while defining and making updates to the organizational structure.

With this background on organization management process, we'll now review how organizations are created and processed.

3.2 Creating and Processing Organizations

To successfully use SAP Sales Cloud, it's important that the organizational structure is set up correctly and accurately reflects your functional organizational structure. In sales, the most important organizational function is the sales organization because it defines the organizational unit of your sales hierarchy under the topmost organizational unit, which is company. This is where you will need to define all related master data relevant for your sales process. All other sales units must be placed below their head of organization counterparts. Before we start setting up the organizational structure, let's review some important concepts:

- **Definitions**
  These describe the role of the organizational unit in the structure, for example, company, reporting line unit, and so on.

- **Functions**
  These reflect the business function or purpose of the organizational unit, such as sales organization, service unit, and so on.

- **Addresses**
  These provide all the address details for the organizational unit, including the email addresses for outbound emails (for autoresponding emails for organizational units).

In the following sections, we review how to set up a new organizational structure in SAP Sales Cloud, how to assign the responsible employees to the organizational units, and how organizational units are referenced in the customer master and sales transactions.

3.2.1 Setting Up an Organizational Structure

To create an organizational structure, log in to HTML5 UI in SAP Sales Cloud as an administrator by choosing **Administrator • General Settings • Org Structures**. Figure 3.2 shows the link to maintain **Org Structures** under the heading **Company**.

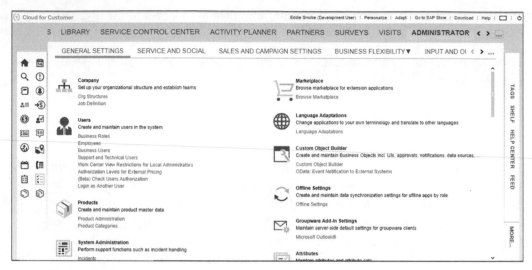

Figure 3.2 Link to Maintain Organizational structures in SAP Sales Cloud

When you click on **Org Structures**, you're taken to the **Org Structures** screen shown in Figure 3.3. All the existing organizational structures are displayed on this screen. If you are newly implementing SAP Sales Cloud, you won't see any organizational structures here. Instead, you'll see a blank page for you to create a new organizational structure from the root.

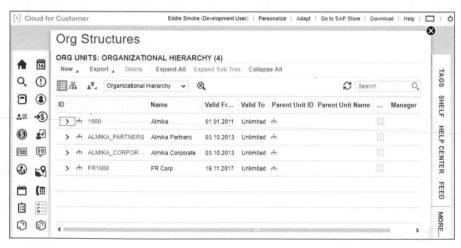

Figure 3.3 Organizational Structures Screen to Create or Edit an Organizational Structure

By default, the system displays all the organizational units in the search result list if the organizational unit validity belongs to the current date. The advanced search option allows you to filter the organizational units based on attributes and validity dates, as shown in Figure 3.4.

Figure 3.4 Advanced Search Option with Additional Filters

You can display the organizational units in an organizational hierarchy as shown earlier in Figure 3.3, expand the organizational unit to see the underlying organizational units, and switch the organizational units view from **List** view to **Organizational Hierarchy** view (Figure 3.5).

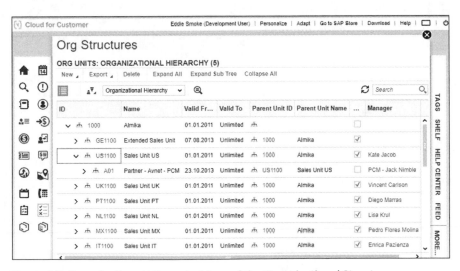

Figure 3.5 Organizational Hierarchy View of the Organizational Structure

To create a new organizational unit, click on **New,** and select **Org Unit**. The **New Org Unit** screen pops up, as shown in Figure 3.6.

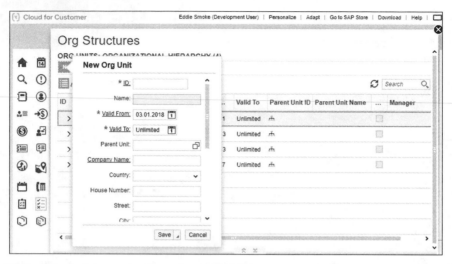

Figure 3.6 Creating a New Organizational Unit

On this popup, enter the **ID** and the **Valid From** and **Valid To** dates as minimum required entries to create a new organizational unit. In addition, you can maintain additional information such as **Name, Parent Unit, Company Name, Country, House Number, Street, City, Function (Sales, Service, Reporting Line), Manager**, and so on. After maintaining all these details, click **Save and Open**, and the organizational unit is created and opened, as shown in Figure 3.7.

Figure 3.7 Newly Created Organizational Unit

You can also maintain information about the organizational unit on the **GENERAL**, **FUNCTIONS**, and **EMPLOYEES** tabs. On the **GENERAL** tab, add the parent unit for the organizational unit by clicking on **Add**, as shown in Figure 3.8. In the **PARENT UNIT** popup, select the required **Parent Unit ID** from the options, and click **Add** to include the parent organizational unit.

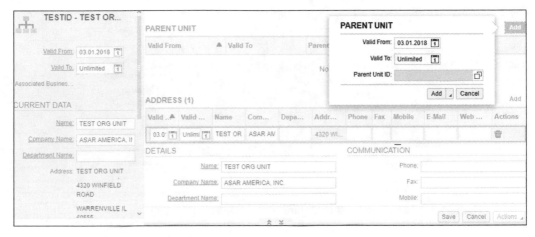

Figure 3.8 Adding a Parent to an Organizational Unit

On the **FUNCTIONS** tab, select whether this organizational unit is **Company**, **Sales Organization**, **Sales**, or **Service**. Note that **Sales Office** and **Sales Group** functions reflect the SAP ERP integration. SAP Sales Cloud doesn't support assignment of sales office and sales group to multiple organizational units. These functions can be used as master data in the account's sales data, which are copied to the sales transactions from the account's data.

You can also select **Currency** for the organizational unit. Currency on the company level is used for reporting purposes, currency on the sales organization level is used to default in sales transactions, and currency on the sales unit level is used for analysis from employees. In the next section, we'll review how to assign employees to organizational structures.

You can maintain validity dates for functions by clicking on **Add**, as shown in Figure 3.9.

If you've integrated SAP Sales Cloud with an SAP ERP system, you can add distribution channels to the organizational unit, as shown in Figure 3.10. By defining distribution channel rules, you can limit the relevant distribution channel selection for an account's or an employee's sales data. The system considers those distribution channels for business document processing. However, you can still change the distribution channel in the business document.

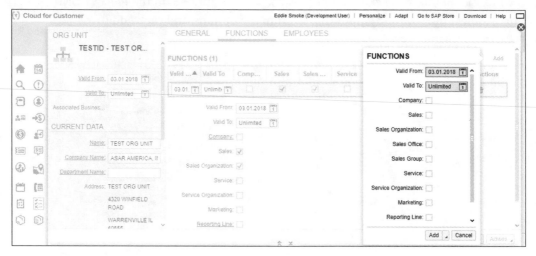

Figure 3.9 Adding Functions to Organizational Units

Figure 3.10 Adding Distribution Channels to an Organizational Unit

After maintaining all the details, click **Save**, and the organizational unit is created. This organizational unit can be used to cluster master data such as accounts, prices, and products. In reporting, sales data can be aggregated at each organizational unit level. The reporting line function can be used for notifications or approval workflow for managers.

In the next section, we'll show you how to assign employees to organizational structure.

3.2.2 Assigning Employees to an Organizational Structure

Employees and managers are assigned to organizational units to define their responsibilities for specific organizational units. To assign employees and managers, open an organizational unit by choosing **Administrator • General Settings • Org Structures**, and then click on the organizational unit you want to assign the employee to. You're taken to the organizational unit's **GENERAL** tab. Click on the **EMPLOYEES** tab to open the **EMPLOYEES** part of the screen, as shown in Figure 3.11.

Figure 3.11 Assigning Employees to an Organizational Structure

The organizational unit manager assignment defines the applicable manager for the organizational unit or team based on the reporting line function. You can only assign one manager at a time to an organizational unit; however, a manager can be assigned to multiple organizational units. To add a manager to an organizational unit, click on the **Add** button as shown in Figure 3.12, and maintain the **Valid From** and **Valid To** dates. Select the manager from the search options, and click **Add** to assign the manager to the organizational unit.

You can assign employees to an organizational unit if they need to work as a team for the organizational unit. The team assignments for the organizational unit are reflected in the search for business objects when they are searched under My Team.

The organizational unit's employee assignment defines its applicable manager based on the reporting line function within the organizational hierarchy. To add employees to the organizational unit, click **Add** as shown in Figure 3.13, maintain the **Valid From** and **Valid To** dates, and select the responsible **Employee** from the search options. After that, click **Add** to add the employee to the organizational unit. Repeat the process to assign all the employees for that organizational unit.

Figure 3.12 Assigning a Manager to an Organizational Unit

Figure 3.13 Assigning Employees to an Organizational Unit

An employee can be assigned to multiple organizational units in the **EMPLOYEES** table. However, the employee is assigned as a primary for one organizational unit and as a secondary to more than one organizational units. For distribution of works based on organizational units, only primary employee assignments are considered. Similarly, a manager can be responsible for multiple organizational units defined by an entry in the **MANAGERS** table. An employee needs to be assigned to an organizational unit as primary. A manager can also be assigned as an employee in the **EMPLOYEES** table to represent his reporting line.

3.2.3   Organizational Data in Transactions

References to organizational data in transactions are indirectly based on the employee responsible for those transactions. The determination of an organizational unit, such as a sales unit, can depend on the owner of a transaction or on the party determination step. For example, the seller party (company) in a quote is derived from the sales unit.

Assigning a responsible employee to an organizational unit determines the organizational unit's responsibility in associated transactions. This is mainly relevant for analytics and reporting purposes at the organizational unit level based on the assignment of the employee responsible.

3.3   Configuring Organizations

Organization management has no configuration requirements. It basically involves setting up the organizational structure manually or through data migration.

To create an organizational structure manually, choose **Administrator • General Settings • Org Structures**, and click on **New • Org Unit**. The **New Org Unit** popup appears, as shown in Figure 3.14.

Figure 3.14 Creating a New Organizational Unit

On this popup, maintain the required details such as **ID**, **Name**, **Valid From** and **Valid To**, and so on. If you're creating this organizational unit as subunit under another organizational unit, then select the parent organizational unit from search options in the **Parent Unit** field, and then click **Save**. The new organizational unit is successfully created. You follow this process to create an organizational hierarchy directly from the root organizational unit to all the nodes in the hierarchical structure.

Instead of manually creating organizational units, you can also use the data workbench capability to import an organizational unit from a template available in SAP Sales Cloud. For this, you log in to SAP Sales Cloud in the responsive user interface (RUI) and choose **Data Workbench • Import** to go to the **Import Data** screen shown in Figure 3.15.

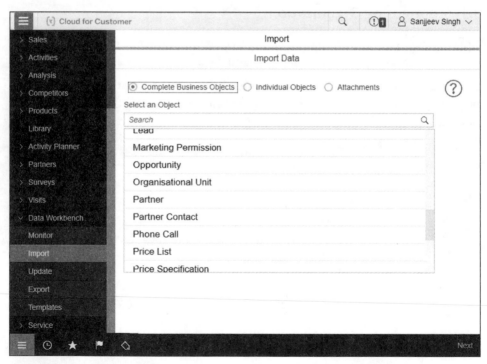

Figure 3.15 Importing an Organizational Unit through the Data Workbench

Select the **Complete Business Objects** radio button, and then select the **Organisational Unit** option from the list. You'll then see the **Download Metadata** link for the organizational unit, as shown in Figure 3.16. It's recommended that you download the metadata to use as a template to update the data for organizational units you want to create.

Figure 3.16 Link to Download Metadata for the Organizational Unit

After you download the metadata, you'll see the templates to update data for the organizational unit, employee assignment, organizational unit functions, name and address, and parent organizational unit (Figure 3.17).

Name	Type	Compressed size	Password ...	Size
OrganisationalUnit	Microsoft Office Excel Co...	1 KB	No	
OrganisationalUnitDistributionChannelAndDivision	Microsoft Office Excel Co...	1 KB	No	
OrganisationalUnitEmployeeAssignment	Microsoft Office Excel Co...	1 KB	No	
OrganisationalUnitFunctions	Microsoft Office Excel Co...	1 KB	No	
OrganisationalUnitNameAndAddress	Microsoft Office Excel Co...	1 KB	No	
OrganisationalUnitParentOrganisationalUnitAssign...	Microsoft Office Excel Co...	1 KB	No	

Figure 3.17 Templates for Organizational Unit Data

You update these templates with your own organizational data and then save them on your local machine. To continue the organizational unit upload process, choose

Data Workbench • Import, and select **Organisational Unit** under **Complete Business Objects**. Click **Next** to go to the **Upload zip file** screen, as shown in Figure 3.18.

Figure 3.18 Importing Organizational Units through the Data Workbench

On this screen, click **Browse**, and then select the template ZIP file from your local machine. For uploading, you can upload as an initial upload or as a delta upload by selecting the **On** or **Off** switch for **Initial Load**, as shown in Figure 3.18. Before executing the actual upload, you have the option of simulating the upload process by selecting the **On** or **Off** switch next to **Simulation Mode**. After that, click **Upload,** and the organizational units will be created in your SAP Sales Cloud tenant from the data provided in your template file.

Note that integration with on-premise SAP applications such as SAP ERP and SAP Customer Relationship Management (SAP CRM) require adoption as the data model because the organizational structures between SAP Sales Cloud and SAP on-premise solutions don't fully match. For example, assigning a sales office and sales group to several sales organizations isn't supported in SAP Sales Cloud. However, via message severity fine-tuning, you can enable a sales unit in such a way that it doesn't need to match the sales organization in the transaction. You set up the organizational structure once to closely reflect your functional organization and then make tweaks as needed, such as assigning employees or managers to organizational units or updating organizational units. You can also delete an organizational unit at the lowest level. When you delete an organizational unit, the system performs a check and provides an update if the organizational unit is already used in transactions.

3.4   Summary

This chapter discussed how organization management in SAP Sales Cloud enables you to graphically represent functional organization, organizational units, and responsible employees and managers. We also reviewed how to set up an organizational structure from scratch, add suborganizational units, and assign employees and managers to the organizational units. In the next chapter, we'll cover managing accounts and contacts in SAP Sales Cloud.

Chapter 4

Account and Contact Management

Accounts and contacts are foundational master data for all transactions in SAP Sales Cloud, such as activities, leads, opportunities, quotes, and sales orders.

Accounts and contacts are master data in SAP Sales Cloud and are crucial for all transactions. *Accounts* are the master data records you want to maintain for companies or customers and prospects you interact with. For example, if you want to do business with company ABC, then you'll create a master data record for this company as an account in your SAP Sales Cloud system. Then you'll use this account record in all lead, activity, appointment, task, opportunity, quote, sales order, and sales planning transactions.

Whereas accounts represent companies or organizations you want to do business with, *contacts* represent the master data of people working at those companies and serving as your contacts. For example, if you're dealing with Mr. John Smith at company ABC, then you'll create John Smith as contact master data in your SAP Sales Cloud system for company ABC. Although you can have more than one contact for one account, you can also mark one as the primary contact that is assigned for that account in the transactions.

In this chapter, we'll review how to create account and contacts for those accounts. We'll also review the key information you can maintain at in accounts and contacts. Some unique features are available in SAP Sales Cloud to influence these capabilities through a scoping exercise. Finally, we'll introduce you to the fine-tuning exercise for accounts available in SAP Sales Cloud.

4.1 Creating Accounts and Contacts

In this section, we'll go over the step-by-step instructions on how to create accounts and contacts in SAP Sales Cloud. To create an account, you log in to your SAP Sales Cloud system in the responsive user interface (RUI), which is SAP Fiori, and navigate to **Customers • Accounts**. The **Accounts** screen appears, as shown in Figure 4.1. The list of accounts in your system is available under **My Accounts**. You can change the filter from **My Accounts** to **My Team's Accounts**, **All**, or **My Territory Team's Accounts** to view additional accounts for these filters.

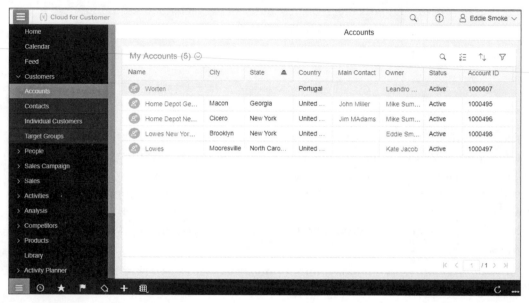

Figure 4.1 Accounts Screen

To create a new account, follow these steps:

1. Click on the **+** button at the bottom of the screen shown previously in Figure 4.1 to go to the **NEW ACCOUNT** screen (see Figure 4.2).

2. At a minimum, maintain the **Name**, **Role**, and **Country** fields to create an account. In addition to entering these fields, you can maintain **Web Site**, **ABC Classification**, **City**, **State**, **Owner** (sales rep for account), and **Parent Account** (if any). It's worth noting that when you create an account, you can assign the **Role** as **Prospect** or **Customer**. At a high level, **Prospect** is an account you haven't created any sales order for yet. As soon as an account is ready to do business with your organization, you'll change the role from **Prospect** to **Customer**.

3. Select **Save and Open** at the bottom of the screen. The new account is created in your SAP Sales Cloud system, and you're taken to the account **OVERVIEW** screen, as shown in Figure 4.3. Information about the account is presented in various tabs, which we'll review in the next section.

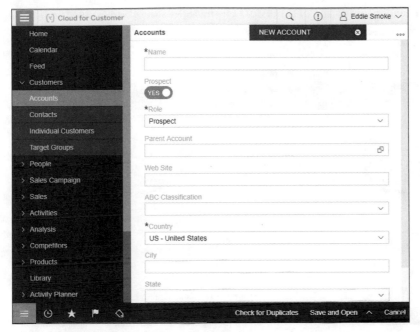

Figure 4.2 Creating a New Account

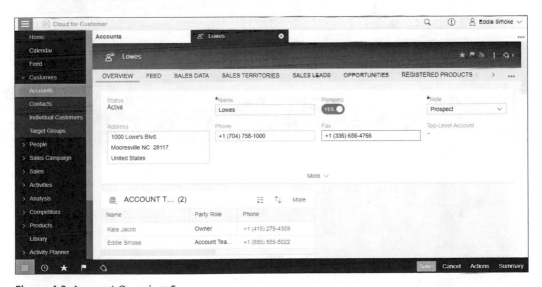

Figure 4.3 Account Overview Screen

After creating the account, you need to create a contact for the account by following these steps:

1. Click on the icon consisting of three dots on the right side, and you see the link to view contacts, as shown in Figure 4.4.

Figure 4.4 Viewing Contacts for the Account

2. Click on **Contacts** to go to the **CONTACTS** tab for the account, as shown in Figure 4.5. Here you have an option to add an existing account (already created in your SAP Sales Cloud system) or create a new contact.

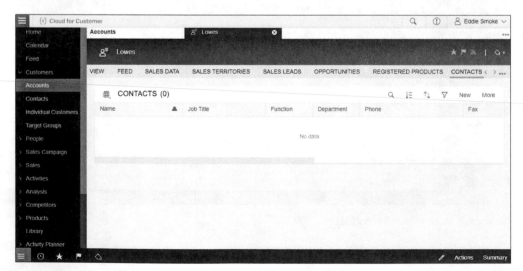

Figure 4.5 Contacts Tab for the Account

3. To create a new contact, click on **New** to go to the **NEW CONTACT** screen, as shown in Figure 4.6.

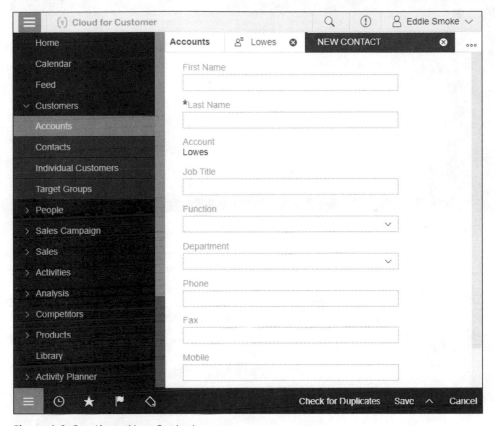

Figure 4.6 Creating a New Contact

4. Maintain **First Name**, **Last Name**, job **Title**, **Job Function**, **Phone** number fields, and click **Save**. The new contact (for this example, John Smith) is created, as shown in Figure 4.7.

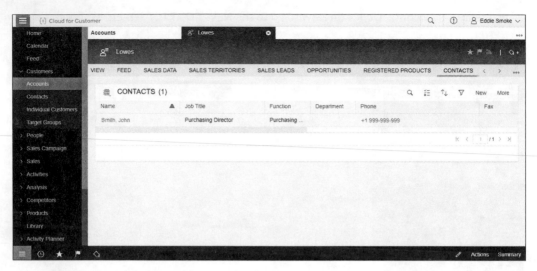

Figure 4.7 Newly Created Contact for the Account

5. If you want to add an existing contact to this account, click on **More • Add**, as shown in Figure 4.8.

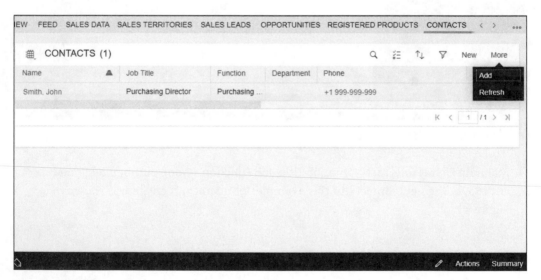

Figure 4.8 Option to Add an Existing Contact to the Account

6. When prompted, select the contact, as shown in Figure 4.9. You can also search for contacts from this screen.

Figure 4.9 Add Contact Search Option

7. Click **OK** to add the contact to the account. For this example, contact Gerd Meyer has been added, as shown in Figure 4.10.

Figure 4.10 Adding a Contact to the Account

8. You can also create a contact directly from the **Contacts** work center in the navigation bar on the left side of the screen. To do so, navigate to **Accounts • Contacts**, as shown in Figure 4.11.

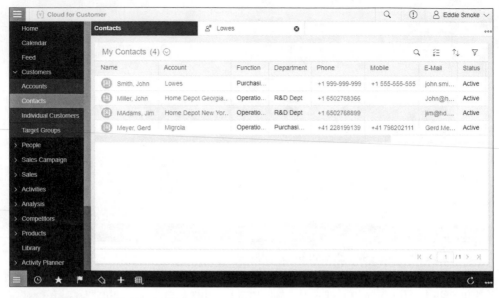

Figure 4.11 Contacts Work Center

9. On this screen, you can display **My Contacts**, **All**, and **My Team's Contacts**. To create a new contact, click on the **+** button at the bottom of the screen. The **NEW CONTACT** screen appears, as shown in Figure 4.12.

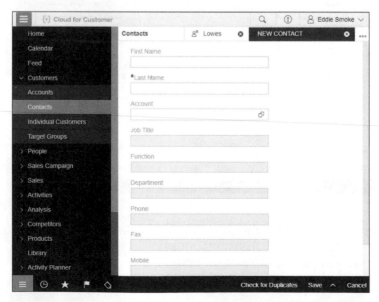

Figure 4.12 Creating a New Contact Directly from the Contacts Work Center

10. Maintain the contact details, and click **Save** to create the contact exactly as explained earlier in this section.

In the next section, we'll review the important tabs on which to maintain information for accounts and contacts.

4.2   Account and Contact Details

Accounts and contacts are the fundamental components of the sales process, and details and information from these master data drive all the sales transactions (leads, opportunities, activities, quotes, sales orders, etc.), so it's important to review how SAP Sales Cloud enables you to maintain the required details. In this section, we'll first review the details for accounts and then for contacts.

4.2.1   Account Details

To see the account details, you choose **Customers • Accounts**. From the account list, open one of the accounts to go to the account **OVERVIEW** screen, as shown in Figure 4.13.

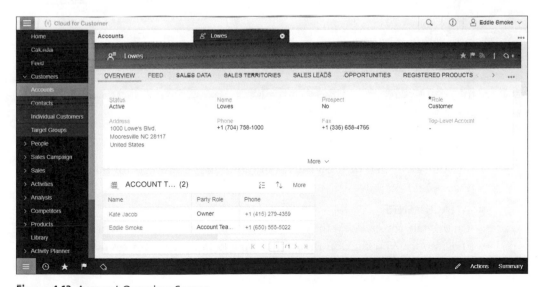

Figure 4.13 Account Overview Screen

On the account **OVERVIEW** screen, you can a snapshot of account information, including status, name, role, address, and phone. Information is presented in tabular format for easy navigation. More than 25 tabs are available out of the box in SAP Sales Cloud, but you don't need to maintain all the tabs. For example, if you don't maintain registered products in accounts, you won't use the **REGISTERED PRODUCTS** tab. Let's review some of the important tabs for accounts:

- **OPPORTUNITIES**

    Although we'll cover opportunities in Chapter 7, the **OPPORTUNITIES** tab shows all the opportunities for an account, as shown in Figure 4.14.

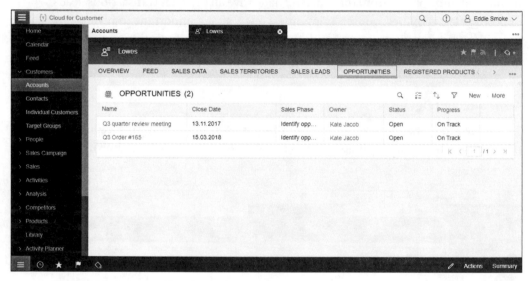

Figure 4.14 Opportunities for an Account

- **CONTACTS**

    As you saw earlier, the **CONTACTS** tab shows all the contacts for that account (see Figure 4.15).

- **ATTACHMENTS**

    On this tab, you can view the current attachments or add your own attachments to the account. You click on the **ATTACHMENTS** tab, then click on **Add**, and choose **Local File**, **Web Link**, or **From Library**, as shown in Figure 4.16.

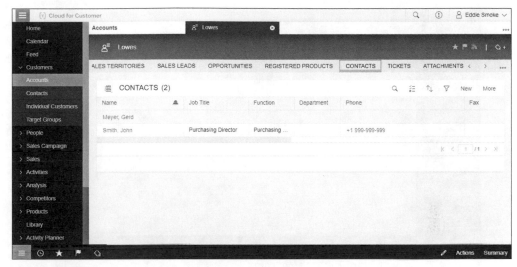

Figure 4.15 Contacts Tab Showing All the Contacts for an Account

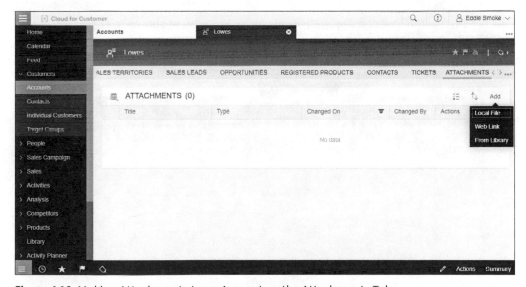

Figure 4.16 Making Attachments to an Account on the Attachments Tab

- **ACCOUNT TEAM**

  Multiple team members, such as the account owner, team member, solution consultant, and partners, often collaborate on an account. On the **ACCOUNT TEAM** tab,
  you can view all the team members for the account, as shown in Figure 4.17.

Figure 4.17 Account Team Tab for an Account

- **LEADS**

  On this tab, you can see all the leads for an account, as shown in Figure 4.18. You'll learn more about leads in Chapter 6.

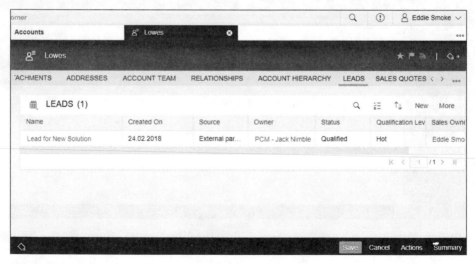

Figure 4.18 Leads Tab Displaying Leads for an Account

- **SALES QUOTES**

  Any sales quotes created for this account are shown on this tab. We'll cover more on quotation management in Chapter 10.

- **ACTIVITIES**

  This tab shows all the activities and tasks created for an account, as shown in Figure 4.19. Here you can view all the types for activities created for an account, such as appointments, tasks, phone calls, and emails. You'll learn more about activity management in Chapter 8.

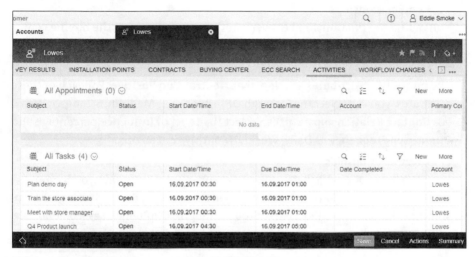

Figure 4.19 Activities for an Account on the Activities Tab

- **RELATIONSHIPS**

  On this tab, you can keep track of other entities, such as ship-to, bill-to, or payers related to the account, as shown in Figure 4.20.

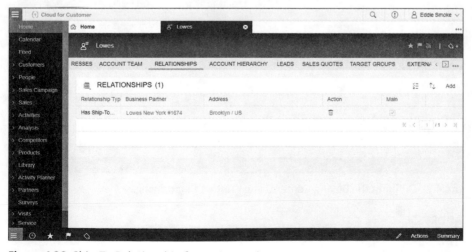

Figure 4.20 Ship-To Relationship for an Account

■ **BUYING CENTER**

This tab lets you map the buying center or decision makers at the account so you can understand the buying center dynamics, influencers, political map, supporters, and so on. You have two options for representing the buying center, as shown in Figure 4.21:

– **Contact Relationships**

You define the relationship between contacts and then map the buying center using attributes, as shown in Figure 4.21. The available **Relationship Types** for contacts are **Directed By** and **Dotted Line To**.

The options for **Attributes** are **Negative**, **Neutral**, and **Positive**. For each of these attributes, you can select the **Strength OF Influence** as **Medium**, **Strong**, or **Weak**. For **Contact Relationships**, you can select the **Level of Influence** percentage and **Interaction Frequency** as **Daily**, **Weekly**, **Monthly**, and so on.

– **Employee Relationships**

You map the relationship between contact and employee (within your company) under the relationship type **Main Employee Responsible**. For each such relationship, you define the attributes of **Attitude**, **Strength of Influence**, **Level of Influence**, and **Interaction Frequency** exactly as described for **Contact Relationships**.

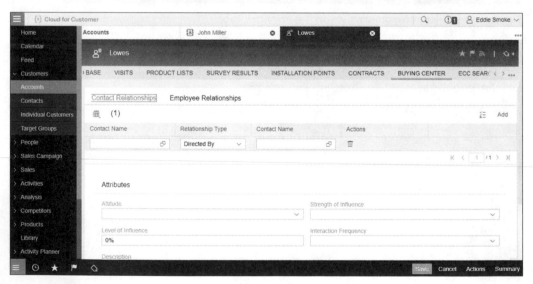

Figure 4.21 Defining the Buying Center Using Contact Relationships

■ **ADDRESSES**

On this tab, you can maintain multiple addresses for an account, as shown in Figure 4.22.

Figure 4.22 Addresses Maintained for an Account on the ADDRESSES Tab

Now that we've covered some of the important tabs to view information related to accounts, let's review tabs available for contacts in the next section.

4.2.2 Contact Details

To view the information available for contacts, you navigate to **Customers • Contacts**, and click on any contact from the list to open the contact **OVERVIEW** screen (see Figure 4.23). The contact **OVERVIEW** screen provides details regarding the **Name**, **Account**, **Job Title**, **Function**, **Department**, **Business Address**, **Personal Address**, **Phone Number**, **Email**, and so on.

Similar to accounts, contact information is provided on 15 tabs. Let's review some of the important tabs for contacts:

- **ADDRESSES**
  Similar to accounts, this tab lists all the personal and business addresses for a contact.

- **RELATIONSHIPS**
  If a contact has relationships with multiple contacts or individuals, you can view all those under this tab, as shown in Figure 4.24. Although there are multiple relationships for one contact, one relationship is marked as the primary, as shown in Figure 4.24.

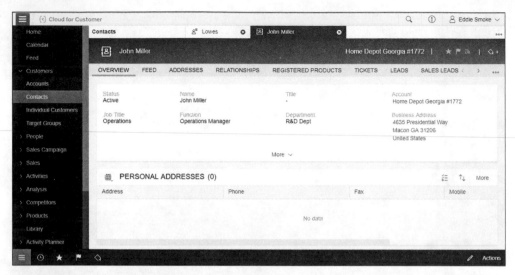

Figure 4.23 Contact Overview Screen

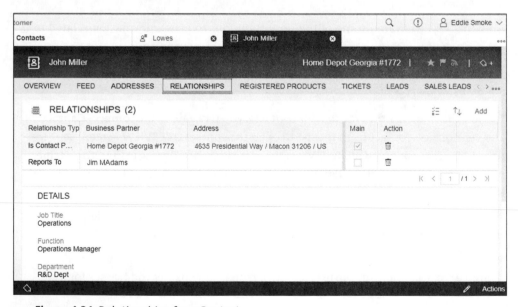

Figure 4.24 Relationships for a Contact

- **LEADS**

   Similar to the **LEADS** tab for an account, if a contact is assigned to any leads, all those leads will be visible under this tab for the contact, as shown in Figure 4.25.

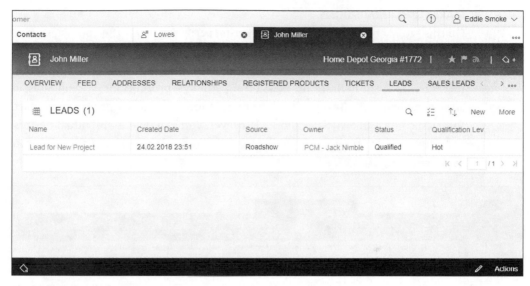

Figure 4.25 Leads for Contacts

- **OPPORTUNITIES**

  If a contact is assigned to any opportunities, you can see those opportunities on this tab, as shown in Figure 4.26.

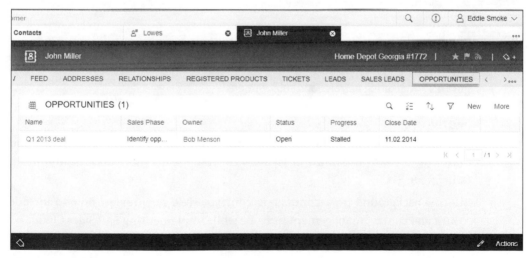

Figure 4.26 Opportunities for a Contact

- **MARKETING PERMISSIONS**

  On this tab, you can maintain the marketing permissions for the contact, such as whether the contact would like to be contacted through email, phone, or text. In addition, you can maintain the communication categories subscribed by a contact, such as event invitations, newsletters, surveys, promotions, and updates, as shown in Figure 4.27. By default, all the permissions and subscriptions are enabled for each contact in SAP Sales Cloud. However, you can delete individual permissions and subscriptions through the delete (trashcan icon) in the **Action** column, as shown in Figure 4.27.

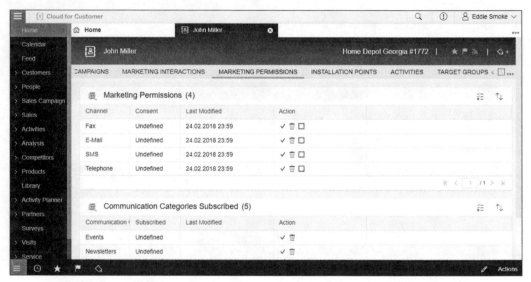

Figure 4.27 Marketing Permissions Subscriptions

- **ACTIVITIES**

  If a contact is involved in activities and tasks, you can view all those activities and tasks on this tab, as shown in Figure 4.28. You'll learn more about activities in Chapter 8.

With this background on accounts and contacts, we'll now review how to include account and contact management in scope while implementing SAP Sales Cloud.

Figure 4.28 Activities Tab for a Contact

4.3   Configuring Accounts and Contacts

To make the necessary settings in SAP Sales Cloud for including accounts and contacts management in the scope of implementation, you log in to SAP Sales Cloud as admin under the HTML5 user interface (UI) and navigate to **Business Configuration • Implementation Projects • Edit Project Scope • Implementation Focus • Scoping • Questions**, then expand **Account and Activity Management**, and click on **Account Management** (see Figure 4.29).

On this screen, you have five questions to review. Depending on your business requirements, you review and enable the following questions to include the appropriate capabilities within the scope of your SAP Sales Cloud solution:

- **Account Hierarchy: Do you want to use account hierarchies?**
  An account hierarchy is a grouping of accounts in a hierarchical manner. It allows accounts to be related in a hierarchy by using a parent account field to link them together, and then one or more accounts are created or linked to each level of hierarchy using that parent account field. If you do business with a group of companies, then account hierarchies are very useful. An account hierarchy helps you offer special pricing to all accounts in the hierarchy. If you enable this in scope for

your solution, you'll be able to set up an account hierarchy in your SAP Sales Cloud solution.

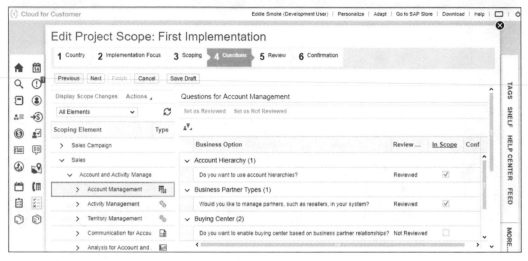

Figure 4.29 Scoping Account Management

- **Business Partner Types: Would you like to manage partners, such as resellers, in your system?**
  If you want to use your partners in the SAP Sales Cloud system, then you need to enable this in scope.

- **Buying Center: Do you want to enable buying center based on business partner relationships?**
  The buying center, covered in Section 4.2.1 earlier in this chapter, helps you understand the relationships involved between buying partners. Knowing their relationship network is the deciding factor for success in an account. If you enable this in your business scope, you'll be able to leverage these business partner relationships in the buying center.

- **Buying Center: Do you want to enable buying center based on buying center relationships?**
  In this option, you can enable relationships within buying center to understand how well you're aligned with decision makers in an account.

- **Distribution Channel: Do you sell products and services using multiple distribution channels?**
  Distribution channels define how you're offering your products and services in the marketplace, for example, selling directly or indirectly through resellers or selling through an online storefront. All of these are methods are distribution channels. If you're selling your products and services through multiple distribution channels, then you'll enable this question.

After you've included accounts and contacts in your business scope, you can move on to fine-tuning activities by logging in to SAP Sales Cloud in the HTML5 UI with the admin role. Then, navigate to **Business Configuration • Implementation Projects • Open Activity List**, choose the **Fine-Tune** tab, and search for "*accounts*", as shown in Figure 4.30.

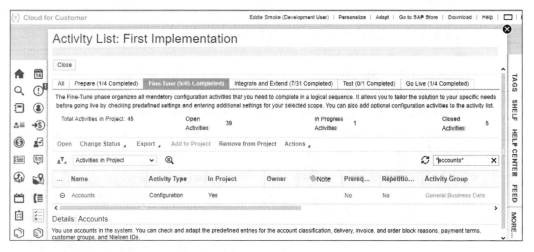

Figure 4.30 Searching for Accounts in the Fine-Tuning Activity

Click on **Accounts** from the search results to see the fine-tuning options for accounts, as shown in Figure 4.31. Under this fine-tuning activity, you can check and adapt the predefined entries for the account in **ABC Classifications**, **Payment Terms**, **Customer Groups**, **Nielsen IDs**, **Customer Roles**, and **Delivery Block Reasons**.

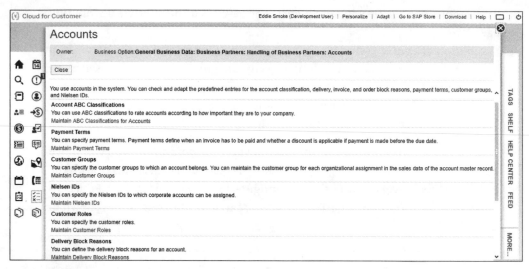

Figure 4.31 Fine-Tuning Activities for Accounts

Let's review these activities as follows:

- **Account ABC Classifications**

  You can use ABC classifications to rate accounts according to how important they are to your company. To adapt this list, click on **Maintain ABC Classifications for Accounts**, as shown in Figure 4.31, and you'll be taken to the **ABC Classifications** screen shown in Figure 4.32.

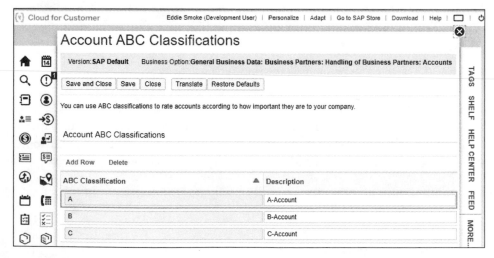

Figure 4.32 Fine-Tuning for Account ABC Classifications

Here you can click on **Add Row** to add your own classification by entering the **ABC Classification** ID and **Description**.

- **Payment Terms**

  Payment terms define when an invoice has to be paid and whether a discount is applicable if payment is made before the due date. Under this fine-tuning activity, you can specify your own payment terms. Click on the **Maintain Payment Terms** link to go to the **Payment Terms** screen shown in Figure 4.33.

  SAP Sales Cloud delivers standard out-of-the-box entries for payment terms such as **Payable immediately due net**, **20 days net**, **30 days net**, and **45 days net**. Review this list if you need to define a new payment term, and then click on **Add Now**, enter the **Payment Terms ID** (starting with "Z") and the **Description**, and save your entry.

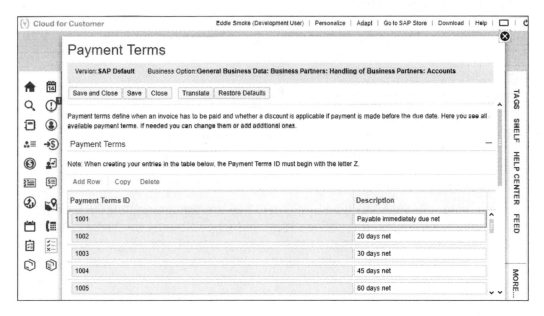

Figure 4.33 Maintaining Payment Terms

- **Customer Groups**

  Customer groups are a way of classifying similar accounts together in one group. You can specify the customer groups to which an account belongs and maintain the customer group for each organizational assignment in the sales data of the account master record. To fine-tune customer groups, click on the **Maintain Customer Groups** link, and to go to the **Customer Groups** screen, as shown in Figure 4.34.

Standard customer groups, such as **Industrial customer**, **Development partner**, and **Wholly-owned subsidiary**, are delivered out of the box. If you need to add your own customer group, click on **Add Row**, enter a new **Customer Group** ID and **Description**, and save. Your new customer group is created.

Figure 4.34 Maintaining Customer Groups

- **Nielsen IDs**

  Here you can specify the Nielsen IDs to which corporate accounts can be assigned. To adapt Nielsen IDs, click on **Maintain Nielsen IDs**, and the **Nielsen IDs** screen appears, as shown in Figure 4.35. Similar to previous fine-tuning, if you need a new Nielsen ID, you can click **Add Row**, enter a new **Nielson ID** and **Description**, and save.

- **Customer Roles**

  Here you can review out-of-the-box customer roles and add a new one if necessary. Click on the **Maintain Customer Roles** link to go to the **Customer Roles** screen shown in Figure 4.36. You can define the customer roles and specify a default customer role for each customer type. If you create a new customer, the chosen default role will be assigned by default to the new customer. You can also change the description of the roles defined by SAP. The original descriptions are **Prospect** for **Role Code BUP002** and **Customer** for **Role Code CRM000**. When you're adding a new **Role Code**, it must start with "Z".

Figure 4.35 Maintaining Nielsen IDs

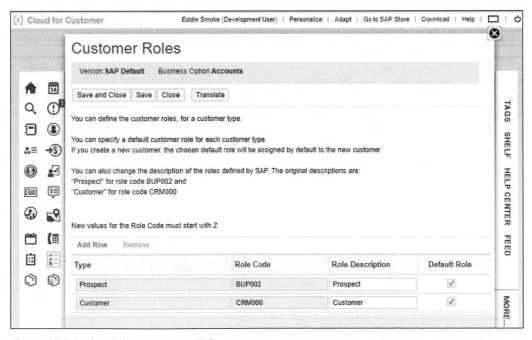

Figure 4.36 Maintaining Customer Roles

- **Delivery Block Reasons**

  Delivery block reasons are helpful if you want to block any sales orders from being delivered to a specific customer. For example, let's say that you want to stop any future products from being delivered to a customer due to outstanding invoices. In that case, you would want to activate the delivery block status for that customer. However, you would also want to assign a delivery block reason so that anyone looking at the customer record would know why the customer has been put on delivery block. In this part of the configuration, you can define your delivery block reasons. SAP Sales Cloud comes with several standard delivery block reasons including credit limit, political reason, bottleneck product, down payment required, and customer request. If needed, you can add your own delivery block reasons.

4.4   Summary

In this chapter, you learned the concepts behind accounts and contacts and how they are created in SAP Sales Cloud. We reviewed what information is maintained for accounts and contacts in various tabs. To influence the scope for accounts, we covered how to include account management in the scope of your implementation, and, finally, we provided step-by-step instructions to fine-tune accounts in SAP Sales Cloud to adapt per your unique requirements. In the next chapter, we'll cover the territory management functionality in SAP Sales Cloud.

Chapter 5

Territory Management

Territory management helps you achieve optimal coverage of your sales market by defining a matrix organization and lets you control data access based on territory hierarchy.

A territory is a geographic area or customer group over which an individual salesperson or sales team has responsibility. These territories are usually defined based on geography (city, ZIP codes, area codes, etc.), sales potential, products groups, historical data, or a combination of these factors. The ultimate aim of territory management is to maximize the market coverage by optimally using the sales resources.

In this chapter, we'll cover the key features of territory management in SAP Sales Cloud and how the solution can be set up to accurately reflect your sales territory. We'll also cover the definition of territory rules, territory realignment, and steps to enable territory management in the scope of your SAP Sales Cloud implementation.

5.1 Territory Management Process

Sales management mostly employs territory management for the following three reasons:

- **Customers**
  Territory management can be used to increase market coverage and provide better customer service.

- **Sales team**
  Territory management provides greater accountability, enthusiasm, and motivation in the sales team. It's great for effective performance evaluation.

- **Management and reporting**
  Territory management enables enhanced control and provides the potential for sales incentives and better allocation of costs and resources per territory.

Territory management can help spread out the workload for your sales team, allowing them to plan and complete tasks more efficiently and effectively, build better customer relationships, and follow through on each sales lead brought to their attention. Just as important is the motivation it provides to sales team if they feel like they are being productive and accomplishing a lot of the sales goals they set out to do.

SAP Sales Cloud enables you to define complex territory hierarchy structures using the highly intuitive territory management capability. In the territory hierarchy, you can assign an owner and team members to each territory node. You can also assign a salesperson to multiple territory nodes with a specific role to support the matrix organization. Similarly, you can assign the same account to one or more territories. Using account attributes, you can define account assignment rules to help you map who covers what territory, which allows quick and easy realignment of territories to ensure optimal sales market coverage.

With that, let's review the key capabilities of territory management in SAP Sales Cloud:

- **Territory hierarchy**
  You can define complex territory hierarchy structures and adjust your territory hierarchy structure according to changing sales markets. Territory management allows you to upload territory hierarchy from Microsoft Excel, data workbench, or application programming interfaces (APIs), as shown in Figure 5.1.

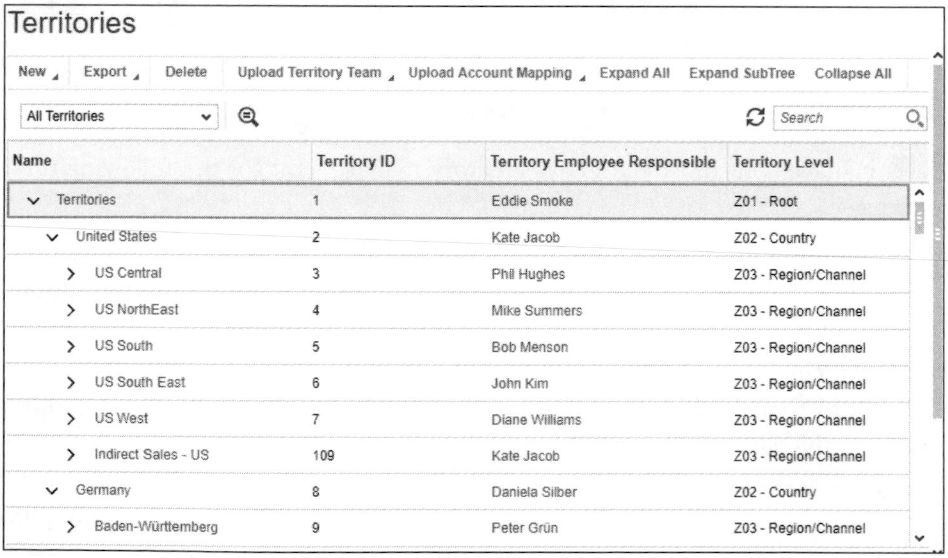

Figure 5.1 Territory Hierarchy Structure

> **Note**
> Similar to territory hierarchy, you can upload the territory team and account territory mapping, including delta uploads from Microsoft Excel or via APIs, as shown in Figure 5.1.

- **Territory team with roles**
  To support the matrix organization, you can assign the same person to multiple territories with a specific role, as shown in Figure 5.2.

Figure 5.2 Assigning a Person to Territories under Specific Roles

You can easily handle reassignment of employees and partner contacts to territories when they leave or move to another territory by updating the territory team. Due to indirect assignment via territory, when an employee or partner contact is removed from the territory team, that person loses access to accounts, contacts, and individual customer and business documents (leads, opportunities, activities, sales quotes, etc.) that are tied to the territory. You can determine and redetermine involved parties in business transactions based on the territory team role.

- **Auto calculate territory**
  Using workflow rules, you can define a rule to call the **Derive Territory** action when an individual customer or account is saved and when certain conditions are met. This will ensure that the **Derive Territory** action is called for every account created manually or brought in from an external application.

- **Sales analysis using the territory dimension**
  SAP Sales Cloud delivers standard territory data sources for out-of-the-box analytics, as shown in Figure 5.3. These data sources include territory hierarchy (territory model), territory account assignment, territory team, and all transactions that support a territory or have territory as a characteristic.

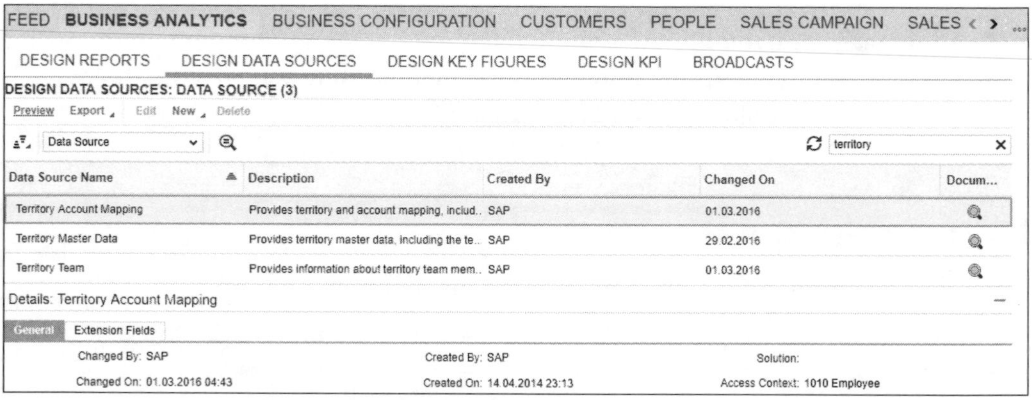

Figure 5.3 Territory-Related Data Sources

5.2   Creating and Processing Territories

If your user is granted both read and write access to update territories, you can do so in both the responsive user interface (RUI) and the HTML5 UI. In the next sections, we'll go over the steps to create and work through a territory hierarchy structure.

5.2.1   Setting Up a Territory Hierarchy

To create a territory hierarchy, you log in to SAP Cloud for Customer and click on **Territories** under **Sales** to navigate to the **Territories** screen shown in Figure 5.4.

For new SAP Cloud for Customer implementations, you won't have any territories predefined, so you need to start with a new territory. To create a new territory, you have two options: upload the territory from Excel or create a new territory manually. To create a new territory, click on **New** (see Figure 5.5), and then choose to create a **New Territory**, **New Sub Territory**, or **Territories from Microsoft Excel**.

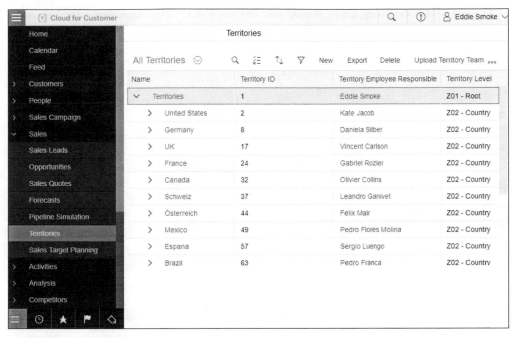

Figure 5.4 Territory Hierarchy Structure in SAP Sales Cloud

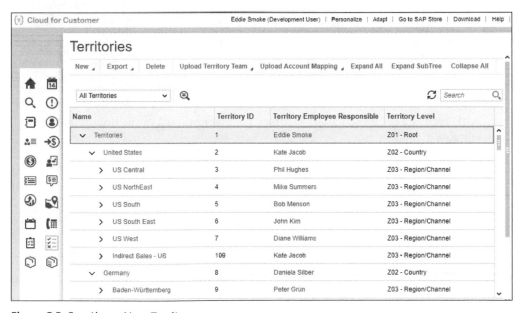

Figure 5.5 Creating a New Territory

Select **New Territory**, and a popup appears for you to enter new territory details, as shown in Figure 5.6.

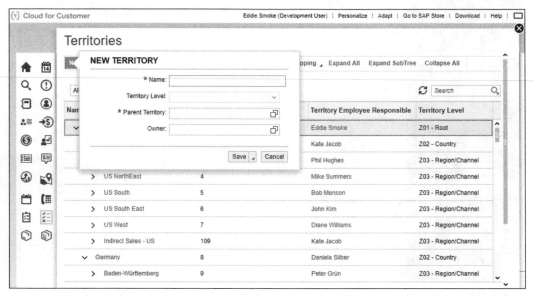

Figure 5.6 New Territory Popup

On this screen, you can't select the **Territory Level** because you're creating a new territory. In this case, you need to select the **Parent Territory** from the search option, select the territory **Owner** (optional), and click **Save**.

If you're creating a subterritory, select the territory under which you want to create the subterritory (refer to Figure 5.5), click **New**, and select **Sub Territory**. In this case, both **Territory Level** and **Parent Territory** are prepopulated in the popup, as shown in Figure 5.7.

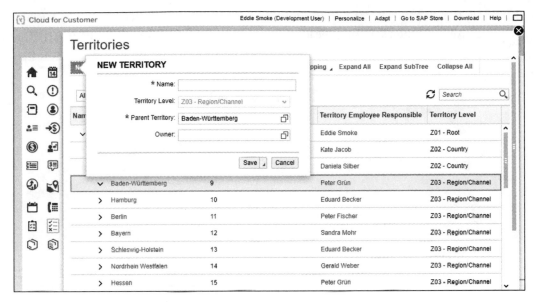

Figure 5.7 Creating a New Subterritory

If you click on **Save and Open**, you're taken to the territory details, as shown in Figure 5.8.

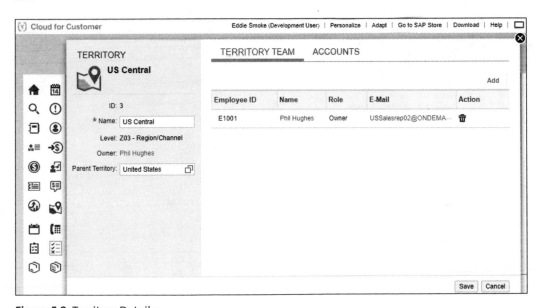

Figure 5.8 Territory Details

On this screen, you can add territory team members under specific roles by clicking on **Add** and then selecting the **Party Role** and **Name**, as shown in Figure 5.9.

Figure 5.9 Adding Territory Team Members

To see the accounts under this territory, click on the **ACCOUNTS** tab, as shown in Figure 5.10.

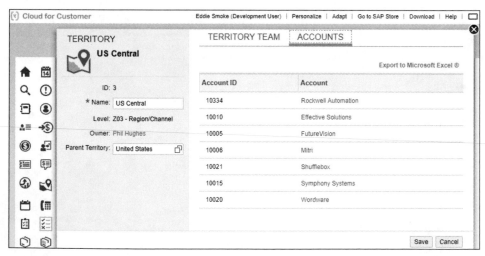

Figure 5.10 Viewing the Accounts under a Specific Territory

Similar to the HTML5 UI, you can log in to the RUI with the administrator role and navigate to **Sales • Territories** to create and update territories, as shown in Figure 5.11.

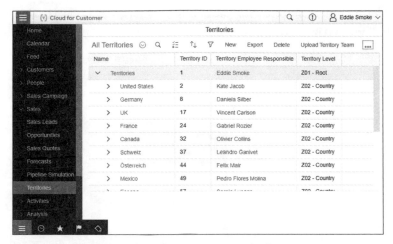

Figure 5.11 Creating and Updating a Territory in the RUI

If you select and open a particular territory, the screen shown in Figure 5.12 appears with basic information about the territory, including the **ID** number, **Name**, **Parent Territory**, **Level**, and **Owner**. At the bottom of the screen, you'll also find the employees assigned to the territory. You can add new employees to the territory by clicking **Add**.

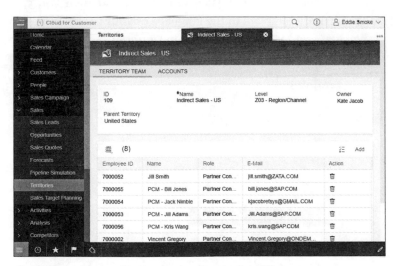

Figure 5.12 Viewing the Territories Map in the RUI

We've touched on uploading territory structures to SAP Sales Cloud from Excel. Now let's review how to upload a territory structure from your local machine using an

Excel template instead of manually creating each and every territory node. For this, log in to SAP Sales Cloud, navigate to **Sales • Territories**. Choose **New** to see your dropdown options, as shown in Figure 5.13.

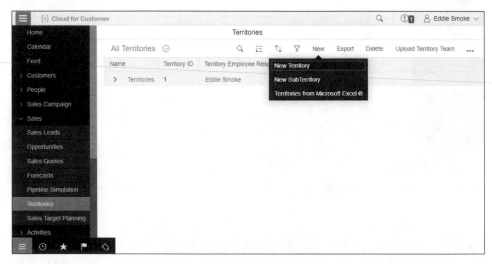

Figure 5.13 Option to Create a New Territory from Microsoft Excel

From the dropdown, select **Territories from Microsoft Excel®**, and then you can choose to download the territory template in the language of your choice from the popup. By default, **Language** is set to **English**, as shown in Figure 5.14.

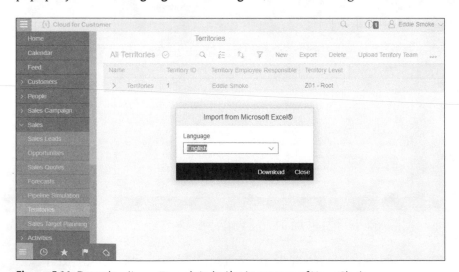

Figure 5.14 Downloading a Template in the Language of Your Choice

Select the language, and click **Download** to download the template to your local machine. Note that you should have already installed the SAP Cloud for Customer Add-In for Microsoft Excel from the **Download** section in SAP Sales Cloud. Open the downloaded Excel territory template, and select the **SAP Hybris Cloud for Customer** tab, as shown in Figure 5.15.

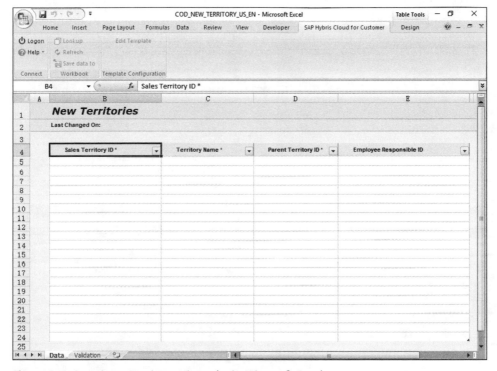

Figure 5.15 Opening a Territory Hierarchy in Microsoft Excel

Before you update this template, select **Logon** to connect to the SAP Sales Cloud system through Excel, and you'll be prompted to enter the login details, as shown in Figure 5.16. Enter the **SAP System URL**, **User Name,** and **Password,** and then select **Log On** to be connected to the system.

After you're connected, you can maintain the **Sales Territory ID**, **Territory Name**, **Parent Territory ID**, and **Employee Responsible ID** per your territory structure. After all the territory details have been maintained in the Excel sheet, you can select **Save data to** in the top-left corner, as shown in Figure 5.17. This step ensures that territory data from Excel is uploaded to the SAP Sales Cloud system.

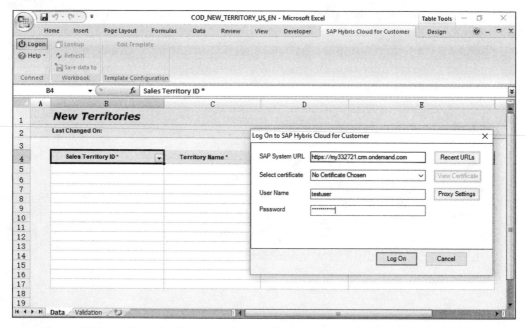

Figure 5.16 Logging In to the SAP Sales Cloud System through Microsoft Excel

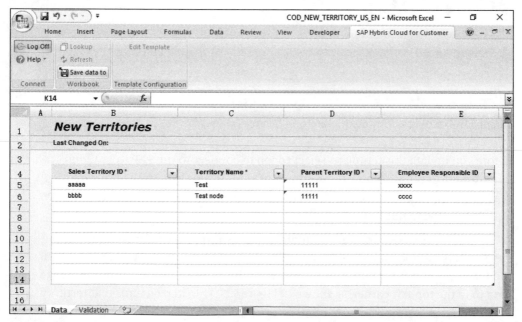

Figure 5.17 Saving the Territory Data from Microsoft Excel to SAP Sales Cloud

In the next section, you'll learn about the territory rules.

5.2.2 Using Territory Rules

The territory assignment rules define the accounts included in the territory based on the account attributes. Account attributes can be used to define rules and calculate territory assignments on accounts. The standard account attributes supported by SAP Sales Cloud are ABC classification, status, role, prospect, address (country, city, state, and postal codes), SAP ERP sales area (sales org, distribution channel, division, customer group), account owner, and any extension field added to the account header. For individual customers (persons), available attributes are date of birth, gender, marital status, nationality, and occupation. For accounts (companies), additional attributes are industry and account hierarchy (top-level account).

To define territory assignment rules, log in to the HTML5 UI under the administrator role, and navigate to **Administrator • Sales and Campaign Settings • Define Rules for Territory Realignment**, as shown in Figure 5.18.

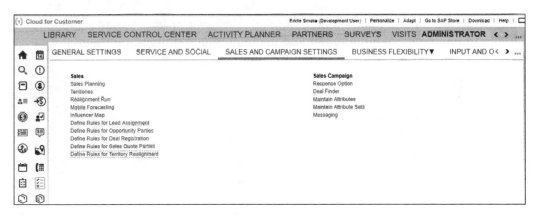

Figure 5.18 Navigation for Defining Rules for Territory Realignment

Click on **Define Rules for Territory Realignment**, and the **Territory Management Rules** screen appears, as shown in Figure 5.19.

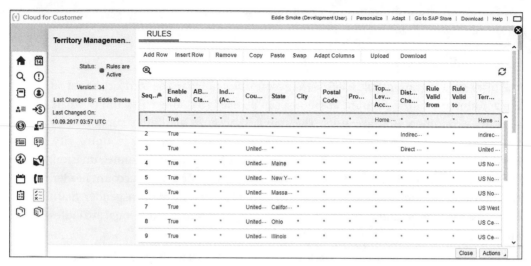

Figure 5.19 Rules for Territory Alignment

The sequence of rules is displayed under the rules with their attributes. You can adapt columns to change the fields used for rule definition by clicking on **Adapt Columns** in Figure 5.19. The **Decision Table Configuration** screen appears, as shown in Figure 5.20.

Figure 5.20 Decision Table Configuration by Rearranging Columns

Using the arrow keys in the **Decision Table Configuration** screen, you can move attributes between **AVAILABLE COLUMNS** and **CURRENT COLUMNS** per your needs. The available attributes are the ones delivered standard with SAP Sales Cloud, and the current attributes are the ones you're using for your territory rules from the standard ones. Depending on your business requirements for territory rules, move the attributes from the **AVAILABLE COLUMNS** to the **CURRENT COLUMNS** and vice versa. The territory rules created here won't take effect unless you activate these rules. To activate a rule, select it, and then click on **Activate Rule** under **Actions**.

5.2.3 Territory Realignment

Whenever there are changes in the territory alignment rules, you need to run the territory realignment to make sure accounts and territory owners are realigned per the new territory definition and coverage. To start territory realignment, follow the navigation **Administrator • Sales and Campaign Settings • Realignment Run**, as shown in Figure 5.21.

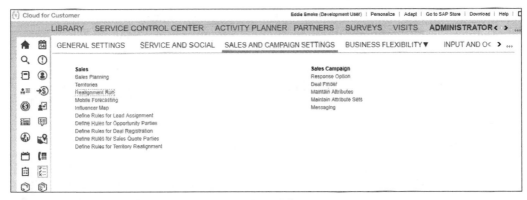

Figure 5.21 Link for the Territory Realignment Run

When you click on **Realignment Run** in Figure 5.21, you're taken to the **Realignment Runs** screen where you can see all the previous realignment runs, as shown in Figure 5.22. Here you have the option of creating a new realignment run (**New** button), scheduling a future realignment run (**Schedule** button), or setting one of the previous realignment runs as obsolete (under the **Actions** button).

Figure 5.22 Realignment Runs

To create a new realignment run, you have two options: realignment resulting in a single territory per account and realignment resulting in multiple territories per account. We'll review both scenarios in the following sections.

Realignment Run for a Single Territory per Account

In a single territory per account, the account-territory relationship can be overwritten manually by a user using an **Override** flag on the account, the account-territory relationship can be uploaded via Excel (same as override but mass action), and the account-territory relationship can be calculated based on rules in the system (accounts flagged as **Manual Override** are skipped in the calculation).

The realignment will take care of recalculating the account-territory relationship based on changes in the rule. The territory realignment for accounts not only updates open leads and opportunities but also realigns open sales quotes and activities (appointments, phone calls, and emails). When you create transactions, such as opportunities, you auto determine the territory on the opportunity based on that of the associated account.

To start the realignment run, follow these steps:

1. Select **New** (refer to Figure 5.22) to go to the **Define New Realignment Run** screen, as shown in Figure 5.23.

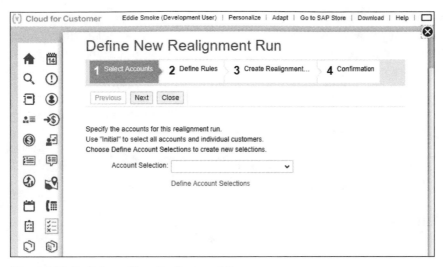

Figure 5.23 Defining a New Realignment Run

2. Select **Initial** from the **Account Selection** dropdown to process all accounts and individual customers. If you want to further filter the account selection, click on **Define Account Selection** to make additional account selections and to process a subset of accounts, as shown in Figure 5.24.

Figure 5.24 Account Selection before the Realignment Run

3. Select the required filters for accounts. You can realign all accounts or filter the accounts that you want to realign by country, region, or any other attribute. After you've made the accounts selection, click **Next** to go to second step, **Define Rules**. In this step, you define the territory, as shown in Figure 5.25.

Figure 5.25 Maintaining Territory Rules for a New Realignment

4. Click on **Maintain Territory Rules** to maintain the territory rules as explained previously in Figure 5.19. The account-territory relationship is calculated based on this central condition table. The first rule that meets the criteria determines the territory, so you need to ensure that more specific rules are on top and more generic rules are at the end. After maintaining the territory rules, click **Next** to go to the third step, **Create Realignment**, as shown in Figure 5.26.

5. Enter the **Title** for the realignment run, and then click **Create** to start the realignment. You're taken to the final step in the process, **Confirmation**, which confirms that the realignment has started (see Figure 5.27).

To check the status of this realignment run, click on the **Open Realignment Run** link in Figure 5.27. The status will show if realignment has started or finished.

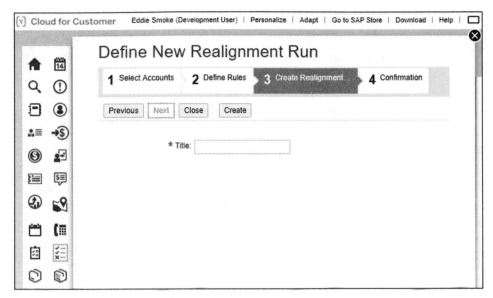

Figure 5.26 Step to Create the Realignment Run

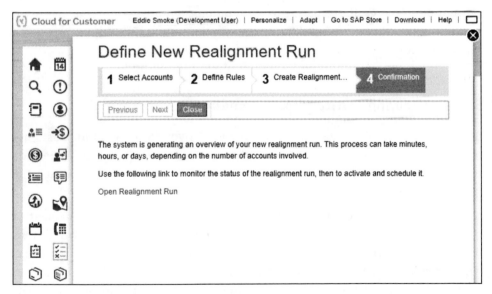

Figure 5.27 Starting a New Realignment Run

Realignment Run for Multiple Territories per Account

In multiple territories per account, the account-territory relationship can be manually maintained or be uploaded using Excel upload as the dedicated territory assignment, and the account-territory relationship can be calculated based on rules in the system. The realignment will take care of recalculating the account territory relationship based on changes in the rules. Realignment won't update the territory in open business documents because there can be multiple territories per account, and you can't programmatically determine the unique territory. When creating a transaction, such as an opportunity, you automatically determine the territory for the opportunity only if the account has one territory; otherwise, the system gives a warning message to the user to select a territory manually from the available territories on the account.

The key difference as compared to a single territory per account is that all rules are executed against each account, potentially resulting in the assignment of multiple territories per account. The advantage of using multiple territories per account is that you can use the SAP ERP sales area (sales org, distribution channel, division, sales office, sales group, customer group) because it results in multiple territories per account by sales area. If you decide to use multiple territories per account, existing business documents won't be realigned because the system isn't able to resolve the unique territory to realign the transactions.

5.3   Configuring Territory Management

Before you can configure territory management in your SAP Cloud for Customer tenant, you need to include territory management in your project scope. To include territory management in the project scope, you need to edit the scope and enable the questions for territory management, as shown in Figure 5.28.

Navigate to **Sales • Account and Activity Management • Territory Management** to review all the scoping-relevant questions for territory management. These questions determine whether you want to include territory management in your scope, whether you want to use a single territory per account or multiple territories per account, whether you want to use account filters for realignment runs, and so on. The scoping questions related to territory management are as follows:

- **Do you want to assign an account to more than one territory?**
  You will enable this if your territory rules are such that same account can be aligned to more than one territory.

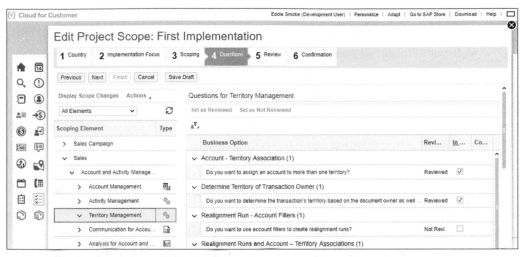

Figure 5.28 Including Territory Management in the Project Scope

- **Do you want to determine the transaction's territory based on the document owner as well as the account?**
  Normally in transactions, you determine the territory ID based on the territory that the account belongs to. However, if you want the territory to be determined based on the territory that the employee responsible belongs to, you would enable this in your scope.

- **Do you want to use account filters to create realignment runs?**
  Realignment rules move accounts from one territory to another. Instead of creating realignment runs for a set of accounts (based on some filters), you can enable this question.

- **Do you want realignment runs to remove territory assignments for accounts that, based on current rules, qualify for no territories?**
  If you enable this question, it will render accounts as without territory if they don't meet the criteria for new territory rules.

- **Do you want to use territory management?**
  If you want to use territory management in your SAP Sales Cloud solution then you will enable this; otherwise you will keep it unchecked.

- **Do you want the territory changes you make to an account, to be automatically updated in the open documents associated with the account?**
  When you do territory realignment, accounts move from one territory to another; it is understandable that you may want transactions associated with those

accounts to be realigned as well so that they reflect accurate territory. Enable this question so that open transactions are realigned as per accounts territory changes.

- **Include closed documents as part of realignment run and if update of open documents is enabled, also include closed documents in that update?**
  Similar to the previous question, if you want closed transactions to be realigned when transactions are realigned, then you will enable this question. This mostly depends on how you want to report on your territories. If you want to compare old territories to current territories, you may not want to move the closed transactions from the old territory to the new one.

After enabling the appropriate questions, click **Next** and save the new scope.

After including territory management in your project scope, you need to perform some fine-tuning activities before setting up your territory hierarchy and territory alignment rules. Click on **Open Activity List** to see the two fine-tuning activities related to territory management, as shown in Figure 5.29.

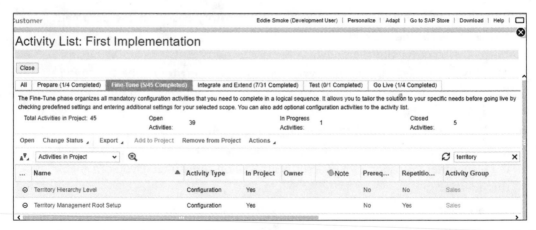

Figure 5.29 Fine-Tuning Activities for Territory Management

In the first activity, **Territory Hierarchy Level**, you can create territory hierarchy levels such as country, region, city, and postal codes. To maintain territory hierarchy levels, click on the **Territory Hierarchy Level** link in Figure 5.29 to go to the **Territory Hierarchy Level** screen, as shown in Figure 5.30. Here you can maintain territory hierarchy levels starting from the root by entering the **Territory Level Code** and **Description**. Click **Save** to confirm the change.

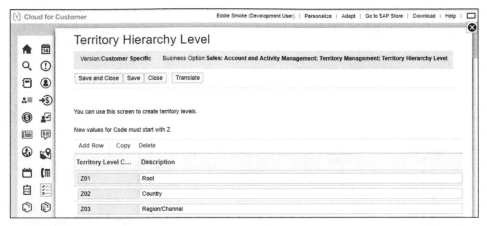

Figure 5.30 Maintaining Territory Hierarchy Levels

The second fine-tuning activity for territory management, **Territory Management Root Setup**, enables you to create a root for your territory. Clicking the link takes you to the **Territory Management Root Setup** screen, as shown in Figure 5.31.

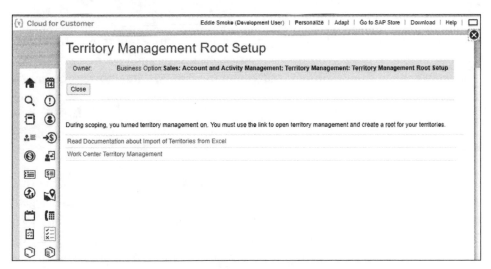

Figure 5.31 Fine-Tuning Activity for Territory Management Root Setup

Here you have a documentation link about importing territories from Excel. To set up the territory root, click on the second link, **Work Center Territory Management**, to go to the **Territory** screen, as shown in Figure 5.32.

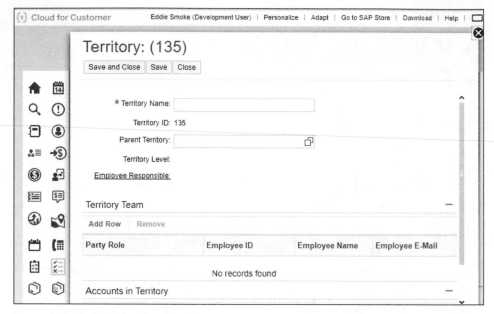

Figure 5.32 Maintaining Territory Root

Here you can maintain the **Territory Name**, **Territory Team**, **Accounts in Territory**, and so on. After maintaining all the details, you can click **Save**, and your configuration is complete for setting up territory management in your SAP Cloud for Customer system.

5.4   Summary

In this chapter, you learned that territory management includes all the activities that are required to create and configure a hierarchy of sales territories and to delegate responsibility at each level of hierarchy to the appropriate employees. We also covered all territory rules by defining the responsibilities of territory and how to set up the territory alignment rules. To account for changes in sales territories, you can use territory realignment runs to make changes to your account-territory assignments and corresponding sales transactions. We also reviewed how to include territory management in the project scope and the corresponding fine-tuning activities. In the next chapter, you'll learn about the lead management functionality in SAP Sales Cloud.

Chapter 6

Lead Management

Leads are fuel for your sales funnel. The quality of leads determines your pipeline performance and forecast commitments. For any successful sales and marketing team, it's absolutely critical to have an effective lead management process and system in place. In this chapter, we'll discuss how SAP Sales Cloud can be used to realize the most effective lead management process.

For sales and marketing professionals, leads are music to their ears. Leads fuel and fill sales funnels, and, most importantly, the quality of leads defines sales performance and converts leads into tangible business opportunities. Although leads can be defined and interpreted in many ways, essentially they signify possible business interest from a prospect or a potential buyer in a company's products or services. Leads can arise from encounters at trade shows, social gatherings, and business networking events that cause interest in your offerings. Sometimes you don't necessarily need to meet someone to get a lead. Interest in your products and services from prospective buyers may come in any form, for example, a phone call or email request from a prospective customer, request for information from your website, response to a survey, and so on.

Leads are about capturing information on prospects or potential buyers that can be as basic as the prospect's or buyer's name and contact information or as elaborate as contact details, company name, products and services of interest, and so on. A lead is the starting point for any sales pursuit, and the more information the lead includes, the easier it is for the sales team to qualify and make informed decisions regarding whether this lead is worth following.

In this chapter, we'll cover the lead management process and how SAP Sales Cloud enables you to manage lead processing for your sales team. Starting with the key capabilities of lead management in SAP Sales Cloud, we'll discuss how leads are created and processed as well as how to configure lead management in your SAP Sales Cloud system per your business requirements.

6.1   Lead Management Process

Regardless of industry or sales processes, there are two types of leads:

- **Active leads**
  With active leads, potential buyers or prospects have expressed interest in your products or services by directly contacting your company, or you've captured their interest in one of your interactions with them. In active leads, you already have an initial communication with prospects.

- **Passive leads**
  Passive leads are perceived interests in your products and services, but not necessarily the explicitly expressed interests from potential buyers or prospects in your offerings. Based on the profiles of your buyers or customers, you can extrapolate potential targets for your products and services. For example, if you're in the business of selling SAP consulting services, than any organization that uses SAP software is a potential target or buyer for your services. If you get a list of 100 organizations running SAP software, they are all passive leads for your business because you perceive them as potential buyers for your services. Because they haven't expressed interest in your services, they aren't active leads but rather passive leads.

Although active leads are preferred over passive leads, the ability to generate active leads is limited. Most companies work from passive leads even though their conversion rate is much lower than active leads. Passive leads are part of demand generation or marketing activities (internal events), whereas active leads are predominantly driven by external events. The key is to have a system and process in place to capture and pursue each lead through the sales process. As Figure 6.1 shows, sales funnels include both active and passive leads. All the leads in the sales funnel go through their individual lifecycle and qualification process before they are either converted or discontinued from further processing.

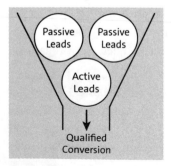

Figure 6.1 Sales Funnel Made Up of Active and Passive Leads

Irrespective of type (active or passive), each lead has some unique characteristics that determine the lead management process, as shown in Figure 6.2.

Figure 6.2 Important Characteristics of Leads

These three important characteristics of leads are described as follows:

- **Time sensitive**
  As you know, a lead captures a possible buying interest from a potential prospect or a buyer who might have a need for your product or services. Because needs change, your potential buyer's interests are also constantly changing, hence the time sensitiveness of leads. Leads have to be acted upon within a stipulated time depending on the industry and line of business. Due to time sensitivity, information on a lead may not be constant and often changes with time. A hot lead might not remain hot after a few days or few weeks because either the prospect's requirements changed or they might already be redlining a contract with your competitor. Hence, it's critical that the lead processor takes into account the time sensitiveness of leads. The lead management process needs to have notifications and workflows in place to trigger workflows and reminders to team members and managers if leads aren't acted upon in a predefined time period.

- **Definite lifecycle**
  Every lead follow a definite lifecycle from creation to close. Due to the time sensitiveness of a lead, it must follow a lifecycle and must be closed within a specified time. Leads can't remain open forever. Leads pass through various stages (or statuses) such as open, accepted by sales, rejected by sales, canceled, converted, and so on. The lead qualification process guides users to work leads through these stages or statuses.

- **Conversion**
  If a lead is qualified, it must be either converted to an opportunity or to an account/contact (if the lead is for a new account). Although the goal is to convert all qualified leads into opportunities, it might not be possible to convert every lead to an opportunity for various reasons, including the lead isn't qualified, the prospect's requirements are no longer valid, the lead isn't worth pursuing for commercial reasons, and so on. The conversion of leads involves creating a follow-up

opportunity from the lead or an account and contact (if the lead was created for an account that doesn't exist in your system yet).

A lead triggers a sales pursuit, and the lead's quality along with the sales process determine the fate of the lead. Whether you're able to take a lead all the way to win the pursuit or you're forced to abandon the pursuit on the way largely depends on the quality of the lead. Lead processing involves taking the lead through its qualification process. As we discussed earlier, leads have some unique characteristics, which the lead management process needs to take into account (i.e., time sensitiveness, lifecycle management, and conversion process).

Although lead processing requirements might vary from industry to industry and from company to company, a set of features serves as a common denominator for the lead qualification process. The following must-have features of lead processing enable you to manage each lead effectively through its lifecycle:

- **Lead routing**
  Lead routing is the process of assigning leads to sales reps so that the leads can be worked on and followed through. When leads are created, you need to have either an automated or manual process to route the leads to appropriate individuals or teams for lead qualification. Automatic lead routing can be based on rules regarding geographical coverage, product category, responsible marketing team or sales team, and so on. The territory management functionality available in SAP Sales Cloud can be used to automate lead routing to sales reps.

- **Lead scoring**
  To measure the quality and effectiveness of leads, you need to assign scores to them so that you can compare various lead sources for their effectiveness.

- **Lead acceptance or rejection**
  When leads are assigned to a sales team for processing, the team can either accept the lead if it's qualified or reject the lead if it's not worth pursuing. The lead acceptance and rejection process is handled through accepted and rejected lead statuses. You can also assign a reason for rejection so that you can track the root cause of the lead rejection.

- **Lead nurturing**
  Lead nurturing is the process of qualifying leads with additional information to help bring the lead to its logical end. You can carry out specific lead qualifying activities to determine if and when a lead can be converted to an opportunity.

- **Integration with lead generation systems**
  To constantly feed your sales funnel with new leads, the lead management process should be integrated with the lead generation system. Many lead-generation tools are available that you can integrate with SAP Sales Cloud, including Hoovers, Marketo, and Avention.

- **Standard conversion analytics**
  One of the critical features for lead management is the ability to measure the conversion of leads to sales opportunities. Because you acquire leads from various sources, it's important to measure the effectiveness of each lead so that you're not wasting time and resources on ineffective lead sources. SAP Sales Cloud offers standard analytics and reports to measure the effectiveness of the lead conversion process.

- **Rule-based notifications**
  The time sensitivity of leads requires rule-based notifications and workflows to trigger reminders for the sales team so that leads are acted on within a stipulated time period, and no sales opportunities are lost. In SAP Sales Cloud, you can trigger rule-based tasks and emails as notifications to the sales team. For example, you can set up a task notification for a sales rep if the lead has been assigned but hasn't been accepted or rejected by a sales rep for 24 hours. You can also set up escalation notifications to management if no action is taken on a lead within 48 hours.

- **Lead conversion process**
  For a lead to meet its logical end, you need to have a lead conversion process in place. Qualified leads can either be converted to opportunities or to accounts and contacts. If you believe that a lead should be pursued for a tangible sales opportunity, you convert the lead to a follow-up opportunity transaction, and the lead is marked as converted. Otherwise, you convert the lead to an account and contact if the lead was created for a new account and contact, which hasn't been created in your system yet.

  Figure 6.3 shows the lead conversion process. After a lead is converted either to an opportunity or an account and contact, the lead is marked as converted, and you can't work on or edit that lead anymore. In SAP Sales Cloud, you can control how many opportunities can be converted from a lead through configuration, which is covered in Section 6.3.

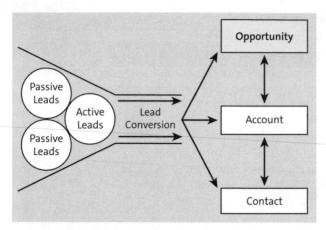

Figure 6.3 Lead Conversion Process

6.2   Creating and Processing Leads

In SAP Sales Cloud, leads can be created manually by users or automatically by a marketing campaign or through integrated lead generation systems (e.g., Marketo, Avention, and Hoovers). Irrespective of how leads are created in the system, the information needed to create leads, nurture them, and subsequently convert them to opportunities largely remains the same. The SAP Sales Cloud system has a very intuitive lead management process that can be used by any industry or organization to enable the most efficient lead generation and qualification engine. The key is to define such an effective and optimal process that the sales team can leverage the system to reinforce the process to achieve the most value for your leads and allow nothing to fall through the cracks as far as following up and nurturing new leads are concerned.

Before we walk through the lead creation and processing, let's briefly discuss how leads are represented in SAP Sales Cloud to provide a preview and a refresher for those who have used other customer relationship management (CRM) solutions. Leads used to be represented as transactional data, requiring a three-step process in which you needed to create a prospect and contacts before you could create the lead.

In SAP Sales Cloud, however, a lead is a transaction that you can create with very basic information per your requirements, such as company name, contact person, phone, email, and so on. These details are entered in the lead document, and no master record for the prospect or contact is created at that point. You should think of a lead as an interim document with a lifecycle. The lead lifecycle defines the processing of the lead and the subsequent step when the lead lifecycle ends. There are three possible outcomes for the lead, as shown in Table 6.1.

Action in Lead	Action Details
Lead rejected	The lead is rejected, and no follow-up process is needed for the lead.
Lead accepted and converted to an account and contact	The lead is qualified for a prospect and contact, but there is no evident opportunity on the horizon. In this case, the lead will be converted to an account and a contact, and the lead will be closed.
Lead accepted and converted to opportunity	The best outcome is that the lead is qualified, and there is an immediate opportunity. In this scenario, the lead will be converted to an opportunity. As part of the conversion process, an account, contact, and opportunity are created with just one click.

Table 6.1 Available Actions for Leads

Leads are not only created for new accounts and contacts but also for existing accounts and contacts as well. For existing accounts and contacts, when leads are converted to opportunities, the accounts and contacts aren't created as part of the lead conversion process because they already exist in the system.

As mentioned earlier, a lead is a time-sensitive document because it captures the interest of ever-changing prospects at a point in time. It's critical that the lead is acted on within a specified time period. SAP Sales Cloud allows you to configure thresholds and notifications for lead processing to ensure that leads are followed up on and converted to opportunities or accounts and contacts as the case may be. Depending on our business, industry and market dynamics, or product lines, your lead qualification threshold could vary from one hour to one week.

The key is to have the threshold built in to the system so that notifications are triggered as tasks and emails to respective team members as a reminder to follow up on the leads. If a lead is rejected by the sales team with a reason for rejection, no further action is needed on the lead; however, if the lead is accepted by a sales rep, the lead can be converted either to an account and contact or to an opportunity. If a lead has been converted to an account, the lead is marked converted, and no further action is needed or carried out on the lead. However, if a lead is converted to an opportunity, you have an option to keep the lead open for further processing, for example, if you need to create more than one opportunity as a follow-up from that lead.

The option to keep the lead open for conversion to an opportunity is controlled through SAP Sales Cloud configuration. Suppose you configure this limit to be two. In that case, when you create a follow-up opportunity from the lead, the lead still allows you to create one more opportunity as a follow-up transaction from the lead. However, after creating the second opportunity, the lead is marked converted, and you can't create another opportunity from this lead because you've already created two opportunities and reached the maximum limit of two set through the configuration.

In the following sections, we review the step-by-step process for creating and processing leads in SAP Sales Cloud. We also cover the logical follow-up process or transaction from a lead.

6.2.1   Creating Leads

We'll only cover the process of creating manual leads because automatic lead creation through marketing campaigns and other lead-generation systems such as third-party marketing systems or SAP Marketing Cloud is outside the scope of this book. In SAP Sales Cloud, leads can be created manually in many ways and from different sections of the application. You can manually create leads in the system one lead at a time, which we'll demonstrate in this section. You also have the option to mass create the leads in SAP Sales Cloud through a data migration template.

To create leads from the **Sales Campaign** work center, follow these steps:

1. Log in to SAP Sales Cloud.
2. In the navigation bar on the left side of the screen, select **Sales Campaign** and then **Leads** (Figure 6.4). **Leads** is part of marketing under the **Sales Campaign** work center.
3. Select **My Leads** from the dropdown to enter the **Leads** view and see a list of leads. Figure 6.5 shows the dropdown variants available: **All**, **Converted**, **In Approval Leads**, **Leads for My Territories**, **My Leads**, **My Team's Leads**, **Qualified**, and **Unassigned**.
4. To create a new lead, click on **Create** (+ in bottom-left menu bar), and the **New Lead** screen appears, as shown in Figure 6.6.

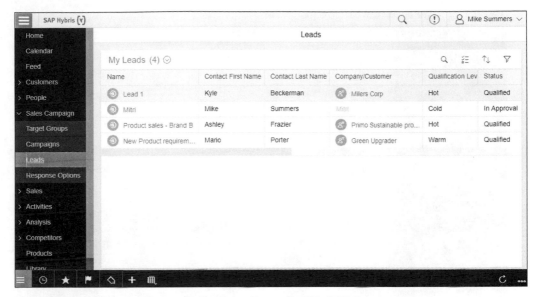

Figure 6.4 Leads Navigation under the Sales Campaign Work Center

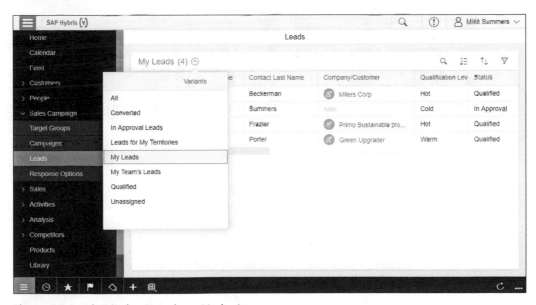

Figure 6.5 Leads Display Dropdown Variants

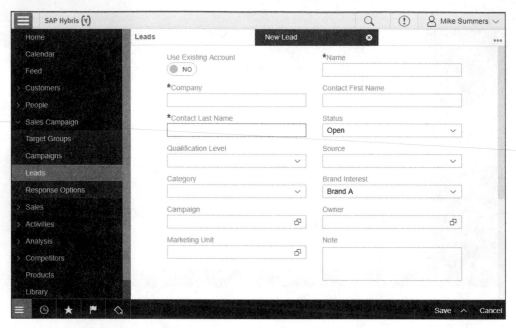

Figure 6.6 New Lead Creation Screen

5. While creating a new lead, first select whether this lead is created for an existing account or a new account. If you select **NO** under **Use Existing Account**, you're presented with a free-text field to enter the **Account Name**. However, if you select **YES** for **Use Existing Account**, then you need to select one of the existing accounts, as shown in Figure 6.7.

Following are descriptions of some of the important fields in a lead transaction:

– **Status**

Statuses such as **Open**, **Qualified**, **Accepted**, and **Declined** are assigned to the leads for better processing and reporting. In addition to the standard lead statuses, custom entries can be added using business configuration.

– **Qualification Level**

To better classify the leads, you can assign qualification levels such as **Hot**, **Cold**, and **Warm** to the leads.

– **Source**

To help differentiate the quality and effectiveness of leads, you can assign a source to the leads such as **Campaign**, **Road Show**, **Trade Fair**, **Telephone Inquiry**, and so on.

Figure 6.7 Lead Creation for an Existing Account

- **Category**
  Assigning categories further classifies leads based on your internal assignments such as **Prospect for Products**, **Prospects for Service**, and **Prospects for Training**.

- **Campaign**
  If a lead has been created as part of a campaign, then you can assign the campaign ID to the lead for identification and reporting purposes.

6. Maintain all the required information on the **New Lead** creation screen, and click **Save** to successfully create the lead. After maintaining the pertinent information in the lead, you have three options to save it:

   - **Save**
     Saves the lead and closes the **New Lead** screen.

   - **Save and New**
     Saves the lead, and the **New Lead** screen is presented to enter details for the next lead. If you're planning to create more than one lead at a time, **Save and New** is a good option to enter all the leads one after another into the system.

   - **Save and Open**
     Saves and opens the lead so that you can maintain additional lead details as needed.

7. For this example, select **Save and Open**, and the lead is created and opened for editing and processing as shown is Figure 6.8.

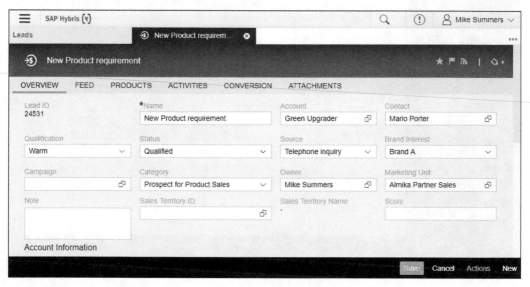

Figure 6.8 Lead Overview Screen and Tabs for Additional Details

As evident from Figure 6.8, SAP Sales Cloud offers a very intuitive user interface (UI) for displaying leads. The lead information is presented in different tabs, including **OVERVIEW**, **FEED**, **PRODUCTS**, **ACTIVITIES**, **CONVERSION**, and **ATTACHMENTS**, as shown in Figure 6.8. These tabs can be configured and personalized based on the scope of the project. There are more UI tabs that you can configure SAP Sales Cloud to enable or hide as needed to support your business requirements. (For more information on personalization, see Chapter 18.) For now, let's review the standard UI tabs available in a lead:

- **OVERVIEW**
  Displays lead details such as **Lead ID**, **Name**, **Account**, **Contact**, **Qualification**, **Status**, **Source**, and **Category**.

- **FEED**
  Provides details on any lead updates. It's a great tool if a team is working on the lead.

- **PRODUCTS**
  Enables you to assign products to the lead.

- **ACTIVITIES**
  Lists all the activities created for the lead such as appointments, tasks, phone calls, and emails.

- **Contacts**
  Enables you to add customer contacts for the lead.

- **Sales and Marketing Team**
  Allows you to add internal team members from sales and marketing who are working on the lead.

- **Involved Parties**
  Allows you to add all the external parties, such as customers and partners involved, who are collaborating on the lead.

- **CONVERSION**
  Shows the leads that have been converted to opportunities.

- **ATTACHMENTS**
  Enables you to attach documents and images to the lead.

- **Changes**
  Shows the change log of what and who changed the lead.

- **Surveys**
  We can attach surveys to qualified leads. For surveys, newer versions of the same survey can be created if needed. Activating a newer version of a survey will inactivate the previous version. When you attach the survey to the lead, only the newer active version will be attached. If you used the previous version of the survey in the lead, those surveys will remain unchanged.

- **Tickets**
  Enables you to add service tickets to the lead.

- **Sales Quotes**
  Shows the sales quotes created with reference to the lead.

- **Sales Orders**
  Shows the sales orders created with reference to the lead.

- **Approvals**
  Shows all the approval details and enables you to start a formal approval process for the lead.

- **Document Flow**
  Shows all the preceding and subsequent documents linked to the lead such as the preceding lead, follow-up opportunity, or quotation.

- **Workflow Changes**
  Shows the workflow changes if you've enabled workflow for the lead.
- **Notes**
  Allows you to add free notes to the lead.

6.2.2   Processing Leads

Processing leads refers to uncovering additional information to determine whether the lead is worth pursuing and should be converted to an opportunity or whether the lead should be discontinued. Let's discuss the key features of leads in SAP Sales Cloud and how they are processed:

- **Lead scores**
  These scores are used to determine the viability of the lead in terms of its likelihood to convert. Scores can also be used to automatically qualify leads if they exceed a certain threshold. SAP Sales Cloud offers the following types of lead scores:

  - **Engagement score**
    A score is assigned to a lead based on the level of engagement from the customer. Scoring models can be set up under **Sales Campaign • Lead Scores** based on a customer's response to sales campaigns.

  - **Predictive score in the deal finder**
    In the deal finder, sales reps can select any topic of interest and add leads to the funnel. After the leads have been added to the funnel, integration with predictive analytics help them prioritize the leads based on their lead scores. Sales reps can use these scores to review leads and convert them to opportunities.

  - **Survey score**
    Lead qualification questionnaires can be set up in the **Survey** work center with scores assigned to potential answers. Using the activity planner and routing rules, you can assign these lead qualification questionnaires to leads based on type, geography, customer category, and so on. These questionnaires serve as the checklists, guidelines, and fact-gathering tools for sales reps to qualify the leads. Based on the responses, the system aggregates the score into a total survey score for the lead. Figure 6.9 shows an example of a score assigned to a lead.

- **Lead routing or distribution rules**
  These rules can be set up as route leads to a person, marketing unit, or territory based on the attributes of the lead or associated account and contact. Lead routing rules can be administered by local or global administrators, and they can be uploaded from Microsoft Excel as well. Administrators set up lead routing by

choosing **Administrator • Sales and Campaign Settings • Define Rules** for lead assignment, as shown in Figure 6.10.

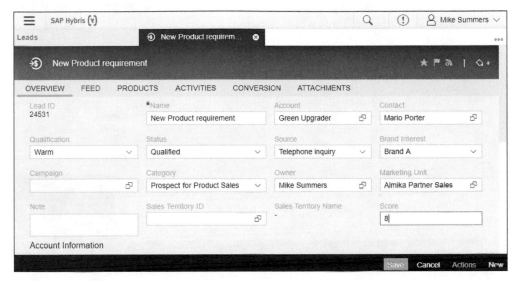

Figure 6.9 Assigning a Score to a Lead

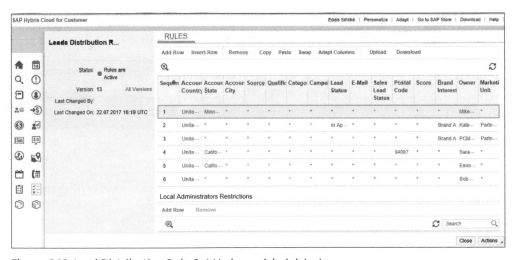

Figure 6.10 Lead Distribution Rule Set Up by an Administrator

- **Lead routing execution**

  Routing is triggered on the creation of a lead, and the lead owner is assigned per the applicable rule. Rules can also be executed at a later stage in the lead's lifecycle if certain lead attributes have changed after creation or if the rules are changed by using the action **Assign Selected Leads Using Rules**, as shown in Figure 6.11. In addition, using workflow rules, lead distribution rules can be triggered every time a lead is saved or specifically when certain routing-relevant attributes change.

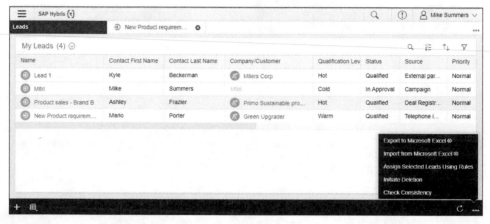

Figure 6.11 Lead Routing Execution

- **Lead status**
  Statuses enable you to maintain leads through their lifecycles such as **Open, Qualified**, **Accepted**, **Accepted**, and **Declined**, as shown in Figure 6.12.

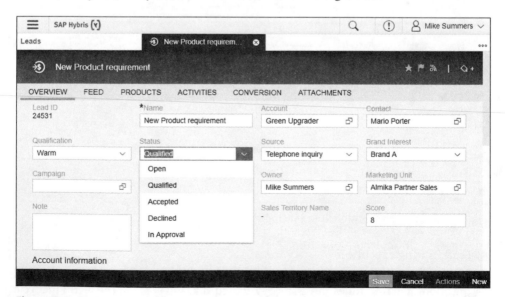

Figure 6.12 Statuses on Leads

In addition to the standard statuses delivered, custom statuses can be added using business configuration. The **Converted** status is the logical end of the status chain. You can't assign this status manually to lead; it's system assigned as and when the lead is converted to an opportunity.

- **Lead qualification**
  Qualification levels represent the likelihood of the lead to be converted to an opportunity. The standard qualification levels available in SAP Sales Cloud are **Cold**, **Hot**, and **Warm**, as shown in Figure 6.13.

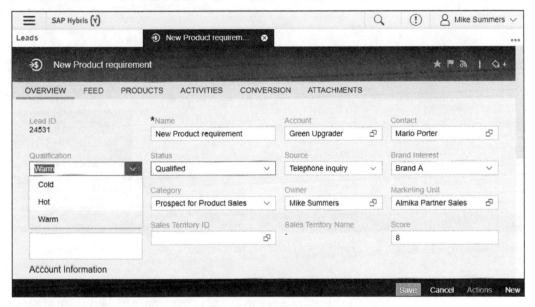

Figure 6.13 Standard Qualification Levels Available for a Lead

If needed, you can define additional custom qualification levels in configuration. Lead qualification levels can be manually maintained or automatically updated based on any business criteria using workflow rules.

- **Lead aging notification**
  The manager of a sales rep can be notified if a lead remains too long in a certain phase (known as *aging*). By default, notification has a high priority and automatically expires 14 days after creation. You can modify the notification process for lead aging through configuration.

- **Converting leads**
  You can convert leads to an opportunities or account and contact as the final stage of the lead lifecycle. Figure 6.14 shows the action to convert a lead to an opportunity.

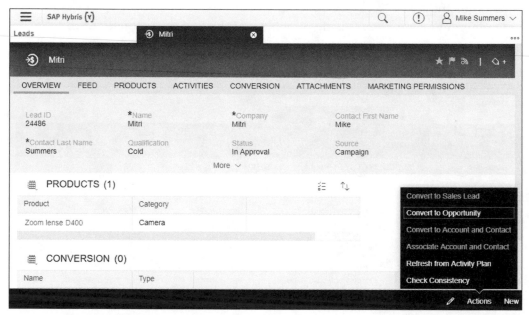

Figure 6.14 Action to Convert a Lead to an Opportunity

The link between an opportunity and its lead is maintained to track the effectiveness of the demand-generation process. A lead can be converted into one or more opportunities as set in configuration.

- **Avention (now called D&B Hoovers) and SAP InfiniteInsight**
  The integration of these solutions with SAP Sales Cloud allows you to automatically create and score leads. After you've defined triggers in Avention and activated the integration, data from Avention is automatically imported on the basis of triggers and results as leads in SAP Sales Cloud. With SAP InfiniteInsight active integration, each lead is enriched with a lead score derived from SAP InfiniteInsight evaluations. Sales reps use the lead scores to decide which leads to pursue. Sales reps also use the deal finder feature to view the scored leads brought in by SAP Sales Cloud and to determine whether they want to convert them into opportunities.

> **Note**
>
> SAP InfiniteInsight is a suite of tools for predictive analytics that allows automated creation of accurate and robust predictive models.
>
> Avention provides business lead generation, qualification tools, and a business contact database.

- **Business card scanner**

  You can quickly create leads directly in SAP Sales Cloud by scanning business cards from mobile devices, as shown in Figure 6.15.

Figure 6.15 Lead Created from a Business Card via Mobile Device

This capability is enabled by a software from partner company ABBYY. You'll need to obtain a license from ABBYY before using these capabilities. For more details, visit *http://cloud.ocrsdk.com*.

- **Mobile access to lead**

  Mobile access is available for iOS, Android, and Windows mobile devices. Users can view and edit leads from mobile devices based on their authorizations, as shown in Figure 6.16.

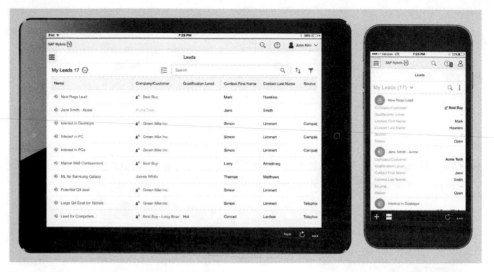

Figure 6.16 Lead Access from Mobile Devices

Reports, graphical views, and offline support for leads are available from mobile devices. Due to the responsive user interface (RUI) layout configuration in the desktop version, adaptation and personalization remain intact in mobile devices.

- **Lead change history**
  History can be activated to keep track of all changes made to the lead over a period of time, as shown in Figure 6.17.

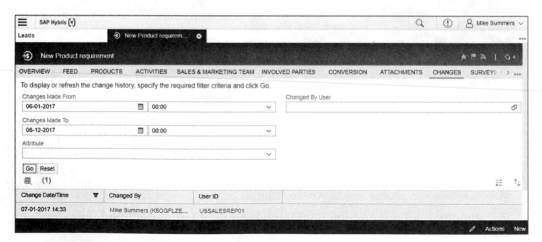

Figure 6.17 Lead Change History

- **Lead copying**

  Copying leads allows you to create a new lead from an existing lead, as shown in Figure 6.18. The main information is copied to simplify the lead creation process.

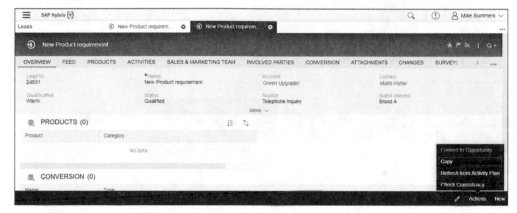

Figure 6.18 Copying a Lead to Create Another Lead

- **Lead attachments**

  You can attach files of different formats to leads by choosing **Local File**, **Web Link**, or **From Library**, as shown in Figure 6.19.

Figure 6.19 File Attachment Options

- **Activities in leads**

  You can track all the activities (**APPOINTMENTS**, **TASKS**, **PHONE CALLS**, **E-MAILS**) carried for a lead, as shown in Figure 6.20. Activities can be created from the **Leads** work center, and lead information will be defaulted in the activity.

- **Integration with LinkedIn Sales Navigator**

  This integration for SAP Sales Cloud allows you to leverage LinkedIn Sales Navigator from the **LEADS** overview screen and view additional details about the account such as size, location, LinkedIn connections, common connections, etc. This functionality can help you find additional leads at a company, get introductions through common connections, or save a lead for future use. Additionally, on the **CONTACT** tab in leads management, you can see the details of the LinkedIn connections for the lead. This is a very powerful feature you can use from the LinkedIn Sales Navigator without leaving your SAP Sales Cloud application.

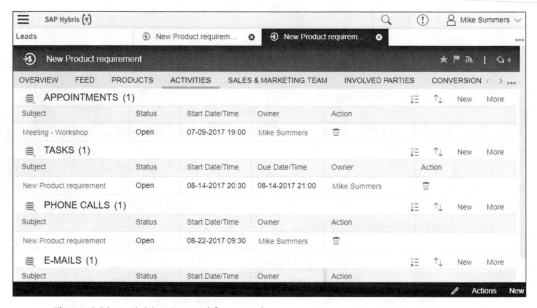

Figure 6.20 Activities Created for a Lead

6.2.3   Following Up Leads

There are three options to follow up leads, as follows:

- **Convert to opportunity**
  Sales reps expect to convert leads to opportunities so that the lead can be followed up methodically through the sales cycle until business in won. The opportunity is the logical next step in the sales process from the lead. Figure 6.21 shows that through the **Actions** menu, a lead can be converted to an opportunity. In this case, information from the lead is copied to the newly created opportunity, and the lead is marked as converted.

- **Create new account or contact**
  If a lead isn't qualified to be converted to an opportunity, sales reps can convert

the lead to an account and contact (if the lead is for a new account and contact) by choosing **Convert to Account and Contact** from the **Actions** menu.

- **Associate with existing account and contact**
  If a lead is for an existing account and contact in the system, then sales reps can select **Associate Account and Contact** from the **Actions** menu to associate the lead to an existing account and contact.

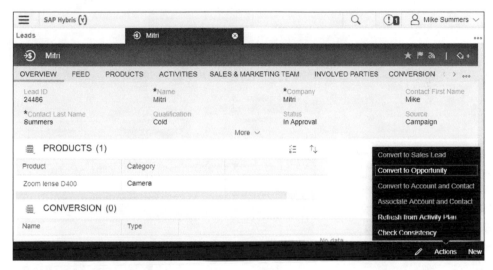

Figure 6.21 Following Up a Lead

> **Note**
>
> For more information on opportunities, see Chapter 7. To learn how to create a new account and contact or associate a lead with an existing account and contact, see Chapter 4.

6.3 Configuring Lead Management

Currently, SAP Sales Cloud configuration is only allowed in an HTML5 UI. On the top right of your SAP Sales Cloud RUI screen (when you log in), click on the user's name followed by **Launch HTML5**. Before you start configuring leads per your business requirements, you must include the leads and also review all the questions as part of a project scoping exercise. Although we covered project scoping in Chapter 2, we'll now discuss the additional steps specific to lead management for updating the scope.

6.3.1   Adding Lead Management to the Project Scope

To include lead management in the project scope, follow these steps:

1. Navigate to the work center, and then choose **BUSINESS CONFIGURATION • IMPLE-MENTATION PROJECTS** (see Figure 6.22).

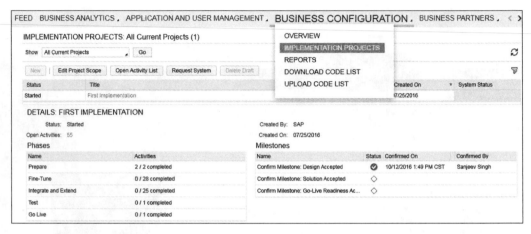

Figure 6.22 Business Configuration to Edit the Project Scope

2. Select the **Edit Project Scope** button (Figure 6.23) to begin the configuration.

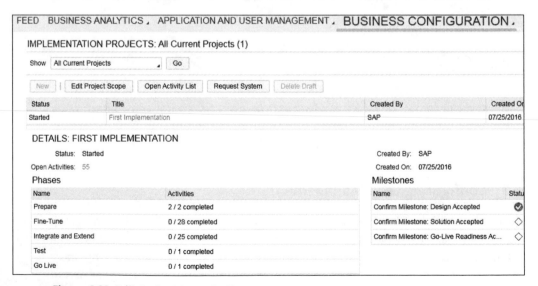

Figure 6.23 Edit Project Scope Button

3. One the first step, **1 Country and Type of Business** (Figure 6.24), verify that the correct country was preselected, and click **Next**.

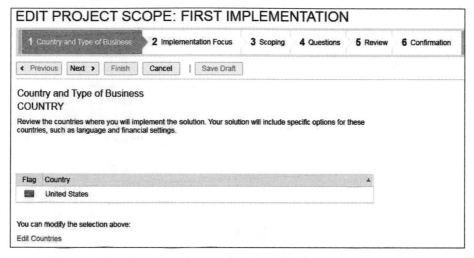

Figure 6.24 Selecting Country and Type of Business for the Project Scope

4. On the second step, **2 Implementation Focus** (Figure 6.25), verify that the information regarding your implementation focus is correct, and click **Next**.

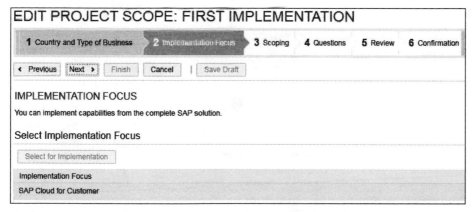

Figure 6.25 Selecting SAP Cloud for Customer as the Implementation Focus

5. The third step, **3 Scoping**, lists all the scoping elements to be included in the project scope. Under **Scoping Element**, you can see that **Lead Management** is part of **Sales**. To include lead management in the scope of your implementation, select **Lead Management** and the **Leads** subelement, as shown in Figure 6.26.

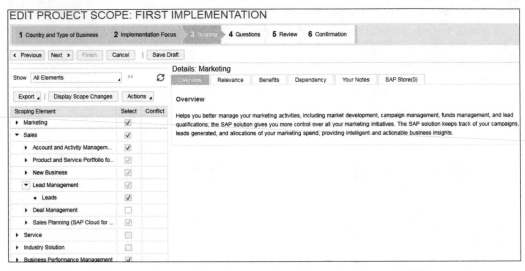

Figure 6.26 Selecting the Scope of Project from the Available Scoping Elements

6. In this first implementation of SAP Sales Cloud, select all the required scoping elements.

7. In the fourth step, **4 Questions**, review the scoping questions related to lead management by clicking on the two gears icon in the **Type** column for **Leads**, as shown in Figure 6.27.

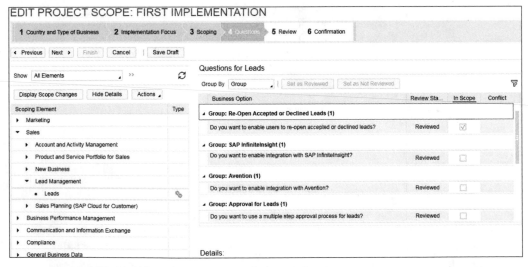

Figure 6.27 Questions for Scoping Lead Management

8. All the questions related to lead management are displayed on this screen. If you agree with the questions, enable the checkboxes in the **In Scope** column; otherwise, leave the checkboxes unchecked.

Let's review some of these questions to understand how they influence the scope and functionality of your lead management process:

- **Do you want to disable historical analysis of leads?**
  Enabling this question will disable the historical analysis of leads.

- **Do you wish to trigger lead aging notifications only when relevant, for better performance?**
  This triggers aging notifications for stalled or aging leads.

- **Compatibility mode for lead aging.**
  This enables compatibility mode for lead aging.

- **Do you want to enable duplicate check for lead?**
  If you want to perform duplicate checks on leads when they are created, you need to enable this functionality.

- **Do you want to enable users to edit or delete notes in the note history?**
  Under normal circumstances, we don't recommend that you change the historical notes on leads; however, if you enable this question, you can change as well as delete historical notes.

- **Do you want to keep your Lead's Sales Area Data (Sales Org, Distribution Channel, Division, etc.) when converting a lead to a customer?**
  When leads are converted to accounts, sales area data from the lead will be copied to the account if you enable this question.

- **Do you want to enable users to specify, per lead, a predetermined combination of sales organization, distribution channel, and division?**
  By enabling this, you can allow users to specify default sales areas for leads.

- **Do you want to enable users to reopen accepted or declined leads?**
  By default you can't reopen accepted or declined leads; however, enabling this question will allow you to do so.

- **Would you like to assign leads to territories using lead routing rules?**
  By enabling this you can assign leads to territories using lead routing rules.

- **Re-Open Accepted or Declined Leads (Do you want to enable users to re-open accepted or declined leads?)**
  If this isn't included in the project scope, you can't edit leads if the lead status has been set to **Accepted** or **Declined**.

- **SAP InfiniteInsight (Do you want to enable integration with SAP InfiniteInsight?)**
  To integrate SAP InfiniteInsight with SAP Sales Cloud, you need to enable this checkbox to include it in the scope.

- **Avention (Do you want to enable integration with Avention?)**
  To integrate Avention with SAP Sales Cloud, you need to enable this checkbox to include it in the scope.

- **Approvals for Leads (Do you want to use a multiple step approval process for leads?)**
  Enable this in scope only if you need to have a multistep lead approval process.

- **Automatic Submission of Leads for Approval (Do you want the system to automatically submit a lead for approval?)**
  Include this in scope if you want leads to be submitted for approval.

- **Contact for Leads (Do you want to make contact for leads an optional field?)**
  Although you can enable this checkbox to make the contact field optional when creating a lead, it isn't recommended. You should always require a contact to create a lead.

- **Lead Creation Using an Existing Account (Do you want to always set "Use Existing Account" checkbox as checked during lead creation?)**
  If you enable this, you can only create leads for existing accounts, but not for new accounts. It's better to have this unchecked so that you have a choice when creating leads.

9. After reviewing all the questions related to leads, go to the fifth step, **5 Review**, by accepting the popup. Complete the subsequent steps, and close the final step to confirm the project scope.

6.3.2   Configuring Leads

Now that leads management is part of the scope, you can configure it, as follows:

1. To configure leads, like configuring any other functionality in SAP Sales Cloud, click the **Open Activity List** button (Figure 6.28).

2. Select the **Fine-Tune** tab, which contains all of the configuration activities. The fine-tune phase organizes all configuration activities so you can tailor the solution to your specific needs. Figure 6.29 shows **Leads** under **Activities in Project**.

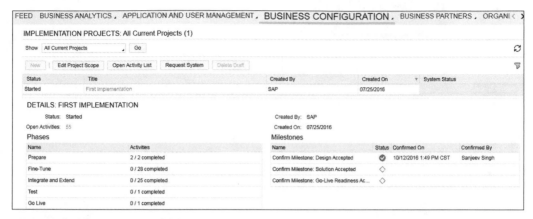

Figure 6.28 Open Activity List Button

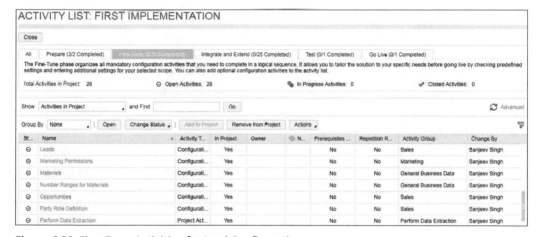

Figure 6.29 Fine-Tune Activities for Lead Configuration

3. You can scroll down the table to find leads in the list or search for leads through search field.

4. Open the **Leads** link to start the configuration activities for all lead-influencing parameters such as **Number Range**, **Status**, and **Qualifications**, as shown in Figure 6.30. These settings are enabled by the system based on the scope you've selected in project scoping (**Scoping Elements**) and the questions you've checked in the scoping exercise in the previous section.

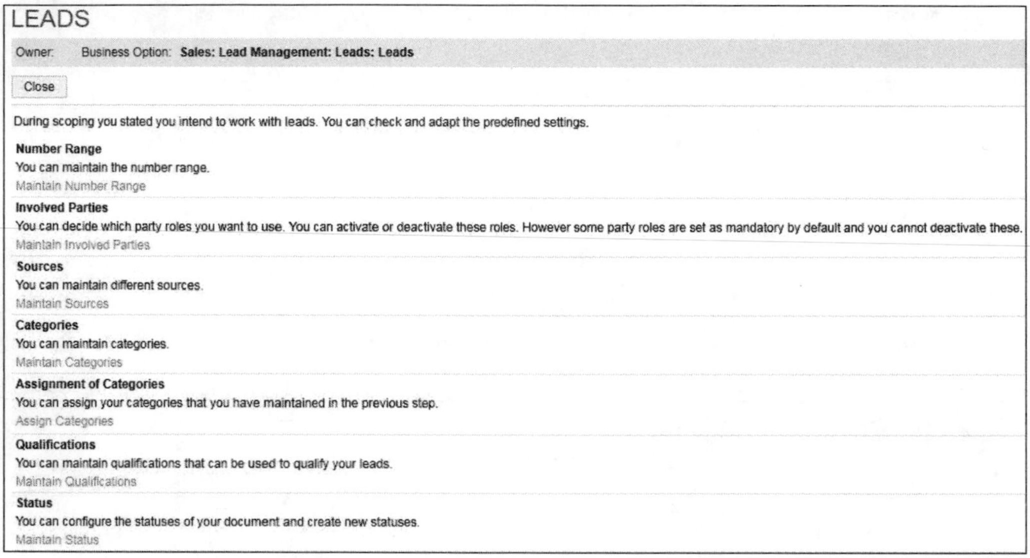

Figure 6.30 Configuration Settings for Leads

We'll cover the configuration of all the elements under **Leads** in sequential order as follows:

- **Number Range**

  When you create a lead, the system assigns an internally generated ID to the lead. Through configuration, you can control what number range is assigned to the lead. The standard SAP Sales Cloud system provides an automatic number range for leads between 0000000001 and 8999999999. You can change the current number in this range so that leads will be assigned a number from a new number range.

  For example, if you change the current number to 100001, the system will assign IDs to leads from 100001 onward until 8999999999. To change the number range for a lead, click the **Maintain Number Range** link. Figure 6.31 shows **Begin Number** and **End Number** for a lead with **Type Automatic**. To alter the number range, select **Change Current Number,** and navigate to the **Change Current Number** screen that shows the current number assigned to the lead. Here, you can change the number to a higher number than the current number so that the next time a lead is created, it will start from the new number entered here.

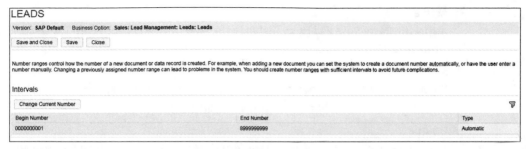

Figure 6.31 Number Range for Leads

- **Involved Parties**

  Involved parties refer to a list of employees and partners you can maintain for leads. The most common partners are account, employee responsible, contact person, marketing manager, and lead qualifier. Depending on your requirements, you can configure the list of involved parties for the lead. Figure 6.32 shows all the party roles available for leads and their corresponding settings.

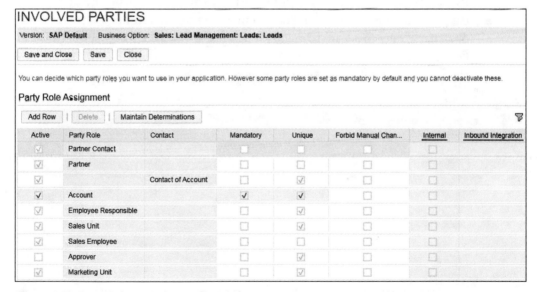

Figure 6.32 Party Role Assignment for Leads

Let's review all the configuration controls available for involved parties:

- **Active**

  A specific **Party Role** will be available in the lead only if it's active in this table. If a role is unchecked, you won't see this party in the lead.

- **Mandatory**

  If you enable this checkbox for a **Party Role**, it will be required for the lead. You can't create a lead without assigning this **Party Role**.

- **Unique**

  This checkbox ensures the uniqueness of the **Party Role** in the lead because you can't have more than one account in a lead. Similarly, **Employee Responsible**, **Approver**, and **Sales Unit** can be unique in a lead. You may have more than one contact for a lead, so it isn't recommended to have **Contact** set as **Unique** for the **Party Role**.

- **Forbidden Manual Change**

  Select this checkbox if you don't want users to change any specific **Party Role** in a lead.

Parties can be manually entered in a lead or can be automatically determined based on determination rules. You can maintain the determination rules for any or all party roles in a lead. To maintain party determination rules, select the **Party Role** in the table, and click on the **Maintain Determination** button. Figure 6.33 shows the **Party Role Sales Employee** selected for this example.

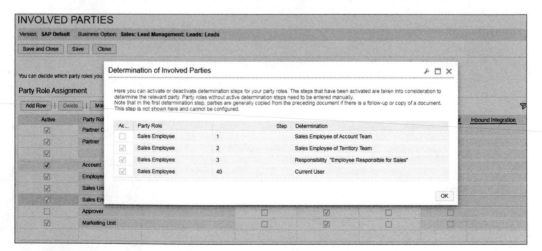

Figure 6.33 Determination of Involved Parties in Leads

The system displays the **Determination of Involved Parties** popup screen where you can activate or deactivate determination steps for the **Party Role** as needed. Let's review all the available determination options for **Sales Employee**, as follows:

- **Step 1 – Sales Employee of Account Team**
  Figure 6.33 shows the first step of determination rule as **Active**. When the lead is created for an account, the system looks for the sales employee assigned to the account team and the populated **Sales Employee Party Role** in the lead from the account team. If the first step determination isn't active, the system will skip it.

- **Step 2 – Sales Employee of Territory Team**
  If either the first step is inactive or there is no sales employee assigned to the account team, the system reads the second step. If you've implemented territory management, and sales employees are assigned to territories, the system determines the territory for the account and finds the assigned sales employee to populate the **Party Role** in the lead.

- **Step 3 – Responsibility "Employee Responsible for Sales"**
  If the system isn't able to find the sales employee in the preceding two steps, then the third step is used based on sales responsibility.

- **Step 4 – Current User**
  The last place to search for the sales employee is the user itself. The system populates the user as **Sales Employee** for the lead.

For each partner role, the system provides a set of determination steps that you can fine-tune to meet your requirements to automatically assign party roles in a lead.

Finally, if you want to add a new party role that hasn't been provided by the standard SAP Sales Cloud, you can choose the **Add Row** button (see Figure 6.34). This is possible as long as those roles are already configured in system.

- **Sources**
  Leads can originate from many sources, for example, trade shows, referrals, and D&B. Depending on the sources you acquire leads from, you can configure the list of sources in your system. Assigning these sources to the leads helps you report on the leads and measure the effectiveness of lead sources. Standard SAP Sales Cloud provides a list of sources, but you can remove and add your own sources as needed. To configure lead sources, click on the **Maintain Sources** link (refer to Figure 6.30), and you'll see the list of **Available Sources** (delivered by SAP) as shown in Figure 6.35.

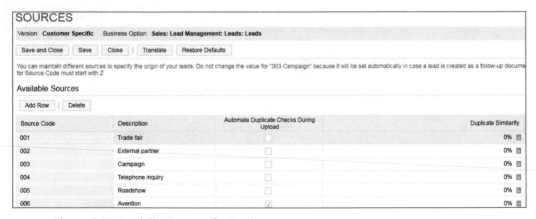

Figure 6.34 Adding a New Party Role to a Lead

SOURCES

Version: **Customer Specific**   Business Option: **Sales: Lead Management: Leads: Leads**

Save and Close   Save   Close | Translate   Restore Defaults

You can maintain different sources to specify the origin of your leads. Do not change the value for "003 Campaign" because it will be set automatically in case a lead is created as a follow-up docume
for Source Code must start with Z

Available Sources

Add Row | Delete

Source Code	Description	Automate Duplicate Checks During Upload	Duplicate Similarity
001	Trade fair	☐	0% 🗔
002	External partner	☐	0% 🗔
003	Campaign	☐	0% 🗔
004	Telephone inquiry	☐	0% 🗔
005	Roadshow	☐	0% 🗔
006	Avention	☑	0% 🗔

Figure 6.35 Available Sources for Leads

The source codes are unique IDs mapped to each source. It's important that you don't change the value for **003 Campaign** because it's set automatically in case a lead is created as a follow-up document of a campaign. If you want to create a new source, select **Add Row**, and enter a **Source Code** and **Description** for the new source you want to add. It's critical that you assign the **Source Code** starting with

"Z" (see Figure 6.36). If you want to remove a source from this list, select the row, and then click on the **Delete** button to remove that entry from **Available Sources**.

The **Duplicate Similarity** is a threshold value used during lead creation using application programming interfaces (APIs). If **Automate Duplicate Checks During Upload** is turned on and the similarity match of the incoming lead with existing leads in the system exceeds this threshold, a new lead (with new account and contact) isn't created.

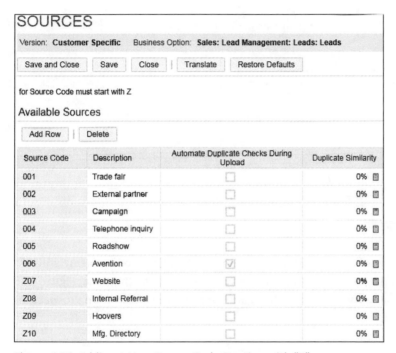

Source Code	Description	Automate Duplicate Checks During Upload	Duplicate Similarity	
001	Trade fair	☐	0%	▦
002	External partner	☐	0%	▦
003	Campaign	☐	0%	▦
004	Telephone inquiry	☐	0%	▦
005	Roadshow	☐	0%	▦
006	Avention	☑	0%	▦
Z07	Website	☐	0%	▦
Z08	Internal Referral	☐	0%	▦
Z09	Hoovers	☐	0%	▦
Z10	Mfg. Directory	☐	0%	▦

Figure 6.36 Adding a New Source Code Starting with "Z"

- **Categories**

  This field helps you categorize leads based on criteria you choose. You may want to categorize leads based on your line of business, product categories, product sales leads, consulting sales leads, and so on. Categorization of leads can be used in routing the leads to the appropriate sales team as well as reporting on the effectiveness of leads compared to their sources. To configure categories, click on **Maintain Categories** link (refer to Figure 6.30). Figure 6.37 shows all standard SAP-delivered **Available Categories** with **Category Code** and corresponding **Description**.

Figure 6.37 shows a new category added with **Category Code Z01** and **Description Prospect for Productivity**.

Figure 6.37 Available Categories for Leads

To add a new category, click on **Add Row**, enter a **Category Code** starting with "Z" and a description, and then save the newly added entry to the table. Figure 6.38 shows a new category added with **Category Code Z01** and **Description Prospect for Productivity**.

- **Assignment of Categories**

  The categories just configured won't be available for selection in leads unless categories are assigned to be part of the leads. To configure the assignment of categories, click on the **Assign Categories** link (refer to Figure 6.30) to see all the available categories assigned to leads. To assign a new category, click on **Add Row**, and maintain the new category assignment from the dropdown selection.

  Figure 6.39 shows the newly created assignment **Z01 (Prospect for Productivity)** chosen from the dropdown (the category previously configured). Assignment of categories is only possible for existing categories, so you need to first create a new category starting with "Z" and then assign that category to a lead.

Figure 6.38 New Category Code Z01 (Prospect for Productivity)

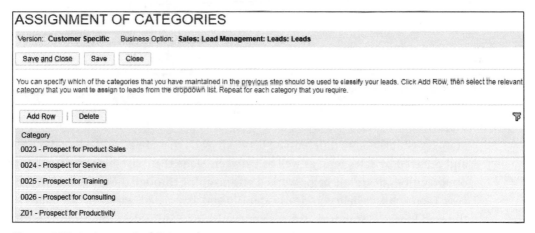

Figure 6.39 Assignment of Categories

- **Qualifications**

  The quality of leads determines the follow-up actions. Qualifications can be the standard **Cold**, **Warm**, or **Hot,** or you can configure any other qualifications to meet your requirements. A **Hot** lead definitely requires attention sooner than a **Cold** lead. Qualification levels help you measure the quality or urgency of leads. To configure qualifications, select the **Maintain Qualifications** link (refer to Figure 6.30). SAP-delivered qualifications (**Cold**, **Warm**, and **Hot**) are available for leads.

However, if the available qualifications aren't sufficient to meet your qualification requirements, you can change, remove, or add new qualifications per your business requirements. To add a new qualification, select **Add Row,** and enter **Qualification Code** "Z1" and a **Qualification Description** as "Very Hot" for this example (see Figure 6.40).

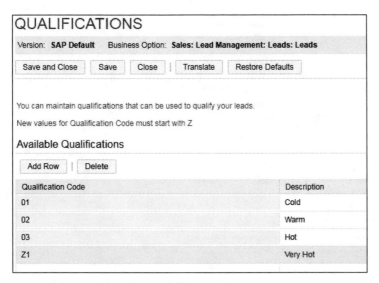

Figure 6.40 Adding a New Qualification Code

- **Status**
  Statuses enable you to differentiate between leads that are accepted by sales reps and rejected by sales reps, as well as between leads that have been converted to opportunities or are still being worked on and going through the qualification process. Lead statuses help you clearly identify and associate leads to all the stages in the lead lifecycle. Standard statuses are available in SAP Sales Cloud, and you can add new statuses through configuration per your requirements. However, there are some restrictions in configuring statuses. To understand the options, click on the Maintain Status link (refer to Figure 6.30), and you're presented with all the available statuses for leads, as shown in Figure 6.41.

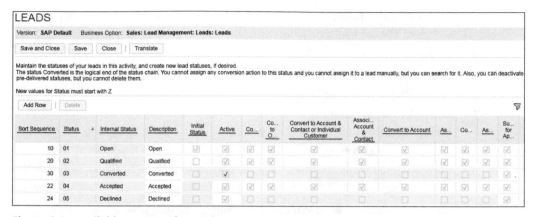

Figure 6.41 Available Statuses for Leads

Before we discuss all the controls and options in this status table, notice in Figure 6.41 that the **Delete** button next to **Add Row** is grayed out, which means you can't delete any of the lead statuses available in the system. Statuses can only be activated or inactivated, but they can never be deleted. With that in mind, let's review the available options or controls for all the statuses in a lead lifecyle, as follows:

- **Sort Sequence**

  This sequence determines the order in which these statuses will be available in the lead for users to select.

- **Status**

  This is the number assigned for each status. If you configure a new status to meet your business requirements, you must start the new status with "Z".

- **Internal Status**

  There are four types of internal status available for leads: **Accepted**, **Declined**, **Open**, and **Qualified**. You can't add any new internal statuses. If you add a new status for your requirements, you must assign one of these four internal statuses to your new status. It's important to note that **Internal Status Converted** isn't available for users to set on leads. This status is set by the system based on the conversion activity of a lead to an opportunity or of a lead to account and contact.

- **Description**

  This is a free-text field to describe the lead status.

- **Initial Status**

  When a new lead is created, this is the initial status you want the system to assign to the lead. Depending on which status you enable with this control, that status will be set while creating the lead.

– **Active**

Only statuses with the **Active** checkbox enabled will be available on leads. You can uncheck any status that isn't applicable so that it's not available in the lead.

– **Convert to Opportunity**

If you enable this checkbox for a status, the system will allow you to convert a lead to an opportunity only in that status. For example, if you want to convert only qualified leads to opportunities, you enable this checkbox only for the **Qualified** status.

– **Convert to Account & Contact or Individual Customer**

If you enable this for a status, the system allows you to convert a lead to an account and contact only in that status.

– **Associate Account & Contact**

In this status, a lead can be associated with an account and contact or an individual customer.

– **Convert to Account**

If you enable this checkbox for a status, the system allows you to convert a lead to an account only in that status.

– **Associate Account**

If enabled for a status, you can associate an account to a lead in that status.

– **Convert to Contact**

If enabled for this status, a lead can be converted to a contact.

– **Associate Contact**

In this status, you can associate a lead to a contact.

– **Submit for Approval**

If you're using a lead approval process, you can trigger the approval process in this status.

If you add a new status, you can give a **Sort Sequence** as needed, **Status** starting with "Z", and a **Description** of your choice; however, you must assign one of the four SAP-delivered **Internal Statuses** (**Accepted**, **Declined**, **Open**, and **Qualified**). You can't add a new status without one of these four internal statuses.

■ **Reasons**

Many times, you may want to track why a specific status was set for a lead, particularly when a lead is accepted or rejected. For example, a lead might be rejected by a sales rep for various reasons such as incorrect information, customer changed requirements, or lead not worth pursuing. Having reasons associated with a status helps you track and report on the status and corresponding reasons. You can maintain your own reasons in addition to those delivered by SAP. To configure reasons, select the **Maintain Reasons** link (refer to Figure 6.30). Figure 6.42 shows the **Available Reasons** with **Reason Code** and **Description** fields. You can add a new **Reason Code** starting with "Z" and assign a corresponding **Description** as required.

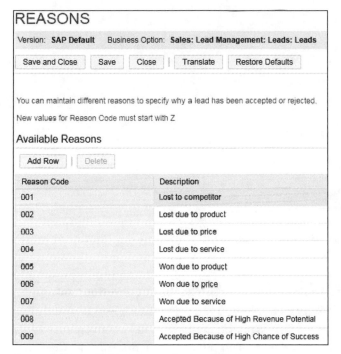

Figure 6.42 is shown below.

REASONS	
Version: **SAP Default** Business Option: **Sales: Lead Management: Leads: Leads**	

| Save and Close | Save | Close | Translate | Restore Defaults |

You can maintain different reasons to specify why a lead has been accepted or rejected.

New values for Reason Code must start with Z

Available Reasons

| Add Row | Delete |

Reason Code	Description
001	Lost to competitor
002	Lost due to product
003	Lost due to price
004	Lost due to service
005	Won due to product
006	Won due to price
007	Won due to service
008	Accepted Because of High Revenue Potential
009	Accepted Because of High Chance of Success

Figure 6.42 Available Reasons for Lead Statuses

- **Assignment of Reasons**

    After you've configured reasons, you need to assign the reasons to the statuses so that users can select those reasons for corresponding statuses. To configure **Assignment of Reasons**, click on the **Assign Reasons** link (refer to Figure 6.30). Figure 6.43 shows the **Available Status** list and the corresponding **Assigned Reasons** list. Reasons are only expected for **Accepted** and **Rejected** statuses. If you select the **Status Accepted**, as shown in Figure 6.43, you'll see all the **Assigned Reasons** for **Accepted Status**. You can select **Add Row** if you need to assign a new reason, or you can select a reason and then click on **Delete** if that reason is no longer needed for that status.

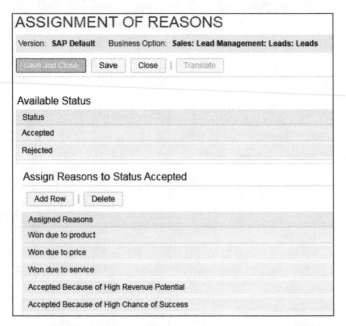

Figure 6.43 Available Lead Statuses and Their Assigned Reasons

- **Conversion Limit**

  This configuration limits the number of times a lead can be converted to an opportunity. If the limit is set to 2, for example, you can convert each lead to exactly two opportunities. Otherwise, if nothing is maintained in this field, conversion to only one opportunity is permitted by default. You can configure this through the **Maintain Conversion Limit** link (refer to Figure 6.30). Figure 6.44 shows the **Define Number** field entering how many times a lead can be converted to an opportunity.

LEAD CONVERSION

Version: **SAP Default**   Business Option: **Sales: Lead Management: Leads: Leads**

Save and Close   Close

YOU CAN ENTER THE NUMBER TO SPECIFY HOW MANY OPPORTUNITIES A LEAD CAN BE CONVERTED TO

Define Number:

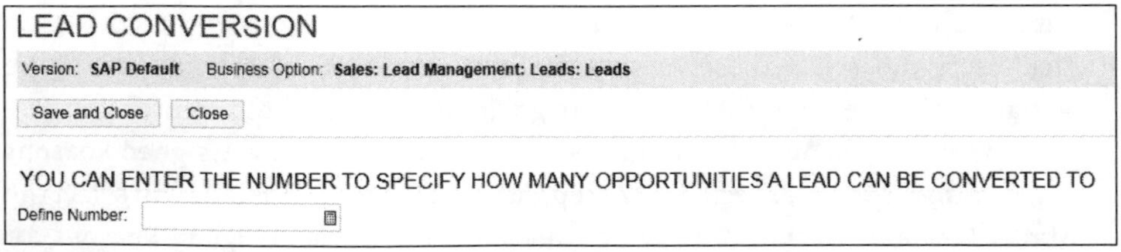

Figure 6.44 Lead Conversion Limit to Restrict the Number of Opportunities Created from a Lead

With this, we've covered all the configuration options available in SAP Sales Cloud. Using these fine-tuning activities, you can configure the lead management process in your SAP Sales Cloud system to meet your unique business requirements.

6.4 Summary

In this chapter, we covered the lead management process and how leads are created and processed in SAP Sales Cloud. We reviewed all the details of leads and the information crucial for working through a lead lifecycle and follow-up to either an opportunity or account and contact. Finally, we covered all the important configuration and fine-tuning steps for the lead management process in SAP Sales Cloud. With this background on lead management, we'll cover opportunity management in the next chapter.

Chapter 7
Opportunity Management

*Opportunity management enforces a structured process and method-
ology to deliver expected sales results. It helps you move sales deals
forward through the funnel by being in complete control of the sales
cycle. Without effective opportunity management as the engine of a
sales machine, successful sales pursuits are merely accidents.*

Sales opportunity management or simply opportunity management is a well-de-
fined process to pursue a real sales possibility. In the previous chapter, you learned
that a lead is a potential buying interest in your products and services that can be real
or perceived. An opportunity is a qualified sales possibility that might result in an actual business transaction. Sales pursuits can be repeated by following predefined processes and activities, and opportunity management forces you to put a structure and
discipline to your sales process and guide your sales activities toward anticipated
results.

Your sales methodology is the backbone of any opportunity management process. It
provides you with a road map to guide your sales efforts toward success by following
a predefined sales process. Opportunity management provides you dimensions or
yardsticks to evaluate your sales pursuits and real-time assessment of how aligned
your sales efforts are with winning the deal and what actions are needed for course
correction if opportunities aren't aligned toward out expected results.

In this chapter, you'll learn about the standard opportunity management process
flow in SAP Sales Cloud, its features, and how they can be used to implement your
unique sales methodology and sales processes. Opportunities are created as a follow-
up from a lead or another opportunity. They can also be created standalone without
reference to any lead or opportunity. Later in this chapter, you'll see how opportunities are created from leads, opportunities, or standalone, as well as the subsequent
process to drive the sales pursuits. Processing opportunities involves carrying out
suggested activities per an assigned sales methodology, moving forward opportunities though sales stages (per an assigned sale cycle), managing statuses, managing

team members, working through rule-based approval processes, splitting revenue with sales team and partners, and so on. The opportunities can be followed up with a sales quotation or sale order as required by your sales process.

The opportunity management process in SAP Sales Cloud can be configured to meet any sales process or sales methodology. Based on the defined scope of implementation per your business requirements, you can configure SAP Sales Cloud to meet your unique business scenarios. In the configuration section, we'll go through step-by-step instructions to configure all the aspects and controlling parameters for opportunity management, including opportunity types, sources, statuses and status reasons, involved parties, activity timeline, sales cycle and phases, and sales assistants.

7.1   Opportunity Management Process

The opportunity management process is the most important and critical link between lead and sales order processing. This process controls or enables the conversion of a qualified lead to a sales quotation or sales order. Opportunities are created as a follow-up transaction from leads and opportunities and are followed up by sales quotes or sales orders per your order management process requirements. There are many benefits when using opportunity management, but some of the most important are described as follows:

- **Standardizes the sales process and keeps the sales funnel moving forward**
  The opportunity management process based on an established sales methodology helps you formulate the sales process so that successful sales pursuits aren't accidents, but predefined and repeatable. When you follow the sales methodology, you move forward opportunities through the sales funnel.

- **Wins more business**
  By following the opportunity management process, you're in control of the sales cycle and hence the sales results. You improve the conversion ratio of winning opportunities.

- **Provides forecast visibility**
  Opportunity management provides visibility to your sales pipeline and accuracy to your sales forecasts and commitments.

Figure 7.1 shows that an opportunity can be referenced to a marketing campaign and can be created as a follow-up from a lead or as a copy from itself. A sales quote or sales order in SAP ERP can be created as a follow-up transaction from an opportunity in SAP Sales Cloud to maintain the link from lead to order.

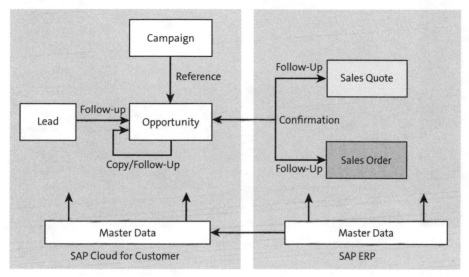

Figure 7.1 Opportunity Process Flow

To help you understand how opportunities are processed in SAP Sales Cloud to achieve various sales processes, let's review some of the important features of opportunity management as follows:

- **Opportunity advanced search and queries**
  You can search for opportunities contextually and efficiently. Predefined queries are available to display **My Opportunities**, **My Team's Opportunities**, and **Opportunities for My Territories**, as shown in Figure 7.2. In addition to these, you can set up custom queries as needed. You can navigate to **Opportunities**, **Accounts**, **Contacts**, and **Opportunity Owner** from the result list. The basic find feature is a text-based search, and you can also sort across available fields in the result set.

- **Opportunity details (overview)**
  You can maintain general opportunity information in the opportunity **OVERVIEW** screen such as **Status**, **Phase**, **Campaign**, **Primary Contact**, **Account**, and **Expected Revenue**, as shown in Figure 7.3. You can also capture start and close dates for an opportunity along with the sales organization unit, distribution channel, and division information.

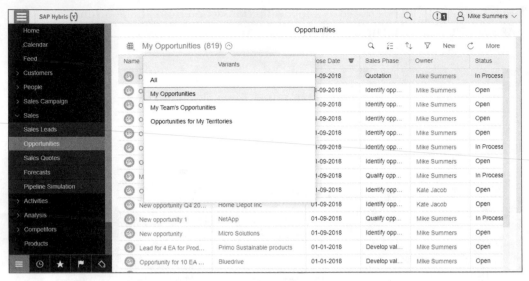

Figure 7.2 Predefined Queries to Display Opportunities

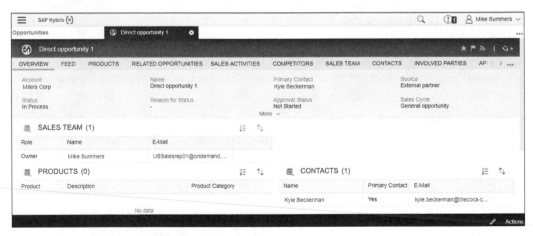

Figure 7.3 Opportunity Overview Screen

- **Contact management**

    The contacts from an account that are relevant to an opportunity can be added to the **CONTACTS** tab of an opportunity (see Figure 7.4). When adding a contact, you can identify it as the main contact for the opportunity and also add a role in which the contact participates in the opportunity such as purchasing manager, decision maker, and approver.

Figure 7.4 Contacts for an Opportunity

- **Opportunity buying center**
  This opportunity relationships management tool allows sales reps to leverage relationships to reach decision makers and influencers. It helps you define Custom relationships on the **Buying Center** screen to identify relationships such as reports to, indirectly reports to, is a friend of, or went to school with. Using this sales team can identify and maintain employees that may have connections to key customer contacts. You can define any relationship attribute as desired to further qualify the nature of the relationship between two individuals.

- **Track and manage sales activities**
  You can create and manage appointments, phone calls, tasks, visits, and emails on opportunities, as shown in Figure 7.5. Statuses are available on activities to allow users to complete/close activities that have been completed directly from an opportunity. Activities show up on your calendar and can be synced to groupware applications such as Microsoft Outlook and Lotus Notes.

- **Opportunity activity advisor**
  The **Activity Advisor** area of the screen guides the sales rep with suggested activities and tasks based on the sales phase the opportunity is in. This feature can be used to tailor the system to fit your unique sales methodology. Users can select activities that are relevant and add them to the list of sales activities for the opportunity, as shown in Figure 7.5. The administrator configures the suggested activities for the sales phases.

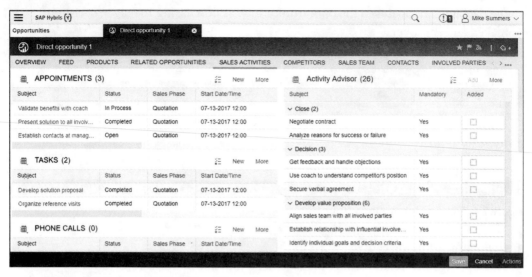

Figure 7.5 Sales Activities for an Opportunity

- **Opportunity activities timeline**

  The activities timeline is a graphical display of the spread of sales activities that have been performed and are scheduled to be performed between the start and close dates of the opportunity (see Figure 7.6). External (customer-facing) activities are shown above the line, and internal activities are shown below the line. Users can filter down activities based on the type and status to show only the relevant activities on the timeline.

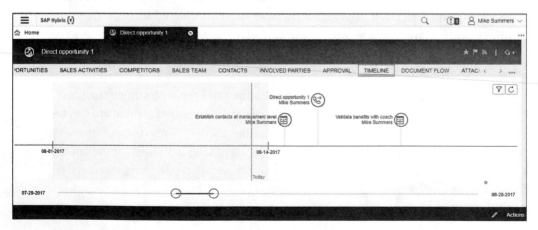

Figure 7.6 Activities Timeline in Opportunities Tab

- **Opportunity hierarchy**

  Using this capability, you can establish a hierarchical relationship between opportunities to support the organization of more complex sales engagements, as shown in Figure 7.7. You can either add an existing opportunity to this hierarchical structure or create a new opportunity.

Figure 7.7 Opportunity Hierarchy

- **Influencer map**

  The influencer map for an opportunity displays the spiral of influence around a contact, as shown in Figure 7.8.

Figure 7.8 Spiral of Influence for an Opportunity

Based on an employee's or contact's participation in activities, opportunities, and so on in the past, the likelihood of employees or contacts knowing the central contact increases and therefore determines their position in the spiral. Based on real-world experience, if the sales rep believes that an employee or contact has been displayed too close or too far from the central contact, the rep can drag and change the position. The system will remember it for the next time. By dragging an employee into the **Add to Opportunity** frame, he can be added to the sales team directly.

- **Evernote integration for opportunity notes**
  SAP Sales Cloud offers out-of-the-box integration of Evernote with opportunities. Any note taken in a user's Evernote account can be brought over and pinned in SAP Sales Cloud. Searches across notes are available, and notes are grouped by notebooks as maintained in Evernote. Suggested notes are also shown based on textual matches between opportunity and notes content.

- **Integration with LinkedIn Sales Navigator**
  As covered in the previous chapter, SAP Sales Cloud has out-of-the-box integration with the LinkedIn Sales Navigator. Similar to how its functionality works with leads, on the **Opportunities** overview screen, you can use the LinkedIn Sales Navigator to view LinkedIn-related details for an opportunity. On the **Contact** tab in opportunities management, the LinkedIn Sales Navigator will show the LinkedIn connections for the contact.

We'll review the additional opportunity details in Section 7.2.2.

7.2   Creating and Processing Opportunities

In the previous chapter, you saw that opportunities can be created from leads as part of the lead conversion process, and most of the information from a lead is copied on to an opportunity. In this section, we'll create standalone opportunities by manually entering all the required details (not copied from a preceding document) in order to review the information required to create an opportunity. Regardless of how opportunities are created, their processing remains the same. Processing and follow-ups from opportunities are covered later this section.

7.2.1   Creating Opportunities

A new opportunity can be created under by choosing **Sales • Opportunities** and then clicking on the **+** button. The **New Opportunity** screen presented for creating a new opportunity is shown in Figure 7.9.

Let's review the details you can maintain to create an opportunity:

- **Document Type**
  Selected as **Opportunity** by default. You can select other opportunity types if they are configured in the system (covered later in Section 7.3).

- **Name**
  Free-text field to enter the description of an opportunity.

- **Account**
  The account (customer) you're creating the opportunity for.

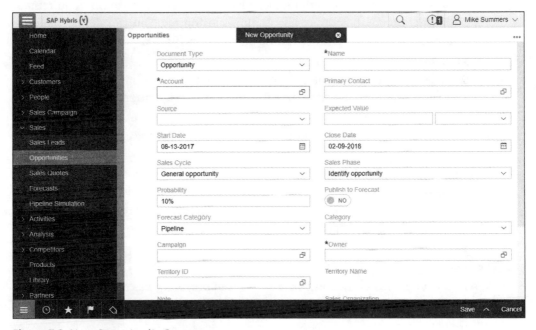

Figure 7.9 New Opportunity Screen

- **Primary Contact**
  The primary contact for the opportunity.

- **Source**
  The source of the opportunity; these values can be changed through configuration.

- **Expected Value**
  The expected value of the opportunity to show the expected revenue.

- **Start Date**
  The start date of the opportunity. By default, this is the current system date, but it can be changed by user.

- **Close Date**
  The expected date of winning the opportunity.

- **Sales Cycle**
  Based on the sales methodology followed in the opportunity. By default, SAP Sales Cloud offers the **General opportunity** sales cycle. The sales cycle controls the sales phases in the opportunity.

- **Sales Phase**
  A sales cycle can have multiple sales phases such as qualification, requirement gathering, proposal, contract negotiation, closing etc. You can define the sales phases for your sales cycle depending on your specific sales methodology.

- **Probability**
  The chance of success or the chance of winning the opportunity. This is controlled by the probability assigned to the sales phase in configuration.

- **Publish to Forecast**
  Controls whether this opportunity should be included in the opportunity forecast.

- **Forecast Category**
  Allows you to include this opportunity in one of the forecast categories.

- **Category**
  Allows you to categorize this opportunity as **Prospect for Service**, **Prospect for Training**, **Prospect for Product**, and so on. These categories can be changed or added in configuration.

- **Campaign**
  Allows you to enter the campaign ID if this opportunity has resulted from a campaign.

- **Owner**
  Can by updated with the sales rep responsible for working this opportunity.

- **Territory ID**
  Can be updated to identify the opportunity based on the territory it belongs to.

- **Notes**
  Free-text field for the user to capture notes while creating the opportunity.

- **Sales Organization**
  Can be updated to identify this opportunity based on the sales organization it belongs to.

- **Distribution Channel**
  Defines the distribution channel this opportunity belongs to.

- **Division**
  Identifies which division this opportunity belongs to.

After maintaining all these details, you have three options—**Save**, **Save and New**, or **Save and Open**, as shown in Figure 7.10.

In the next section, you'll learn how to process opportunities and leverage some of the unique capabilities available in SAP Sales Cloud to better manage opportunities.

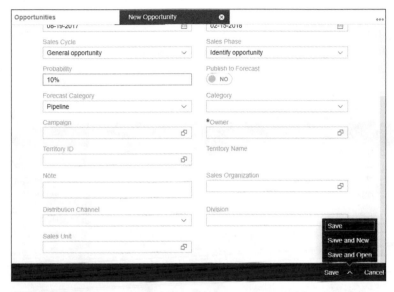

Figure 7.10 Options to Save, Save and New, or Save and Open

7.2.2   Processing Opportunities

As you've seen earlier, opportunities have a definite timeline, that is, a **Start Date** and **Close Date**. During this time period, you manage the opportunity through various sales stages in your sales cycle. You're performing various activities and tasks per your sales methodology to progress the opportunity through the sales funnel to a higher probability of winning the deal. Opportunities feed your sales forecast, so it's critical that opportunities accurately reflect the status and conditions of your sales pursuits. The opportunities in SAP Sales Cloud are processed by managing details on various opportunity tabs or tabs. In the following sections, we'll review some of these important tabs.

Overview

In the **Opportunities OVERVIEW** screen, the following important fields are available to influence opportunity processing:

- **Status**

  You can assign statuses to an opportunity to accurately define what it reflects; for example, whether the opportunity is still being worked on by the sales team, has been won, or has been lost. Some of the statuses available in opportunities are **Open**, **In Process**, **Won**, **Lost**, and **Stopped**. You can't feely change the status in the opportunity **Status** field. Rather, you can set the desired status through the **Actions** popup menu, as shown in Figure 7.11. The current status of the opportunity is **In Process,** and you can set any of the subsequent statuses (e.g., **Won**, **Lost**, or **Stopped)** to the opportunity.

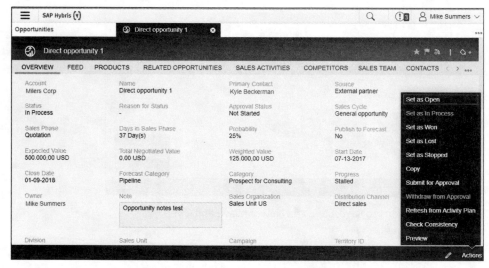

Figure 7.11 Setting the Opportunity Status through the Actions Menu

- **Reason for Status**

  Along with **Status**, another important field available to complement opportunity processing is **Reason for Status**. Sometimes it's important to trace the reason for specific opportunity statuses to get more insight into sales pursuits. For example, if you set the opportunity to **Lost**, you need to select a reason for the loss. You could lose an opportunity for various reasons, but capturing the reason for the **Lost** status will help you evaluate and take corrective actions as needed to improve the opportunity win ratio. **Reason for Status** is mainly required for **Won** and **Lost** statuses; however, you can configure your own reasons for various statuses as needed.

- **Sale Cycle/Sales Phase**

  You process opportunities through various stages in the sales process by assigning appropriate sales phases. A sales cycle is assigned to an opportunity at its creation, but sales stages (within the sales cycle) are updated per the progress made on an opportunity in moving forward through the sales funnel. Figure 7.12 shows the assigned **Sales Cycle** of **General opportunity** with six distinct **Sales Phases**: **Identify opportunity**, **Qualify opportunity**, **Develop value proposition**, **Quotation**, **Decision**, and **Close**.

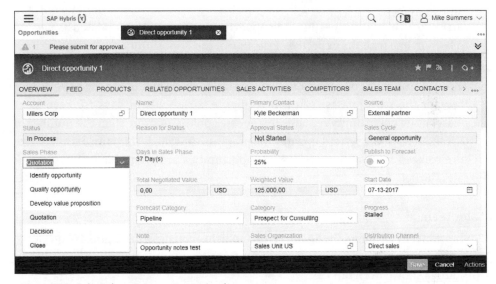

Figure 7.12 Sales Phases in an Opportunity

These sales phases are in increasing order of their probability of success. Through configuration, you assign probability or chance of success as a percentage to these **Sales Phases** so that the sales pipeline is adjusted per the probability of success. Sales cycle and sales phases are unique to each sales organization, and the sales team needs to pay special attention to define and map these processes before they are configured in SAP Sales Cloud.

- **Expected Value/Weighted Value**
  These are the expected size of the sales deal you're pursuing through an opportunity. The **Expected Value** is the amount in absolute terms. For example, if you're chasing a $150,000 deal, then the expected value of the opportunity is $150,000. The weighted value is the adjusted opportunity value based on the probability associated with the sales phase. As the opportunity progresses through higher sales phases, the **Weighted Value** keeps increasing due to the associated higher probability of success.

Another value field, **Total Negotiated Value**, appears between **Expected Value** and **Weighted Value**, but you can't maintain the value for this field at the header level. It can only be maintained from the **Products** tab, which we'll cover later in this chapter.

- **Start Date/Close Date**
  The opportunity **Start Date** is by default the opportunity creation date, but you can update this date as needed. The opportunity **Close Date** is updated as needed to keep in line with the expected close date of the opportunity.

- **Progress**
  Through this field, you can evaluate the progress made in moving the opportunity through the sales phases. You can configure thresholds in days for each sales phase; if the opportunity remains in any sales phase for more than the number of threshold days, the system updates the progress to **Stalled**. This is an excellent feature to keep track of how well your opportunities are progressing though your sales funnel.

Sales Team

For better team visibility, the **SALES TEAM** tab helps you determine and assign all the sales team members on one tab. If needed, new sales team members can be added on this tab, as shown in Figure 7.13.

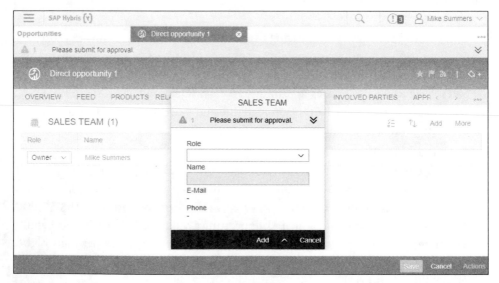

Figure 7.13 Adding a New Sales Team Member to the Opportunity

When adding the team member, you can select the **Role** the team member will be playing in the opportunity. The standard roles are available as shown in Figure 7.14; however, you can update these roles through configuration per your business requirements.

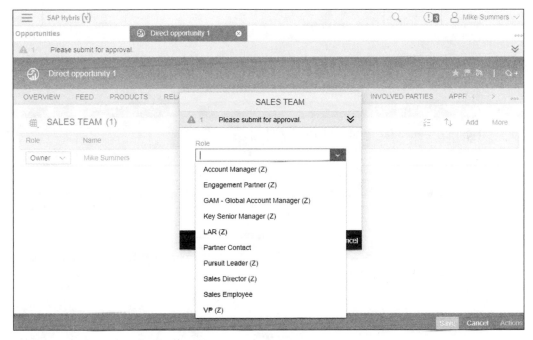

Figure 7.14 Available Roles for the New Team Member

Feed

The **FEED** tab offers a collaboration platform to share updates, discuss ideas, and communicate with colleagues about a specific opportunity, as shown in Figure 7.15. Based on configuration, the feed shows who made which updates to the key fields of an opportunity. Feed integrates with SAP Jam.

Contacts

On this tab, all the displayed contacts are either determined from an account or manually entered by the user when the opportunity is created. Additional contacts can be assigned to the opportunity during its lifecycle if such new contacts are uncovered and relationships are established, as shown in Figure 7.16.

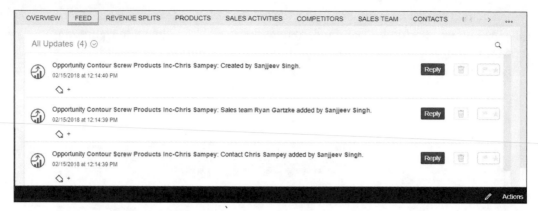

Figure 7.15 Feed Tab in an Opportunity

Figure 7.16 Adding a Contact to an Opportunity

Involved Parties

Involved parties are mostly external entities or parties who are involved in influencing opportunities, such as channel partners, resellers, and consultants. You can add additional **Involved Parties** on this tab similar to on the **Contacts** and **Sales Team** tabs. Figure 7.17 shows how you can add a new partner under **INVOLVED PARTIES** for the opportunity. While adding a new partner, you can also select from the **Role** dropdown to determine the role of the partner in the opportunity: **Reseller**, **Distributor**, **Consultant**, **Influencer**, and so on. You can define and update these roles through configuration per your business requirements.

Figure 7.17 Adding a New Partner under Involved Parties

Products

On this tab, you assign all the products and services you're trying to sell through this opportunity. While assigning products to the opportunity, you enter the product **Quantity, Negotiated Value, Notes,** and timeline (revenue from and revenue to dates to realize the negotiated value). Figure 7.18 shows an example of adding a new product to the opportunity. Normally, products are assigned to the opportunity as you move higher in the sales phases and get closer to winning the opportunity. The negotiated value for the products and the timeline when you expect to realize the revenue help you to accurately forecast revenue distribution with time and among sales teams as covered in revenue splits.

Products can be added to an opportunity one at a time or in bulk from a preexisting product list. Pricing is automatically fetched, and the negotiated value is calculated for products for which the list price is maintained in SAP Sales Cloud. Pricing can also be retrieved from SAP ERP using a standard pricing call between SAP Sales Cloud and SAP ERP. The description of the added product is fetched from the product master but can be overridden in the opportunity as needed. In addition, notes can be captured for every product line item that is added to the opportunity.

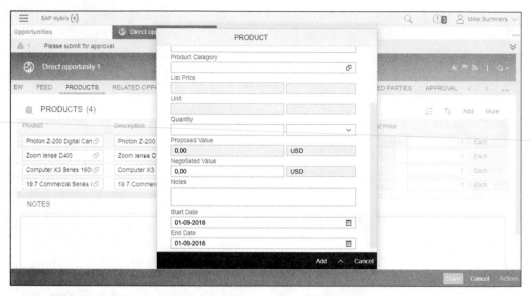

Figure 7.18 Adding a Product to the Opportunity on the Products Tab

As discussed earlier, in team selling scenarios, you may need to split sales credit for the opportunity among team member both internal and or external. The revenue splits functionality works in conjunction with item revenue scheduling for the negotiated value of the opportunity. Only the negotiated value of an opportunity is split among the team members, not the expected value or weighted value. In the **Revenue Splits** work center, you click on **Add** to enter a team member with whom you need to split the revenue.

Competitors

You can maintain competitors as well as competitor products to your opportunity on this tab. Before you can assign competitors or competitor products to an opportunity, you must create the competitors and competitor products in the system. On the **COMPETITORS** tab, you can only add one of the existing competitors available in the system to an opportunity, as shown in Figure 7.19.

Sales Activities

As you know, processing opportunities means working through various tasks and activities to move the opportunity ahead in the sale funnel from one sales stage to another and toward a higher chance of success. Figure 7.20 shows all the **Appoint-**

ments, **Tasks**, **Phone Calls**, and **Emails** for this opportunity displayed on the **SALES ACTIVITIES** tab. You can click on **New** under **Appointments**, **Tasks**, and **Phone Calls** to create new activities from this tab as needed.

Figure 7.19 Adding a Competitor to an Opportunity

Figure 7.20 Sales Activities and Activity Advisor in an Opportunity

The **Activity Advisor** area of the screen helps you implement the sales methodology for an opportunity. You can configure recommended or mandatory activities and tasks for each sales phase under **Activity Advisor** per your sale methodology. Figure 7.20 shows recommended activities for each sales phase. To add any of these activities to an opportunity from **Activity Advisor**, select that activity and then click **Add** under **Activity Advisor**.

Sales Documents

Follow-up sales quotes and sales orders can be created here. If you've scoped SAP ERP integration in your SAP Sales Cloud solution, you can create follow-up sales quotes and sales orders in SAP ERP from the **SALES DOCUMENTS** tab in the opportunity. When follow-up transactions are created in SAP ERP from the **SALES DOCUMENTS** tab of the opportunity, all the required information flows through from the opportunity to the transaction automatically. Figure 7.21 shows the **SALES DOCUMENTS** tab in an opportunity.

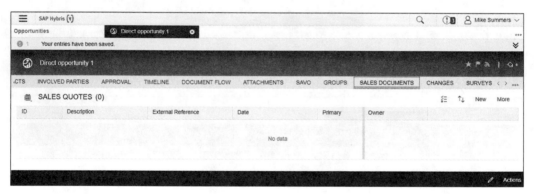

Figure 7.21 Sales Documents Tab in an Opportunity

Surveys

Figure 7.22 shows that you can add surveys or questionnaires to the opportunity by clicking **Add** on the **SURVEYS** tab. Surveys must be designed and assigned to the right activity plan and routing rules prior to assigning them to the opportunities. To automatically assign surveys to opportunities, you can leverage workflow rules.

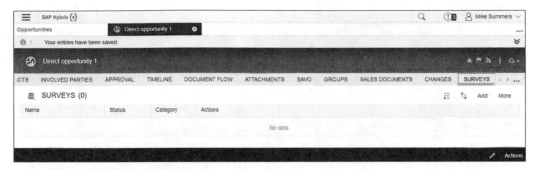

Figure 7.22 Surveys in an Opportunity

Related Opportunities

On this tab of an opportunity, you can add and track related opportunities. You can click **Add** to link an existing opportunity under **Related Opportunities**, or you can click **New** to create a new opportunity (see Figure 7.23). Both **Add** and **New** link such opportunities and list them on the **RELATED OPPORTUNITIES** tab of the original opportunity.

Figure 7.23 Adding Related Opportunities to the Original Opportunity

Approval

The opportunity approval process can be set up on opportunities as desired based on conditional rules. Approvers can be determined based on roles, and they can receive notifications to approve an opportunity. Figure 7.24 shows the details of the opportunity **APPROVAL** tab.

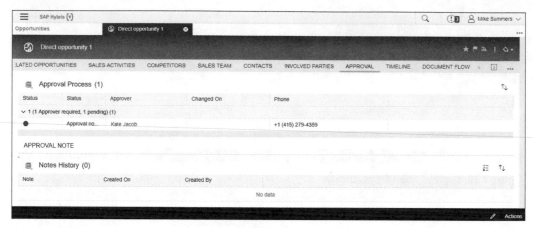

Figure 7.24 Approval Tab in an Opportunity

Rule-based notifications and workflow rules based on conditions can be set up to trigger when the conditions are either met on creation or on every save of the opportunity. Notifications can be issued within the system or as emails with placeholders identified. Recipients of the notifications are picked from the participating involved parties in the opportunity. Workflow rules to update a field or trigger an action can also be set up on a conditional basis per your business requirements.

Document Flow

The **DOCUMENT FLOW** tab shows any preceding documents the opportunity may have originated from and any follow-up documents that may have been created from the opportunity, as shown in Figure 7.25.

Mobile Access

Mobile access for opportunities is available for iPad, iPhone, Android, and Windows tablets. Users can view and edit opportunities based on their authorizations. Reports, graphical views, and offline capabilities are supported in opportunities. Layout configurations once made in the desktop version using adaptations or personalizations are honored in the mobile devices.

In the next section, you'll learn about the follow-up process used with opportunities.

Figure 7.25 Document Flow for an Opportunity

7.2.3   Follow-Up Process for Opportunities

You learned in the previous chapter that normally opportunities are created as a follow-up process from leads. In the sales cycle, a follow-up from an opportunity either results in a sales quotation or sales order. Figure 7.26 shows that in SAP Sales Cloud, it's possible to create follow-up sales quotations or sales orders in SAP ERP from an SAP Sales Cloud opportunity.

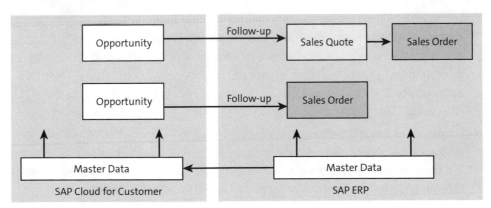

Figure 7.26 Opportunity Follow-Up Process from SAP Sales Cloud to SAP ERP

You've seen earlier that sales quote and sales order follow-up transactions in SAP ERP can be created from the **SALES DOCUMENTS** tab of an opportunity. During this process, all the required information from the source document (opportunity) is copied to the target document (sales quote or sales order) automatically, and the document flow for the opportunity is updated with the SAP ERP document numbers.

With this understanding of opportunities in SAP Sales Cloud, in the next section, you'll learn how to configure opportunities and influence parameters via fine-tuning.

7.3   Configuring Opportunities

Before you configure all the aspects of opportunities in SAP Sales Cloud, you need to ensure that opportunity management is included in the scope of your project. If opportunity management isn't included in the project scope, you can't see the opportunity-related configuration **Activities** in the fine-tune phase.

7.3.1   Getting Started

To include opportunities in the project scope, select **Business Configuration**, click **Edit Project Scope**, and then click **Next** until you get to the **Scoping** phase. Navigate to the **New Business • Opportunities** checkbox to include opportunities in the scope of your implementation. Click **Next** to review the following questions for opportunities in the next stage:

- **Do you want to use a multiple step approval process for opportunities?**
  Normally you would use an approval process in opportunities that ensures that a sales manager approves before a customer is given a sales quotation as part of an opportunity. If you want a multistep approval process in opportunities, then you will enable this question.

- **Do you want the system to automatically submit an opportunity for approval?**
  If you want all opportunities created in the system to automatically be submitted for approval before they can be worked on, include this in your scope. Enabling this question will automatically submit all opportunities for approval.

- **Do you want to enable users to view top influencers for contacts and employees on the Influencer Map?**
  The influencers map shows the relationship between contacts and employees. If

you want all the opportunity users to be able to view the influencers map for account contacts, you will include this in your scope.

- **Do you want to enable users to capture registered products in opportunities?**
  This functionality is useful if you are an equipment manufacturer and trying to sell additional products and services to an existing customer. Including registered products (the products customer has already bought from you and you have them registered in your system) in opportunity gives you additional insights on how you want to manage this opportunity. If you want capture registered products on opportunities, then you will enable this.

- **Do you want to enable historical analysis of opportunities?**
  Enabling this question will allow you to do historical analysis on opportunities. This will help you evaluate what went right and what could have been done differently in winning the opportunity.

- **Do you want to enable users to see earlier versions of opportunity notes?**
  This allows users to see earlier opportunity notes. It is recommended to keep this log so that you are able to review all the historical notes on the opportunity.

- **Do you want to enable users to edit or delete notes in the note history?**
  This enables users to edit or delete historical notes on opportunities. It is not recommended to allow the users to edit or delete the historical notes, as it's a best practice to keep a clean log of all the notes on opportunities.

- **Do you want to automatically redetermine opportunity parties based on changes to the account team of the associated account?**
  If you enable this question, the account team for an opportunity will be automatically updated whenever the account team is updated for an account. It is recommended that opportunities reflect the current account team, hence enabling this will keep your account and opportunities team in sync.

- **Do you want to enable sales phase progress for opportunities?**
  This will enable the opportunity sales phase to progress. A sales cycle has multiple phases such as qualification, demo, proposal, negotiation, etc. An opportunity progresses through various sales phases from lower probability of success to higher probability of success. We recommend that you include this in your scope.

- **Do you want to add products during opportunity creation?**
  Normally when you create an opportunity you may not have enough information on the opportunity to add products; however, enabling this question allows you to add products to an opportunity at the time of creation.

- **Do you want to enable quantity scheduling for opportunities on a monthly, quarterly, or yearly basis?**
  This enables quantity scheduling for opportunities. This is useful when you are working on a scheduling or consignment contract opportunity where the opportunity value is scheduled for the product quantity over a period of time.

- **Do you want an automatic update of the product revenue schedule based on the quantity schedule?**
  Similar to the previous question, if enabled, this question allows you to automatically update the product revenue schedule based on the quantity schedule in the opportunity.

- **Do you want to split revenue per opportunity among sales team members?**
  When you have more than one sales rep working on the same opportunity, you might need to split the sales credit among those sales reps. If you want to split the opportunity revenue among sales team members, then you will enable this question.

- **Do you want to enable revenue scheduling for opportunities on a monthly, quarterly, or yearly basis?**
  Similar to quantity scheduling, if you want revenue scheduling for this opportunity then you include this in scope. Enabling this will allow you to schedule revenue for opportunities over a time period defined in the opportunity.

- **Do you want to enable users to specify, per opportunity, a predetermined combination of sales organization, distribution channel, and division?**
  If you want to maintain a sales area (a combination of sales organization, distribution channel, and division) for an opportunity, using this setting you can set a default sales area for all the opportunities when they are created.

- **Do you want to default the sales organization, distribution channel, and division based on the account and employee sales data?**
  If you want to have a default sales area data for opportunities when they are created based on the sales area of the account or employee responsible for the opportunity, you will enable this question.

- **You can assign sales cycles and phases to your opportunity.**
  Normally you have a default sales cycle (and corresponding sales phases) assigned to opportunities out of the box. However, if you want to assign your own sales cycle and sales phases to opportunities, then you will enable this question. It allows you to assign sales cycle and sales phases to your opportunity types.

- **Would you like to use a sales assistant that proposes activities that you have to do in a certain phase of your opportunity?**
  If you have sales methodology you want sales reps to follow that requires them to perform certain predefined activities for each phase in sales cycle, this question is relevant. For example, you might want sales rep to confirm the budget with the customer before submitting a formal sales quote. In that case, you would want to automatically create an activity or task for the sales rep to confirm the budget. The sales assistant functionality in SAP Sales Cloud lets you propose certain activities in the opportunity for each sales phase. This question lets you enable the sales assistant functionality.

Once you have completed scoping, to begin configuration, follow these steps:

1. Hover the mouse over **Business Configuration** in the work center, and then click on **Implementation Projects** from the dropdown.

2. Click on **Open Activity List.**

3. Click on **Fine-Tune**. Figure 7.27 shows all the **Activities in Project** that are available for configuration. You open the activities related to opportunities as explained in the next sections.

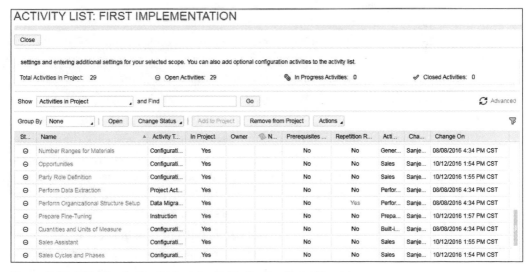

Figure 7.27 Activities in the Project Available for Configuration

7.3.2   Opportunities

When you click on **Opportunities** in the **Project Activities** screen, all the available configuration settings are displayed, as shown in Figure 7.28.

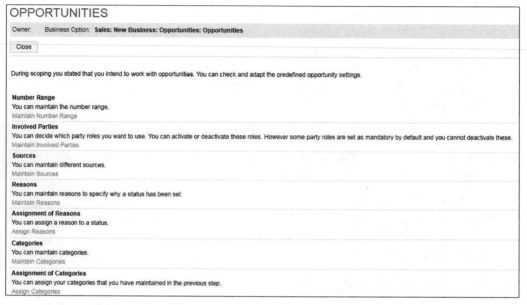

Figure 7.28 Predefined Opportunity Settings Available for Configuration

You can change these settings based on your business requirements, as follows:

- **Number Range**

  The number range controls what document identification number (ID) is assigned when a new opportunity is created. Under **Number Range**, you click the **Maintain Number Range** link to open intervals and change the current number, as shown in Figure 7.29. The **Begin Number** (**0000000001**) and **End Number** (**8999999999**) with the Type set as **Automatic** shows that the system will automatically assign opportunity IDs between these two numbers when opportunities are created.

  To change the number range, click on **Change Current Number**, and enter a number higher than the current number in this field, as shown in Figure 7.30. After saving this, all the new opportunities created in the system will get new numbers that are higher than the entered **Current Number**. Once saved, you can't enter a number lower than the current number.

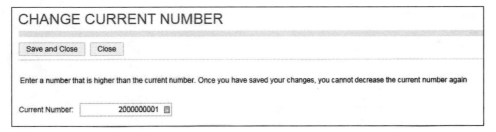

OPPORTUNITIES

Version: **SAP Default**   Business Option: **Sales: New Business: Opportunities: Opportunities**

| Save and Close | Save | Close |

Number ranges control how the number of a new document or data record is created. For example, when adding a new document you can set the system to create a document number automatically, or have the user enter a number manually. Changing a previously assigned number range can lead to problems in the system. You should create number ranges with sufficient intervals to avoid future complications.

Intervals

| Change Current Number |

Begin Number	End Number	Type
0000000001	8999999999	Automatic

Figure 7.29 Default Number Range Available for Opportunities

CHANGE CURRENT NUMBER

| Save and Close | Close |

Enter a number that is higher than the current number. Once you have saved your changes, you cannot decrease the current number again

Current Number: 2000000001

Figure 7.30 Changing the Current Number for an Opportunity Number Range

- **Involved Parties**

  You've seen in an earlier section that the **INVOLVED PARTIES** tab in opportunities helps you maintain all the roles involved in the opportunity. In this configuration activity, you can activate and deactivate roles per your business requirements, and you can further control which roles are mandatory and which roles need to be determined in the opportunity. Under **Involved Parties**, you click on **Maintain Involved Parties** to see the **Party Role Assignment** settings. On this screen, you can decide what party roles you want in opportunities. Some of the roles are selected by default and can't be changed, as shown in Figure 7.31.

  To include a party role on the **INVOLVED PARTIES** tab for opportunities, you need to enable the **Active** checkbox for that **Role** in the **Party Role Assignment** table. For each party role, you have three additional controls: **Mandatory, Unique**, and **Forbid Manual Change**. If a **Party Role** is **Mandatory** in an opportunity, you can't create that opportunity without the mandatory party role. System-defaulted mandatory party roles are **Account, Sales Employee**, and **Sales Unit**. You can enable additional party roles as mandatory if required to support your unique business process. **Unique** Party roles can be assigned only once in an opportunity, and party roles marked **Forbid Manual Change** can't be changed by users in opportunities.

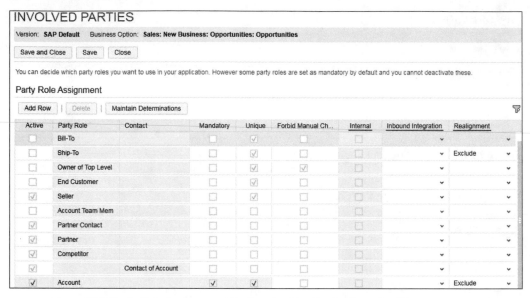

Figure 7.31 Party Role Assignment for Involved Parties in Opportunities

If the SAP Sales Cloud standard-delivered party roles aren't sufficient to meet your requirements, you can add new party roles by clicking the **Add Row** button. You need to configure such party roles before adding them to the **Party Role Assignment** table. For each **Party Role**, you have the option of configuring the determination rules. The party roles are determined from various sources such as the preceding document (if the opportunity is created as a follow-up transaction from a lead or copy from another opportunity), business partner relationship, organization structure, or territory structure.

To configure determination for a party role, select that partner, and click **Maintain Determinations**. The **Determination of Involved Parties** popup appears, as shown in Figure 7.32. Here you can activate determination rules as applicable. The first rule, **Business partner relationship of Account**, means if a partner is assigned a relationship with an account, then the party role will be determined from the account relationship. In the second rule, **Business partner relationship of Partner Contact**, the partner is determined from the partner relationship. Partner determination is only carried out if it's activated. If the system doesn't find a partner per active determination rules, then that partner will be missing in the opportunity.

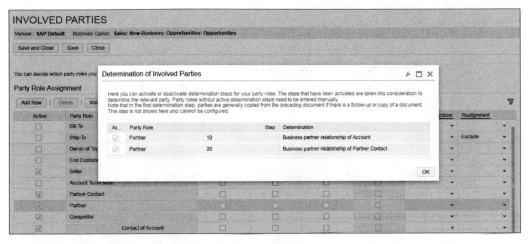

Figure 7.32 Determination Options for the Involved Parties

1. **Sources**

   You can maintain different sources to specify the origin of opportunities. These sources are the same as those configured for leads. Whatever sources you maintain for leads will be available for opportunities as well and vice versa.

   Click **Maintain Sources** to see the **Available Sources** in the system. You can create additional entries in this table with more sources (source codes starting with "Z") as needed (see Figure 7.33).

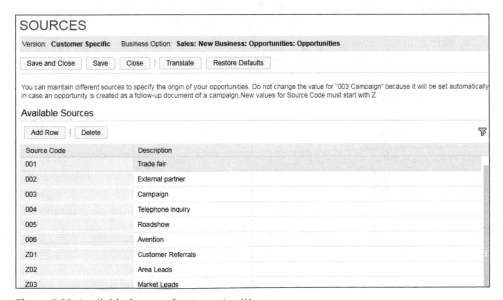

Figure 7.33 Available Sources for Opportunities

- **Reasons**

  In this configuration activity, you maintain reasons to specify why a status has been set for an opportunity. To maintain reasons for opportunity statuses, click on **Maintain Reasons,** and the **Available Reasons** list appears, as shown in Figure 7.34. If the SAP-delivered reasons aren't sufficient, you can add your own status reasons by providing reason codes starting with "Z" and a description as needed.

Figure 7.34 List of Available Status Reasons for Opportunities

- **Assignment of Reasons**

  After configuring the reasons, you need to assign those reasons to statuses so that users are presented with reasons to select when corresponding opportunity statuses are set. Click on **Assign Reasons** to open the **Assignment of Reasons** screen, as shown in Figure 7.35. Opportunities can be set with one of the five statuses: **Open, In Process, Stopped, Won,** and **Lost.**

  To assign reasons to a status, select the required status from the **Available Status** column, and then add **Reasons** as needed under **Assigned Reasons.** Figure 7.35 shows that the **Assigned Reasons to Status Lost** as **Lost to competitor, Lost due to product, Lost due to price,** and **Lost due to service.** You can add or remove these status reasons as needed to meet your unique business requirements.

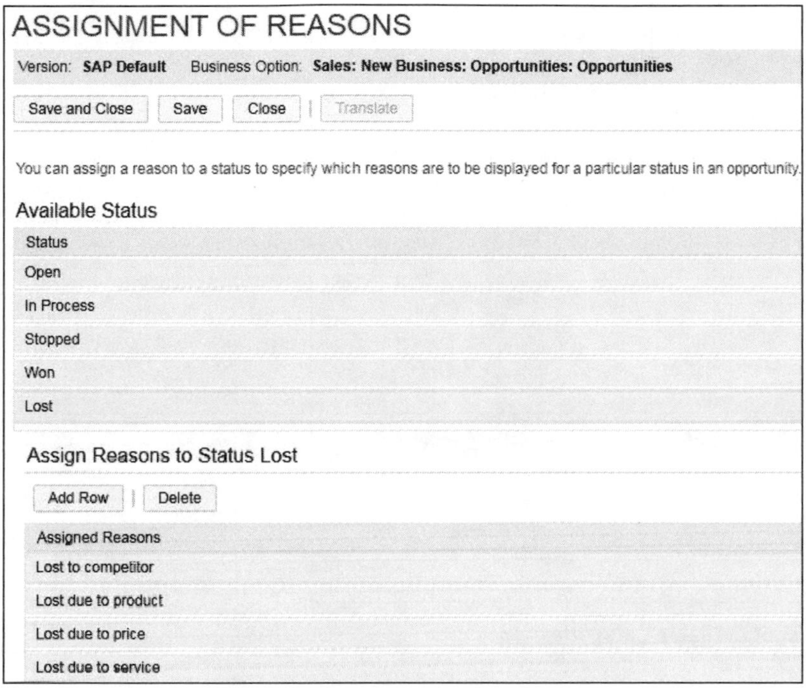

ASSIGNMENT OF REASONS

Version: **SAP Default**   Business Option: **Sales: New Business: Opportunities: Opportunities**

| Save and Close | Save | Close | Translate |

You can assign a reason to a status to specify which reasons are to be displayed for a particular status in an opportunity.

Available Status

Status
Open
In Process
Stopped
Won
Lost

Assign Reasons to Status Lost

| Add Row | Delete |

Assigned Reasons
Lost to competitor
Lost due to product
Lost due to price
Lost due to service

Figure 7.35 Assignment of Reasons to Opportunity Statuses

- **Categories**

  You can maintain a list of **Categories** to classify opportunities. You can open the standard SAP-delivered list of categories for opportunities by clicking on **Maintain Categories** (see Figure 7.36). This is a comprehensive list of categories in the system, but only assigned categories for opportunities will be available for users to select in an opportunity. You can add new categories by creating category codes starting with "Z" if you need additional categories to meet your business requirements.

- **Assignment of Categories**

  As mentioned earlier, **Categories** need to be assigned to opportunities to be selectable in opportunities. To assign categories to opportunities, click **Assign Categories**, and a list of categories for opportunities appears, as shown in Figure 7.37. To add a new category to the list, click **Add Row,** and select that **Category** from the dropdown. To delete a category from this list, select that **Category**, and click **Delete** so that it doesn't appear under the categories drop down in the opportunity. After making changes, click **Save and Close** to exit the **ASSIGNMENT OF CATEGORIES** screen.

201

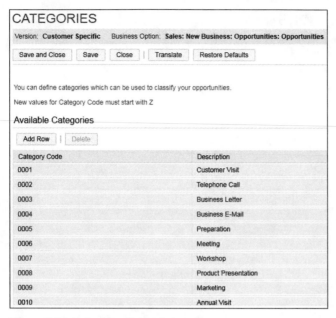

Figure 7.36 List of Available Categories

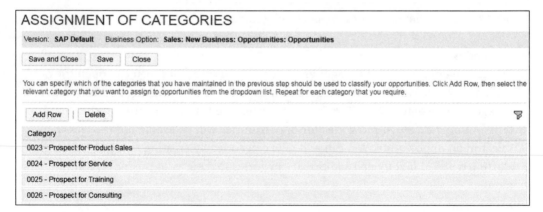

Figure 7.37 List of Categories Assigned to Opportunities

- **Contact Roles**

    If you need to add new contact roles (e.g., decision maker, gatekeeper, and contract approver) for opportunities, you can add these contact roles through this configuration. Click **Maintain Contact Roles** to display the **Available Contact Roles** list, as shown in Figure 7.38. You can add new contact roles by clicking **Add Row**. Figure 7.38 shows a new **Contact Role Code** of **Z001** with **Decision Maker** as the **Description**.

You can add as many contact roles for an opportunity as required. Click **Save and Close** to exit the **CONTACT ROLES** screen.

CONTACT ROLES

Version: **SAP Default**   Business Option: **Sales: New Business: Opportunities: Opportunities**

| Save and Close | Save | Close | Translate |

You can create new contact roles.

Note: When creating your entries in the table below, the Contact Role Code must begin with the letter Z.

Available Contact Roles

| Add Row | Delete |

Contact Role Code	Description	Color
Z001	Decision Maker	

Figure 7.38 Adding a New Contact Role for an Opportunity

- **Document Types**

  If you follow multiple sales cycles to cater to your different lines of business or sales organizations, you may need to create different opportunity types in your SAP Sales Cloud system with their own settings. A default opportunity type is delivered as part of SAP Sales Cloud, but if you choose to create additional opportunity types, click **Maintain Document Types** under **Document Types**.

  Figure 7.39 shows an example of adding a new **Document Type Z01** with **Project Opportunity** as the **Description**. Just like any other configuration, you can create a new opportunity type by clicking **Add Row** and entering an opportunity type starting with "Z". Click **Save** (or **Save and Close**) to make the new document type effective in your system.

DOCUMENT TYPES

Version: **SAP Default**   Business Option: **Opportunities**

| Save and Close | Save | Close | Translate |

You can define new document types. Only for newly created document types you can configure its settings.

Note: When creating your entries in the table below, the Document Type must begin with the letter Z.

Document Types

| Add Row | Delete |

Document Type	Description
Z01	Project Opportunity

Figure 7.39 Adding a New Document Type for an Opportunity

- **Custom Status**

  SAP Sales Cloud provides system-delivered statuses such as **Open**, **In Process**, **Stopped**, and **Lost**. If these statuses aren't sufficient, and you need additional statuses for your opportunities, SAP Sales Cloud allows you to create your own custom statuses for specific opportunity types. To create new statuses, click **Maintain Custom Status**. Figure 7.40 shows the **Available Document Types** list and options to add custom statuses to that opportunity type.

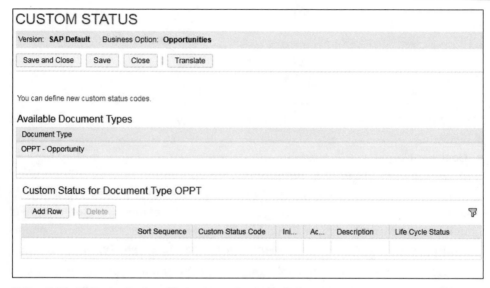

Figure 7.40 Adding a Custom Status to an Opportunity

To add a new custom status, select the **Document Type** under **Available Document Types**, and click **Add Row** under **Custom Status**, as shown in Figure 7.41. To add a new custom code, you need to enter a **Sort Sequence** for the new status, a **Custom Status Code** (a five-character code), and a **Description**. If you want the custom status to be the initial status for an opportunity, enable the **Initial Status** checkbox. The **Active** checkbox must be enabled for the custom status to be available in opportunities. Figure 7.41 shows the **Life Cycle Status** dropdown from which you can select one of the five statuses to map to your newly added custom status.

These five statuses are basically system statuses that control the internal functions of opportunities. It's important to map your Custom Status to one of these system statuses. For example, the custom status added in this example, **Contract Review**, can be mapped to **Won** (in the **Life Cycle Status** column) because the opportunity has already been won and is going through the contract execution process. Unlike the standard statuses that can be set using from the **Actions** menu, custom status can only be set via the dropdown field. If any custom status is maintained, the standard statuses can't be used.

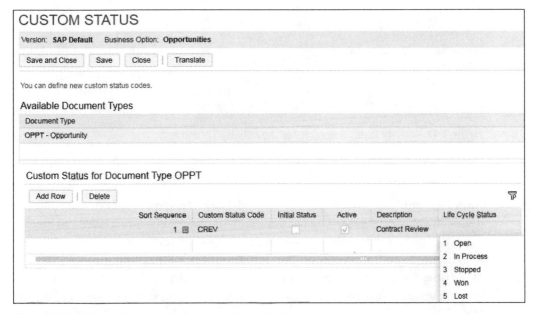

Figure 7.41 Adding a Custom Status to an Opportunity

- **Activity Timeline**

  To configure the activity timeline, you click **Maintain Timeline** under **Activity Timeline**, and the activity types included in the activity timeline appear, as shown in Figure 7.42. The four activity types (**Appointment**, **Phone Call**, **Activity Task**, and **Visit**) available for opportunities can be activated if you want those to be included in the opportunity activity timeline. Figure 7.42 shows that you can mark the activity types as **Internal** if you want those to appear on the activity timeline as internal activities. Activity tasks are normally internal activities because they are carried out by internal team members.

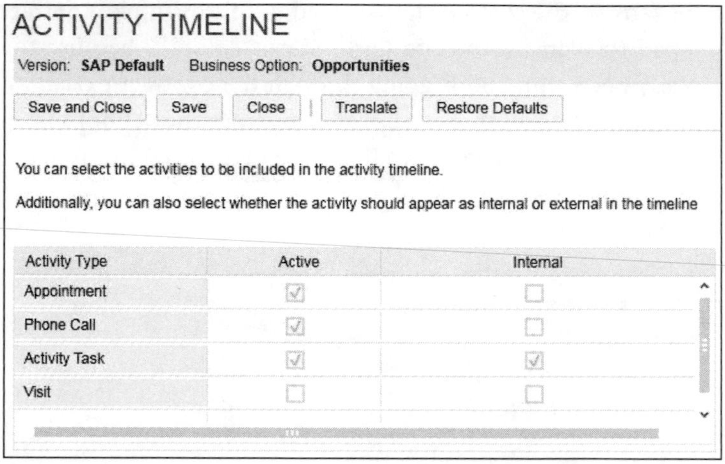

Figure 7.42 Activity Types Available for the Activity Timeline

7.3.3   Sales Assistant

Sales assistant (also referred to as activity advisor) refers to a set of activities you can define to enable guided selling per your sales methodology. Using sales assistant in opportunities provides a set of suggested activities and tasks for users to select while working through opportunities. You can also mark certain activities and tasks as **Mandatory** for the users to carry out in specific sales phases. To configure sales assistant per your business requirements, click **Sales Assistant** in the **Activities in Project** list, as shown in Figure 7.43.

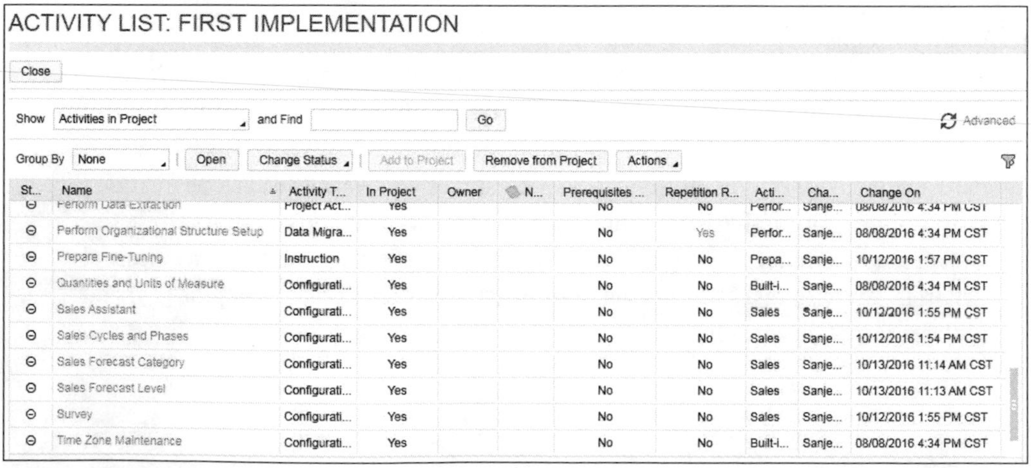

Figure 7.43 Fine-Tuning the Activities List

Before you assign activities and tasks to **Sales Assistant**, you need to maintain such activities by clicking on **Maintain Activities** under **Activities**, as shown in Figure 7.44.

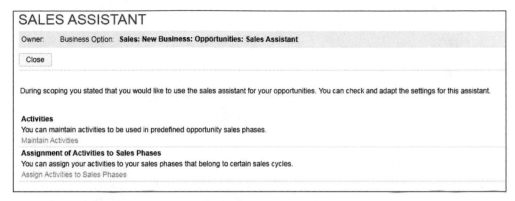

Figure 7.44 Maintain Activities and Assign Activities to Sales Phases

Figure 7.45 shows all the activity types that can be included in **Sales Assistant**. You can add and remove activities by clicking on **Add Row** and **Delete** as needed.

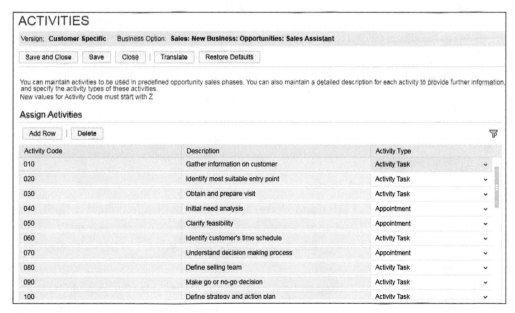

Figure 7.45 Available Activity Types for Sales Assistant

Each sales cycle has a set of sales phases. To assign the required activities and tasks to each sales phase, click on the **Sales Phase**, as shown in Figure 7.46. Under

Assign Activities to General Opportunity-identify opportunity, click on **Add Row** and **Delete** to add or remove activities from sales phases as needed. You can select the **Mandatory** checkbox for any activity, and users will be required to add those activities to the opportunities whenever the corresponding sales phase is set for the opportunity.

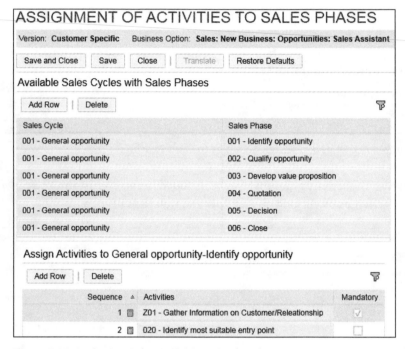

Figure 7.46 Assigning Sales Activities to Sales Phases

7.3.4   Sales Cycles and Phases

You can click on **Sales Cycles and Phases** from the **Activities in Project** list in Figure 7.43 to configure all the settings related to sales cycles and phases. Figure 7.47 shows links to configure **Analysis Phases**, **Sales Phases**, **Sales Cycles**, and **Default Sales Cycle for Opportunities**.

Let's review all the configuration options available under **Sales Cycles and Phases**:

- **Analysis Phases**
  Analysis phases is used for company-wide reporting of opportunities. To check the analysis phases available in standard SAP Sales Cloud and add new analysis phases per your business requirements, click on **Maintain Analysis Phases** shown in Fig-

ure 7.47. The **Available Analysis Phases** list is displayed in Figure 7.48 with the **Analysis Phase Code** and corresponding **Description**. You can add new analysis phases as needed in this table by clicking on **Add Row**. The new analysis phase code should begin with "Z".

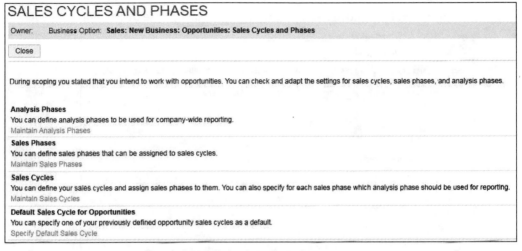

Figure 7.47 Settings to Configure Sales Cycle and Phases

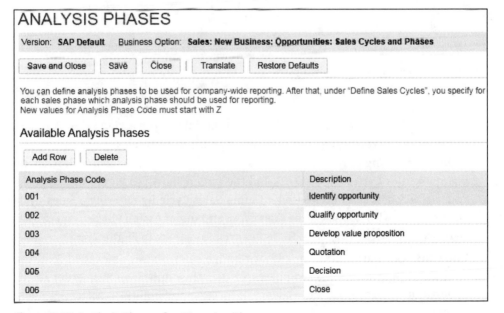

Figure 7.48 Analysis Phases for Opportunities

- **Sales Phases**

  Sales phases are unique stages in opportunities that you want to track and plan your sales activities around. To add sales phases for your opportunity sales cycle, click on **Maintain Sales Phases** shown in Figure 7.47. You can add new entries to the **Available Sales Phases** list shown in Figure 7.49 by clicking on **Add Row** and entering a new **Sales Phase Code** starting with "Z" and a sales phase **Description** as needed.

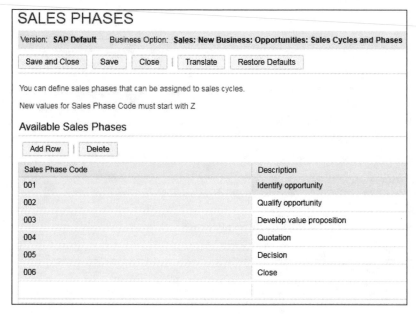

Figure 7.49 Sales Phases for Sales Cycles

- **Sales Cycle**

  You define the sales cycle per your sales methodology and assign sales phases to that sales cycle. You also assign an analysis phase to each sales phase in the sales cycle for reporting purposes. To maintain the settings for the sales cycle, click on **Maintain Sales Cycles** (Figure 7.47), and the screen shown in Figure 7.50 appears. You can add new sales cycles under **Define Sales Cycle** by entering a **Sales Cycle Code** starting with "Z". Select the sales cycle, and under **Assign Phases**, you can see all the sales phases assigned to that sales cycle, as shown in Figure 7.50.

  Under **Assign Phases**, you can add or remove sales phases as needed. You can assign a sequence to the sales phases so that they appear in that order in the opportunity. You can also add a chance of success (probability) to each sales phase so that the sales pipeline reflects the weighted value of opportunities. To track the progress of opportunities in each sales phase and make sure that opportunities are progressing through the sales funnel, you can define thresholds for the number of days that opportunities may remain in each sales stage. If opportunities remain in a sales phase over the threshold days, the progress of such opportunities are marked as slow or stalled as the case may be.

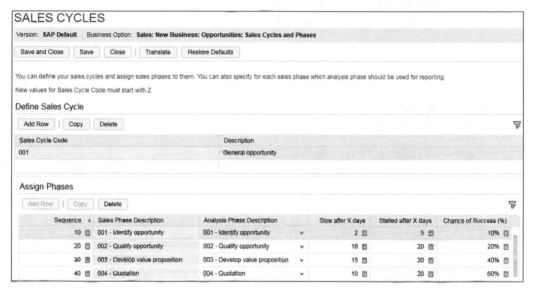

Figure 7.50 Assigning Sales Phases to the Sales Cycle

Figure 7.50 shows that the threshold days for sales phase **002 – Qualify Opportunity** have been set to 10 days for slow and 20 days for stalled. If an opportunity remains in the Sales Phase 002 – Qualify Opportunity phase for more than 10 days, then the opportunity progress will be marked as **Slow**. If the opportunity remains in Sales Phase 002 – Qualify Opportunity phase for more than 20 days, the opportunity progress will be marked as **Stalled**. You can maintain the values for these days and chance of success for each sales phase per your business requirements.

- **Default Sales Cycle for Opportunities**
  If you've configured more than one sales cycle for opportunities, you can set a sales cycle as the default so that whenever an opportunity is created, that particular sales cycle is defaulted. In an opportunity, you can change the default sales cycle and select another sales cycle from the dropdown if needed; however, the default sales cycle is always prompted whenever an opportunity is created irrespective of the opportunity type. To enable the settings for **Default Sales Cycle for Opportunities**, click on **Specify Default Sales Cycle** in Figure 7.47.

Figure 7.51 shows that **001 – General opportunity** has been selected from **Sales Cycle Code** as the default sales cycle. To set another sales cycle as the default, select that **Sales Cycle Code** from the **Define Default Sales Cycle** dropdown, and then click **Save** or **Save and Close** to make it effective in your opportunities.

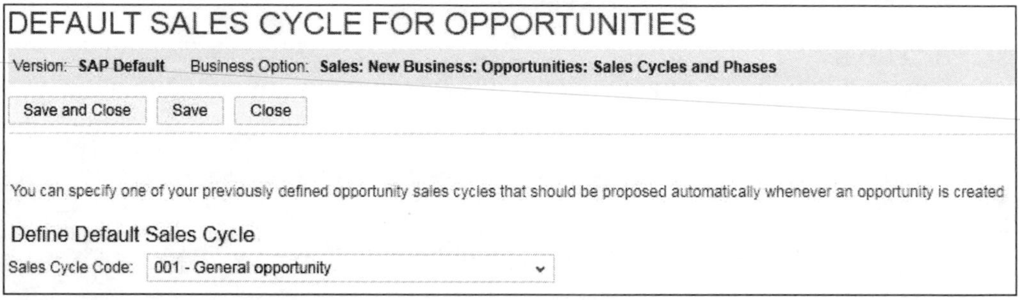

DEFAULT SALES CYCLE FOR OPPORTUNITIES

Version: **SAP Default**   Business Option: **Sales: New Business: Opportunities: Sales Cycles and Phases**

| Save and Close | Save | Close |

You can specify one of your previously defined opportunity sales cycles that should be proposed automatically whenever an opportunity is created

Define Default Sales Cycle

Sales Cycle Code: 001 - General opportunity   ⌄

Figure 7.51 Defining the Default Sales Cycle for an Opportunity

7.3.5   Sales Forecast Category

The **Activities in Project** list shown earlier in Figure 7.43 includes forecast categories. Using sales forecast categories, you can further categorize your opportunities based on these additional parameters. To configure sales forecast categories, click on **Sales Forecast Category** shown in Figure 7.43. The standard SAP Sales Cloud sales forecast categories are shown in Figure 7.52. You can add new sales forecast categories to this list as needed.

Figure 7.52 Sales Forecast Categories for Opportunities

7.4   Summary

In this chapter, you've learned about the opportunity management process and how opportunities are created and processed in SAP Sales Cloud. We've reviewed the key information maintained in various opportunity tabs and their significance, including account, contact, expected value, probability, closing date, sale cycle, sales phases, sales activities, products, revenue splits, sales documents, involved parties, and sales team. These details help you work with opportunities through all the sales stages.

You also learned the follow-up process from an opportunity to create a sales quote or sales opportunity in SAP ERP. Finally, you learned how to fine-tune various opportunity configuration activities, such as opportunity number range, categories, status reasons, custom statuses, contact roles, opportunity document types, activity timeline, sales assistant, sales cycle and sales phases, and sales forecast categories. As you've seen, the success of opportunities hinges on the activities and tasks carried out to move the opportunities ahead in the sales cycle.

In the next chapter, you'll learn about all the activity types—appointment, phone calls, and tasks—available in SAP Sales Cloud, how to create them, and how to fine-tune them to meet your unique business requirements.

7

Chapter 8
Activity Management

Activity management is the process of recording relevant sales activities that you want to track and report on. The key is to define the relevance of activities that are unique to every organization. Predefined sales activities help organizations drive the sales process forward to achieve revenue goals.

Activity management deals with creating, tracking, and reporting on all the activities carried out by the sales team on a daily basis. The goal of activity management is not only to track the activities of the sales team but also act as a sales assistant and guide the team toward successful sales pursuits. Working through various steps in the sales process from lead qualification to advancing sales opportunities toward winning the deals, you're required to carry out a set of activities and tasks to accomplish certain objectives. Because every sales organization differs in its sales methodology and sales process, requirements for recording and managing activities are unique to every organization.

While defining the needs for activity management for any sales team, you need to consider the day-to-day activities that are carried out by your sales team, the internal versus external activities you need to record, the activity types you want the sales team to carry out in various sales phases, and, most importantly, the activities you want to record and track in the system. You need to have these questions answered and agreed upon between the sales team and sale managers before implementing any activity management solution for your team. Based on your sales methodology and best practices, you can define sales assistants with a set of activities for various sales stages in opportunities, as covered in the previous chapter. The set of activities defined for each sales stage can be required or recommended per your unique sale process. All the activities may not be required for each sales opportunity.

To give comprehensive details on activity management in SAP Sales Cloud, we'll start by introducing the activity management process and the four different types of activities—appointments, phone calls, emails, and tasks—with their unique characteristics.

We'll review the key differences between activities and tasks, external and internal team interactions, calendar maintenance of activities, and their key features. In a section dedicated to creating and processing activities, you'll learn how to create all the activity types available in SAP Sales Cloud and learn about their data requirements, which activity types are visible on the calendar and which aren't, and how they are linked to groupware (Microsoft Outlook). We'll go through screenshots and step-by-step instructions to create and process all activity types and discuss the relevance of all the activity tabs and data fields available to capture and track activities. We'll identify and explain the key differences in creation and processing of different types of activities in the relevant sections to help you map your requirements to appropriate activity types in SAP Sales Cloud.

SAP Sales Cloud has delivered standard fine-tuning settings for activity management to configure your unique business requirements and scenarios. In Section 8.3, we'll review the fine-tuning settings available for activities, such as maintaining/assigning categories and maintaining involved parties for appointments, tasks, emails, phone calls, and chats, as well as how you can tweak those settings to meet your unique requirements for activity management.

8.1   Activity Management Process

Using the activity management process in SAP Sales Cloud, you record your interactions with external customers as well as tasks assigned to internal team members. These interactions and tasks are carried out to meet specific goals in the sales process. Capturing activities provides a history of interactions between the sales team and account contacts, and it also improves communication between all the team members working together in the sales process. Activity management can also be used to recommend appropriate activities to sales reps for each sales stage to move the opportunity forward. More than just a transaction to record and report on sales rep interactions and activities, activity management is also a very powerful sales enablement tool to guide the sales team toward achieving sales goals through a set of predefined tasks and activities. Figure 8.1 shows that activities are created with reference to accounts, contacts, leads processing, and opportunities processing.

The SAP Sales Cloud activity types—appointments, tasks, phone calls, and emails—and their unique features, including a calendar view for activities, will be discussed in the following sections.

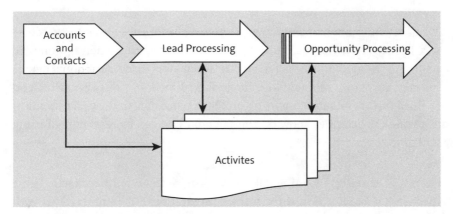

Figure 8.1 Activities Created for Accounts, Contacts, Leads, and Opportunities

8.1.1   Activity Types

Following are descriptions of the four types of activities available in SAP Sales Cloud in line with the general day-to-day business activities carried out by sales teams:

- **Appointments**

  These types of interactions or activities represent scheduled meetings or visits with account contacts. Appointment activities are similar to Microsoft Outlook appointments, and they show on your SAP Sales Cloud calendar when scheduled. Microsoft Outlook appointments will also show up on your SAP Sales Cloud calendar if you've integrated Microsoft Outlook with your SAP Sales Cloud. You can drag and drop appointment activities on the calendar to reschedule appointments as needed.

  To create appointment activities, you need account contacts (or meeting attendees) and scheduled start and end dates and times. In the next section, we'll explain how to create and work through appointment activities.

- **Tasks**

  Tasks are activities carried out by a user or team members. Task activities are created for internal team members and not for account contacts. These activity types are assigned to a processor or task executor for task completion within a specific due date and time. If needed, you can also maintain a percentage of completion for such activities to accurately reflect the status of such tasks.

- **Phone calls**

  Phone call activities are basically interaction records for calls made to customer contacts. In such activities, you capture a time stamp to specify when a phone call was made and the account contact to whom the call was made. Additional details are captured in phone call activities, including direction, priority, status, and notes, which further enhance reporting on these types of activities. Like appointments, phone call activities show on the calendar and can be rescheduled using drag and drop.

- **Emails**

  These types of activities record email interactions with account contacts. These activities work in conjunction with Outlook integration. Email interactions with contacts in Outlook can be linked with account contacts as email activities. Email activities don't appear on the calendar.

8.1.2   General Features

General features of activity management (e.g., maintaining notes and attachments, tracking the lifecycle of an activity through various statuses, and referring to accounts, contacts, leads, and opportunities) enable you to effectively manage your unique business activity-related requirements. These general features are as follows:

- **Notes**

  You can maintain notes on activities with a user name and time stamp. Notes help you record activity interaction for future reference and sales team transparency.

- **Attachments**

  Activities allow you to make different types of attachments such as local files, web links, and files from a library. You can make these attachments to the activities as needed.

- **Statuses**

  To track the progress of activities, you can maintain different statuses, including **Open**, **In Process**, **Canceled**, and **Complete**. These statuses are set on activities through the **Actions** menu. When an activity is created, the system defaults the status as **Open**, regardless of the activity type and how it was created.

- **Reference to an account and contact**

  When activities are created, you can enter account and contact details to establish a reference.

- **Reference to lead or opportunity**
  Activities are mostly created with reference to a lead or an opportunity. Such references appear in the activities document flow.

- **Groupware integration with Microsoft Outlook**
  SAP Sales Cloud activity management integration with Microsoft Outlook allows users to work seamlessly between SAP Sales Cloud and Outlook. Activities from Outlook are easily linked to accounts, contacts, leads, and opportunities in SAP Sales Cloud.

- **Quickly create activities**
  SAP Sales Cloud navigation provides shortcut links to quickly create activities.

- **Flag and favorite activities**
  You can flag, tag, and mark favorite activities as needed for easy tracking and ready reference.

- **Mobile access to activities**
  SAP Sales Cloud mobile apps for iPhone, Android, and iPad allow easy access to and processing of activities from mobile devices as needed.

- **Changing the history view**
  Like any transaction in SAP, changing the history view on activities allows you to track all the changes. It offers a time stamp along with user IDs for a complete change of history view.

- **Feeds**
  By default, all the activities provide feeds with change updates. Unless you unfollow, an activity feed constantly gets updated with all the updates related to changes made to that activity. The generated feed notifies you when a new activity is created and when an existing activity is updated.

8.1.3   Activity Management Calendar View

The appointment and phone call activity types appear on the activity calendar view. In calendar view, it's much easier to view and reschedule activities as needed. You can view user activity for day, week, month, and agenda. It also allows you to view the activity calendars of team members as needed (if allowed). To open the activity calendar view, click **Calendar** on the navigation bar on the left side of the screen, as shown in Figure 8.2.

Figure 8.2 Activity Calendar View for User Appointments and Phone Calls

You can alter the activity calendar view to **Work Week**, **Week**, **Month**, **Day**, or **Agenda** by clicking on the view option at the bottom of the screen shown in Figure 8.3 and selecting the appropriate view.

Figure 8.3 Option to Change the Activity Calendar View

SAP Sales Cloud also allows you to view the activity calendar views of team members. Figure 8.4 shows how you can choose the **Team Calendar** option by clicking on the **Employee** icon in the bottom-right corner. You can go back to your own calendar by clicking on **My Calendar**.

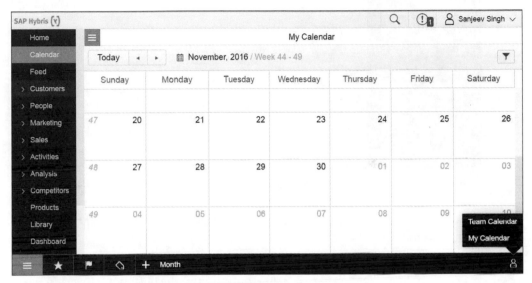

Figure 8.4 Choosing to View the Team Calendar

8.2   Creating and Processing Activities

The information required to create and process activities depends on the activity type you select to create. To understand the key differences in creating and processing various activity types, we'll review step-by-step instructions to create and process all the four types of activities (appointments, phone calls, tasks, and emails) with appropriate details in the following sections.

8.2.1   Creating Appointment Activity Types

You've seen in the previous section that appointment activity types are visible on the activity calendar. These types of activities can be created either from **Calendar** or from **Appointments** under the **Activities** work center on the navigation bar, as shown in Figure 8.5.

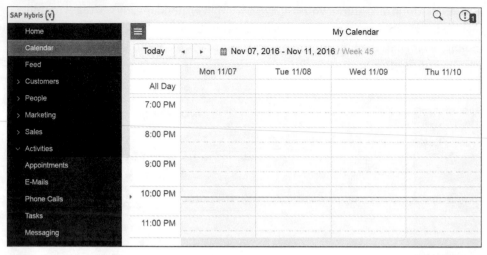

Figure 8.5 Activities Navigation Expanded to Select Appointments

Let's create an appointment activity from both the **Calendar** and **Appointments** work centers, as follows:

1. To create an appointment from the **Calendar** work center, click the **Calendar** work center in the navigation bar, click the **+** button from the bottom toolbar, and select **Appointment** (see Figure 8.6). Because **Calendar** only displays appointment and phone call activity types, when you create an activity from **Calendar**, those are your only prompt options.

2. In the **New Appointment** create screen that appears, the appointment **subject** field is required (see the **Please make an entry. Otherwise, system will enter one when you save.** warning at the top of the screen). However, SAP Sales Cloud auto populates this field if you don't enter the appointment subject. In this screen, you can maintain the following to create an appointment:

   – **Subject**: Describe and identify the appointment in this free-text field. If you don't enter your own text, the system adds a default subject when the appointment is saved. It's recommended to have a subject naming convention for the appointments.

   – **Account**: Select an account from the value selection you're creating this appointment for. Although **Account** isn't required to create an appointment, it's a good practice to include it in appointments so that you can report on the sales reps appointments for specific accounts or vice versa as needed.

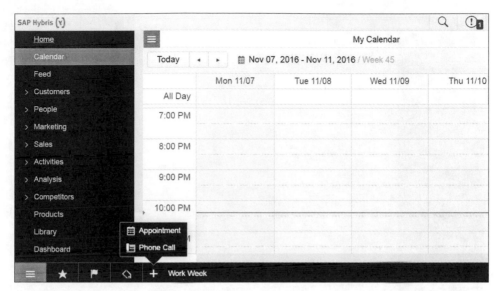

Figure 8.6 Choosing Appointment or Phone Call Activities from Calendar View

- **Primary Contact**: Depending on the account you select for the appointment, the primary contact for the account is auto populated (if the primary contact has been maintained on the account) in this field. The primary contact isn't necessarily the attendee for this appointment.

- **Location**: Enter the location of the appointment in this free-text field.

- **All-Day Event**: By default, this is set to **No**, but you can change this to **Yes** if you're creating an all-day event. In that case, you don't need to select the **Start Time** and **End Time** for the appointment, similar to an appointment created in Outlook.

- **Start Date/Time** : Select the appointment start date and time in these two fields. The system defaults both the start date and time for the appointment, but you can change these as needed.

- **End Date/Time**: Per the start date and time selected for the appointment, enter the end date and time as needed.

- **Category**: To categorize appointments based on categories configured in the system, select one of the categories from the dropdown. Figure 8.7 shows **Customer Visit** selected under **Category**.

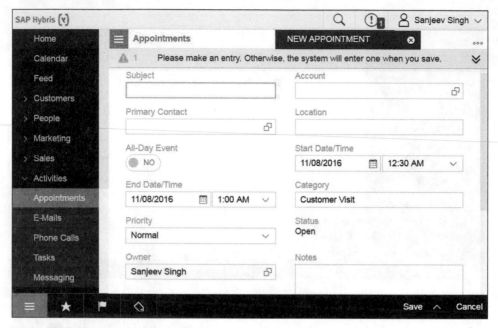

Figure 8.7 New Appointment Screen

- **Priority**: The importance of an appointment is designated through its priority. Select one of the priorities (**Immediate**, **Low**, **Normal**, or **Urgent**) configured in the system for your appointment.

- **Status**: Appointments can have **Open**, **In Process**, **Canceled**, or **Complete** statuses. By default, the **Open** status is set on appointments when they are created, but you can set other statuses as needed through the **Actions** menu, which we'll explain in the "Appointments" subsection under Section 8.2.5.

- **Owner**: The owner is the organizer of appointments. By default, the user creating the appointment is set as the owner of the meeting, as shown in Figure 8.8. You can select another owner though the search option if you're creating an appointment on behalf of another team member.

- **Notes**: Enter meeting notes and other details to be communicated with all the meeting attendees in the **Notes** free-text field.

- **Attendees**: Include all the attendees for an appointment by clicking **Add** and selecting the attendees (could be internal employees or external contacts or partners) to add them to the appointment, as shown in Figure 8.9.

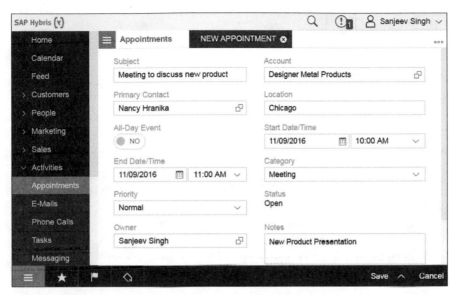

Figure 8.8 Appointment Details Added to the New Appointment

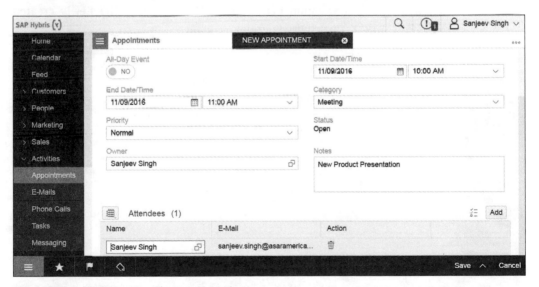

Figure 8.9 Adding an Attendee to a Meeting

3. After entering all the details on an appointment, click **Save** to create the appointment in your system. Figure 8.10 shows the newly created appointment under **My Appointments**.

Appointments

My Appointments (8)

Subject	Status	Start Date/Time	End Date/Time	Account
Meeting to discuss new product	Open	11/09/2016 10:...	11/09/2016 11:...	Designer Metal Products
New Services Lead	Open	11/09/2016 9:0...	11/09/2016 11:...	The Best Corp
C4C Example Opportunity	Open	11/08/2016 3:3...	11/08/2016 4:0...	Designer Metal Products
C4C Example Opportunity	Open	11/08/2016 10:...	11/08/2016 10:...	Designer Metal Products
New Services Lead	Open	11/07/2016 10:...	11/07/2016 10:...	The Best Corp
Test Quote Lead from Mobile ...	Open	11/04/2016 8:3...	11/04/2016 9:0...	Quote (Test Company)
Initial need analysis	Open	10/11/2016 12:...	10/11/2016 12:...	MTS Systems
TEST APPT	Completed	10/11/2016 9:3...	10/11/2016 10:...	

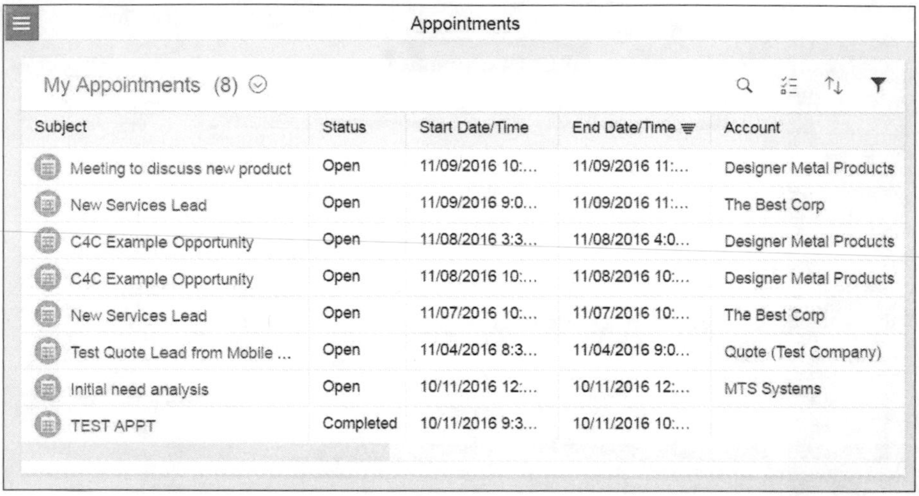

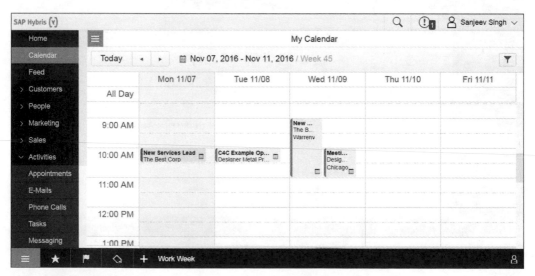

Figure 8.10 Newly Created Appointment Appears under My Appointments

4. Verify that the newly created appointment appears on your calendar by clicking on **Calendar** in the navigation bar. Figure 8.11 shows that the newly created appointment appears on activity calendar.

Figure 8.11 Newly Created Appointment on the Activity Calendar

Switching gears, let's now create an appointment from the **Activities** work center by following these steps:

1. From the navigation bar, expand **Activities**, and click on the **Appointments** work center.

2. Click on the **+** button at the bottom of the screen to create a new appointment (Figure 8.12).

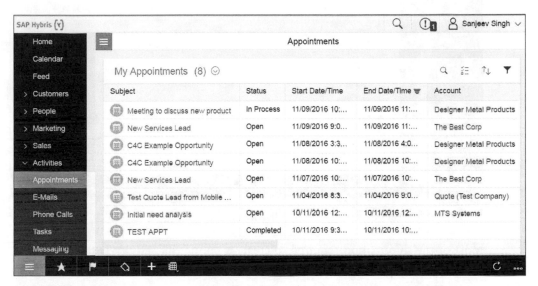

Figure 8.12 Creating an Appointment by Clicking the Plus Button on the Appointments Screen

3. The **New Appointment** screen launches, as shown in Figure 8.7. Enter the appointment details as needed.

4. Click **Save** to create the appointment.

8.2.2 Creating Phone Call Activities

Similar to the appointment activity types, you can create phone call activities either from the calendar or from **Phone Calls** under **Activities** in the navigation bar. You can click on the work center **Phone Call** under **Activities** as shown earlier in Figure 8.6, and click on create button (plus sign and a **NEW PHONE CALL** screen appears, as shown in Figure 8.13.

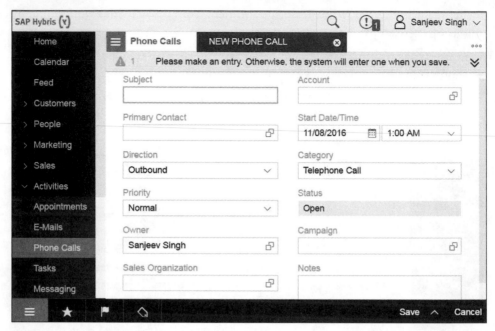

Figure 8.13 Creation of a New Phone Call Activity

Most of the information required to create a phone call activity is the same as is required to create an appointment activity, except the following:

- **Start Date/Time**
  Unlike the appointment activity, the phone call activity only has **Start Date/Time** and not **End Date/Time**.

- **Direction**
  Phone calls can be outbound to account contacts or inbound from account contacts to you. To differentiate between these types of phone calls, assign **Direction** as **Inbound** or **Outbound** to activity.

- **Campaign**
  Phone calls with prospects or customers can be part of a campaign. To track such campaigns in phone calls, enter the **Campaign** ID in the phone call activities.

In addition, you don't need to add attendees for creating phone call activities (as is needed for appointment activities). As shown in Figure 8.14, maintain all the required details in the phone call activity, and click **Save** to create it.

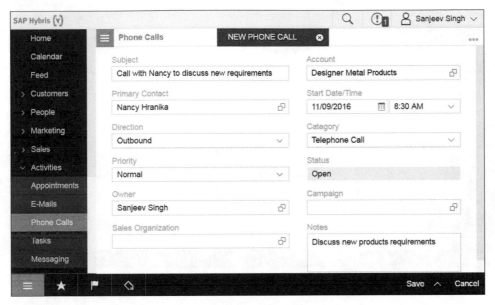

Figure 8.14 Information Filled in for the New Phone Call Activity

You can click on **Phone Calls** on the navigation bar to see the newly created phone call activity under **My Phone Calls**, as shown in Figure 8.15.

Figure 8.15 Newly Created Phone Call Activity under My Phone Calls

You can click on **Calendar** in the navigation bar to see the newly created phone call activity visible on the activity calendar, as shown in Figure 8.16.

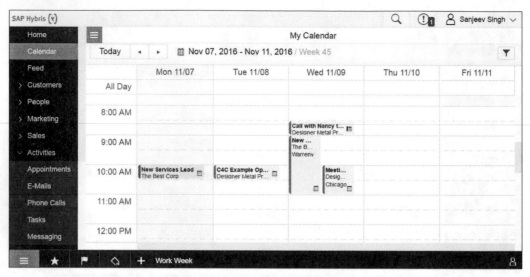

Figure 8.16 Newly Created Phone Call on the Activity Calendar

8.2.3   Creating Task Activities

Task activities are fundamentally different from the previous two activity types in a couple of unique ways. First, task activities aren't displayed on the activity calendar. You can neither create task activities from the calendar nor can you see the created tasks on the calendar like you can appointments and phone calls. Secondly, task activities are created for internal team members only and not for external partners or account contacts. Although you can assign accounts and contacts on task activities, only the task owner can process the task.

To create a task activity, navigate to **Tasks** under **Activities**, and click on the **+** button. The **NEW TASK** screen appears, as shown in Figure 8.17.

The fields unique to task activities are as follows:

- **Processor**
  This refers to the partner responsible for executing the task. The processor is only relevant for tasks, not appointments or phone calls.

- **Completion**
  Enter the percentage as appropriate to reflect the percentage of task completion.

- **Due Date/Time**
  Unlike the **End Date/Time** field in an appointment activity, tasks have a **Due Date/**

Time field because they are assigned activities and are expected to be completed by the processor within a specific date and time.

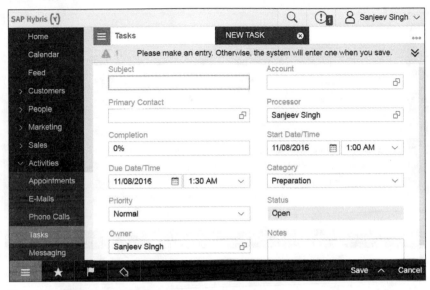

Figure 8.17 Creating a New Task Activity

Enter the task details as shown in Figure 8.18, and click **Save** to create the task activity.

Figure 8.18 Entering Details for a New Task Activity

Figure 8.19 shows the newly created task activity under **My Tasks**.

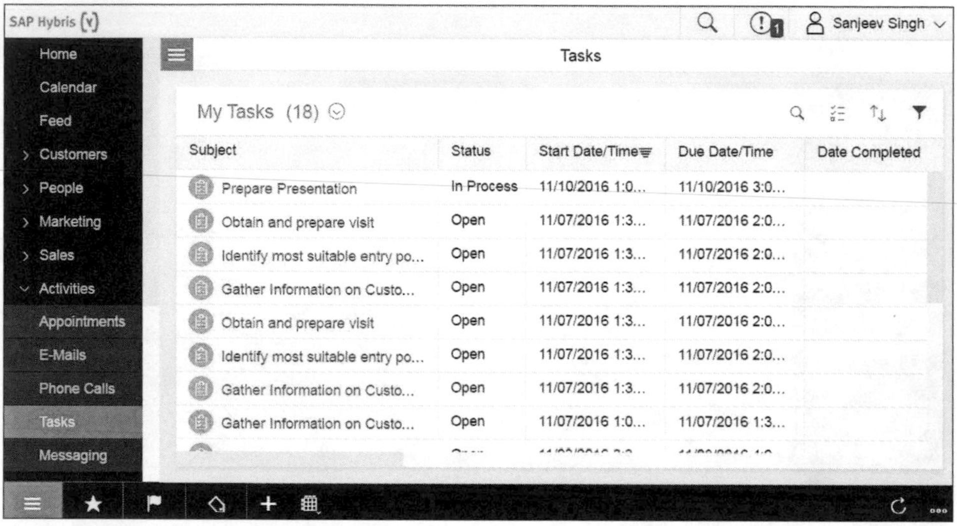

Figure 8.19 Newly Created Tasks under My Tasks

8.2.4   Creating Email Activities

Email activities are created by transferring inbound or outbound emails from Microsoft Outlook to SAP Sales Cloud. You don't create email activities like you do appointments, phone calls, or task activities. Email activities are synchronized with Outlook 2007, 2010, or 2013. To enable email integration, you need to download the SAP Cloud for Customer Add-In for Microsoft Outlook. You'll log in to your SAP Sales Cloud through your local Outlook client, and then you can drag and drop emails from your inbox to activities in SAP Sales Cloud.

You can link email activities to accounts, contacts, leads, and opportunities from Outlook to SAP Sales Cloud. Figure 8.20 shows email activities in SAP Sales Cloud synched from Outlook.

To link activities to accounts, contacts, leads, and opportunities, choose **Activities • E-mails**. On the **OVERVIEW** screen that appears, open one of the email activities, as shown in Figure 8.21.

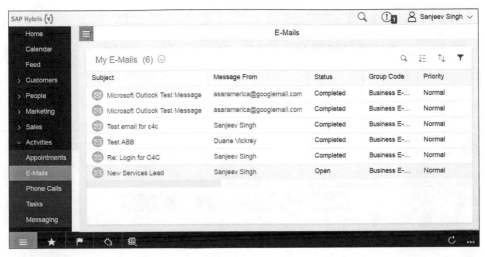

Figure 8.20 List View of My E-Mails Activities

Figure 8.21 E-Mails Activity Overview Screen

Click on the **RELATED ITEMS** tab, and then click on **Add** to go to the **Add Reference** popup shown in Figure 8.22. In the **Type** dropdown, select the object type you want to link, and then use the search option in the **Name** field from to select the specific object you want to link.

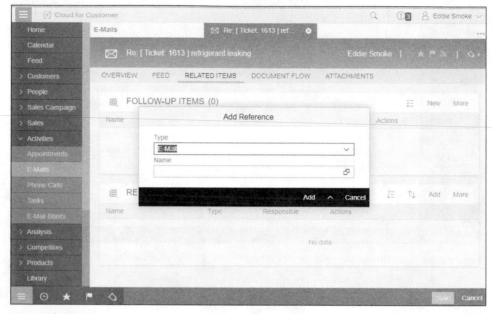

Figure 8.22 Add Reference Popup

For this example, select the object **Type** as **Lead**, and then select the corresponding lead object in the **Name** field, as shown in Figure 8.23.

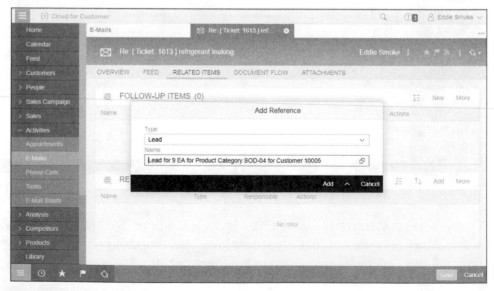

Figure 8.23 Linking a Lead to an Email Activity

When you click **Add**, your object is added to the email activity, as shown in Figure 8.24. You can see the **Lead** is added under **RELATED ITEMS** for the email activity.

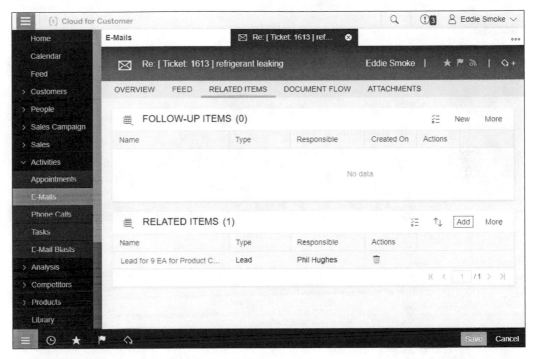

Figure 8.24 Lead Added as a Related Item for Email

8.2.5   Processing Activities

In the previous sections, you learned how to create all four types of activities (appointments, phone calls, tasks, and emails) in SAP Sales Cloud. In this section, we'll review how all of these activity types are processed and the additional details you can maintain to effectively manage and work through these activities. You've seen that appointment and phone call activities are displayed on the calendar. You can work through these activities from the calendar in addition to opening and processing these activity types individually. Before we go through each on these activity types for processing, let's review what options are available from the calendar. Figure 8.25 shows all the **Work Week** activities in an example calendar.

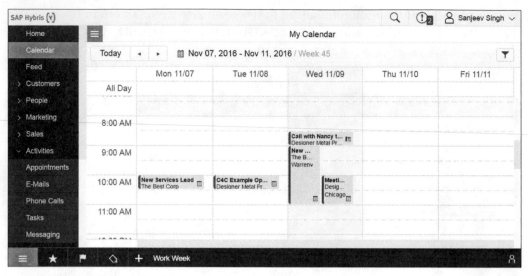

Figure 8.25 My Calendar View with Work Week Activities

To view the details of these activities on the calendar, click on the activity and a new popup window appears, as shown in Figure 8.26.

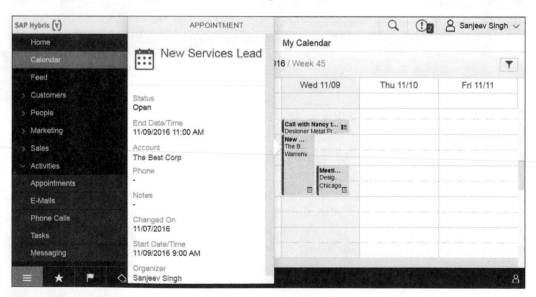

Figure 8.26 Appointment Details from the Calendar

In this view, you can only see the high-level details about the activity, and you can't make any changes. However, the activity calendar allows you to drag and drop activities on the calendar to change the date and time of your activity. The preceding Figure 8.26 shows the **New Services Lead** appointment with a **Start Date/Time** of **11/09/2016 9:00 AM** and an **End Date/Time** of **11/09/2016 11:00 AM**. To reschedule this appointment from 11/09/2016 (9:00 AM to 11:00 AM) to 11/11/2016 (8:00 AM to 10:00 AM), you simply drag and drop this activity on the calendar to the new date and time, as shown in Figure 8.27. The drag and drop feature is very useful for rescheduling appointment and phone call activities directly from the calendar.

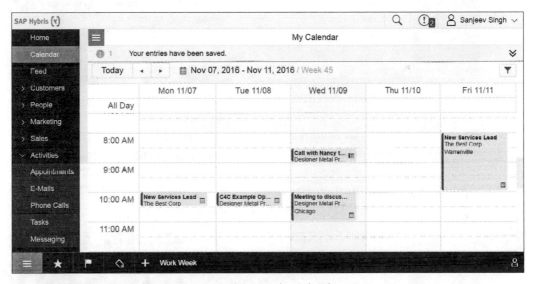

Figure 8.27 Dragging and Dropping an Activity on the Calendar

In the following sections, we'll now review all the processing options available from within the activities as opposed to using the calendar.

Appointments

To open an existing appointment, click **Appointments** under **Activities** in the navigation bar. By default, **My appointments** are displayed, as shown in Figure 8.28. Open the appointment created earlier by clicking on the meeting **Subject** link **Meeting to discuss new product**.

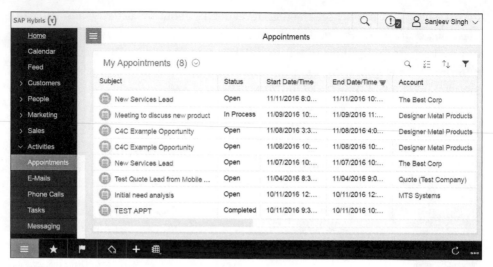

Figure 8.28 My Appointments List

Figure 8.29 shows the **OVERVIEW** screen of the opened appointment, which provides detail about the appointment such as header information, attachments, notes, and involved parties. On the top-right corner of the screen, icons are available to mark appointment as **Favorite Item**, **Flag Item**, **Follow**, **Post Update**, and **Add Tags**. The **FEED** tab provides all the updates made to the appointment.

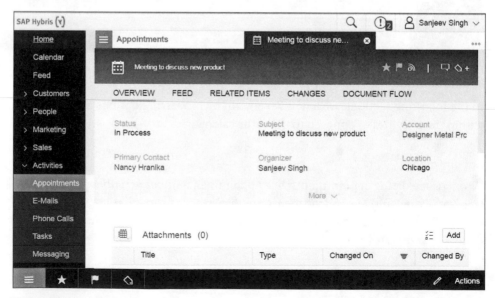

Figure 8.29 Activity Overview Screen

The **RELATED ITEMS** tab displays details about **FOLLOW-UP ITEMS** and **RELATED ITEMS**, as shown in Figure 8.30.

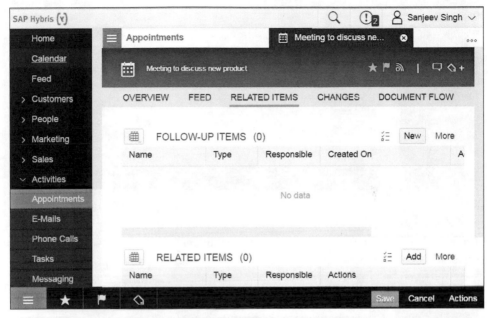

Figure 8.30 Related Items Tab for Appointments

Under **RELATED ITEMS**, click **Add** to link or add a reference to related activities (appointments, phone calls, emails, or tasks), leads, and opportunities. Figure 8.31 shows the **Add Reference** popup to link related items by selecting the **Type** from the dropdown and linking the item by selecting it from the **Name** field. After making the related item selection in the **Add Reference** popup, click **Add**, and the item appears under **RELATED ITEMS**.

Under **FOLLOW-UP ITEMS**, you can create follow-up activities, leads, and opportunities as needed. Click **New** and then select the item type (**Appointment**, **Task**, **Phone Call**, **Lead**, **Sales Lead**, or **Opportunity**) you want to create, as shown in Figure 8.32.

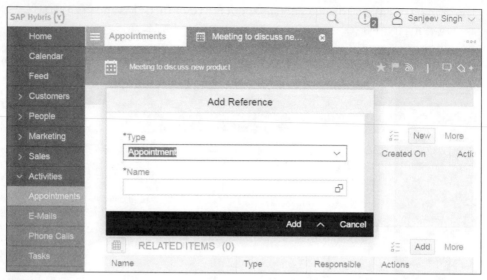

Figure 8.31 Adding a Reference to an Appointment under Related Items

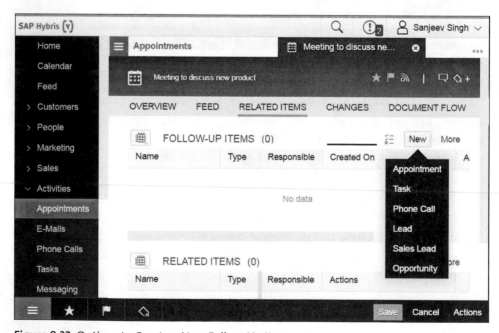

Figure 8.32 Options to Create a New Follow-Up Item

SAP Sales Cloud keeps a log of all the changes made to transactions. You can display the change history for all the changes made to appointments in the **CHANGES** tab. Figure 8.33 shows the **CHANGES** tab with the change log, including **Changes Made From**, **Changes Made To**, **Changed by User**, and **Attribute**.

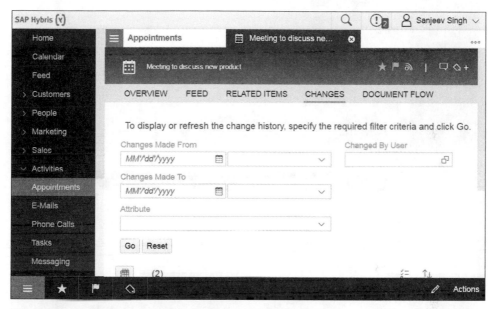

Figure 8.33 Displaying Change History with Various Filer Criteria

The **DOCUMENT FLOW** tab provides an overview of the link between preceding and follow-up activities or transactions from appointments. If an appointment is created from a lead or an opportunity, then you see a document flow on this tab with a link established between the appointment and the preceding lead or opportunity. Because this appointment was created as a standalone and not as a follow-up activity from another transaction, Figure 8.34 shows only one element for the current appointment.

Click on the **Edit** (pencil) icon at the bottom-right corner of the screen to enable edit mode so you can make changes. Next to that icon, the **Actions** button can be used to change the status on the appointment. Both **Actions** and **Edit** (pencil) are common on all the activity screens to make changes and update the status. Figure 8.35 shows the **Actions** menu status options of **Set as In Process**, **Set as Complete**, and **Set as Canceled**. When an appointment is created, the **Open** status is set by default for the appointment.

Figure 8.34 Document Flow Tab Showing the Link between Preceding and Follow-Up Transactions

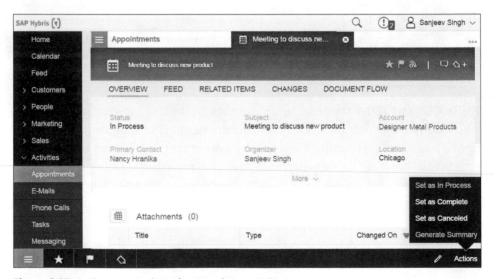

Figure 8.35 Actions to Update the Appointment Status

Phone Calls

To see the details of phone call activities, click **Activities** and then **Phone Calls** in the navigation bar to see the **My Phone Calls** list, as shown in Figure 8.36.

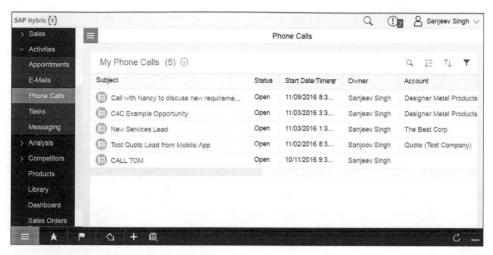

Figure 8.36 List of Phone Call Activities

You can select other variants to display additional phone call activities, such as **My Completed Phone Calls**, **My Open Phone Calls**, **My Calls Today**, and **My Calls This Week**, as shown in Figure 8.37.

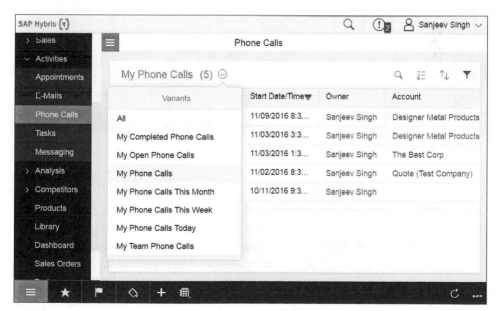

Figure 8.37 Dropdown with Additional Variants to Display Phone Calls

From the **My Phone Calls** list, click on the **Subject** of the phone calls activity you created in a previous section to open the activity, as shown in Figure 8.38. The same tabs are available for phone call activities—**OVERVIEW, FEED, CHANGES, RELATED ITEMS**, and **DOCUMENT FLOW**—as were used for appointments in the previous section. To process phone calls, you can update information in these tabs as needed and use options from the **Actions** menu to set appropriate statuses. You can also attach surveys to the phone call activities.

You can maintain multiple versions of the same survey and attach a specific, active version of survey to the activity as needed. Only one version of a survey can remain active at a time.

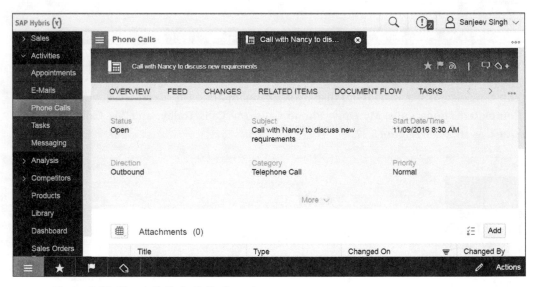

Figure 8.38 Phone Calls Activity Overview

Tasks

Like other activity types, you can open the list of task activities by clicking on **Tasks** under **Activities** in the navigation bar. From the list of tasks, open the task you need to process. Figure 8.39 shows the task you created in the previous section. You can update the information on the task **OVERVIEW** and **RELATED ITEMS** tabs as needed just as you've done for the other activity types. Clicking **Actions** provides options for you to change the task status to **Cancelled** or **Complete**, as the case may be.

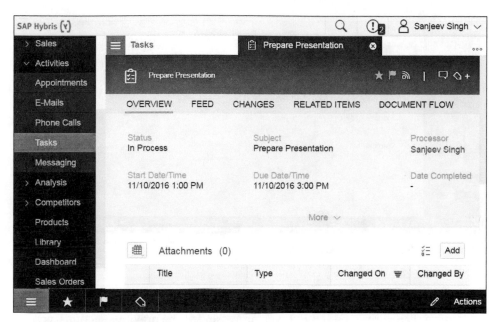

Figure 8.39 Task Overview Screen

Emails

Unlike the other activity types, email activities aren't manually created from the **Activities** view in SAP Sales Cloud. Basically, email activities are synced from groupware applications (Outlook or Lotus Notes) if they are integrated. Email activities syncing from groupware applications is only a one-direction transfer from the groupware to SAP Sales Cloud—not the other way.

Because emails are only synced from groupware, you can make very limited changes to email activities in SAP Sales Cloud. You can open email activities by clicking on **E-Mails** under **Activities** in the navigation bar. Figure 8.40 shows the **OVERVIEW** screen for one of the email activities with grayed-out fields, as you're not able to edit any information on this screen. You can only make updates to the **RELATED ITEMS** tab in email activities because you can create follow-up items (appointments, tasks, phone calls, leads, or opportunities) as needed.

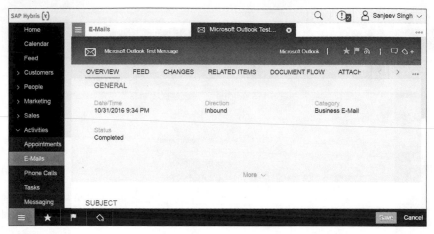

Figure 8.40 E-Mails Activity Overview

8.2.6 Follow-Up from Activities

As you've seen during the activity type processing in the previous sections, you can create follow-up items as needed from the **RELATED ITEMS** tab. The follow-up items can be another activity (phone call, appointment, or task), lead, or opportunity. You can't create follow-up email activities here because email activities are only synced from groupware. Follow-up items create links with the activities for reference and also copy data from the activity to follow-up items at the time of creation. Figure 8.41 shows the types of follow-up items you can create from an activity.

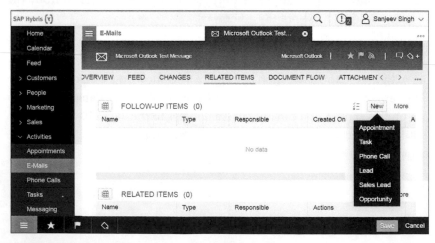

Figure 8.41 Follow-Up Items to Create from an Activity

8.3   Configuring Activities

Before you configure activity management, you need to make sure that it's included in the project scope of your implementation.

8.3.1   Getting Started

To include activity management in the project scope, select **Business Configuration**, click **Edit Project Scope**, and then click **Next** until you get to the **Scoping** phase, as shown in Figure 8.42. You enable the **Activity Management** checkbox to include activity management in the scope of your implementation.

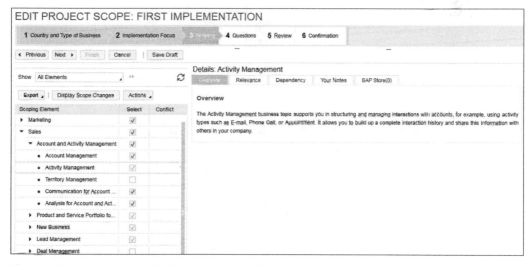

Figure 8.42 Including Activity Management in the Project Scope

Click **Next** to review the questions for activity management in the next stage. Figure 8.43 shows the list of questions under **Business Option**, which you review and check to include in the scope and uncheck to exclude from the scope of your implementation. The scoping questions related to opportunities are as follows:

- **Do you want to enable an enhanced activities facet to search and query for activities in account, contact, and individual customer work centers?**
  If you enable this question, it allows you to use the enhanced activities work center to search and query activities in accounts, contacts, and individual customer work centers.

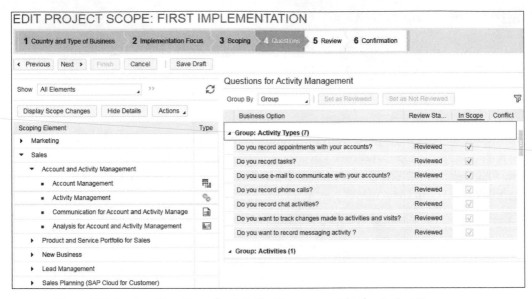

Figure 8.43 Review Questions for Activity Management in the Project Scope

- **Do you want to record information from activity lists in your system?**
  The activity list is a group of activities. They are used for mass creation of activities for either one person or for multiple people. You can enable activity list function-ality in your SAP Sales Cloud system with this question.

- **Do you want to maintain activity planners in the system?**
  The activity planner can be used to plan activities, such as surveys and tasks, to be used when conducting customer visits. This question enables you to maintain the activity planner in your system.

- **Do you want to default Organizational Unit of logged in user for Activity Plans/ Routing Rules?**
  With this question, you can allow activity plans and routing rules to have default organizational units based on logged-in users' organizational unit.

- **Do you record appointments with your accounts?**
  If you want to create appointments for accounts you will enable this question.

- **Do you record tasks?**
  Enabling this question will allow you to create tasks in your SAP Sales Cloud system.

- **Do you use e-mail to communicate with your accounts?**
  Enable this question allows you to communicate through email with accounts. It will allow you to create e-mail activity types in your system.

- **Do you record phone calls?**
  This question enables phone calls activities in your SAP Sales Cloud system. You can create phone call activities by including this in your scope.

- **Do you record chat activities?**
  This question allows you to enable chat activities in your system. Chat activities are useful for customer service scenarios where you want to capture customer chats as activities in your system.

- **Do you want to track changes made to activities and visits?**
  If you want to keep a log of all the changes made to activities and visits, include this in your scope. Enabling this question will let you track changes made to activities and visits.

- **Do you want to record messaging activity?**
  If you want to enable text messaging (SMS) in your SAP Sales Cloud system so that customers can communicate with you through text messages, then you will include this in your scope. It allows you to record text messages as activities—this is usually applicable for customer service scenarios.

- **Do you want to send personalized mass e-mails to many accounts at the same time?**
  This question allows you to send mass emails to accounts.

- **You would be able to execute e-mail blasts for employees added in the target groups.**
  This allows you to blast emails for employees in specific target groups.

- **You can synchronize activities in your SAP Cloud Solution with your users' local e-mail application (Microsoft Outlook or IBM Lotus Notes).**
  This setting enables groupware integration with SAP Sales Cloud. If you want to integrate your SAP Sales Cloud application with your groupware (Microsoft Outlook or Lotus Notes) then you will include this in scope.

- **Do you want to use route templates to schedule periodic creation of routes?**
  You can enable this question if you want to schedule periodic creation of routes (for customer visits) using a template in your system.

- **Do you want to enable users to specify, per activity, a predetermined combination of sales organization, distribution channel, and division?**
  If you want users to assign a predefined sales area (a combination of sales organization, distribution channel, and division) to an activity, then you will enable this question. It allows you to specify a default sales area for activities.

- **Do you want to default the sales organization, distribution channel, and division based on the account and employee sales data?**
  If you enable this question, the default sales area for an activity depends on the account and employee's sales area data.

- **Do you want to use summaries as meeting minutes for appointments, phone calls, and visits in the system?**
  This setting allows you to maintain summaries for activities. You can use summaries as meeting notes for all activity types such as appointments, phone calls, and visits.

- **Do you want to prevent summaries from being sent to external parties?**
  Enable this if you don't want activity summaries to go to external recipients, such as your contacts for customer meeting attendees.

- **Do you want to maintain surveys in the system?**
  If you want to use surveys in your activities then you will enable this.

- **For Survey Execution in Extended Edition, do you want to display the product image along with the ID and Description?**
  Enabling this question will allow you to display a product image along with product ID and description during survey execution.

- **For Survey Execution in Extended Edition, do you want to hide Product ID?**
  Similar to the last question, including this in scope will allow you to hide product IDs on the survey execution screen.

- **For Survey Execution in Extended Edition, do you want to hide Product description?**
  With this question, you can hide product description from the survey execution screen.

- **For Survey Execution in Extended Edition, do you want to enable adding products from past orders?**
  This question allows you to add products from past orders during survey execution.

- **Do you want to execute tasks and surveys during phone calls?**
  You enable this questions if you need to execute tasks and surveys during phone calls.

- **Instead of the sender's name "on behalf of" the system's e-mail address, do you want to use only the employee's e-mail address as the sender?**
  If you enable this, employees' email addresses' will be shown as the sender's email address when an email is sent from SAP Sales Cloud.

- **You go to your customers' physical locations periodically. Do you want to record information from these visits in your system?**
  You can record physical information from previous customer visits in your system by enabling this question.

- **Do you want to deactivate the check-in/check-out buttons for visits?**
  If you don't want to use the check-in/check-out functionality available in visits, you can disable it by enabling this question.

- **Do you want to ensure that sales and service reps complete mandatory tasks and surveys before allowing them to close visits?**
  By enabling this question, you can make it mandatory for sales reps to complete the survey and some mandatory tasks before closing a visit.

- **Do you want to disable execution actions before check-in?**
  You can disable the **Execution** button before check-in functionality in visits using this question.

- **Upon checking into a visit, do you want to update the visit status to "In Process"?**
  If you enable this, when you check-in to a visit, the status is updated to in-process.

- **Do you want to disable the "Do you want to create a new visit?" prompt when users check out from a visit?**
  When a user checks out from visit, by default the system prompts you to create a new visit. This question allows you to disable that feature.

- **Do you want to prevent the deletion of completed visits?**
  By enabling this question, you can prevent completed visits from being deleted from the system.

- **Do you want to prevent users from checking into multiple visits?**
  Users should be normally checked-in to one meeting at a time. With this question, you can prevent users from checking into multiple meetings at the same time.

- **Do you want to enable image recognition (planogram) for visits?**
  You can enable image recognition for visits with this question.

- **Do you want to deactivate the business partner visiting information feature?**
  Enabling this will allow you to disable the business partner visiting information feature in your SAP Sales Cloud system.

Some of the questions are checked by default, and you can't change those settings. Scroll down to the end to review all the questions for activity management. Then click **Next** and **Finish** to save and confirm the project scope.

As you know from previous chapters, all SAP Sales Cloud configurations are included in the fine-tuning activities. From your implementation project, click **Open Activity List**, and then click the **Fine-Tune** tab to open all the activities in the project, as shown in Figure 8.44.

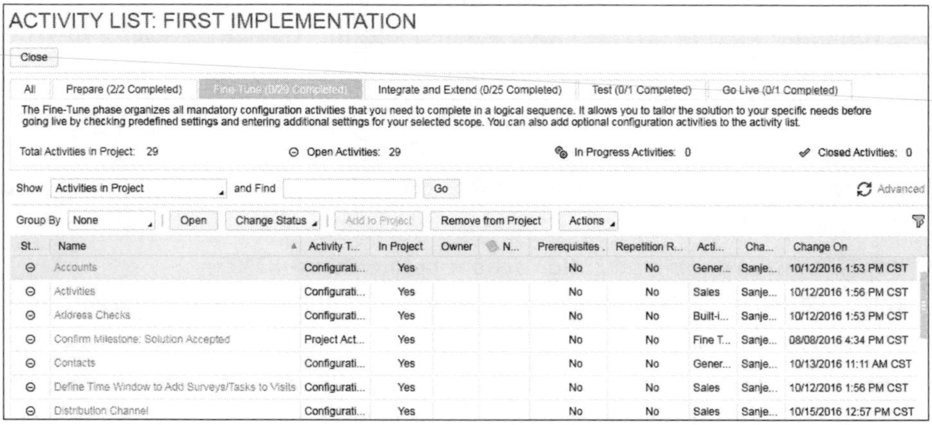

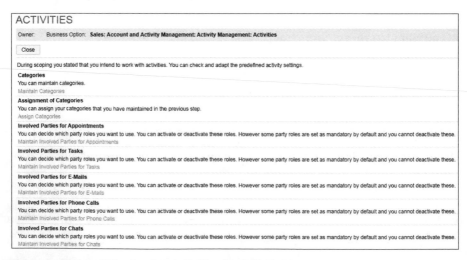

Figure 8.44 Fine-Tuning Activities

To see the settings available under the fine-tune activities, click **Activities** under **Activities in Project**. Figure 8.45 shows a list of fine-tuning activities available to tweak activity management for your implementation. We'll go through each one of these settings in the following sections.

Figure 8.45 List of Fine-tuning Activities for Activity Management

8.3.2 Categories

You've seen in earlier sections that when you create an activity, you can assign **Category** from the dropdown. Assigning categories to activities can help you classify so that it's easier to report on those activities and take actions as needed. SAP Sales Cloud delivers standard categories, such as **Customer Visit**, **Telephone Call**, and **Business Letter**, and you can add your own categories if these categories don't meet your requirements. To view the current list of categories, click **Maintain Categories** (refer to Figure 8.45) under **Categories** in the activity settings.

Figure 8.46 shows the list of available categories. You can also add a new category to this list by clicking **Add Row** and entering a new entry with a **Category Code** starting with "Z" and a **Description** as required.

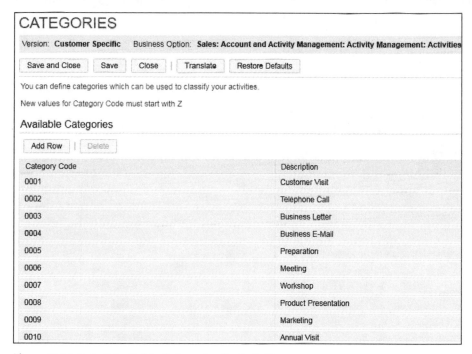

Figure 8.46 List of Available Categories for Activities

8.3.3 Assignment of Categories

In this section of the activity settings, the **Categories** are assigned to the activity types. The list of categories reviewed in the previous section includes categories that could be applicable for all the activity types. Unless you assign a category to an activity type, you can't see that category in the activity. For example when you create an activity you select the activity category. So it is critical that categories created for an activity is assigned to the activity type.. The same category can be assigned to more than one activity type. To review the assigned categories to all the activity types, click **Assign Categories** under **Assignment of Categories**, as shown earlier in Figure 8.45.

Figure 8.47 shows the **Available Activity Types** and corresponding **Available Categories for Appointment**. Click on the **12-Appointment** under **Activity Type** in first table, and the assigned **Categories** are displayed under **Available Categories for Appointment**. You can add or remove categories from assignments as well. To remove a category, select that category, and then click **Delete**. If you've created a new category that you want to assign to an appointment activity, select the appointment under **Available Activity Types**, and click **Add Row**. From the dropdown categories, select the desired category, and click **Save and Close**.

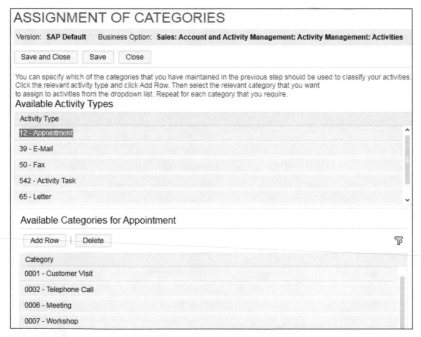

Figure 8.47 Assignment of Categories to Activity Types

8.3.4   Involved Parties

Through this setting you can maintain different types of partner roles involved in various activities and their determination rules. You can configure partner roles for each activity type (appointments, tasks, phone calls, and emails), as shown earlier in Figure 8.45. The following links are available for involved parties settings:

- **Maintain Involved Parties for Appointments**
- **Maintain Involved Parties for Tasks**
- **Maintain Involved Parties for Phone Calls**
- **Maintain Involved Parties for E-Mails**

Because the procedures for maintaining the involved parties are similar for all the activity types, we'll review the settings for involved parties for appointments in this section as an example for all activity types.

To view and add **Party Role Assignment** for appointments, click **Maintain Involved Parties for Appointments**. Figure 8.48 shows the **Party Role Assignment** list for appointments. To add a new party role, you click **Add Row**, and select the required party role from the dropdown. You can't delete any party roles from this assignment; you can only enable and disable the **Party Role** by checking (or unchecking) the **Active** flag. Additional functions to enable party roles as needed include **Mandatory**, **Unique**, **Forbid Manual Changes**, and **Inbound Integration**.

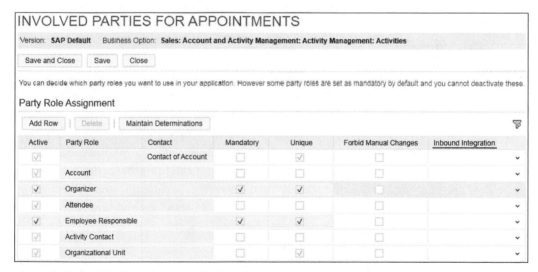

Figure 8.48 Party Role Assignment for Appointments

Partners for these party roles are determined in the appointment per the determination rules assigned to the party roles. To check determination rules for a party role, select that party role, and click **Maintain Determinations**. Figure 8.49 shows the determination rules for employee responsible in an appointment. Three determination rules are assigned to the **Employee Responsible Party Role**, but only the last **Determination** rule (**Current User**) is active. You can only make these determination rules active or inactive; you can't add a new determination rule without using enhancements.

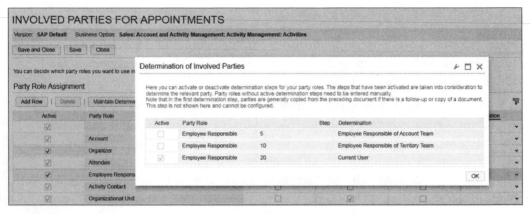

Figure 8.49 Determination Rules for Employee Responsible

8.4   Summary

In this chapter, you learned why activity management is a critical part of the sales process. In SAP Sales Cloud, you can create and process four types of activities: appointments, phone calls, tasks, and emails. Although appointments and phone calls appear on the activity calendar, email activities can only be synced from groupware. We reviewed how you can reschedule appointment and phone call activities through drag and drop on the calendar. Before you can fine-tune activities settings, you need to make sure that activity management is included in the project scope. You saw how to update the project scope to include activities and how you can fine-tune activities settings for categories, assignments, maintaining involved parties, and rules determination in activities. With this comprehensive understanding of activities in SAP Sales Cloud, you're ready to take up partner channel management in the next chapter.

Chapter 9
Partner Channel Management

For organizations selling through channel partners (dealers/resellers), SAP Sales Cloud provides partner channel management capabilities to effectively engage with and grow business through a partner ecosystem.

Partner channel management capabilities available in SAP Cloud for Customer enable effective partner data management from partner registration to collaboration on opportunities. You can streamline the process of lead scoring and routing to partners to maximize coverage of the target market. Some of the benefits of partner channel management include incremental revenue growth through indirect selling, improved value proposition to customers through partner value add, and, most importantly, improved sales coverage, including access to dormant or inaccessible accounts.

In this chapter, we'll review the partner registration process available in partner channel management. After partner registration, we'll discuss how you can provide partners access to the Partner Portal to collaborate with them on marketing and sales activities. We'll also review the deal registration capabilities available in partner channel management, SAP Jam groups, providing direct access to SAP Sales Cloud for partner contacts, and steps to configure partner channel management in SAP Cloud for Customer.

9.1 Partner Registration Process

The partner registration process starts with a prospective partner submitting an online partner application. You can include a link to the partner application on your company portal. When a prospective partner completes the online partner application, a unique ID and password are assigned. Using those credentials, the prospective partner can log in to the portal and check the status of the partner application while you review it. As a partner manager, you can review and approve/reject the application.

If you approve the partner application, it's automatically created in SAP Cloud for Customer, and the partner is given access to the Partner Portal. Your partner can log in to the Partner Portal and access additional information such as partner marketing materials, partner training materials, and sales promotions. Depending on the partner's role and authorization, the new partner can perform the additional functions of creating leads, opportunities, and activities, as well as registering deals, and so on. The new partner can also invite other sales employees in his company to join the Partner Portal to access and collaborate on leads and opportunities.

Figure 9.1 shows the standard partner registration process that can be easily enabled by partner channel management in SAP Cloud for Customer.

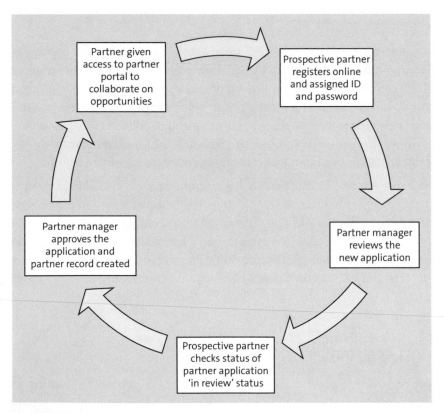

Figure 9.1 Partner Registration Process

To implement the partner registration process in partner channel management, let's review the high-level system landscape, as shown in Figure 9.2. The cloud-based portal let's you manage the registration process until the partner is approved and given access to partner-related pages and applications in SAP Cloud for Customer.

The registration process starts with a prospective partner filling in the registration form in the SAP cloud-based Partner Portal. During the application registration process, a duplicate check is performed against existing records. For unique records, the partner application is created in SAP Sales Cloud (SAP Cloud for Customer). The user receives a notification email with a link to fill in the password (email defaulted) notifying the user that registration is complete. The partner manager can start reviewing the partner application, and, during that process, the prospective partner can log in to the Partner Portal to check the status of the application. After the brand owner approves the partner application, the partner user gets access to SAP Sales Cloud pages and related applications.

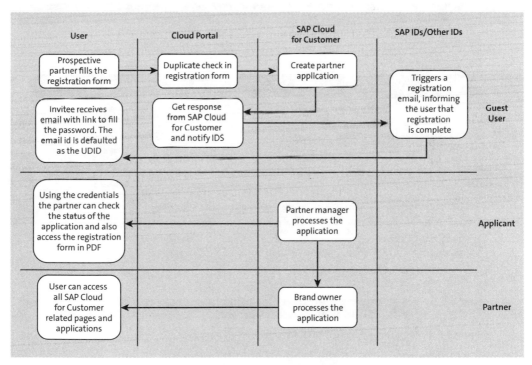

Figure 9.2 High-Level System Landscape for the Partner Registration Flow

Partner registration is a simple, multistep process. Figure 9.3 and Figure 9.4 show two of the steps in the registration process.

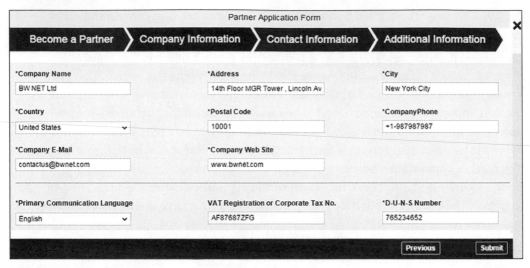

Figure 9.3 Registration: Company Information

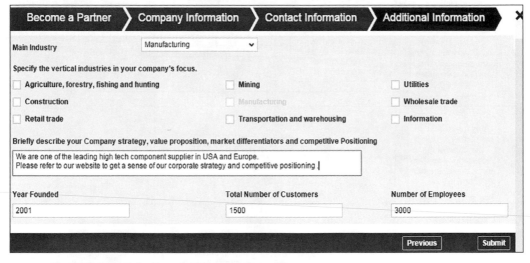

Figure 9.4 Registartion: Additional Information

After partner registration is complete, the new partner is given access to the Partner Portal, as shown in Figure 9.5.

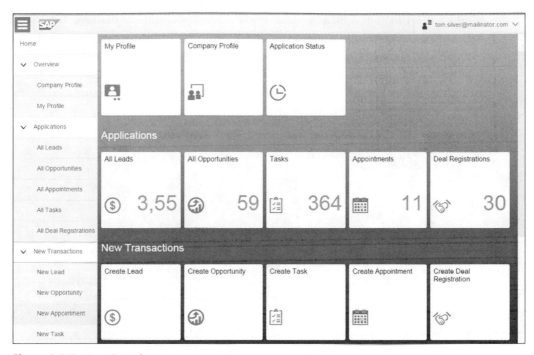

Figure 9.5 Partner Portal

9.2   Partner Portal

As reviewed in the previous section, after the partner application is approved by the company partner program manager, the partner is given access to the Partner Portal or landing page in SAP Cloud for Customer. On the Partner Portal, the partner and his approved users can review the applications available to them, update their profiles, and create or update transactions such as leads, opportunities, and activities. Of course, you can control access to transactions based on user roles so that partner admin roles have more authorizations to create and view transactions compared to partner sales reps who might have limited authorization to view and edit their own transactions.

The Partner Portal helps you design the channel partner portal around a smart content strategy to enable channel partners access to the information they need when they need it. The Partner Portal provides partners with a central, web-based access point to intuitive self-services for managing and tracking their activities. Partners can self-register as a new partner, invite new partner employees, maintain partner contact information, add and track leads and opportunities, manage tasks and appointments, and access important documents and training. The Partner Portal lets you manage your content, receive notifications with workflow service integration, and achieve quick turnaround on approvals through My Inbox integration. You can quickly create role-based portals with SAP Fiori experience and app templates. Figure 9.6 shows the landscape for the Partner Portal.

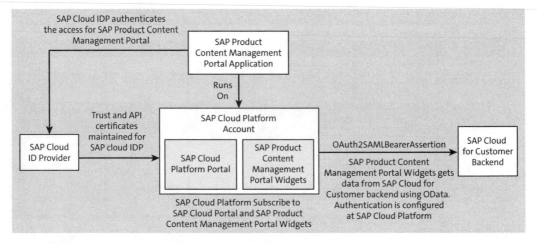

Figure 9.6 Landscape Details for the Partner Portal

The capabilities available to partners through the Partner Portal are as follows:

- **Partner program**
  Partners can review and update their profiles, add and remove additional contacts, create additional users, and so on. They can review partner programs, co-op funds, and loyalty, as well as check the status of their applications.

- **Partner marketing**
  Partners can display, accept, or reject leads from the company. They can also create and edit leads as needed.

- **Partner sales**
  Partners can create new opportunities or follow-up opportunities from leads. They can work through the opportunity cycle and maintain additional details such as status, products, and notes.

- **Partner activities**
  Partners and brand owners can work on common tasks and activities, and have visibility into appointments. They can change the status of activities to mark as complete, update notes, schedule appointments, or create new activities.

9.3   Deal Registration

When you work with multiple partners in the field, one of the key challenges is channel conflict resolution. Partner channel management provides a very powerful deal
registration capability to allow partners to register deals and help brand owners manage the deal registration process. Deal registration is like a lead brought to the brand
owner's attention from partners. Partners can create a deal on the Partner Portal.
Brand owners can either accept or reject the deal, and accepted deals can be converted to opportunities. If a deal is converted to an opportunity, the partner can view
the opportunity ID and then work on the assigned opportunity.

9.3.1   Deal Registration Process

Partners can create deals by assigning an account to the deal or even create a deal
without assigning an account. After submitting a deal, the deal can be routed to the
employee responsible at the brand owner's company. The employee responsible can
view deals individually or group deals together that have been submitted by different
partners for the same customer, products, and dates. The employee responsible can
then accept a deal and convert it into an opportunity. Figure 9.7 shows the typical
deal registration process flow.

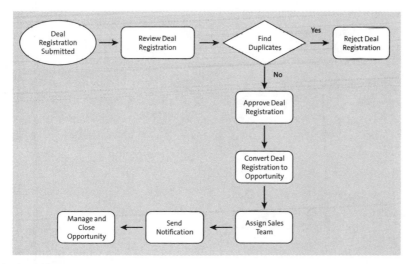

Figure 9.7 Deal Registration Process

A deal effectively represents a kind of prequalified lead that is unique to channel partners. The deal registration process is primarily aimed at reducing channel conflict.
With a deal registration program in place, partners can work with customers without

having to worry about another partner trying to offer the same product to the same customer, as long as brand owners have approved the deals.

Figure 9.8 Figure 9.9 shows the process for deal registration in the Partner Portal. Partners can create deals and check the status of previously registered deals as **Accepted** or **Rejected**.

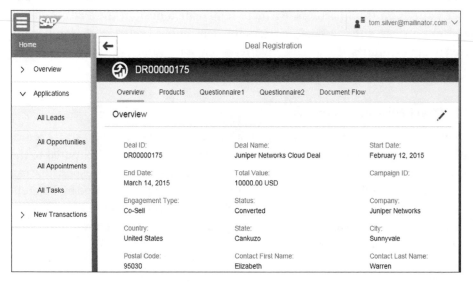

Figure 9.8 Deal Registration Overview

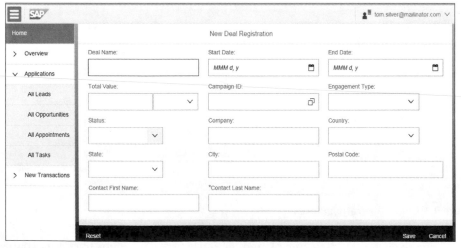

Figure 9.9 New Deal Registration

After a deal has been registered, it's routed to the employee responsible (sales rep) for review. The employee responsible can then accept a deal and convert it to an opportunity, as shown in Figure 9.10.

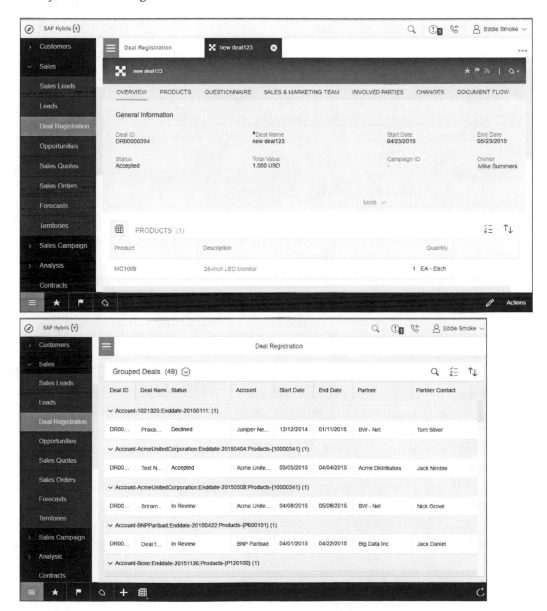

Figure 9.10 Deal Review and Acceptance Process

9.3.2   Deal Registration Conversion to Opportunity

You saw in the previous section that after a deal registration has been submitted by a channel partner, the brand owner can review the deal registration document and compare it with other previously submitted deal registration documents for duplicity of accounts. If a submitted deal is found to be a duplicate, the brand owner can reject the deal, the channel partner is notified about the rejected deal registration, and no further action is needed in the deal registration process.

However, if the deal registration is unique, the brand owner can accept the deal registration and convert it into an opportunity. After that, both the channel partner and brand owner can collaborate and work together on the opportunity.

9.4   SAP Jam as a Collaboration Platform

By integrating SAP Jam with SAP Cloud for Customer, you can extend the capabilities of partner channel management and bring your partners onto a single collaboration platform. Through SAP Jam collaboration, you can increase partner engagement and loyalty by facilitating dedicated communities that are connected to applications. You can directly connect with your partner contacts to exchange ideas, collaborate, and deliver superior content. SAP Jam allows you to engage with your partners in ideation discussion that helps you uncover deeper needs and include them to close the gap and get results faster.

Collaborative workspaces in SAP Jam help you engage internal sales team and partner contacts to keep them up to date with the latest content. You can create SAP Jam groups in the context of account, opportunity, product, and so on. You can view and post SAP Jam group updates in the context of these business objects. These SAP Jam groups can be private, public, or external. In private SAP Jam groups, only invited employees can access the content in the group; however, in a public group, the content is accessible to all the employees who join the group. The external SAP Jam group is accessible to customers, partners, and so on who are invited to join the group. In SAP Jam groups, members can post pictures, documents, multimedia videos, and blog ideas, as well as start a discussion that is relevant for the group.

Following are standard use cases and scenarios available for SAP Sales Cloud for SAP Jam work patterns:

- **Collaborative account planning**
  An account executive uses SAP Sales Cloud as the system of record and leverages

the account management work pattern to gain a 360-degree view into each customer. He inspects live data, such as related opportunities and service requests, and also socializes about the business processes with channel partners to maintain a positive relationship with the customer.

- **Social opportunity management**
  A sales manager uses the deal room work pattern to collaborate with his sales team and channel partners with a goal to win a sales opportunity.

9.5   Partner Contact Direct Access

You can create partners and partner contacts in SAP Cloud for Customer and also assign partner programs and partner types to partners. Using partner contact direct access, you can provide your partner contact direct access to the SAP Cloud for Customer system. Using the **Create User** option under the **Action** menu in the **Partner Contacts** screen, you can create a business user linked to the partner contact (see Figure 9.11).

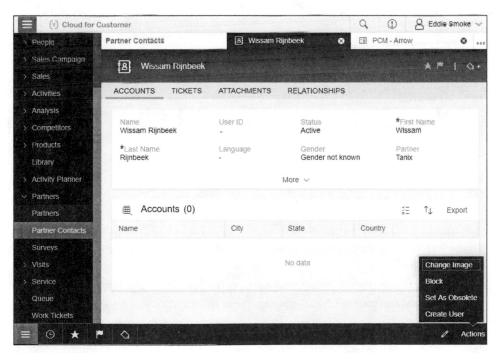

Figure 9.11 Creating a User in Partner Contacts in SAP Cloud for Customer

This business user can then be assigned the needed credentials to directly access the SAP Cloud for Customer system. Based on the business role assignment, the partner contact will be able to access the needed application in SAP Cloud for Customer. Using key user tool capabilities, you can also customize the screen layouts based on business role assignment.

9.6   Configuring Partner Channel Management

To enable partner channel management capabilities in your SAP Cloud for Customer system, you need to include partner program management in your scope, as shown in Figure 9.12.

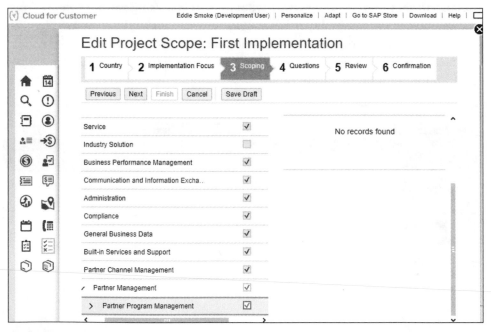

Figure 9.12 Enabling Partner Program Management in the Project Scope

You can configure the solution to capture partner programs, partner types, partner loyalty points, and partner funds management information.

To include partner channel management in the scope of your implementation, log in to SAP Sales Cloud using the admin role under the HTML5 UI, and choose **Business Configuration • Edit Project Scope • Country • Implementation Focus • Scoping.** You'll be taken to the **Scoping** screen, as shown in Figure 9.12. Here you expand **Partner Channel Management** • **Partner Management** • **Partner Program Management**, enable the checkbox, and click **Next**. The **Questions** screen appears, as shown in Figure 9.13. Here you see three questions related to the partner management scope:

- **Fund Management: Do you want to manage funds for these partners, and monitor associated claims?**
  Businesses set up market development funds for partners for joint marketing and promotions activities. If you want to manage funds for partners as a part of partner management in SAP Sales Cloud, then you'll enable this checkbox in the scope of your solution for partner management.

- **Loyalty Management: Do you want to record loyalty management data for these partners?**
  Loyalty management enables you to retain and grow your partner base. If you intend to record loyalty management data in your partner management solution, then enable this checkbox in your scope.

- **Partner Program: Do you want to manage partner programs in your solution?**
  Partner programs enable you to manage multiple tiers of partners, partner levels, and their qualification and certification requirements. If you want to include the management of partner programs in your solution, enable this checkbox.

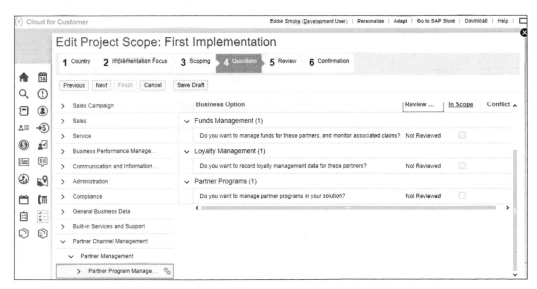

Figure 9.13 Scoping Questions for Partner Channel Management

After you enable the scoping questions for partner program management, you can fine-tune the partner management capability per your unique business requirements.

9.7   Summary

In this chapter, we reviewed the key capabilities of partner channel management available in SAP Cloud for Customer. You saw how brand owners can leverage the deal registration process to improve communication with channel partners and avoid any channel conflict. We also covered how SAP Jam groups can help you collaborate with your partners right from SAP Cloud for Customer. Finally, we covered how to include partner channel management in the project scope of your SAP Cloud for Customer implementation. In the next chapter, we'll review the quotation management functionality available in SAP Cloud for Customer.

Chapter 10
Quotation Management

The quotation management capability available in SAP Sales Cloud enables you to create a sales quote from an opportunity as a follow-up transaction. In this chapter, we'll review the key features of quotation management and how quotations are created, processed, and configured.

Quotation management is an integral part of the sales process. It's a legally binding document that describes the terms of proposed sales and mostly includes customer information, products or services to be sold, quantity and pricing, validity, notes, and so on. Quotations are usually created as follow-up transactions from an opportunity or a preceding transaction from a sales order. Because you can attach multiple quotes to an opportunity, you can indicate one as the primary opportunity for the quote that allows you to update the expected value from the total net value of the quote. Quotations can also be created standalone without any reference to an opportunity. As a best practice, it's recommended that quotations are created as a follow-up from an opportunity or at least a reference to an opportunity should be made in the quotation to keep the link between opportunity and quotation for reporting purposes.

SAP Sales Cloud offers flexible quoting capabilities that enable sales reps to deliver compelling offers to their customers with consistent and accurate pricing. Some of the key differentiators for quotation management in SAP Sales Cloud include the ability to leverage native pricing within SAP Sales Cloud or from the SAP backend system (SAP Customer Relationship Management [SAP CRM] or SAP ERP) and the ability to check product availability and credit limits directly from SAP Sales Cloud. It also provides an out-of-the-box capability to create follow-up sales orders in SAP ERP from SAP Sales Cloud. These capabilities translate into business benefits such as accelerated sales cycles, improved revenue and margins, streamlined quote-to-cash processes, and reduced processing errors.

In this chapter, we'll review the key features that enable the flexible quote management process in SAP Sales Cloud. You'll see how quotations are created and processed, along with the follow-up process from quotations. To see how the quotation management process can be controlled through fine-tuning or configuration, we'll review the key configuration options available in SAP Sales Cloud. Because quotes integrate with SAP ERP for replication and follow-up sales orders, pricing, product availability, and credit checks, separate sections in this chapter are provided to review the integration with SAP ERP as well as pricing capabilities in quotes.

10.1   Quote Management Process

You need a systematic way of creating and processing quotes for your customers. Quote management starts with creating a quote as a follow-up transaction from an opportunity. A quote is a formal response to a customer's request for an offer on your products or services. The customer's request comes in the form of a price request for products and services you're trying to sell to your customer. The main steps in the quote management process are as follows:

1. Look for any open opportunity you're working on. If yes, then you'll create a quote as a follow-up transaction of the opportunity. The advantage of creating a follow-up transaction is that the customer information is copied from the opportunity to the quotation. If a quote request comes without reference to any opportunity, you'll create a standalone quote.

2. Create a quote, and enter critical information in the quote such as customer information, quote validity (i.e., valid to date so that the quote offer is only valid until that date when the customer can accept the quote), products or services, and product quantities and service provision prices that you're willing to accept. The exact information to be maintained in the quote can vary depending on your specific requirements; however, products, prices, customer information, and quote validity are the minimum required fields in a quote.

3. Send the quote to the customer either through email or via physical copy. For some businesses, there may be an intermediate step of getting the quote approved internally by a sales manager or finance team before the quote is sent to the customer.

4. Perform the last step in the process based on the customer's action. If the customer doesn't accept the quote, the quote is invalid after the quote validity date has elapsed. However, if the quote is accepted by the customer, it's a last step in the quote process, and you create a follow-up sales order from the quote. SAP Sales Cloud has extensive features to support the quote management process for modern sales organizations.

Following are the key capabilities of SAP Sales Cloud that primarily drive the quote management process:

- Rich quotation capabilities, such as search, view, create, copy, follow up, submit, update, cancel, and delete, are available in quotations for users to effectively work through and manage quotes in SAP Sales Cloud.

- Basic pricing is supported in quotations natively in SAP Sales Cloud, including price lists, discount lists, surcharges, manual cost, and profit margins.

- Alternative items can be included in the quote but are excluded from the total value of the quote. This allows you to offer some product suggestions (better offers) to customers as a part of the quote.

- For more complex pricing from the SAP backend system, external pricing is supported with SAP ERP/SAP CRM (through live call via simulation).

- To allow product proposals and product substitution in quotations, SAP Sales Cloud offers product proposals by products lists, including cross sell, up sell, and down sell; product exclusion; and product restrictions.

- An end-to-end sales process is supported by allowing the creation of sales orders from sales quotes. The follow-up sales orders can be created either in SAP Sales Cloud or in SAP CRM/SAP ERP. The bidirectional exchange of quotes between SAP Sales Cloud and SAP ERP allows the creation of sales orders in SAP ERP.

- Notes and attachments can be maintained in quotes at the header level as well as item level.

- The output management available for quotes in SAP Sale Cloud allows you to send the quotes to customers directly from the quote screen. While sending these quotes, you can select the form templates, allow output channel determination based on customer preferences, and select the required language so that the customer receives the quote per indicated preferences. Quotes can be sent to customers through hard copy print and mail, fax, or email.

- Internal and external notifications can be sent from the quotation as needed.

- Quotes in SAP Sales Cloud also support a multistep approval process and workflows to meet the requirements for most comprehensive quote management processes.

- Quotations can be accessed and updated from mobile devices. You can also capture digital signatures on quotations from mobile devices.

- From quotes, you can create follow-up transactions such as activities, tasks, and tickets as required for supporting additional follow-up processes.

- Team members can collaborate on quotations using feed postings, favorites, flags, and tags available in SAP Sales Cloud.

These are some of the features of quotation management in SAP Sales Cloud. In the next section, you'll learn how to create and process quotations in SAP Sales Cloud.

10.2   Creating and Processing Quotes

SAP Sales Cloud allows you to create standalone quotes or follow-up quotes from an opportunity transaction. From the **SALES DOCUMENTS** work center in an opportunity, you can create a quote by clicking on **New** (see Figure 10.1). The advantage of creating a quotation as a follow-up from an opportunity is that it provides you with the link between the opportunity and the quotation and, most importantly, copies all the relevant data from the opportunity to the quotation.

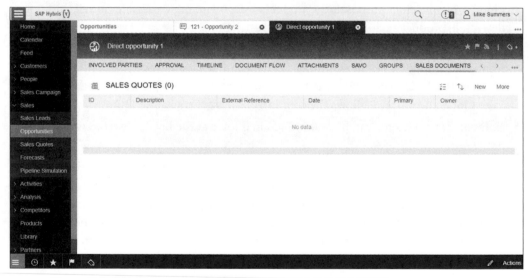

Figure 10.1 Creating a Quote from an Opportunity

You can also create a standalone quote from the **Sales Quotes** work center in the navigation bar, as we'll explain in the following section. We'll also cover processing quotes as well as following-up from quotes.

10.2.1   Creating Quotes

Let's review how to create a standalone quote in SAP Sales Cloud. Click on the **Sales Quotes** work center under **Sales** in the navigation bar on the left side of the screen, and a screen appears for you to create a new quote, as shown in Figure 10.2.

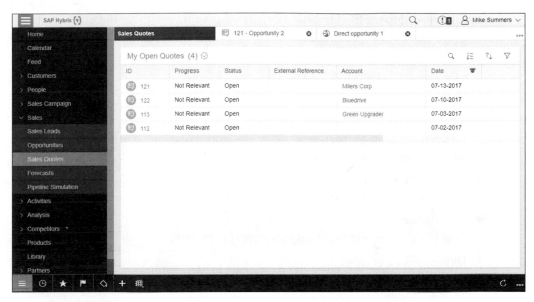

Figure 10.2 Sales Quotes Work Center to Create a New Quote

To create a new quote, click on the **+** button in the bottom status bar, and the **New Quote** screen appears, as shown in Figure 10.3.

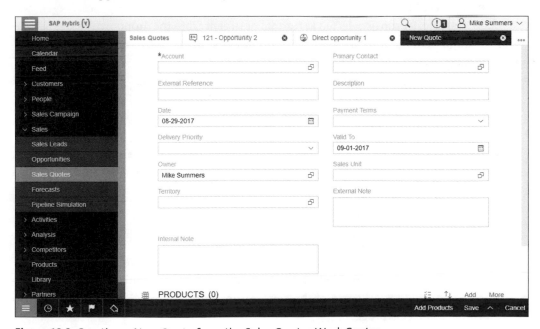

Figure 10.3 Creating a New Quote from the Sales Quotes Work Center

Let's review some of the important details you can maintain on the quote to better manage and track your sales process:

- **Account**
  This is the customer you're creating this quotation for.

- **Primary Contact**
  This is the contact for the account, which can be either manually entered or discovered through partner determination (configuration) if a primary contact is maintained for the account.

- **External Reference**
  This is normally the customer reference for the quotation.

- **Description**
  This is a free-text field to clearly identify the quotation.

- **Date**
  By default, this is the system date when the quote is created; however, you can change this date as needed.

- **Payment Terms**
  These terms can be selected from dropdown values as configured in the system, for example, 20 days net, 30 days net, and payable immediately.

- **Delivery Priority**
  The priority can be selected as **Normal** or **Urgent** from the dropdown values as configured in the system.

- **Valid To**
  This defines the validity date of the quotation. You can select any date.

- **PRODUCTS**
  This section allows you to add products to the quotation.

After maintaining all these quotation details, you can click **Save**, and the system will save the quotation and assign a quote identification number (Quote ID) per the number range configured for the quotation.

10.2.2   Processing Quotes

Quote processing involves working through the quotation and updating it with additional information as needed during the lifecycle of the quotation. In the following sections, we'll review some of the key features available in SAP Sales Cloud to help you in quotation processing.

Products

While processing quotes, you'll spend most of your time on the **PRODUCTS** tab, where you can perform the following actions:

- **Adding quick products to the quotation**
  Products and related quantities can be added to the quotation quickly via the **Actions** menu, as shown in Figure 10.4. Through this, you can add multiple products to the quote by selecting products based on product categories, past quotes, past orders, defined smart product proposals, and valid promotions.

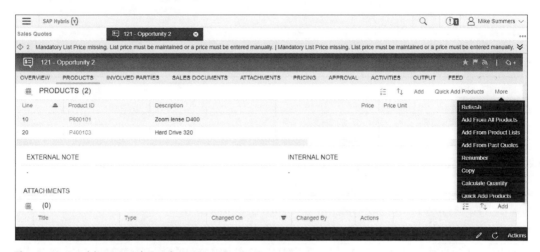

Figure 10.4 Adding Quick Products to a Quotation

- **Free goods determination**
  If free goods have been set up for products in the SAP backend system (SAP CRM or SAP ERP), the action **Request External Pricing** returns free goods from the on-premise system (SAP CRM or SAP ERP) in the quotation, as shown in Figure 10.5. The free goods determination supports both inclusive (e.g., buy 10 and pay for only 9) and exclusive (e.g., buy 10 and get 1 free) setup. The free goods determined in a quotation appear as read-only after the external pricing call. The change of product or product quantity removes free goods subitems from the quotation and requires a new external pricing call.

- **Product availability check**
  The action **Request External Pricing** returns an available to promise (ATP) result from the on-premise system (SAP CRM or SAP ERP). The delivery date confirmation received through the ATP check is nonbinding based on the requested date

(header date is copied to items but is changeable). A simulated delivery schedule for selected products appears in the view, as shown in Figure 10.6.

Figure 10.5 Free Goods Determination in a Quotation

Figure 10.6 Simulated Delivery Schedule Based on ATP

- **Credit limit check**

  You can do a credit limit check for a customer in a quotation using the **Request External Pricing** action that returns **Credit Status**, **Credit Limit**, and **Credit Exposure** from the SAP ERP system, including a message of the exceeded amount, as shown in Figure 10.7. **Credit Status** is part of the approval conditions.

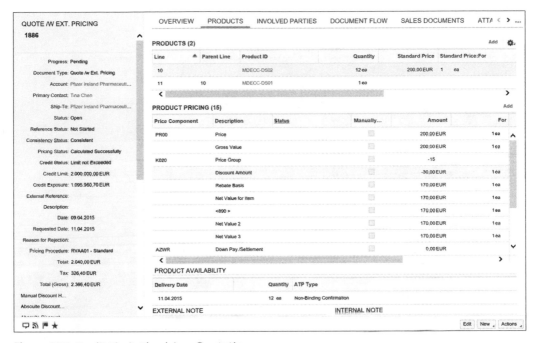

Figure 10.7 Credit Limit Check in a Quotation

- **Bill of materials (BOM) explosion**

  In quotations, you can explode multilevel BOMs (if set up in the SAP backend system) by using the **Request External Pricing** action from SAP CRM or SAP ERP, as shown in Figure 10.8. The price and quantity adjustments for a BOM are only supported on the header item.

- **Product substitution**

  If a product substitution has been set up in the SAP backend system (SAP CRM or SAP ERP), the original product entered in the quotation is replaced by a substitution product via the **External Pricing Call** action. The products will be replaced if substituted, for example, if the entered product is out of stock, as shown in Figure 10.9.

10

Figure 10.8 BOM Explosion in a Quotation

Figure 10.9 Product Substitution in a Quotation

- **Customer part number**

  To support customer part numbers in a quotation, SAP Sales Cloud lets you enter customer part numbers directly into the product **ID** field, as shown in Figure 10.10. These IDs will be directly converted to internal product IDs. The **Description** of the customer part number is language independent.

Figure 10.10 Entering Customer Part Numbers in a Quotation

Involved Parties

Let's review how you can manage involved parties (internal and external partners involved) in quotes both at the header and item levels, as follows:

- **Involved parties**

  Similar to other transactions, you can add and determine further involved parties such as business partners or competitors in quotes, as shown in Figure 10.11. The **INVOLVED PARTIES** tab allows you to change the address for parties and contacts to a document address (one-time address). This address won't change the master data and is only applicable for the document processing itself.

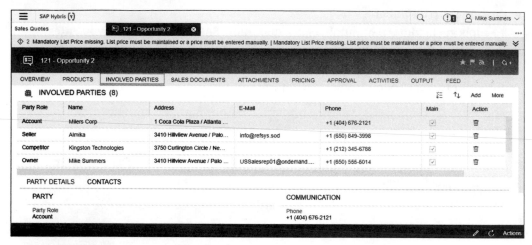

Figure 10.11 Involved Parties in a Quote

- **Ship-to party on the item level**
  You can change the delivery address on the item level by selecting a different ship-to party or ship-to address. You can even make changes to a document address. The document address, also known as a one-time address, is then only applicable for the transaction, as shown in Figure 10.12.

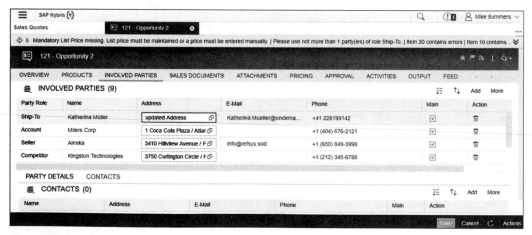

Figure 10.12 Ship-to Party Address Update at the Item Level

- **Approval**

  You can set up a multilevel approval process for sales quotes, as well as edit and view approval notes in the **APPROVAL** tab. You can withdraw from approvals via the **Withdraw from Approval** action. An approval will submit the sales quote automatically based on the output settings of the quote. A manager can approve a quote via notification or directly in the **APPROVAL** tab of the sales quote, as shown in Figure 10.13.

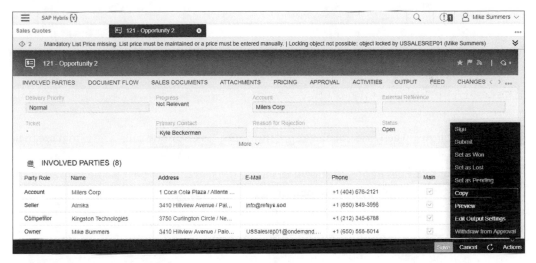

Figure 10.13 Quote Approval Process

- **Signature**

  You can capture a graphical signature on the sales quote via the **Sign** action. The signature is included in the sales quote demo print form. Other print forms need to be enhanced via Adobe Livecycle Designer. Integration of a digital signature, which is legally binding, is supported via partner solutions.

Document Flow

The **DOCUMENT FLOW** tab shows related transactions, such as opportunities or activities for the quote (Figure 10.14). The latest quote sent to the customer can be accessed via the **PDF** icon from the **DOCUMENT FLOW** tab. The follow-up transaction in SAP ERP can be viewed in the document flow, such as follow-up order, delivery, or invoice, including access to the related PDF documents (via a web service).

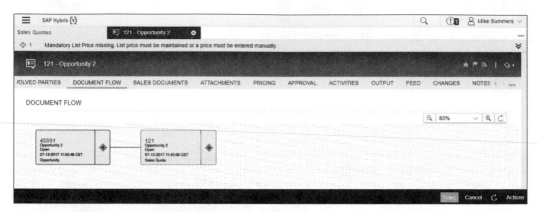

Figure 10.14 A Document Flow for a Quote

Activities

The follow-up activities, such as appointments, tasks, phone calls, and e-mails, can be created directly from the sales quote, and you can keep track of all the activities related to a sales quote, as shown in Figure 10.15. Activities can also be viewed in the document flow of the sales quote. An activity plan supports the creation of tasks that can be used in the context of a sales methodology.

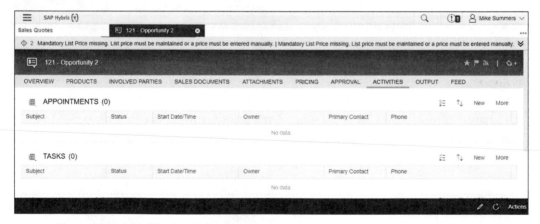

Figure 10.15 Activities in a Sales Quote

You can also use the blocking sales quotes functionality to block the sales quote and prevent a quote from being saved based on an account's order block reason. Using fine-tuning, a sales order can also be blocked, as shown in Figure 10.16.

Figure 10.16 Sales Quote Blocking Based on Sales Document Order Reasons

Notes

You can view and edit quote header notes (plain text or rich text) in the **NOTES** tab, as shown in Figure 10.17. Both internal and external notes can be maintained for the quotes. External notes are part of the standard sales quote output print form.

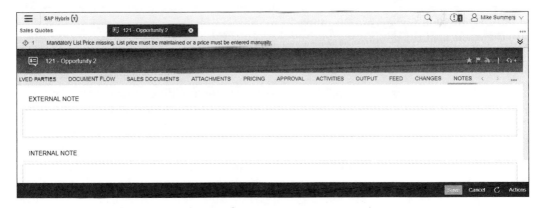

Figure 10.17 Internal and External Notes for Quotes

Surveys

To assist in the assessment of quotations using surveys, you can add predefined questionnaires to sales quotes that can be assigned via the activity planner to the sales quote. Edit, view, and generate survey summaries capabilities are directly available in the sales quote, as shown in Figure 10.18.

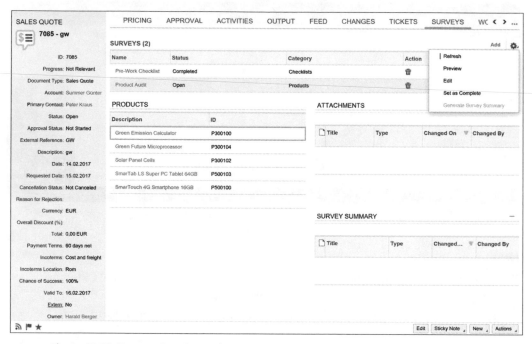

Figure 10.18 Surveys in a Quotation

10.2.3   Follow-Up from Quotes

The sales process from leads or sales connects the building blocks of lead, opportunity, quote, and sales order. For a quote, the preceding document is an opportunity, and an opportunity's preceding document is a lead. Similarly, for a lead, the follow-up transaction is an opportunity, and for an opportunity, the follow-up transaction is a quotation. For a quotation, the follow-up transaction is a sales order. From a quote in SAP Sales Cloud, you can create a follow-up sales order in SAP Sales Cloud, as shown in Figure 10.19.

If you've integrated the SAP backend (SAP CRM or SAP ERP) with SAP Sales Cloud, then you can also create a follow-up sales order in SAP ERP from the quote, as shown in Figure 10.20.

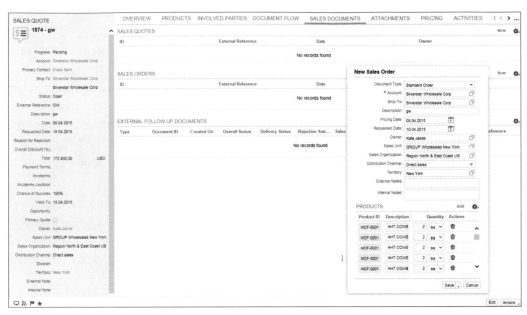

Figure 10.19 Creating a Sales Order as a Follow-Up from a Quote

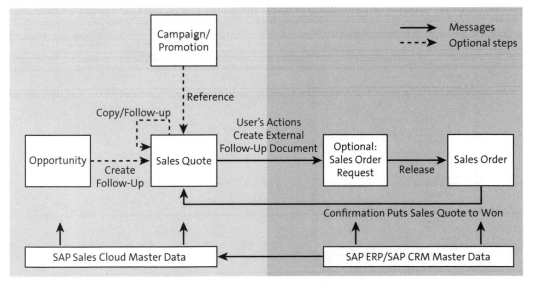

Figure 10.20 Creating a Follow-Up Sales Order in the SAP Backend from a Quote

287

10.3   Configuring Quotes

With that background on the key features of quotation management in SAP Sales Cloud, let's discuss how to enable your unique quotation processes through fine-tuning or configuration. Before you can leverage the quotation management capability in SAP Sales Cloud, you need to include quotation management in the scope of your implementation and then perform fine-tuning activities to exactly map your business requirements for quotes in your SAP Sales Cloud system. In the following sections, we present the key configurations available in SAP Sales Cloud specific to quotation management.

Before you can configure any quotation management settings in SAP Sales Cloud, you must include quotation management in your business scope. To do this, log in to your SAP Sales Cloud system using administrator access, and choose **Business Configuration • Implementation Projects • Edit Project Scope • Next (Implementation Focus) • Next (Scoping) • Sales • New Business • Sales Quotes**, as shown in Figure 10.21.

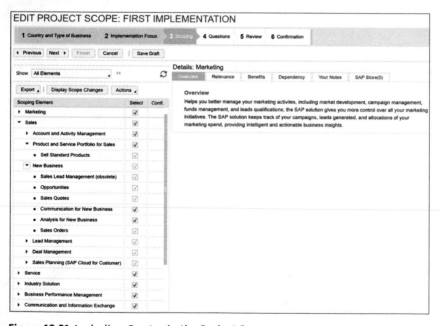

Figure 10.21 Including Quotes in the Project Scope

The quotation-related scoping questions in SAP Sales Cloud are as follows:

- **Do you want to use a multi-step approval process for sales quotes?**
  Under normal circumstances, you might use the approval process for sales quotes

so that a quote needs to be approved by a sales manager if its value is above a certain threshold. This question enables a multistep approval process for quotes.

- **Do you want to use formatted texts for sales quotes?**
  By enabling this question, you can use the formatted texts for quotes.

- **Do you want to capture and attach a graphical signature to the sales quote (Valid for touch enabled devices only)?**
  If you want to capture and attach a graphical signature to your sales quotes, you can enable this question. It allows users to capture signature in quotes on mobile devices.

- **Do you want to enable users to default and specify, per sales quote, a predetermined combination of sale org., distribution channel, and division?**
  If you want a sales area (sales organization, distribution channel, or division) to be the default in your sales quote, then you enable this question.

- **Do you want to control the reset of the approval status and output status via workflow rules?**
  If you enable this question you can reset the approval status on quotes through the workflow.

- **Do you want to submit sales quotes without items?**
  If you want the sales quotes to be submitted without items then you can enable this question. Under normal working conditions, sales quotes without items don't have any meaning. You will always have sales quotes with items, so you don't need to enable this question.

10.3.1 Enable External Pricing in a Quote

If you want to leverage the external pricing capability to price items in sales quotes from the SAP backend, then you need to go through a series of configurations, such as including external pricing in the project scope, selecting document types for which you want to include external pricing, and using pricing authorization, as follows:

1. Set the scope for external pricing by choosing **Business Configuration • Implementation Projects • Edit Project Scope • Next (Implementation Focus) • Next (Scoping) • Next (Questions)**, as shown in Figure 10.22.

2. Set the document types you want to enable the external pricing for by choosing **Fine-Turning Activity • Sales Quotes • Document Types**.

3. Select the **External Pricing** checkbox for **Sales Quote**, as shown in Figure 10.23. Here you can also control the condition types you want to include pricing elements in external pricing.

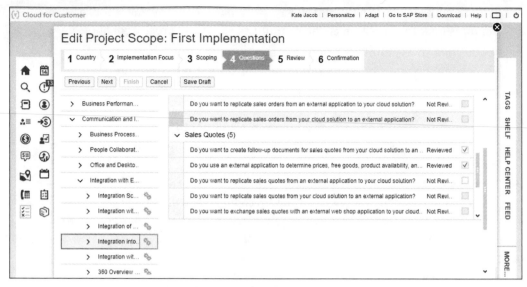

Figure 10.22 Setting the Scope for External Pricing

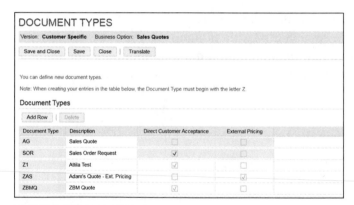

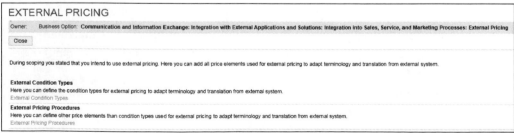

Figure 10.23 External Pricing Configuration

4. Through settings in the **Administration** work center, you can set the authorization levels for external pricing, as shown in Figure 10.24. You can restrict read and write access to price elements for external pricing, which allows you to hide certain conditions, such as profit margin and cost to certain users.

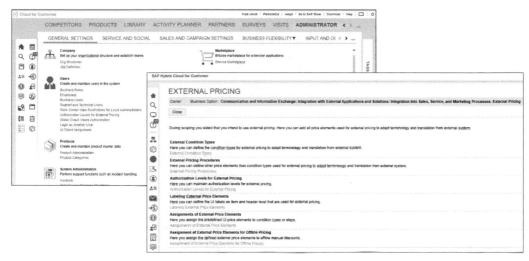

Figure 10.24 Controlling Authorization Levels for External Pricing

10.3.2   Bidirectional Exchange with SAP ERP

To enable bidirectional exchange with SAP ERP, you choose **Business Configuration** • **Scoping Element: Communication and Information Exchange** • **Integration with External Applications and Solutions** • **Integration into Sales, Service, and Marketing Processes** and then enable replication questions, as shown in Figure 10.25.

To replicate quotes between SAP Sales Cloud and SAP ERP, you need to activate the replication of quotes per sales document types, as shown in Figure 10.26.

Selecting the **Replication** checkbox causes the system to transfer sales quotes from the SAP Sales Cloud solution to an SAP ERP system when you choose the **Submit** action. It also allows editing of replicated sales quotes created in SAP ERP in your cloud solution. Selecting the **Direct Customer Acceptance** checkbox disables sales quote output document submission.

Figure 10.25 Settings to Enable Bidirectional Exchange with SAP ERP

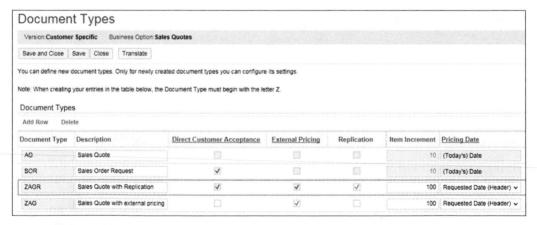

Figure 10.26 Activating Quote Replication with SAP ERP

10.3.3   Reason for Rejection

The **Reasons for Rejection** fine-tuning activity allows you to configure the cancellation codes to cancel a sales quote. Sales quotes can be canceled on the header and item level, and the header cancellation reason will be copied to the items. Canceling a sales quote on the header level will cancel all items.

Figure 10.27 shows how to configure reasons for rejection for quotations. These reasons for rejection force the user to add a reason to a sales quote whenever a quote is rejected. The rejection reason in a quote helps you report and track so that corrective actions can be taken. For example, if a quote is rejected because a competitor is cheaper, you might want to evaluate what the competitor offered and what can you do in the future to counter the competition.

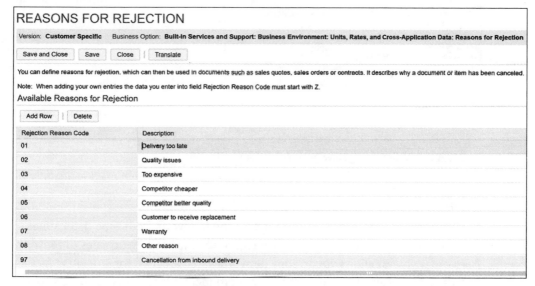

Figure 10.27 Configuring Reasons for Rejection

10.3.4   Maintain Item Types

Figure 10.28 shows how to maintain new item types such as free-of-charge, sample, or text items for quotes. To maintain a new **Item Type**, click on **Add Row** under **Item Types**, and you'll be prompted to enter the **Item Type**, **Description**, and **Base Item Type**, as well as consider a checkbox to indicate whether this item is **Pricing Relevant** (you need to scroll to the right) or not. After maintaining these details, click **Save and Close** to create your item type.

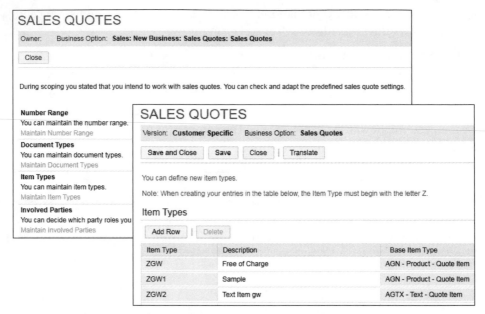

Figure 10.28 Maintaining New Item Types for Quotes

10.3.5   Follow-Up Item Type Determination

Through this configuration, you can define the follow-up item type determination based on the preceding item types (see Figure 10.30). A follow-up sales order to the sales order process allows you to copy item types that are used for SAP ERP/SAP CRM processing. You can add the item type in the product table of the sales quote via adaptation or personalization, which are covered in Chapter 18. You can maintain this configuration by choosing **Maintain Fine-Tuning Activity Sales Quotes • Item Types**.

10.3.6   Maintain Involved Parties

Through this configuration, you can decide which party roles to use in a sales quote. Although some roles are mandatory and can't be changed, you can control other roles in the quotation to meet your business requirements. The mandatory roles for involved parties are preselected in SAP Sales Cloud and can't be altered, as shown in Figure 10.29. These parties are required for successfully processing quotes per standard out-of-the-box functionality in SAP Sales Cloud. To add a new involved party, such as a consultant or external partner, click on **Add Row**, and then maintain all the details as prompted by the system.

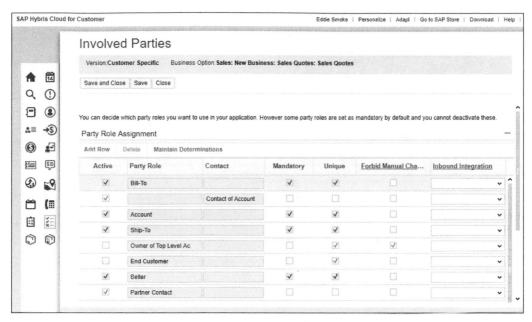

Figure 10.29 Involved Parties Configuration for Sales Quote

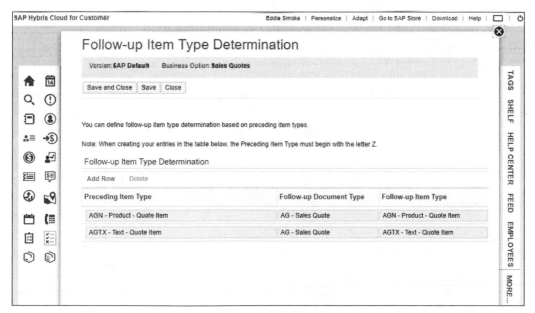

Figure 10.30 Configuring Follow-Up Item Type Determination

For each role, you can activate or deactivate determination steps, as shown in Figure 10.31. The steps that have been activated are taken into consideration to determine the relevant party in a quote.

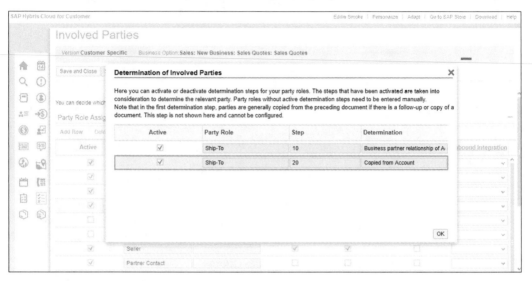

Figure 10.31 Determination of Involved Parties in a Quote

10.3.7   Default Logic for Pricing Date

Through this configuration, you can define the default logic for the pricing date in the system, such as today's date or a requested date, by selecting from the **Pricing Date** dropdown, as shown in Figure 10.32. To enable this configuration, choose **Business Configuration • Implementation Projects • Open Activity List • Fine-Tune**, and then search for "Sales Quote" under **All Activities**. From the search results, click on **Sales Quotes**, and then click on **Maintain Document Types**. Under the document type, select the **Pricing Date** value from the dropdown based on your business requirements.

10.3.8   Default Logic for Quote Validity and Requested Date

The **Date Profile** fine-tuning activity allows you to configure the default of the **Quote Validity** and **Requested Date** (header field) in the sales quote, as shown in Figure 10.33. The requested date on the header is copied to the requested date on the items. Note that manually changed dates on items won't be overwritten by the header date.

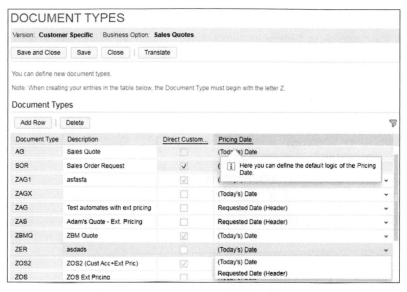

Figure 10.32 Configuring the Default Logic for the Pricing Date

DATE PROFILES

Version: **Customer Specific**   Business Option: **Built-in Services and Support: Business Environment: Units, Rates, and Cross-Application Data: Date Profiles**

| Save and Close | Save | Close |

You can define settings which will then be automatically used as defaults when you create documents.

Date Variable for Sales
SALES QUOTES

Quote Validity = Creation Date + Number of Days:	2 Day(s)
Requested Date = Creation Date + Number of Days:	1 Day(s)

SALES ORDERS

Requested Date = Creation Date + Number of Days:	5 Day(s)

LEADS

Lead Validity = Creation Date + Number of Days:	30 Day(s)

OPPORTUNITIES

Opportunity Validity = Creation Date + Number of Days:	180 Day(s)

Date Variable for Service
WARRANTIES

Warranty Start = Warranty Reference Date + Number of Days:	0 Day(s)

SERVICE REQUESTS

Response Time = Received on Date + Time in Hours:	1 Hour(s)
Completion Time = Received on Date + Time in Hours:	0 Hour(s)

Figure 10.33 Configuring the Default Logic for Quote Validity and Request Date

10.3.9   Workflow Rule Recipient Determination

The **Workflow Rule Recipient Determination** activity allows you to select **Account Team** and **Territory Team** for notifications regarding sales quotes. Figure 10.34 shows the navigation to configure the workflow rule: go to the **Administrator** work center, and choose **View Workflow Rules**.

Figure 10.34 Configuring the Workflow Rule for Recipient Determination

10.3.10   Blocking External Follow-Up Documents for Prospects

If you don't want quotations for prospects to replicate to SAP ERP, you can disable the Create External Follow-Up Document (to SAP ERP) action for prospects (see Figure 10.35). The navigation path for this configuration is **Scoping Element: Communication and Information Exchange • Integration with External Applications and Solutions • Integration with SAP ERP**. Then, enable the answer **Do you want to block prospects created in your cloud solution from being replicated to your SAP ERP solution?**

Figure 10.35 Blocking External Follow-Up Documents for Prospects

10.4   Integration with SAP ERP

In the previous section, you saw that if SAP Sales Cloud is integrated with an SAP backend system (SAP CRM or SAP ERP), you can create a follow-up sales order in the SAP backend from a sales quote in SAP Sales Cloud. To enable SAP ERP integration for quotes, you need to add this scenario to your project scope by choosing **Business Configuration • Implementation Projects • Edit Project Scope • Implementation Focus • Scoping • Questions • Communication and Information Exchange • Integration with SAP ERP**, as shown in Figure 10.36. You need an integration platform/tool such as SAP Cloud Platform Integration or SAP Process Integration (SAP PI) as middleware to integrate SAP ERP and SAP Sales Cloud. This integration is outside the scope of this book.

You can also leverage bidirectional exchange between SAP Sales Cloud and the SAP backend; that is, quotes created in SAP Sales Cloud can be replicated to the SAP backend system. In this case, you can replicate and edit quotes from SAP Sales Cloud to SAP ERP and vice versa, as shown in Figure 10.37. The **Transfer Status**, **Reference Status** for follow-up order creation, and **Cancellation Status** of **Not Started**, **In Process**, or **Finished** enable you to track where exactly the document is in the replication process.

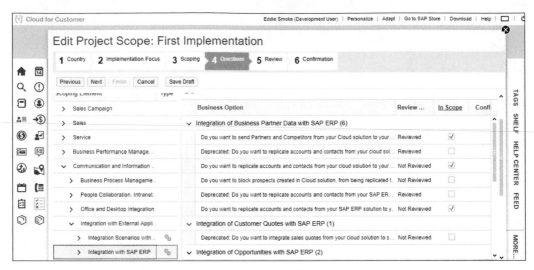

Figure 10.36 Adding Integration to SAP ERP to the Project Scope

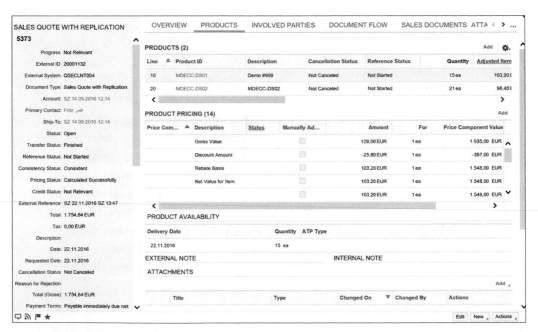

Figure 10.37 Bidirectional Exchange with the SAP ERP Backend

10.5   Pricing in Quotes

For pricing items in quotes, you can use internal pricing in SAP Sales Cloud or external pricing from the SAP backend system (SAP CRM or SAP ERP). For internal pricing,
you need to maintain the product pricing natively in SAP Sales Cloud. If you're using
a standalone SAP Sales Cloud that isn't integrated with the backend SAP ERP system,
you might want to use the internal pricing for products within SAP Sales Cloud. For
the internal pricing, you maintain the price of the products on the product master
data under a price list, as shown in Figure 10.38. When you create a quote, prices for
the products are copied in the quote from the price list maintained on the product
master.

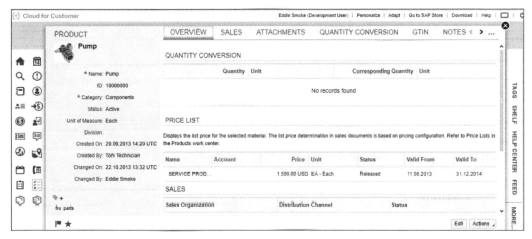

Figure 10.38 Internal Pricing on a Product Master

If you want to price products in a quote based on the product prices maintained in
the backend SAP ERP system, you can use external pricing to maintain a consistent
pricing experience for products across systems. Most organizations maintain pricing
in SAP ERP, so they prefer to use external pricing from SAP ERP. With SAP ERP integrated with SAP Sales Cloud, the quotes created in SAP Sales Cloud can be priced by
making external pricing calls to the SAP backend system. This setting is controlled
though configuration as covered previously in Section 10.3.1 (refer to Figure 10.22)
and also includes tax determinations.

10.6   Summary

In this chapter, you've seen the key capabilities of the quotation management functionality available in SAP Sales Cloud. From creating a quotation to processing a quotation through its lifecycle, we've covered all the critical components. We've also reviewed how quotations can be influenced with SAP ERP integration for pricing, availability check, credit management, and so on. Finally, we covered how to include quotation management in the implementation scope and discussed the key configuration areas available in SAP Sales Cloud for quotations to help you implement your unique business requirements. In the next chapter, we'll cover the next component in the sales process: order management.

Chapter 11

Order Management

Order management in SAP Sales Cloud allows sales reps to create sales orders as follow-up transactions from sales quotations, opportunities, or directly from a visit. Sales orders are transferred to SAP ERP for downstream logistics and billing processing.

Order capture is the last step in the sales process in SAP Sales Cloud before the order is transferred to the backend order fulfillment system. After the order is captured, it's transferred to SAP ERP for downstream processing. Most sales orders are created as a follow-up from a sales quotation or opportunity so that most of the order data is copied from a preceding document (sales quote); however, sales orders can be captured standalone as well, in which case, the user has to manually enter most of the order information.

SAP Sales Cloud allows you to configure the order process to drive your own business objectives with intuitive and expedited order capture capabilities. It offers flexibility to price items in sales orders by leveraging internal pricing from within SAP Sales Cloud or native pricing from SAP ERP, along with product availability and credit limit checks. Further product proposals in sales orders can be influenced on automated product list determinations that are based on account, account hierarchy, or territory.

In this chapter, you'll learn about the key capabilities of order management in SAP Sales Cloud along with how orders are created and processed. We'll also review how order management capabilities in SAP Sales Cloud can be influenced through configuration or fine-tuning. In addition, we'll also briefly discuss how order management is integrated with SAP ERP and how orders are priced.

11.1 Order Management Process

The order management process involves creating sales orders based on customer requirements. Sales orders include customer and contact details, products or services the customer is buying, product pricing, expected delivery date, delivery address, terms of payment, party responsible for payment, notes, and so on. Normally, sales orders are created as follow-up transactions from sales quotes, so all the details from the sales quotes are copied over to the sales order. The follow-up process for sales orders involves order fulfillment, so most sales orders are transferred to the backend for order fulfillment or to the SAP ERP system. SAP Sales Cloud offers rich capabilities to support order processing for various sales scenarios with out-of-the-box integration with SAP ERP.

Let's review some of the key capabilities and unique features of SAP Sales Cloud that help you drive the unique and intuitive order management process:

- **Product proposals**
  Product proposals provide rich order capture capabilities via product lists, including cross sell, up sell, and down sell; product exclusions; and product restrictions.

- **Internal pricing**
  Basic pricing is supported with internal price lists, discount lists, surcharges, manual costs, and profit margins.

- **External pricing**
  For an integrated SAP backend scenario, you can leverage external pricing (from SAP CRM/SAP ERP) via live call simulation to support free goods determination, product availability check, credit limit check, bill of material (BOM) explosion in the sales order, and product substitutions.

- **Notes and attachment**
  You can attach notes and attachments to sales orders at the header level. Attachments at the item levels aren't supported currently in SAP Sales Cloud.

- **Involved parties**
  You can determine involved parties in a sales order based on determination rules (per configuration) and also make document-specific address updates to the involved parties.

- **Notifications**
  You can send both internal and external email notifications, including form templates, output channel determination, and language selection.

- **Multistep approval workflow**
  You can enable multistep approval workflow for sales orders as needed.

- **Mobile support**
  Mobility support is available for sales orders, including the capability to capture signatures for sales orders on mobile devices.

- **Follow-up transactions**
  Follow-up transactions, such as activities and service tickets, can be created from sales orders.

- **Change history**
  Changes made to some of the fields in sales orders are tracked based on user IDs and time stamps. SAP Sales Cloud provides a Business Add-In (BAdI) in case you want to track some specific fields not otherwise tracked.

- **Application programming interface (API) support**
  API support is provided for importing and exporting sales orders from SAP Sales Cloud.

In the next section, you'll learn how to create and process sales orders.

11.2   Creating and Processing Orders

Sales order processing or order fulfillment is a downstream SAP ERP process. SAP Sales Cloud offers an easy order-capture capability for sales reps to maintain the link from the lead to the cash process. In SAP Sales Cloud, sales orders can be created as standalone transactions or as follow-up transactions from an opportunity or sales quotation.

Creating sales orders as a follow-up from sales quotes or opportunities allows you to copy of most of the information, such as customer information, contact, products, pricing, payment terms, and so on, from the preceding document, and it also establishes the link between the quotation and sales order for reporting and tracking purposes. In the following sections, we'll review the step-by-step process for creating and processing sales orders in SAP Sales Cloud.

Follow-Up from Orders

The sales orders created in SAP Sales Cloud are transferred to the SAP ERP system for further processing. All further processing activities from the sales order, such as delivery, picking, packing, post goods issue, and billing, are carried out in SAP ERP. These processes are outside the scope of this book.

11.2.1   Creating Orders

Creating a sales order in SAP Sales Cloud is similar to creating any other sales-related transactions such as opportunities and quotations as covered in previous chapters. Standalone orders can be created from the **Sales** work center on the navigation bar on the left side of the screen or as a follow-up from an opportunity or quotation (from the **Sales Documents** work center).

When you create a sales order, you first select **Document Type** from the dropdown, as shown in Figure 11.1. The **Document Type** here corresponds to the sales order type in the SAP ERP system. On this screen, you can maintain the required order details of **Description**, **Account**, **Owner**, **Ship-To**, **External Reference**, **Pricing Date**, **Requested Date**, **Distribution Channel**, **Division**, and so on. These fields help you capture all the required details to enable an efficient order fulfillment process.

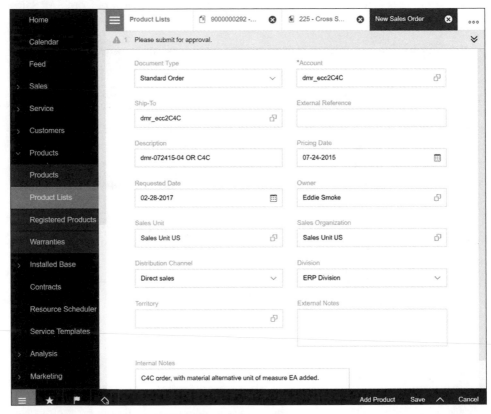

Figure 11.1 Creation of a Sales Order

After maintaining these details, click **Save and Open** to create the sales order in the system. On the **Order Details** page that appears, you can maintain products and order quantity, and accordingly the price will be populated in the sales order based on the pricing setting. You can maintain order details, such as involved parties, various customer order notes, and internal notes, and then save the order for further processing.

11.2.2   Processing Orders

Although sales order processes, such as creating a delivery or creating invoice documents, are performed in the SAP ERP backend system, this section will focus on capabilities available in SAP Sales Cloud to work through the sales order, including how to efficiently enter items in a sales order, how to create activities with reference to a sales order, and how to cross sell and up sell items in a sales order. SAP Sales Cloud offers various features to assist users in efficiently processing sales orders, as follows:

- **Optimized order item entry**

  During order entry, various options are available for users to efficiently and quickly add products to the sales order. Product categories and products within each category, as well as products from the historical sales quotes and sales orders for an account can be listed and selected for entry in a sales order. Product lists can be defined as product proposals for the accounts to allow auto proposal and multiproduct selection in sales orders, as shown in Figure 11.2.

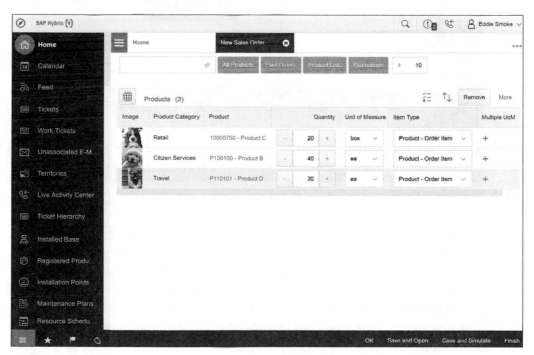

Figure 11.2 Optimized Order Item Entry

For customers who want to set up a list of items to be excluded from a sales order, you can set up product lists with the exclusion type. Whenever an order is created for such customers, the user won't be able to enter products from the exclusion list in the sales order. Similarly, a product list with the restriction type can be created to limit the ordering of a certain set of products. Now it's possible to easily add items in multiple units of measurements in a sales order. Customized number pads make it easier to add quantities, as shown in Figure 11.3.

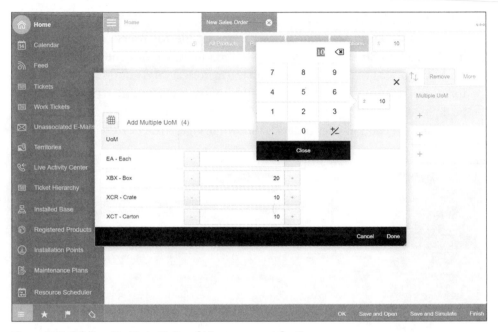

Figure 11.3 Adding Multiple Units of Measurement for Items

Figure 11.4 shows the **Remove Zero-Quantity Items** and **Calculate Quantity** actions, which are used to further streamline orders that have a large number of items. You can remove items with zero quantity from an order to save time during simulation. Similarly, the **Calculate Quantity** action provides a quantity overview, that is, a summation of order items by unit of measurement. This feature provides users with an overview of how many items per unit of measurement are in the order.

- **Cross selling, up selling, and down selling**
  Recommended products can be added via the **+** icon at the bottom of the **PRODUCTS** tab, as shown in Figure 11.5. It allows users to view and sell additional products based on items in the order. The recommended products view only appears if cross selling is applicable. Icons in the products table indicate whether an up sell or

down sell replacement is available for the order item. The **Up/Down Selling Products** action only appears if appropriate product proposals exist.

Figure 11.4 Remove Zero-Quantity Item Action

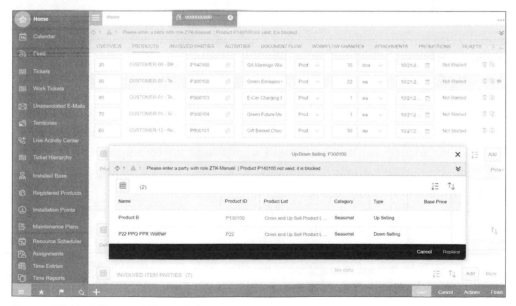

Figure 11.5 Up Selling and Down Selling

- **Activities in an order**

  Follow-up activities, such as appointments, tasks, emails, and phone calls, can be created directly from a sales order to keep track of all the activities related to an order, as shown in Figure 11.6. These activities can also be viewed in the document flow. Email activities can also be assigned to sales orders via Microsoft Outlook integration.

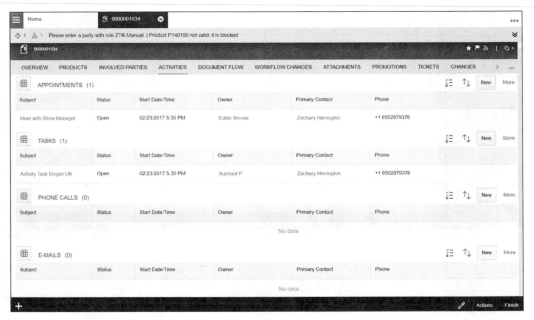

Figure 11.6 Tracking Activities for an Order

- **Language support**

  The print language for the sales order output can be controlled based on the language maintained on the customer master record or the login language of the user. Language can also be changed according to the communication languages selected in the business configuration.

- **Involved parties (document header)**

  Involved business partners (parties) for the sales order, such as partners or competitors, can be determined or added into your sales orders, as shown in Figure 11.7. The **INVOLVED PARTIES** tab also allows you to change the address for parties and contacts to a document address (one-time address). This address won't change master data and is only applicable for the document processing itself.

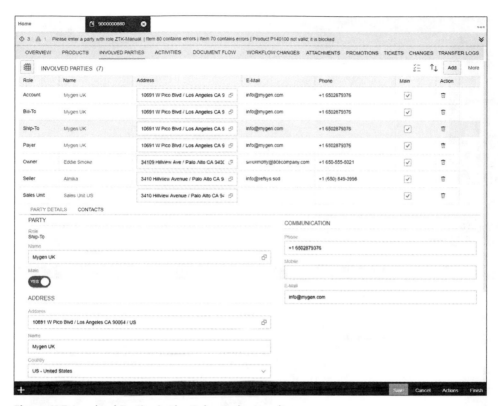

Figure 11.7 Involved Parties in the Sales Order Header

- **Item involved parties**

  Like the sales order header, you can also add and determine further involved business partners (parties), such as partners or competitors, at the item level in an order. The **INVOLVED PARTIES** tab allows you to change the address for parties and contacts to a document address (one-time address). This address won't change master data and is only applicable for the document processing itself.

- **Document flow**

  The document flow shows related transactions for a sales order, such as sales quotation, activities, and opportunities, as shown in Figure 11.8.

- **Capturing signatures in sales orders**

  A graphical signature can be captured via the Sign action. Captured signatures can also be found under the **ATTACHMENTS** tab in an order, as shown in Figure 11.9. A signature can be included in the print form via Adobe LiveCycle Designer. Integration of a digital signature, which is legally binding, is supported via partner solutions.

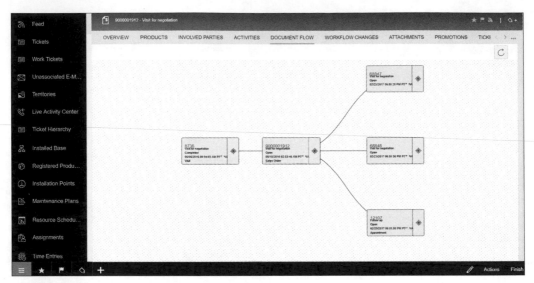

Figure 11.8 Document Flow for a Sales Order

Figure 11.9 Capturing a Signature in a Sales Order

- **Approvals for sales orders**

  To enable a formal approval process for sales orders, you can set up a multilevel approval process based on various conditions. You can edit and view approval notes in the **APPROVAL** tab, as shown in Figure 11.10. If needed, you can also withdraw a sales order from the approval process via the Withdraw from Approval action. As of SAP Sales Cloud 1802, sales orders can be submitted over secured email for approval. Upon submission of a sales order for approval, a manager can approve the sales order via notification or directly in the **APPROVAL** tab of the sales order.

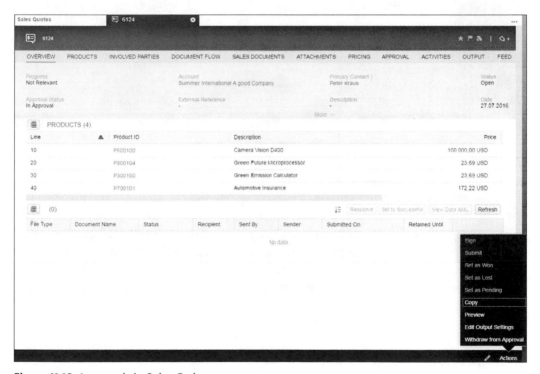

Figure 11.10 Approvals in Sales Orders

- **Minimum order quantity for items in a sales order**

  You can define the minimum order quantity in the material master so that an error message will be displayed in the sales order if the quantity entered by the user is lower than the quantity maintained on the material master (see Figure 11.11). This allows you to make sure that the minimum required quantity is always entered in sales orders for items with a predefined minimum order quantity.

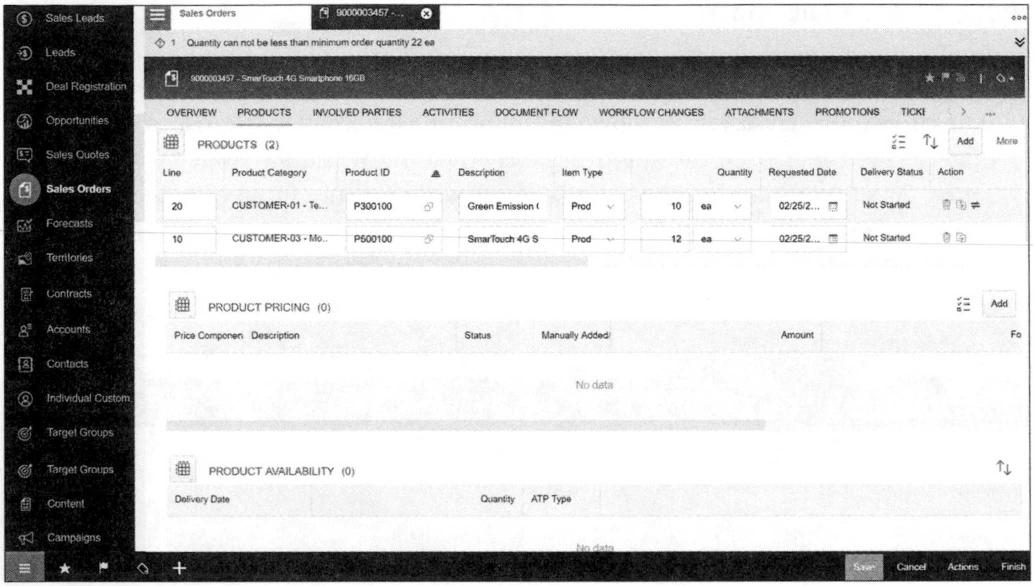

Figure 11.11 Error Message for Minimum Order Quantity

- **Split screen details view**
  In a sales order, you can use the details icon to view all products and involved parties on a split screen. In the sales order, you can select the **Products** or **Involved Parties** tab to use the split screen layout with the list view on the left and individual item details on the right. Clicking on the individual product or involved parties will bring up the split screen. You can scroll through different products and see their details on the same screen in the split screen view. You can use the list to easily switch between items.

11.3 Configuring Orders

Now that we've reviewed all the key capabilities of sales order management in SAP Sales Cloud, let's discuss some of the important configurations and fine-tuning activities related to sales orders in SAP Sales Cloud that allow you to influence your unique sales processes, as follows:

- **Including sales orders in scope**
  Before you can make any configuration-related changes for sales orders in SAP Sales Cloud, you need to include sales orders in **Scoping** under **Business Configuration**, as shown in Figure 11.12.

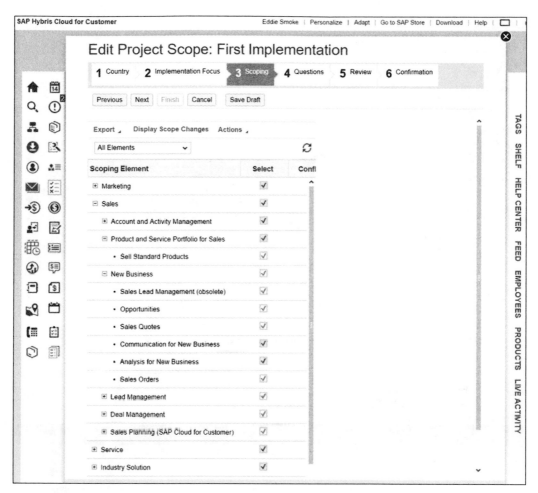

Figure 11.12 Including Sales Orders in the Business Configuration Scope

- **Configuring external pricing**
  If you want to leverage external pricing from SAP ERP for sales orders created in SAP Sales Cloud, you need to set the scope for external pricing, as shown in Figure 11.13.

- **Configure follow-up item type determination**
  The follow-up from the sales order to the sales order process allows you to copy item types that are used for SAP ERP/SAP CRM processing. As shown in Figure 11.14, you can select the **Item Type** in the product table of a sales order via adaptation or personalization.

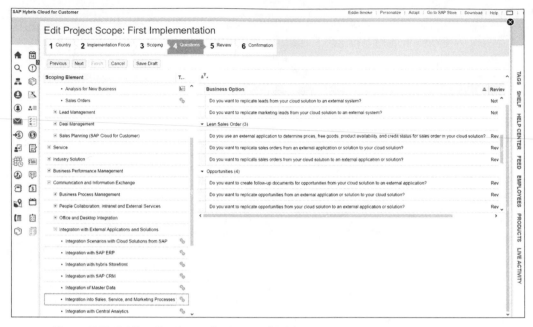

Figure 11.13 Setting the Scope for External Pricing

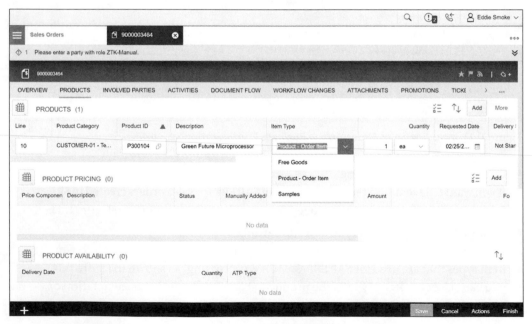

Figure 11.14 Selecting an Item Type in the Product Table

- **Configure item types that aren't pricing relevant**
  Through this configuration, you can define item types that aren't relevant for pricing (i.e., free-of-charge items). This allows users to only add the item type to the item in the sales order without changing the item price to zero or giving a 100% discount, as shown in the first image in Figure 11.15.

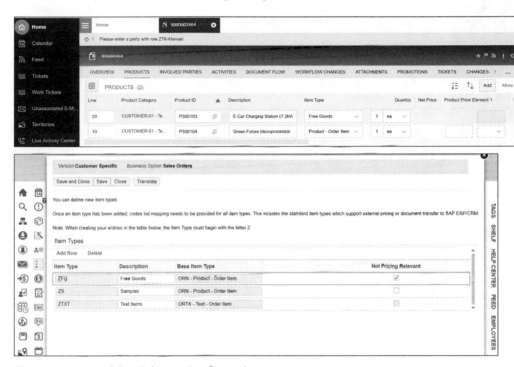

Figure 11.15 Not Pricing Relevant Configuration

To fine-tune item types, navigate to **Sales Orders • Item Types**, and define item types as **Not Pricing Relevant**, as shown in the second image in Figure 11.15.

- **Define item increment per document type**
  Through this configuration, you can define the item increment numbers, for example, 10, 20, 30, and so on, that allow you to control item increment ranges and subitem increment ranges in a sales order. Item increments can be configured by choosing **Sales Orders • Document Types**. Figure 11.16 shows the **Item Increment** in a sales order and the associated fine-tuning activity.

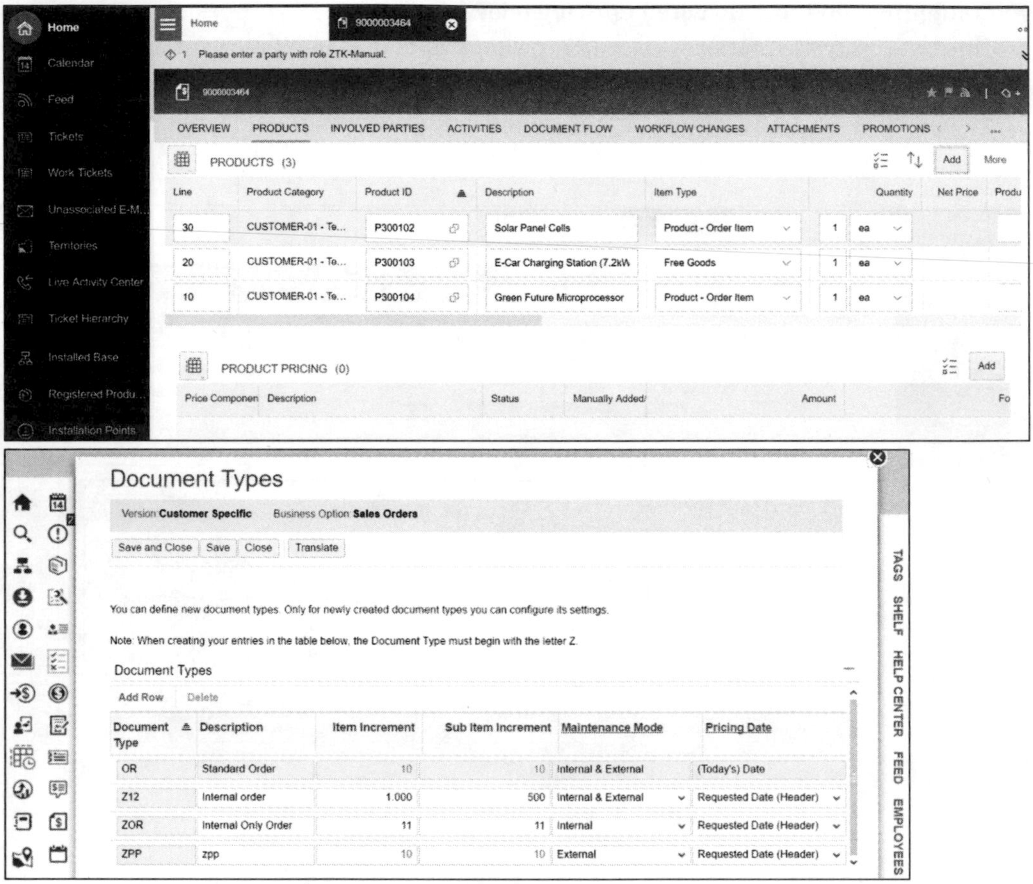

Figure 11.16 Item Increment in a Sales Order

- **Defaulting the sales area in a sales order**

  In a sales order, the default logic for sales area determination follows a sequence. First, the system checks the intersection of the account sales data and employee sales data and populates that into the sales order. It starts with the sales area match (sales organization + distribution channel + division). If that's not found, it then matches sales organization + distribution channel, and finally matches only the sales organization, if previous matches aren't found. Secondly, if the previous search didn't result in any sales areas, then the system defaults the user's employee sales data into the sales order. Finally, if the previous determinations didn't return any sales areas, then the account sales area is defaulted into the sales order.

A sales order also allows **Sales Organization** value selection for users as needed in just one step. Predefined queries available in a sales order are **Account's Sales Data**, **My Sales Data**, and **My Sales Data Matching Account's**, as shown in Figure 11.17.

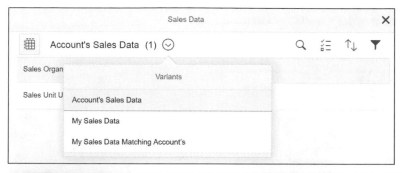

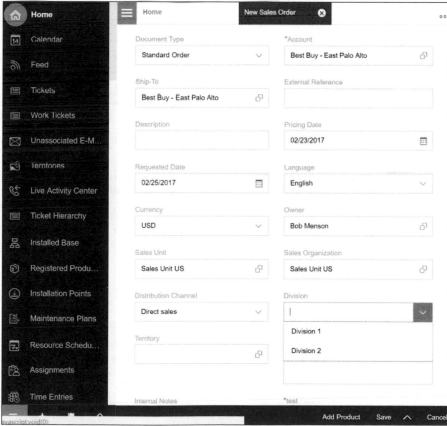

Figure 11.17 Predefined Queries for Sales Area Data

To fine-tune the sales area determination, choose **Business Configuration • Scoping Element: Sales • New Business • Sales Orders**, and then select the question under **Sales Area Determination for Sales Orders**, as shown in Figure 11.18. If sales access is restricted, the key user can set **Distribution Channel** and **Division** as read only in the sales order via adaptation mode.

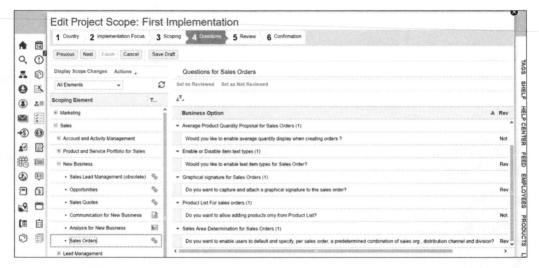

Figure 11.18 Configuring the Default Sales Area in a Sales Order

- **Default logic for pricing date**
  You can default the pricing date in a sales order by navigating to **Sales Order • Document Types** fine-tuning activity. Here you can configure the default behavior of the **Pricing Date** for each **Document Type** by choosing **Today's Date** and **Requested Date (Header)**, as shown in Figure 11.19.

- **Default logic for order header requested date**
  The **Date Profile** fine-tuning activity allows you to configure the default Requested Date on the header in sales orders, as shown in Figure 11.20. Through this configuration, the **Requested Date** on the header is copied to the **Requested Dated** on the items in the sales order. If needed, the user can manually change the dates on the item level, and such dates won't be overwritten by the header date.

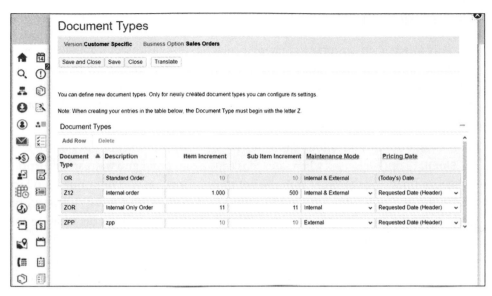

Figure 11.19 Default Price Date in a Sales Order

DATE PROFILES

Version: **Customer Specific**   Business Option: **Built-in Services and Support: Business Environment: Units, Rates, and Cross-Application Data: Date Profiles**

Save and Close   Save   Close

You can define settings which will then be automatically used as defaults when you create documents.

Date Variable for Sales
SALES QUOTES

Quote Validity = Creation Date + Number of Days:	2 Day(s)
Requested Date = Creation Date + Number of Days:	1 Day(s)

SALES ORDERS

Requested Date = Creation Date + Number of Days:	5 Day(s)

LEADS

Lead Validity = Creation Date + Number of Days:	30 Day(s)

OPPORTUNITIES

Opportunity Validity = Creation Date + Number of Days:	180 Day(s)

Date Variable for Service
WARRANTIES

Warranty Start = Warranty Reference Date + Number of Days:	0 Day(s)

SERVICE REQUESTS

Response Time = Received on Date + Time in Hours:	1 Hour(s)
Completion Time = Received on Date + Time in Hours:	0 Hour(s)

Figure 11.20 Configuring the Default Order Header Date on a Sales Order

11.4   Integration with SAP ERP

As briefly touched on earlier in this chapter, all follow-up processes from sales orders, such as delivery, shipping, and billing, are executed outside SAP Cloud for Customer in an order fulfillment system. If you're running SAP ERP for your order fulfillment processes, then you must include SAP ERP integration with SAP Cloud for Customer in the scope to enable the transfer of sales orders to SAP ERP for further processing.

Integration with SAP ERP allows simulate, transfer, and finish actions in sales orders. The **Simulate** option is used when sales reps capture an order and want accurate pricing before finalizing the order with the net price (discounts and net value), product availability (delivery dates, available to promise [ATP] quantities, and ATP types), and statuses (**Credit** and **Rejection**). The **Transfer** option of an order entails creating the order in SAP ERP, which triggers any follow-up processes configured in SAP ERP such as fulfillment and billing. The **Finish** option can be used to combine all the actions (i.e., save, simulate, and transfer), as well as submit for approval if approval is set up, of the order to SAP ERP in a single click.

You can configure the use of internal pricing or external pricing by document type. With SAP ERP integration, you can influence free goods determination, product availability checks, credit limit checks, BOM explosions, and product substitutions in sales orders, as follows:

- **Free goods determination**
  Simulation or transfer of an order returns free goods from SAP ERP if they are set up for the products entered in the sales order. The free goods are only for display, and edits can't be made to such products in the sales order. Free goods are displayed after the external pricing call to SAP ERP, as shown Figure 11.21. Free goods determination supports both *exclusive* (e.g., buy 10 and get 1 free) and *inclusive* (e.g., buy 10 and pay for only 9) procedures.

- **Product availability check**
  Simulation or transfer of an order also returns an ATP result from SAP ERP. Confirmation is nonbinding based on the requested date (header date copied to items). A simulated delivery schedule appears in the sales order, as shown in Figure 11.22.

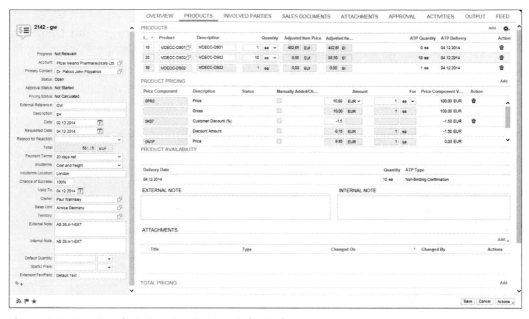

Figure 11.21 Free Goods Determination in a Sales Order

Figure 11.22 Product Availability Check from SAP ERP

- **Credit limit check**

  The simulation or transfer of an order returns **Credit Status**, **Credit Limit**, and **Credit Exposure** information from the SAP ERP system, including a warning message if the amount exceeds the limit as set up under credit management for the customer in SAP ERP (see Figure 11.23). **Credit Status** is part of approval conditions and is determined when an order is simulated or transferred.

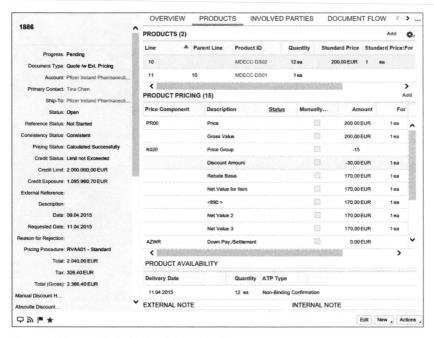

Figure 11.23 Credit Limit Check for SAP ERP

- **BOM explosion**

  If an order is created for a material set up as a BOM in the SAP ERP system, simulation or transfer of an order also "explodes" multilevel BOMs from SAP ERP, as shown in Figure 11.24. Price or quantity adjustments for a BOM are only supported on the header item.

- **Product substitutions**

  If a product substitution has been configured in SAP ERP, then the original product entered in the sales order will be replaced by a substituted product as part of the external pricing call. Figure 11.25 shows the Original Product field with a substituted product. Via external pricing calls, products will be replaced if the condition—such as the entered product is out of stock or has been discontinued—is met.

Figure 11.24 BOM Explosion in a Sales Order

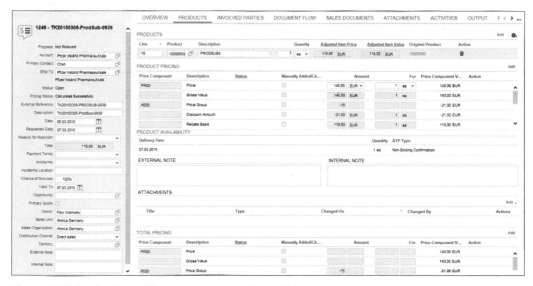

Figure 11.25 Product Substitution via External Price Call

> **Note**
>
> Product substitutions need to be configured in the SAP ERP system.

With bidirectional integration between SAP Cloud for Customer and SAP ERP, sales orders in SAP Cloud for Customer can be replicated to SAP ERP and vice versa. For this bidirectional integration, multiple statuses are available in the sales order to show the progress of sales order replication: **Transfer Status**, **Pricing Status**, and **Cancellation Status** (see Figure 11.26).

Figure 11.26 Sales Order Replication Statuses with SAP ERP

If the transfer status is interrupted, the **TRANSFER LOGS** table provides the details of the error, as shown in Figure 11.27. In this case, saving the sales order will trigger a new replication.

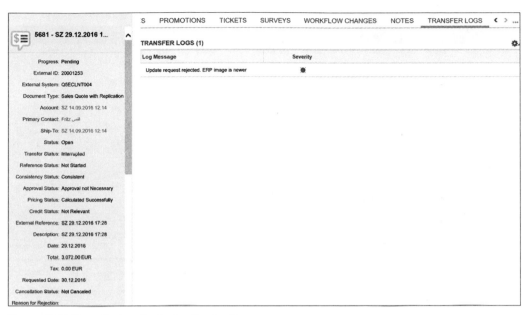

Figure 11.27 Transfer Log for Order Replication

11.5   Pricing in Orders

SAP Cloud for Customer offers both an internal pricing option (pricing data is maintained within SAP Cloud for Customer) and an external pricing option (an external pricing call is made to SAP ERP) to price items in a sales order. Let's review the details of these pricing options, as follows:

- **Internal pricing**

  For simple pricing needs, you can configure sales orders in SAP Cloud for Customer to use the internal pricing capabilities by maintaining the list price, customer-specific price lists, discount lists, and a single pricing procedure. The list price and product discount can be edited in the products table shown in Figure 11.28.

  Internal pricing is much easier to implement, but if you need to calculate taxes for items in a sales order, internal pricing may not work for you because SAP Cloud for Customer internal pricing doesn't support tax determination.

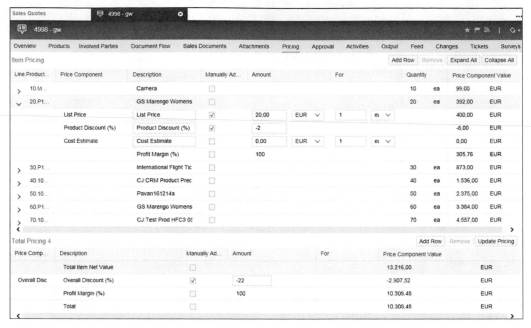

Figure 11.28 Internal Pricing in a Sales Order

- **External pricing**

  The external pricing option with integration into SAP ERP supports comprehensive and holistic order management scenarios and allows users to simulate and request updated pricing from SAP ERP, add manual discounts at the header and item levels in the order, and send back to SAP ERP for final pricing calculations. It also retrieves complete price information in the **PRODUCT PRICING** and **Total Pricing** areas on the **PRODUCTS** tab, including taxes from the SAP ERP/SAP CRM system by user action **Simulate**, **Transfer**, or **Finish**. As shown in Figure 11.29, you can edit and view complete pricing results based on the pricing procedure in SAP ERP. Printing of the pricing element is based on the Customizing settings for the pricing procedure in SAP ERP.

  You can also view and edit external price elements directly on the header in the products table of the sales order.

  External pricing is requested from SAP Cloud for Customer through the **Simulate** action, and the steps in the pricing request process are shown in Figure 11.30.

Figure 11.29 External Pricing from SAP ERP

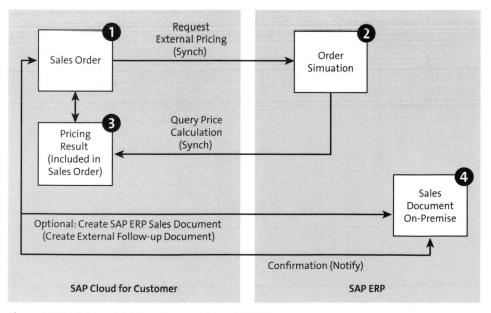

Figure 11.30 External Pricing Request from SAP ERP

The document flow in SAP Sales Cloud is populated from SAP ERP so that users can view whether the invoice or delivery documents were created in SAP ERP.

- **Offline capabilities**
  SAP Sales Cloud offers offline capability from mobile devices such as iPads and Android tablets for capturing sales orders. You can still work in your SAP Sales Cloud application from mobile devices even if no network connection is present. It supports offline sales order capture, including offline order pricing. Users can also view sales orders in offline mode. When a network connection is reestablished, data is synchronized between the mobile device and the SAP Sales Cloud application.

11.6   Summary

In this chapter, you've learned about the key capabilities of sales order management in SAP Sales Cloud. We reviewed how sales orders are created and processed, as well as how you can leverage some of the critical functionalities to meet your unique processes and business requirements. We covered how you can include sales order management in the SAP Sales Cloud implementation scope and configure or fine-tune order management capabilities in SAP Cloud for Customer. We also reviewed SAP Cloud for Customer integration with SAP ERP, along with internal and external pricing options for items within a sales order. In the next chapter, you'll learn about the visit planning and execution capabilities available in SAP Sales Cloud for field sales reps.

Chapter 12

Visit Planning and Execution

SAP Sales Cloud offers comprehensive visit planning and execution capabilities for field sales representatives to not only plan their account visits but also record meeting details as needed.

Sales reps and sales managers often ponder whether they are visiting their customers most effectively and not wasting time and resources in unnecessary custom visits. Properly planning customer visits and routes can help efficiently manage your sales reps' productivity. Visit planning and execution capabilities available in SAP Sales Cloud can help your field sales reps plan and manage their customer visits.

In this chapter, you'll learn about the standard visit process and key capabilities of visit planning and execution available in SAP Sales Cloud. We'll review how visits are planned and executed followed by standard analytics available to measure the effectiveness of visits. We'll also cover the important configuration settings to include visit planning in your project scope. Lastly, we'll cover the retail execution capabilities available in SAP Sales Cloud for the consumer products industry.

12.1 The Visit Process

Visit planning and execution enables field sales reps to plan and record site visits and activities while on-site at accounts. With the SAP Cloud for Customer mobile app, reps can use their smartphones (or tablets) as their personal itinerary planner. They can visit more customers by properly mapping their sales routes and minimizing their distance traveled.

Figure 12.1 shows the process for visit planning and execution. Sales reps can plan for the account visits based on various parameters, such as customer history, corporate key performance indicators (KPIs), or customer specific goals, and then create visits with corresponding activities or tasks. After visits have been planned, sales reps execute the plan by conducting visits to gather information from customers though product audits and surveys. They can perform transactions such as create or update sales orders, check inventory or price information per customer request, update customer information, gather competitive information, and review previous action items.

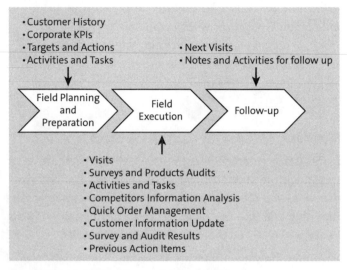

Figure 12.1 Visit Planning and Execution Process

As a follow-up from a visit, sales reps can create next visits and also update notes and activities for the follow-up visit as needed. SAP Sales Cloud provides capabilities to administer, plan, and execute visits, as follows:

- **Visit administration**
  - For visits, you can easily create and manage surveys.
  - Flexible activity planning and routing enables you to define and assign tasks and surveys to be performed at the visit on-site for the account.
  - Enhanced Account 360 provides recommended visit frequency as well as visit history for accounts.
  - Product lists can be maintained to determine account-specific product proposals. You can view/maintain all visits for an account, as well as create and assign account-specific product lists.
  - You can maintain the recommended frequency of visits to help identify the accounts that are overdue for a visit during visit planning.
  - Enhanced reporting is available on survey answers, visits, and visit tasks.

- **Visit planning**
  - Map-based visit planning with integrated calendar view in the browser, along with mobile devices (phones and tablets), enables sales reps to effectively plan their trips. You can also view recommended frequency for accounts that are overdue for a visit and days since last visit.
  - The rule-based determination of recommended tasks and surveys from the activity plans and routine rules enables productive field sales organization.
  - You can select tasks and surveys to be completed in visits. You can also see the recommended list of tasks and surveys assigned to a visit via the activity routing rules.
  - You can add the tasks and surveys intended to be completed during the visit ahead of checking in to the visit. You can also define tasks and surveys that are mandatory to follow up.
- **Visit execution**
  - Visit execution is supported on browsers and mobile devices (phone and tablets) in online as well as offline modes.
  - Sales reps can use check-in and check-out for visits.
  - Tasks and surveys can be completed and/or added during visits.
  - Pictures can be captured and attached to survey results.
  - Follow-up quotes, sales orders, opportunities, activities, tasks, and service tickets are created from visits.
  - Quotes are easily created with product lists.

With this background on visit administration, visit planning, and visit execution process, let's now discuss how to plan and execute visits in SAP Sales Cloud.

12.2   Planning and Executing Visits

In SAP Sales Cloud, you can plan and execute visits by following the work centers on the left-hand navigation. Figure 12.2 shows **Visits**, **Visit Planner**, **Tours**, and **Routes** under the **Visits** work center.

In the next two sections, we'll review how to plan and execute visits before moving on to some information about visit analytics.

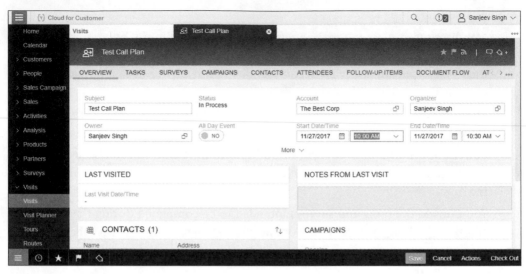

Figure 12.2 Visit Planning and Execution Work Centers

12.2.1   Planning Visits

To plan a new visit, follow these steps:

1. Click on the **Visit Planner** work center in the left side navigation.

2. Click the **+** button at the bottom of the screen to navigate to the **New Visit** screen, as shown in Figure 12.3.

3. Enter the **Subject** of the visit, and then select the **Account**, **Start Date/Time**, and **End Date/Time** of the visit.

4. Select **Save and Open**. Figure 12.4 shows the details of the visit plan. On this screen, you can add **Tasks**, **Surveys**, **Contacts**, **Attendees**, **Notes**, **Attachments**, **Follow-Up Items**, and so on, to help you effectively manage your visit. For example, you might want to create a task for yourself to review a customer's open invoices or sales orders before visiting so that you're prepared to answer any questions from the customer during the visit. Surveys allow you to structure information gathering from the customer during the visit. With specific questions in a survey, you can't miss gathering the required information from the customer.

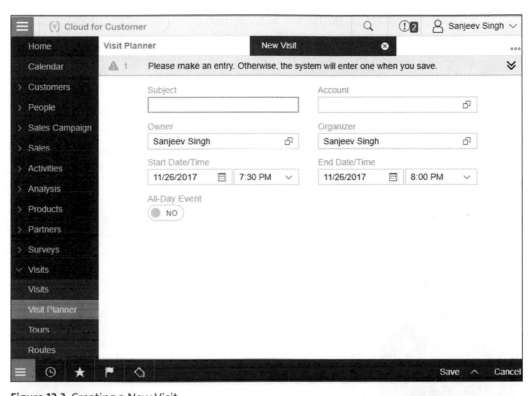

Figure 12.3 Creating a New Visit

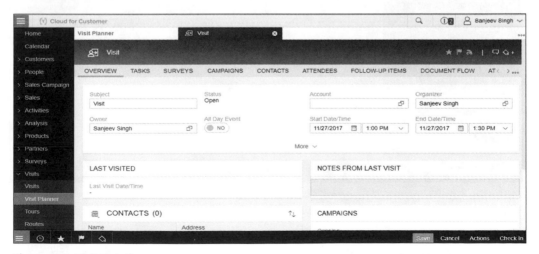

Figure 12.4 Visit Details

5. **Contacts** and **Attendees** let you include contacts you meet at the customer site during your visit. These attendees are existing customer contacts, or, if needed, you can create a new contact and add it to the visit as an attendee. If you want to attach a picture, such as a shelf picture where your products are displayed, you can use **Attachments** to link the pictures to the visit. In addition, **Notes** allows you to capture any free text from the visit that you're not able to capture anywhere else. After maintaining all the details, click **Save** to save the visit in **Open** status.

Along with visits, you can also create tours and routes as part of visit planning.

To create a new tour, follow these steps:

1. Click on the **Tours** work center, and then click on the **+** button to open the **New Tour** screen, as shown in Figure 12.5.

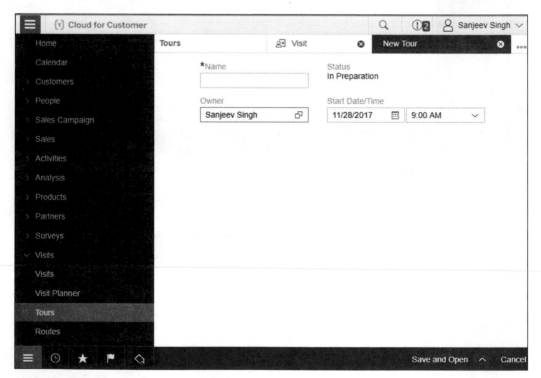

Figure 12.5 Creating a New Tour

2. On this screen, maintain the tour **Name** and **Start Date/Time**, and then click **Save and Open** to maintain additional tour details, as shown in Figure 12.6.

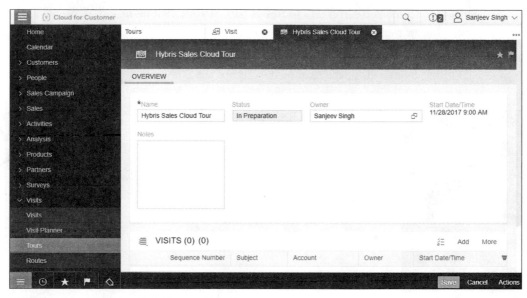

Figure 12.6 Maintaining Details on a New Tour

3. For this tour, add visits by clicking **Add**, as shown in Figure 12.6. After maintaining all the visits for this tour, activate the tour by selecting **Set as Active** in the **Actions** menu, as shown in Figure 12.7.

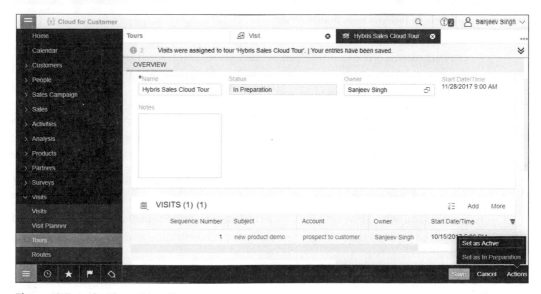

Figure 12.7 Activating a New Tour

Similar to tours, you can create routes as part of your visit planning. To create a new route, follow these steps:

1. Click on **Routes**, and then click the **+** button at the bottom of the screen. The **New Route** screen will appear, as shown in Figure 12.8.

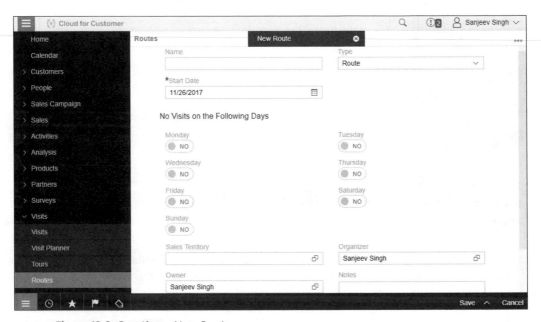

Figure 12.8 Creating a New Route

2. On this screen, maintain the **Name**, **Start Date**, **Sales Territory**, and **Notes** for the new route. You can also create a new **Route** or a route **Template** by selecting the **Type** dropdown shown in Figure 12.8.

3. If you don't want to visit on specific days in a week, select **No Visits** for those days.

4. Maintain the party who will own the route and generated visits in the **Owner** field, or derive the owner from the **Sales Territory** maintained.

5. After maintaining all the details, select **Save and Open**. The **Routes OVERVIEW** screen will appear, as shown in Figure 12.9.

6. For this route, add **Involved Parties**, **Attachments**, and **Proposed Visits**. You can add proposed visits to the route by searching for accounts due and overdue for visiting based on maintained visiting information.

7. After maintaining the proposed visit list, view the proposed daily visit sequences on a map, and visualize your proposed visit plan in a calendar.

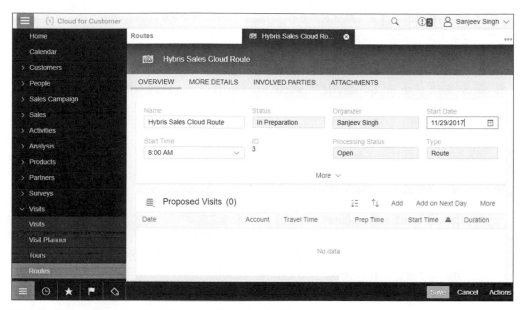

Figure 12.9 Maintaining Details on the New Route Screen

8. After maintaining all the route details, activate the route by selecting **Activate** in the **Actions** menu, as shown in Figure 12.10.

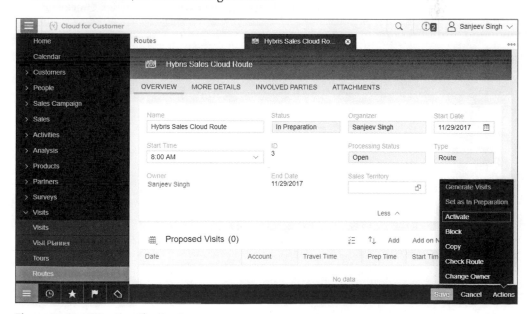

Figure 12.10 Activating the Route

On a final note, as of SAP Sales Cloud 1805, you can use the map view in your calendar to find accounts nearby and create visits on the fly. To do so, on your route in the calendar, once a nearby accounts has been identified, you can drag and drop the account onto your calendar to create a visits. The map will refresh and show your new visit plan for the day. If this visit plan works better for you, it can be saved at a new route or route template.

12.2.2   Executing Visits

Executing visits is nothing but working though the visits and capturing all the details. The key capabilities of visits execution are as follows:

- **Create, read, and update**
  You can create a new visit, display an existing visit, or even make changes to existing visits as needed. Visits are supported in both browsers and mobile devices (including offline access).

- **Check-in and check-out**
  You can capture check-in and check-out information for your visits to track time spent with contacts. When you check in to a visit, the status is updated to **In Process**, and the date/time and geo-location of the user are captured. Figure 12.11 shows an example of a check-in to a visit. As you can see, the **Check-In Date/Time** for the visit has been updated. When you complete your visit, you need to click **Check Out**.

Figure 12.11 Visit Check-In

A visit check-out marks the visit status as **Completed** and records the date/time and geo-location of the user upon check-out. Figure 12.12 shows the visit has been checked out. The **Check-Out Date/Time** field is updated, and the visit is marked as **Completed**.

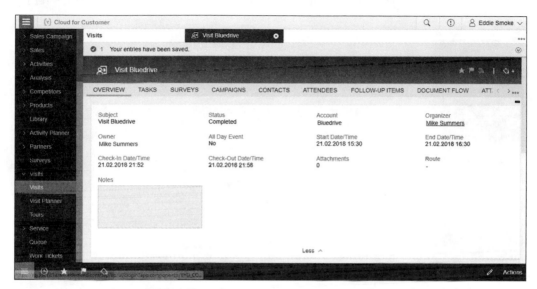

Figure 12.12 Visit Check-Out

- **Tasks or surveys**
  You can add or complete tasks and surveys or use questionnaires to capture specific information. Surveys in visits can also be completed offline through mobile devices.

- **Photos and attachments**
  You can take and upload photos to visits as well as make attachments of documents or survey results.

- **Promotional campaigns**
  You can view current promotional campaigns relevant for the customer or contact visited.

- **Sales documents**
  You can create sales quotations and sales orders for the customer that have resulted from the visit.

- **Follow-up transactions**
  You can easily create follow-up transactions from visits such as appointments, tasks, activities, opportunities, service tickets, and sales orders.

12.2.3 Analytics

Similar to other processes, SAP Sales Cloud offers standard out-of-the-box analytics for visit planning and execution as well. You can use some of these standard reports (see Figure 12.13) or design your own reports and dashboards (covered in Chapter 15).

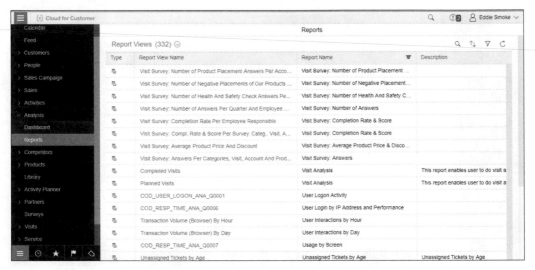

Figure 12.13 Reports Available for Visit Planning and Execution

Analytics provide you advanced content to report on survey responses from visits, visit completion with tasks and survey, and so on. Some of the reporting use cases available for visit planning and execution are as follows:

- Average price of competitor's products across stores
- Discount being offered across stores
- Accounts that are out of compliance
- Visit tracking

To navigate to the reports related to visits in SAP Sales Cloud, log in to SAP Sales Cloud, choose **Analysis • Reports**, and search for "*visit*", as shown in Figure 12.14. The standard visit reports are displayed for you to select from.

Figure 12.14 Searching for Visit Reports

For example, to view the Completed Visits report, click on that report in the list shown in Figure 12.14, select **Run Report**, and the report details will appear, as shown in Figure 12.15. You can now see the list of visits completed in the last 30 days, 90 days, 180 days, and 365 days. You can also change the selection to view completed visits for specific accounts. In a similar way, you can leverage other standard reports for visits to meet your reporting requirements.

Figure 12.15 Completed Visits Report

12.3   Retail Execution

As a specific application of visit planning and execution for the consumer products industry, retail execution enables consumer product companies to create a perfect store, improve product positioning and placement, enhance promotional effectiveness, track competition, and—most importantly—boost sales. The sales and marketing process in the consumer products industry spans across planning, preparation, execution, and analytics.

The retail execution functionality in SAP Sales Cloud allows you to manage your processes from planning to preparation to execution and finally analytics. Let's review the key capabilities available in retail execution to help you through all these processes.

12.3.1   Planning and Preparation

The first step in retail execution is to plan for the customer visits based on your unique market requirements, sales coverage, availability of sales team, and, most importantly, business objectives. Your geographical spread of customers to visit, how many routes you need, whether you want to use templates for the routes instead of creating routes from scratch each time, whether you want to conduct surveys as part of visits, and so on, are all activities in planning and preparation. In this section, we'll review the key capabilities within the retail execution part of SAP Sales Cloud that enable effective planning and preparation.

Routes

A route acts as the single point of entry for visit planning. You can create custom route plans for sales personnel or use templates to conveniently regenerate route plans for frequently used scenarios. Routes can then be used to generate mass visits for the specified sales representative. The key features of route planning in SAP Sales Cloud are as follows:

- Organizes a list of accounts to be visited with a defined schedule
- Adds accounts by search/query, including suggested accounts based on due/overdue accounts with no current visits planned, and honor account/sales-area-based visit frequency and recurrence when planning across proposed date ranges
- Allows the exclusion of days of the week from planning
- Honors account-level visiting hours

- Performs automatic rescheduling
- Realigns correct start and end times automatically for all visits upon time value changes
- Provides a map view of the daily route plan
- Provides a calendar view of the existing/proposed schedule after visit generation
- Manages visit attendees in route
- Generates mass visits from a route/link to generated visits within a route

After you've done the route planning, you need to create routes in your SAP Cloud for Customer system. To efficiently create routes, you should use route templates so that common information can be copied from one template to multiple routes. Route templates can be used to define frequently used route plans to quickly generate routes for any sales personnel in any desired date range. The key features of route templates are as follows:

- Defines sequence of accounts to be visited in a route per day
- Adds accounts by search/query with suggested accounts based on due/overdue accounts with no current visits planned
- Performs automatic rescheduling for quick route updates and realignment of correct start and end times automatically for all visits upon time value changes
- Allows employee/territory-based access control to be enabled in the route planning templates
- Generates new routes from templates
- Allows new route planning templates to be defined based on route generation history

Surveys

One of the key objectives of customer visits is to obtain information from the customer. When you're preparing for visits and creating templates for the routes, it's advisable to create surveys for visits so that customer information can be captured in a more structured way through surveys. In addition, you can define the survey questionnaire to conduct store audits such as how many items are on the shelf, how many items were sold the past week, and what is the performance of any promotions. In-store audits can be defined by creating dynamic surveys that allow you to gain insight by capturing customer information and sentiment anytime, anyplace. The key features of surveys are as follows:

- You can design checklists, product/competitor product audits, and external surveys.
- The survey validity (with start date/end date) as well as mandatory questions on a survey can be maintained to ensure that the required details are captured during a customer visit.
- You can enable prefilling of some answers based on previous answers. If needed, you can also enable the display of the survey form in matrix form.
- Retail execution allows you to design surveys with different question types, such as multiple choice, select single/multiple, amount, quantity, and text.
- You can report on surveys, questions, and answer categories to get complete visibility of your customer visits. You can also score surveys and create survey reports.
- You can use branching logic to move from one question to another question based on the response to questions.
- You can enable access control to surveys by assignment to sales/service organizations.
- You can maintain a question bank for surveys.
- You can search attachments to surveys.
- You can view aggregated results in HTML5, and granular survey results can be exported to Microsoft Excel.

In-Store Activities

You can define in-store activities using activity planner in retail execution. Using activity planner, you can organize tasks, surveys, and notes/attachments for visit determination. The key features of activity planner are as follows:

- You can define tasks and select surveys to be performed as part of an activity.
- You can define mandatory tasks and surveys, as well as enable automatic assignment of a task/survey to a visit.
- You can indicate the frequency of a task/survey to be performed once or every time.

Routing Rules

Routing rules allow you to assign the right activities to the right visits. You can use routing rules to specify conditions that determine which activity plans and relevant worklist items a visit should receive. The key features of routing rules are as follows:

- You can define multiple condition groups in AND/OR form.
- You can assign specific routing rules based on the account and visit attributes, including extension attributes.
- You can compile a list of activity plans to be determined upon a condition criteria match for further use.

Product Lists

Using product lists, you can enable the maintenance of product assortments that are relevant for a key account or point of sale. Product lists allow quick quote/order entry by prepopulating the sales document with the products in the list. The key features of product lists are as follows:

- You can maintain account and product combinations to indicate which products are valid for which accounts with time-based validity at the header and product levels.
- You can assign product lists at an account hierarchy or target group level and also control prepopulation of the list in the quote/order. Product lists can also be maintained at the sales area level.
- You can define a proposed quantity for each product to enable quick order entry.
- Using extension scenarios, you can enable product list fields to be carried forward to sales documents.

Account 360 and Contact Management

Account 360 and contact management delivers a holistic view of the customer and keeps field sales reps informed with the ability to capture, monitor, store, and track all critical information about customers, prospects, contacts, and partners. The key features of Account 360 and contact management are as follows:

- You can maintain key accounts and points of sales with a hierarchical relationship.
- You can view contextual KPIs, reports, and transactions to obtain a holistic view and be informed of any key alerts.
- You can generate an SAP ERP fact sheet for an account from SAP Cloud for Customer for complete transactional information.
- You can manage account teams, territory assignments, sales area assignments, and account relationships.

12

- You can manage prospects and ensure clean data with the configurable duplicate check.

- You can synchronize contacts in SAP Cloud for Customer with groupware such as Microsoft Outlook, Lotus Notes, and Gmail.

- You can enrich account and contact data from external sources such as D&B and InsideView.

12.3.2   Execution in Consumer Products

After completing all the activities related to visit preparation and planning, the next step is to ensure effective execution of visits. The retail execution functionality in SAP Sales Cloud offers key capabilities for sales reps to efficiently execute customer visits, gather information, and take action as needed during those visits.

Visit Execution

Visit execution enables field sales personnel to plan and record site visits and activities while on-site at the account. Decision-making and sales effectiveness are improved due to the real-time customer data and communication. Sales personnel can perform surveys and audits to monitor key areas in stores. The key features of visit execution are as follows:

- You can execute visits online or offline. They can capture visit check-in/check-out information, view last visit notes, and capture survey responses to visits.

- You can take and attach photos or other attachments to the visit or survey response as needed.

- You can manage visit contacts and attendees by adding new and updating existing contacts and attendees.

- You can view current promotional campaigns, collect outstanding payments, and manage follow-up actions such as sales quotes, opportunities, and appointments.

- You can use image recognition to ensure planograph compliance.

Image Intelligence

Image intelligence is the process of gathering information through collection of images. During the visit execution, sales reps can capture images from store product shelves to gather intelligence about how their products are performing in stores. SAP Sales Cloud allows you to capture images of store planograms.

Using image recognition and image intelligence, you can ensure consistent brand experience for planogram compliance. The key features of image intelligence are as follows:

- You can select a planogram and visually review what the planogram looks like in store.

- You can execute picture taking by using Ricoh's Ocutag technology to capture a series of photos and recognize products in store.

- You can analyze photos in real time.

- You can identify issues on the shelf, if any, and deliver corrective actions in store to ensure actual shelf compliance.

- You can evaluate store performance through reporting available in image intelligence.

Collections

Sales reps can review historical invoices and payments and then create payments for any open or overdue invoices online or offline. Key features of collections are as follows:

- You can view invoice and payment information online/offline across a single customer or across multiple customers.

- You can create payments for specific open invoices or assign payments to the oldest invoices.

- You can take payments in various payment methods such as cash or check. You can also capture signature of the payer and/or recipient directly from the app on mobile devices.

- You can configure the payment creation process based on your requirements. You can define whether the signature capture should be captured and stored with the payment, whether the signature capture is mandatory, and whether partial payments are accepted.

Creating and Tracking Orders/Quotes

During visit execution, sales reps need to answer customer questions related to sales quotes, sales orders, delivery, and invoices. With retail execution, sales reps can create and track SAP ERP sales orders and quotes from SAP Sales Cloud. The key features of this functionality are as follows:

- You can configure multiple order types to be downloaded from SAP ERP.
- You can search for and display orders and quotes from SAP ERP directly from SAP Sales Cloud. You can create and update both quotes and orders in SAP Sales Cloud, and changes are immediately updated in SAP ERP.
- You can leverage external pricing from SAP ERP so that items in orders and quotes simulate the exact pricing from SAP ERP.
- Standard SAP ERP capabilities, such as credit checks, order blocking status, cancellation status, and ATP checks, are possible directly from SAP Sales Cloud.

12.3.3   Analytics

Using standard delivered analytics, you can get real insights on data collected in store visits along with real-time access into order volumes to track the effectiveness of sales reps and store performance. The key features of retail execution analytics are as follows:

- The real-time analytical framework provides key insights to end users via interactive dashboards, configurable KPIs, and powerful advanced analysis tools.
- You can get insights into your team's activities and visits, as well as data collected in surveys in real time.
- The sales orders and order statuses can be tracked through dashboards and reports.
- Visibility to real-time analytics lets you manage top-selling products.
- The real-time integration to transaction data lets you identify and respond to exceptions and take corrective actions.
- You can leverage data from external systems to provide a holistic view to end users.

12.4   Configuring Visits

To enable visit planning in your SAP Sales Cloud deployment, you need to include visit planning in your scope. For the scoping questions, select the relevant questions related to visits under **Activity Management**, as shown in Figure 12.16.

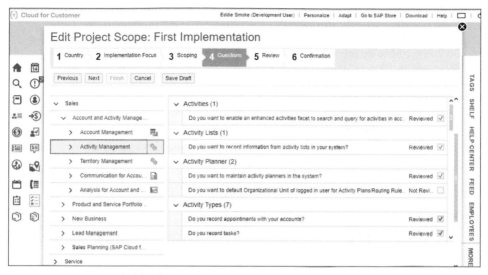

Figure 12.16 Including Visit Planning in the Scope of the Project

Scroll down all the questions for **Activity Management** related to activity planning such as **Activity Planner**, **Route**, and **Visits**, and then select the checkboxes per your activity planning requirements, as shown in Figure 12.16. The scoping questions related to **Activity Planner** are as follows:

- **Do you want to maintain activity planners in the system?**
  If you enable this checkbox, then the activity planner will be available in SAP Cloud for Customer.

- **Do you want to default Organizational Unit of logged in user for Activity Plans/ Routing Rules?**
  If you enable this checkbox, the organizational unit user will be defaulted in the activity plan and routing rules.

Similar to **Activity Planner**, you need to review the questions for **Route** and **Visits**. Figure 12.17 shows the 10 questions scoping questions for visits that you can review and enable as needed to meet your unique business requirements. Most of these questions are self-explanatory, but a few are described for you here:

- **You go to your customers' physical locations periodically. Do you want to record information from these visits in your system?**
  If enabled, the location from the browser will be used to update the location in the

visit. When you log in to the SAP Sales Cloud system, you get a prompt to enable location services in your browser.

- **Do you want to deactivate the check-in/check-out buttons for visits?**
  Standard check-in/check-out capability is available, but if you don't want to use it, you can disable it.

- **do you want to ensure that sales and service reps complete mandatory tasks and surveys before allowing them to close visits?**
  If enabled, users won't be able to close visits if mandatory tasks and surveys aren't completed.

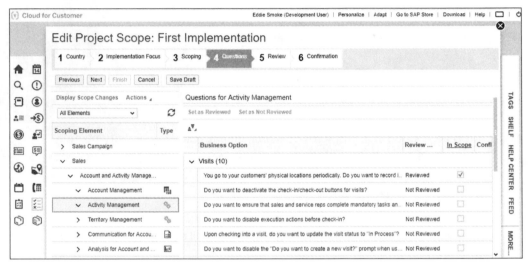

Figure 12.17 Scoping Questions for Visits

After you confirm this scope, activity planning and execution functionality will be enabled for your deployment. Click **Next** to review and finally confirm the scope.

12.5   Summary

In this chapter, we've covered the key components of the visit planning and execution capability available in SAP Sale Cloud that allows you to effectively manage the field activities of sales reps. We also reviewed how to enable visit planning in the scope of your implementation. Finally, we reviewed the application of visit planning and execution, known as retail execution, for the consumer products industry. In the next chapter, you'll learn about the sales planning and forecasting functionality in SAP Sales Cloud.

Chapter 13
Sales Planning and Forecasting

Sales planning and forecasting are sales management tools to carry out top-down sales planning across multiple dimensions, such as accounts, products, and territories, to create sales targets for sales reps and to create sales forecasts.

Sales planning is part of a business strategy to set out sales targets and tactics for your business, and it helps you identify steps to be taken to achieve those sales targets. Planning can help you choose sales strategies that are suited to your target market and identify sales tactics for your sales team to achieve your sales goals. A sales plan is a tool for your business that functions as a road map for your sales team over a set period of time. It's typically developed with a marketing plan or in conjunction with an overall business plan, and it covers a horizon of a few quarters or years.

Using the sales planning capabilities available in SAP Sales Cloud, you can define sales quotas for sales organizations and sales leadership and then distribute the sales quota down the hierarchy to sales reps, enabling companies to carry out top-down sales planning. Multiple dimensions, such as accounts, sales reps, sales organization, products, product categories, and territories, are available to carry out sales target planning and define sales quotas across these dimensions.

Similarly, the sales forecasting functionality available in SAP Sales Cloud allows users to create forecasts based on opportunities, accounts, sales organizations, territories, products, product categories, and forecast categories.

In this chapter, you'll learn how the sales planning and forecasting process works in SAP Sales Cloud, how to create a sales plan and sales forecast, and how to configure sales target planning in SAP Sales Cloud.

13.1 Sales Planning and Forecasting Process

Both sales planning and forecasting are sequential multistep processes from creation to activation. We'll go through those steps in the next section when we create a sales plan and forecast. Unless you activate the sales target plan and forecast, you can't make edits. In this section, we'll review the key features of sales planning as well as sales forecasting.

13.1.1   Sales Planning Features

Figure 13.1 shows an example of a sales target plan. By clicking the hyperlink under the **Plan Name** column, you can navigate to the plan's factsheet. In addition, you can open the plan in Microsoft Excel and work through it there. You can select **Edit**, **New**, **Copy**, **Delete**, and **Change** to work with sales plans as desired.

Figure 13.1 Sales Planning

Some of the unique features of sales plans are as follows:

- **Multiple dimensions**
  As mentioned earlier, sales planning can be carried out on multiple dimensions. While creating sales targets for sales reps in sales planning, you can define sales quotas or targets across many dimensions, such as employees, sales units, accounts, products, product categories, and territories. These planning dimensions allow you to determine the level of granularity for which you can create and track your plan.

- **Multiple horizons**
  The sales planning process allows you to create sales plans across multiple horizons or time periods. The horizon or time period can be as small as a month or as

long as a few years. Depending on your sales planning horizon, you can select the period for your sales plan.

- **Quantity or value**
  The sales target in a sales plan can be selected as quantity or value. For example, sales target for products can be selected in quantity such as the count or volume of products or in terms of absolute value or amount.

- **Multiple versions**
  If necessary, you can create multiple versions of your sales plan, such as a best-case scenario version and a worst-case scenario version. However, it's important to note that only one version of a sales plan can be active over a period of time or horizon at a time.

- **Microsoft Excel support**
  Sales plan integration with Excel enables users to use native Excel capabilities. You can use Excel to maintain your sales plan while still connected to the SAP Cloud for Customer system. For this functionality to work, you need to download SAP Cloud for Customer add-in for Microsoft Excel.

- **Sales plan distribution**
  The sales plan can be maintained in such a way that a sales quota from top management can be viewed by sales managers and then distributed down the hierarchy among their sales reps.

- **Track sales performance**
  Using predelivered analytics, graphical reports, and dashboards in SAP Sales Cloud, you can track your performance against the sales target plan on a real-time basis. Using key performance indicator (KPI) tiles on the home screen, you can keep your team updated on sales performance (planned vs. actual). You can also stay on top of sales in your key regions with the help of **Headlines** on your home screen.

13.1.2 Sales Forecasting

Figure 13.2 shows the example of sales forecasts. Similar to the sales plan, you can click the hyperlink under the **Name** column to navigate to the forecast's factsheet. You can see the forecast period, status, owner, and sales units for the sales forecast. From this screen, you can also open the forecast in Excel.

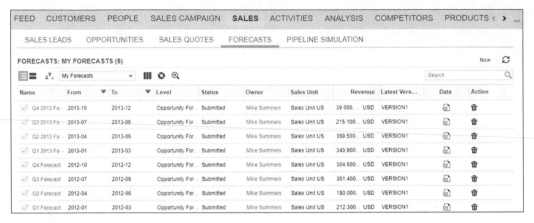

Figure 13.2 Sales Forecasts

Let's review some of the key features of forecasts:

- **Multidimensional forecasting**
  You can prepare a sales forecast based on opportunities, accounts, employees, sales organizations, territories, products, product categories, and forecast categories.

- **Analytical integration**
  Using the reporting interface in Excel, you can maintain and analyze sales forecasts. The predefined specialized dashboard available in SAP Cloud for Customer provides more insights into your sales forecasts.

- **Multilevel overrides**
  Each user can maintain overrides in his own forecasts at every level of the organizational hierarchy.

- **Business-user centricity**
  With a very simple and intuitive user interface (UI), it's much easier to create and update forecasts.

13.2   Planning and Forecasting Sales

With that brief background information on the unique capabilities of sales target planning and sales forecasting in SAP Sales Cloud, let's now review how sales target plans and forecasts are created and activated.

13.2.1   Creating and Activating Sales Target Plans

Before you create a sales target plan, it's worth noting that as of SAP Cloud for Customer version 1711, sales target planning is only available in the HTML5 UI (not in the responsive user interface [RUI]). Therefore, you need to switch to the HTML5 UI (by following the **Launch HTML5** link) before you can see the options to view, edit, or create a sales target plan. In this UI, you need to choose **Sales • Sales Target Planning** to get to the **SALES TARGET PLANNING** screen, as shown in Figure 13.3.

Figure 13.3 Sales Target Planning Screen in HTML5 UI

To create a new sales target plan, click on the **New** button on this screen, and a guided wizard begins with the following steps:

1. **Set General Properties**

   To define parameters for planning, as shown in Figure 13.4, enter the values for **Sales Unit, Horizon From/To** (month and year), **Plan Name**, and **Plan Currency**. The **Plan ID** is an auto-generated unique key based on the combination of sales unit and horizon. If the manager has already set a sales target for a given sales unit and horizon, then this field will get auto-populated. The current logged-in sales manager can then distribute these sales targets to his subordinates further down the organization hierarchy. After maintaining these details, click on **Next**.

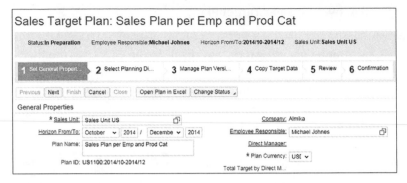

Figure 13.4 Creating a New Sales Target Plan

2. **Select Planning Dimensions**

On this screen, sales targets can be defined for the following six dimensions (see Figure 13.5):

- Territory
- Employee
- Product
- Account
- Product Category
- Sales Unit

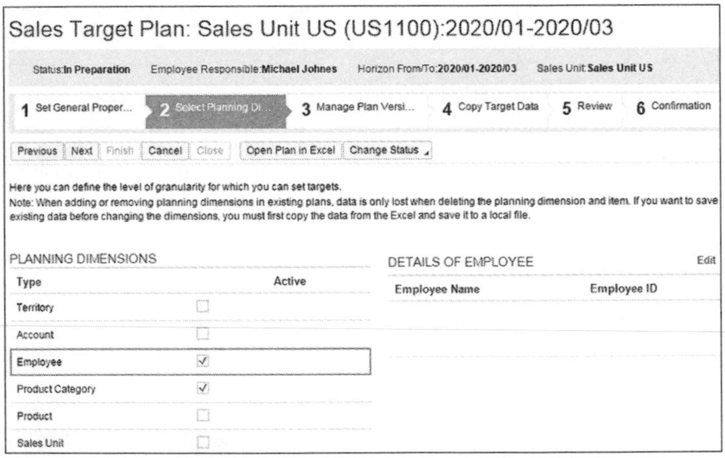

Sales Target Plan: Sales Unit US (US1100):2020/01-2020/03

Figure 13.5 Select Planning Dimension Step in Sales Target Plan Creation

These planning dimensions will determine the level of granularity on which the plan can be created. To add a planning dimension to a sales plan, select the required planning dimensions, and add master data. For example, if you want to add **Employee** as a planning dimension, click the **Edit** button to add employees for whom you want to set targets, as shown in Figure 13.6. Once you're satisfied, click **Next**.

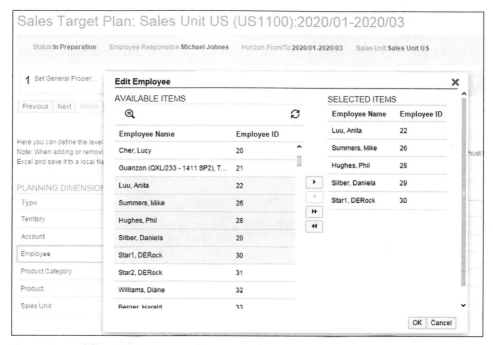

Figure 13.6 Adding Employee as a Planning Dimension

3. **Manage Plan Versions**

   On this screen, you can maintain multiple versions of a plan, for example, one plan for the best-case or optimistic scenario and another one for a more realistic or pessimistic scenario. Although you can have multiple versions of a sales plan, you can keep only one version of a sales plan active at a time, as shown in Figure 13.7. Once you've selected your active plan, click **Next**.

Figure 13.7 Active Version of a Sales Plan

4. **Copy Target Data**

On this screen, you define the target values for the planning dimensions selected in the previous step (see Figure 13.8). If you have a historical sales plan, you can copy the target from the previous plan and make changes as desired. However, if you don't have any historical plan data or targets, you can maintain the target values manually. Copying from the previous plan provides a baseline for planning your new target. For example, you can copy last year's target data and add 20% to that for this year's target.

Figure 13.8 Maintaining Target Data for the Sales Plan

Before making a copy from the previous year, a planner or sales manager can also review the performance through an embedded sales chart, as shown in Figure 13.8. For the copy target functionality to work properly, the source and target horizon should be for the same period (month-wise), although it can be for different years. Once you have copied the relevant data, click **Next**.

5. **Review**

On this screen, you review the sales plan information entered so far to make sure everything looks as expected before confirming the plan. To make changes, open the plan in Excel by clicking on the **Open Plan in Excel** link to maintain target values, as shown in Figure 13.9.

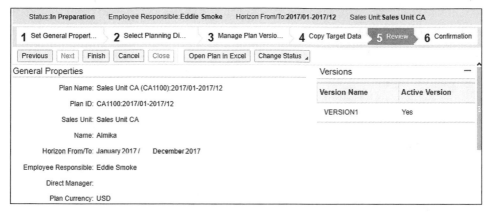

Figure 13.9 Reviewing or Opening the Plan in Excel to Make Updates

To maintain a sales plan in Excel, you need the SAP Cloud for Customer add-in for Microsoft Excel, which can be downloaded and installed from the SAP Cloud for Customer download menu. When you open a plan in Excel, you're required to enter your SAP Cloud for Customer login details before you can maintain the target values in Excel. In Excel, move to the **SAP Cloud for Customer** tab to use commands to maintain the values, as shown in Figure 13.10. If a copy was made from a previous sales plan, then that sales target data will already be available in Excel, and you can build on top of that instead of entering data from scratch. Otherwise, the values will be empty, and you have an option to start fresh.

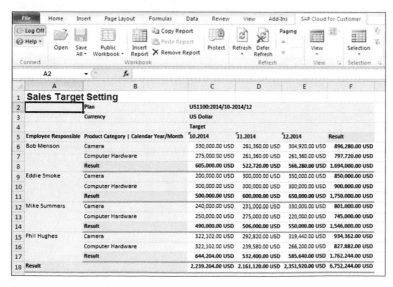

Figure 13.10 SAP Cloud for Customer Tab in the Microsoft Excel Add-In

6. Update the target values in the spreadsheet, and then click **Upload Input** to update the values in the SAP Cloud for Customer backend system, as shown in Figure 13.11.

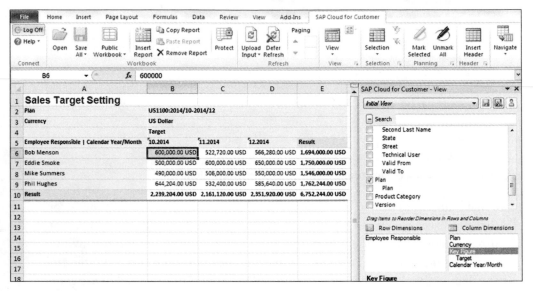

Figure 13.11 Upload Activity to Update Values in SAP Cloud for Customer

7. After you've completed maintaining the target values in the sales plan, the only activity left is to activate the plan. You can change the status to activate your sales target plan, as shown in Figure 13.12. After a sales manager activates a sales target plan, it becomes visible to his team members (direct reports per organizational structure setup in SAP Cloud for Customer).

Figure 13.12 Activating the Sales Target Plan

13.2.2   Creating a Sales Forecast

To create a new sales forecast, you select the **Forecasts** tab under the **Sales** work center, and click on the **+** button, as shown in Figure 13.13.

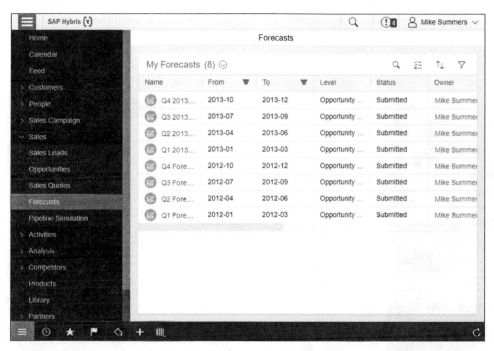

Figure 13.13 Creating a New Sales Forecast

The create screen is defaulted to create a forecast for the current quarter; however, you have the option to change the time horizon as desired. The forecast **Owner** and **Sales Unit** are automatically determined based on the credentials of the user creating the sales forecast. For admin users, the **Owner** and **Sales Unit** fields are editable, enabling an admin to create a sales forecast for any user. For product forecasts, users can forecast based on product quantity by including product quantity in the sales forecast.

As shown in Figure 13.14, the **From Year-Month** and **To Year-Month** dropdowns enable you to define the forecast time horizon. Only those opportunities will be included in the forecast that are marked relevant and that fall within this defined time horizon.

The **Level** field differentiates whether the forecast is based on opportunity header revenue or on product revenue. Under **Level**, you can choose **Opportunity Forecast** to create a forecast for opportunity header revenue, or you can choose **Product Forecast** to create a forecast for product revenue from items in opportunities. The **Opportunity Forecast** and **Product Forecast** choices for **Level** are available only for sales roles. For sales manager roles, you have two additional selections under **Level**: **Opportunity Aggregate** and **Product Aggregate**. The aggregate levels indicate that a manager is aggregating the forecasts submitted by direct reports and not fetching from the opportunities directly.

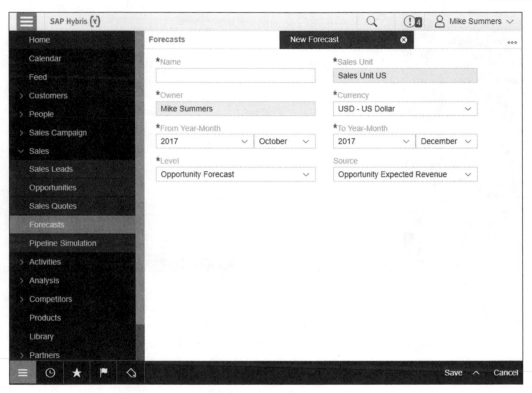

Figure 13.14 Entering Details on a New Forecast

The next important field in the forecast is **Source** (Figure 13.14), which enables you to indicate the source of the initial data. The value selection in this field depends on the **Level** of the forecast. For opportunity forecasts, the **Source** choices are **Expected Revenue** or **Weighted Revenue**. For **Product Forecast**, the only choice for **Source** is **Opportunity Product Revenue** or **Item Revenue**, as shown in Figure 13.15. Under the sales manager role for **Aggregate Forecasts**, the available **Source** is the **Roll-Up Forecast Revenue**.

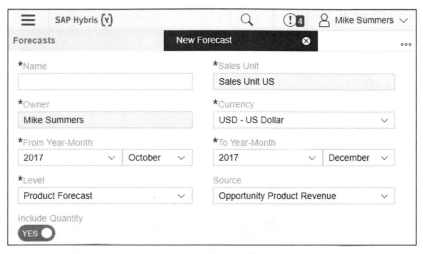

Figure 13.15 Selecting Level and Source in a Forecast

After maintaining the values, click **Save** to create the forecast. To evaluate all the options available to work through the forecast, let's open the recently created forecast, as shown in Figure 13.16. Here you can see that the forecast maintains the versions created with the submission details. It also has the **Active** flag to show if the forecast is active or inactive.

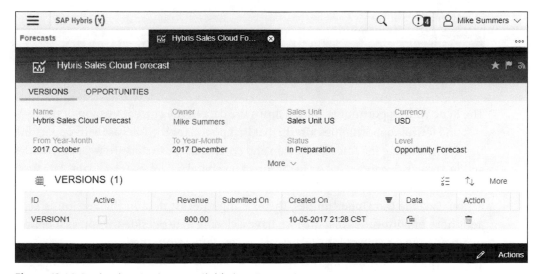

Figure 13.16 Reviewing Options Available in a Forecast

Forecasts can be opened in Excel, as shown in Figure 13.16, to edit values. However, this option to edit the forecast is only available for inactive forecasts. In a forecast, you can use **Submit** from the **Actions** menu to submit the forecast to your manager. After the forecast is submitted, it becomes **Active**, and you can no longer make changes to the forecast. However, your manager has the option to use an **Action** on the forecast to send the forecast back for revision.

In addition to **Submit**, there are additional actions available in forecasts, as shown in Figure 13.17. However, these actions are only available in inactive versions of sales forecasts.

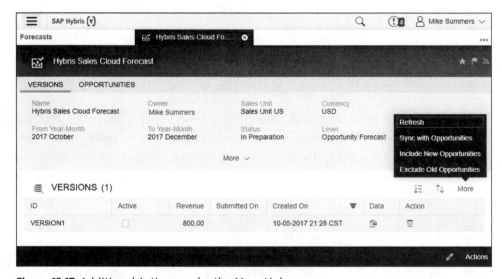

Figure 13.17 Additional Actions under the More Link

The Sync with Opportunities option drops the data in the current version of the forecast and fetches opportunities afresh; that is, it populates the forecast with opportunities data matching the forecast horizon and criteria. In the Include New Opportunities action, the existing forecast data in the forecast version is kept intact, and the data from the newly created opportunities in the forecast time horizon are added. In the last action, **Exclude Old Opportunities**, the existing forecast data in the version is kept, and those opportunities that are lost, have a closing date outside the forecast period, or are no longer relevant for the forecast are removed from the forecast.

To edit the forecast, you open it in Excel, as shown Figure 13.18. You need the SAP Cloud for Customer add-in for Microsoft Excel to edit forecasts in Excel. You can modify **Value/Volume** in the forecast, and click **Upload Input** to maintain changes in the system. The button toggles to Refresh after **Upload**. You can click the Refresh button to monitor whether the input is uploaded.

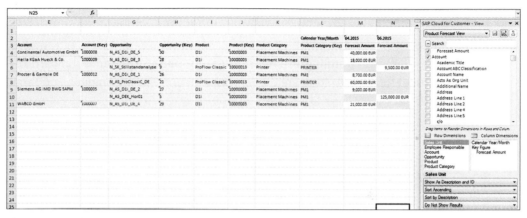

Figure 13.18 Editing Forecast in Excel

13.2.3   Analytics

SAP Sales Cloud offers standard out-of-the-box analytics for both sales target planning and sales forecasting to compare target data versus actual data, as shown in Figure 13.19.

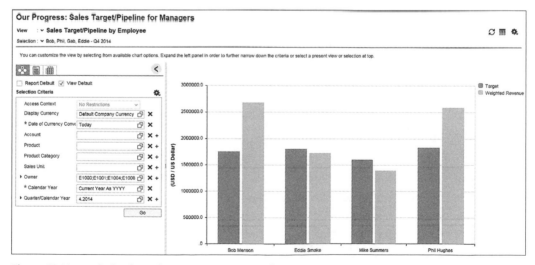

Figure 13.19 Analytics for Sales Target versus Pipeline

367

Sales managers can use the **Sales Target/Pipeline by Employee** report shown in Figure 13.19 to monitor their direct report's progress in relation to the sales targets. Sales managers can toggle the report view between **By Employees**, **By Month**, and so on, and employees can review their performance using My Progress: Sales Target/Pipeline for Employee report screen.

Similar to sales target planning analytics, SAP Sales Cloud also provides standard analytics for sales forecasts to compare the **Forecast Amount, Pipeline Amount**, and **Target Amount**, as shown in Figure 13.20.

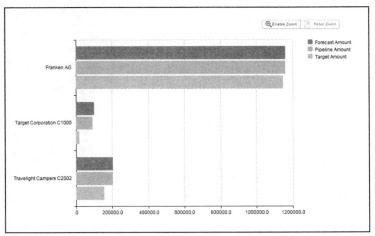

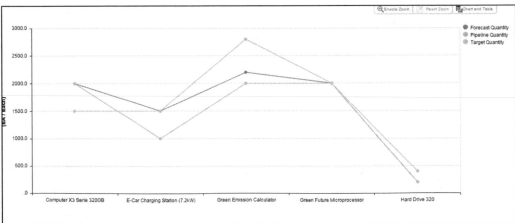

Figure 13.20 Example of Forecast Analytics

Using forecast analytics, you can analyze data based on standard queries. You can compare the forecast with the pipeline and target, review forecast variance between versions, and personalize these reports to add them to the home screen.

You can also create forecasting dashboards to compare target versus pipeline versus opportunity, as shown in Figure 13.21. You can click on a data point to pass a filter to subsequent dashboard reports.

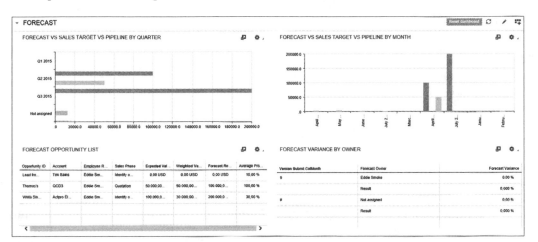

Figure 13.21 Forecasting Dashboards

13.3   Configuring Sales Planning and Forecasting

The configuration or fine-tuning is only relevant for sales target planning. There are no configurations available for sales forecasts. To configure sales target planning, you log in to the system as administrator, and go to **Business Configuration • Implementation Projects • Select a Project • Edit Project Scope**. Under the **Scoping** tab, click on **Sales** (scoping element), and check/select **Sales Planning** along with the other items under it, as shown in Figure 13.22. After that, click **Next** to review and confirm the configuration.

Figure 13.22 Configuring Sales Target Planning

13.4   Summary

In this chapter, you've learned about the importance of sales target planning and sales forecasting in the overall sales management process. You've seen how sales target planning can be done across multiple dimensions, such as accounts, products, employees, and territories, and how you can track plan versus actual data for these sales targets using standard analytics. We also covered how sales forecasts can be created for various levels and sources to conveniently forecast based on opportunity revenue or product revenue. Finally, we covered what configuration options are available for sales target planning. The sales forecast doesn't require any configuration or fine-tuning. With that, we're ready to review Account 360 and sales intelligence as covered in the next chapter.

Chapter 14

Account 360 and Sales Intelligence

Providing a 360-degree view of customers has been the most promised objective of all customer relationship management applications. SAP Sales Cloud provides complete account information from backend systems in the account details view.

Sales reps crave actionable insights and intelligence on their accounts to uncover leads and sales opportunities. One of the critical requirements of any sales application is to provide information, alerts, and sales intelligence about accounts and contacts from internal and external sources. From internal systems such as SAP ERP and SAP Business Warehouse (SAP BW), you can get transactional details about the accounts such as historical sales orders, payments history, and shipment details.

For sales reps to have easy access to information on accounts or prospects, it's important that information from internal and external sources is presented effectively in account views. Using the Account 360 view in SAP Sales Cloud, you can combine these details from SAP ERP and SAP BW and display them on the account details view in SAP Sales Cloud to provide complete account information to sales reps. It helps you get a holistic 360-degree view of accounts in SAP Sales Cloud. In this chapter, you'll learn about the details of Account 360, ERP Cockpit, and ERP Customer Factsheet from SAP CRM and SAP ERP. There are some specific integration requirements for these functionalities to work. We'll cover those requirements as well along with these functionalities.

14.1 Account 360

The Account 360 setup enables you to bring on premise SAP ERP business intelligence sales document data into the account details view to provide you with complete information about the sales transactions for selected accounts, as shown in

Figure 14.1. For the Account 360 functionality to work, SAP Cloud for Customer must be integrated with SAP ERP.

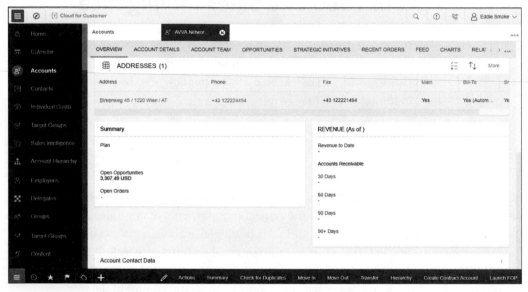

Figure 14.1 Account 360 View

14.1.1 SAP Cloud for Customer Set Up

You must enable **Account 360 Integration** in the **Scoping Element** of **Business Configuration** to include this capability in the solution scope. To do this, log in to the HTML5 user interface (UI) with the admin role, choose **Business Configuration • Implementation Project • Edit Project Scope • Implementation Focus • Scoping,** and then expand the scoping element as **Communication and Information Exchange • Integration with External Applications • 360 Overview – Account**. Then you need to enable the **360 Overview – Account** in scope, as shown in Figure 14.2.

The **360 Overview – Account** page relies on account information from SAP BW. To include SAP BW integration in scope, you need to enable the **Integration with Central Analytics** question by expanding the **Communication and Information Exchange • Integration with External Applications and Solution • Integration with Central Analytics** scoping elements, as shown in Figure 14.3.

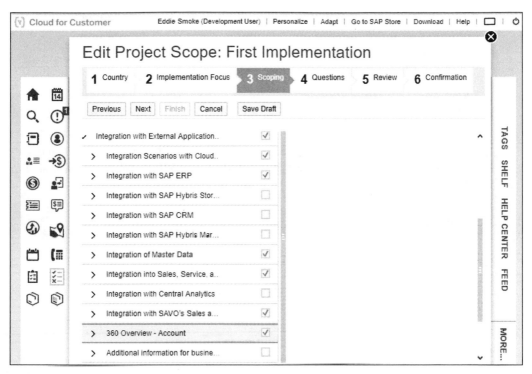

Figure 14.2 Including 360 Overview – Account in Scope

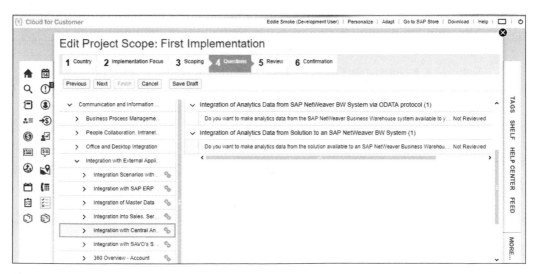

Figure 14.3 Including SAP BW Integration in Scope

After including the required integration in scope for **360 Overview – Account**, you need to set up communication settings in SAP Sales Cloud and SAP ERP.

On the SAP Sales Cloud side, you first need to define a communication system. A communication system represents an external system that is used for application integration. Communication systems can be, for example, external time recording or master data systems. Before you can use a communication system in an application integration scenario, you need to create a communication arrangement. To create a communication system, log in to SAP Sales Cloud under the admin role, and navigate to **ADMINISTRATOR • GENERAL SETTINGS**. Under **Integration**, choose **Communication Systems**, as shown in Figure 14.4.

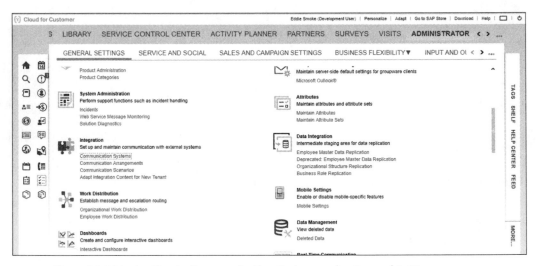

Figure 14.4 Navigation to Communication System under General Settings

When you choose **Communication Systems**, you're taken to **Communication Systems: All Communication Systems**, as shown in Figure 14.5. Here you can see the list of communication systems currently configured in the system.

To create a new communication system, click on **New** to open the **New Communication System** screen, as shown in Figure 14.6.

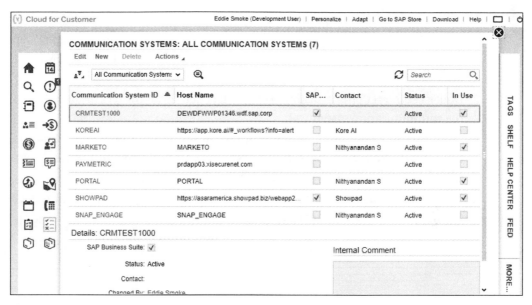

Figure 14.5 All Communication Systems Configured in the System

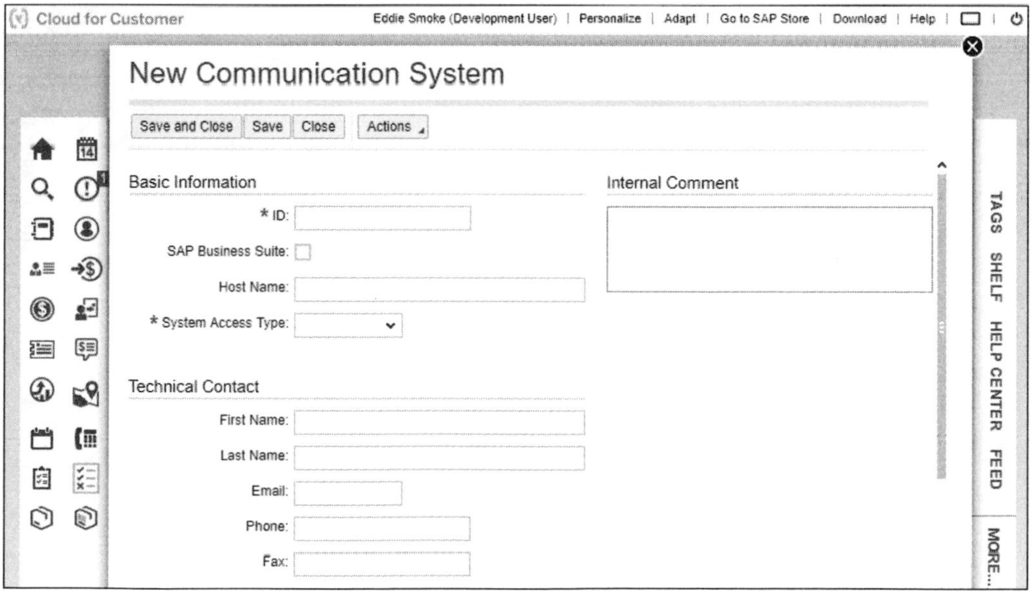

Figure 14.6 Creating a New Communication System

Here you maintain the details of the new communication system as follows:

1. Under **Basic Information** section, enter the details of the communication system such as **ID** (a unique identification for the communication system), **Host Name** of the system you're connecting to, and **System Access Type** (choose **Internet**).

2. Under **Technical Contact**, maintain the contact details for the technical contact for the communication system.

3. Scroll further down to see the **System Instances** section. Choose **Add Row**, and maintain the **System Instance ID** (of the system you're connecting to) and the **Preferred Application Protocol** as applicable (see Figure 14.7).

4. After maintaining all the details, save and activate the newly created communication system by choosing **Actions • Set to Active**.

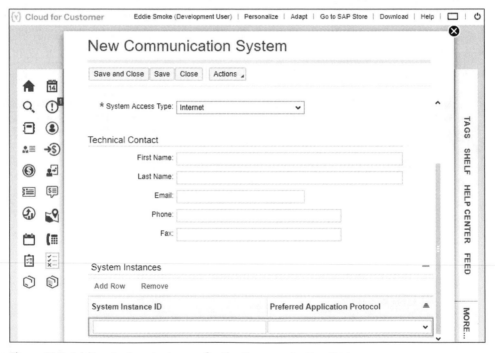

Figure 14.7 Adding System Instances for the Communication System

To use the communication system just created, you need to create a communication arrangement under administrator by choosing **ADMINISTRATOR • GENERAL SETTINGS** and then clicking on **Communication Arrangements**, as shown in Figure 14.8.

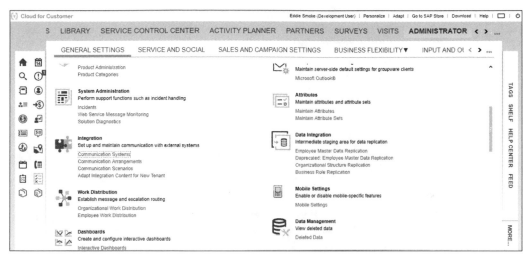

Figure 14.8 Navigating to Communication Arrangements

You're taken to the **COMMUNICATION ARRANGEMENTS: ALL COMMUNICATION ARRANGEMENTS** screen, as shown in Figure 14.9.

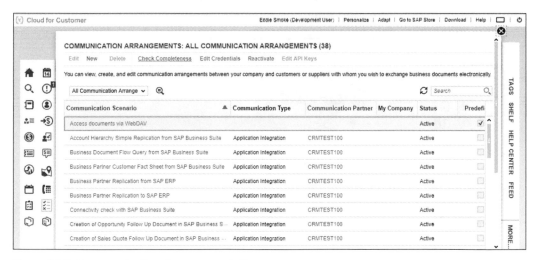

Figure 14.9 Communication Arrangements Screen

To create a new communication arrangement, choose **New**. You're taken to a guided process to create a new communication arrangement, as shown in Figure 14.10.

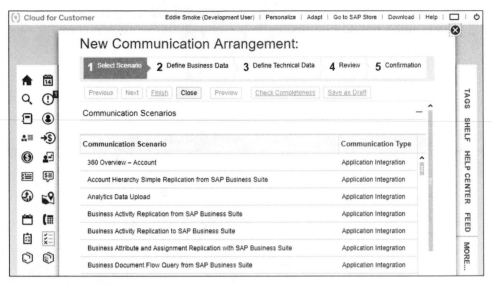

Figure 14.10 Creating a New Communication Arrangement

First, select the communication scenario **360 Overview – Account**, and then choose **Next**. You're taken to the **Define Business Data** step, as shown in Figure 14.11.

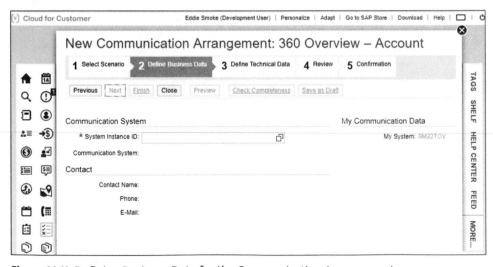

Figure 14.11 Defining Business Data for the Communication Arrangement

Here you maintain the **System Instance ID** (of the communication system created earlier in this section) and choose **Next** to go to the **Define Technical Data** step, as shown in Figure 14.12.

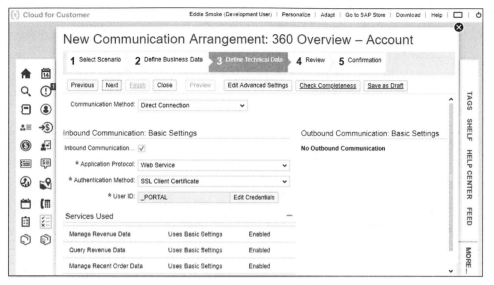

Figure 14.12 Setting Up Technical Data for the Communication Arrangement

Here you maintain the inbound communication settings and then choose **Next** to review and finally confirm the settings to activate the communication arrangement.

As a final step of integration configuration in SAP Sales Cloud, you expose the data source for ID mapping by going to **ADMINISTRATOR • BUSINESS ANALYTICS • Design Data Sources**, and select **Object ID Mapping** (Figure 14.13).

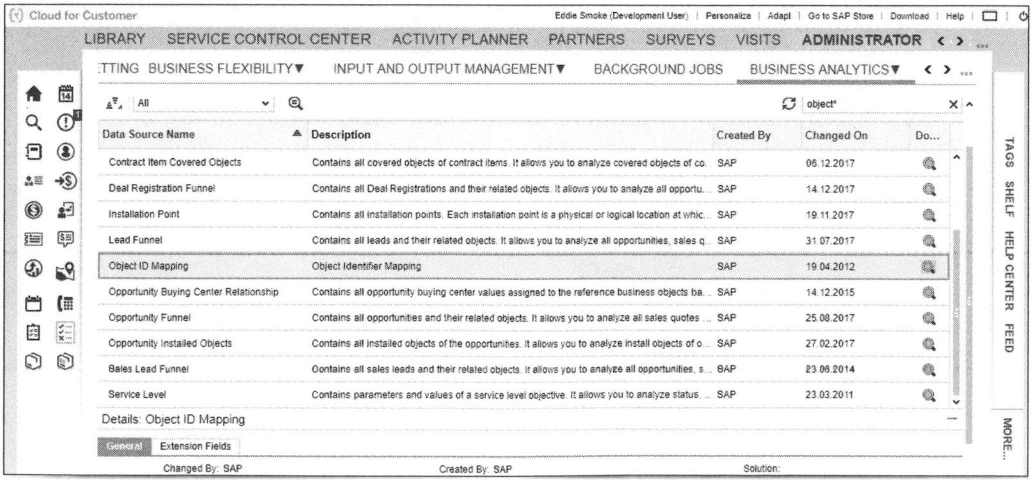

Figure 14.13 Enabling Object ID Mapping

14.1.2   SAP ERP Set Up

After completing the required settings in SAP Sales Cloud, you need to set up the SAP ERP system. First, you create consumer proxies in the SAP ERP system, and then create and configure logical ports via Transaction SOAMANAGER in the SAP ERP system. Open Transaction SOAMANAGER in your SAP ERP system to go to the **Web Service Configuration** screen, as shown in Figure 14.14.

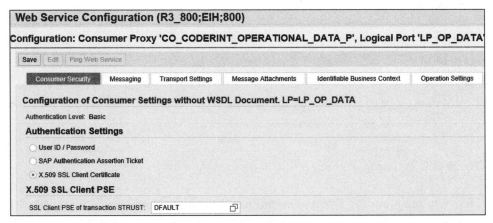

Figure 14.14 Web Service Configuration in SAP ERP

Here you maintain the **Authentication Settings** and then go to the **Messaging** step, as shown in Figure 14.15. Select the **Reliable Messaging** protocol as well as **Message ID (Synchronous)** for transfer.

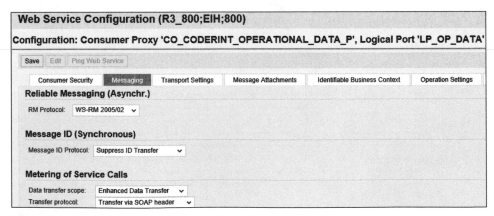

Figure 14.15 Messaging Settings for Web Service Configuration

After maintaining the messaging setting, choose the **Transport Settings** tab, as shown in Figure 14.16. Here you maintain the **URL Access Path, Computer Name of Access URL, Port Number of Access URL, URL Protocol Information**, and so on. After making these settings, choose **Save** to save your changes. You've now successfully completed the required SAP ERP settings.

Web Service Configuration (R3_800;EIH;800)

Configuration: Consumer Proxy 'CO_CODERINT_OPERATIONAL_DATA_P', Logical Port 'LP_OP_DATA'

| Save | Edit | Ping Web Service |

| Consumer Security | Messaging | Transport Settings | Message Attachments | Identifiable Business Context | Operation Settings |

Transport Binding

* URL Access Path:	/cxf/COD/ERP/queryidmapping
Computer Name of Access URL:	iflmaptr101aaio110avtaiot-aaio110.intaas.hana.ondem;
Port Number of Access URL:	443
URL Protocol Information:	HTTPS ⌄
Logon Language:	Language of User Context ⌄
Name of Proxy Host:	
Port Number of Proxy Host:	
User Name for Proxy Access:	
Password of Proxy User:	
Make Local Call:	No Call in Local System ⌄
* Transport Binding Type:	SOAP 1.1 ⌄
Maximum Wait for WS Consumer:	0
Optimized XML Transfer:	None ⌄
Compress HTTP Message:	Inactive ⌄
Compress Response:	True ⌄

Figure 14.16 Transport Settings for Web Service Configuration

In the next section, you'll learn about the ERP Cockpit.

14.2   ERP Cockpit

Sometimes while working in SAP Cloud for Customer, you might need to make changes to transactions in SAP ERP. For that, you first need to log in to SAP ERP, which isn't a very effective way of working. SAP Cloud for Customer offers the ERP Cockpit to make changes to SAP ERP transactions directly from SAP Cloud for Customer. Figure 14.17 shows an example of launching the ERP Cockpit from SAP Sales Cloud.

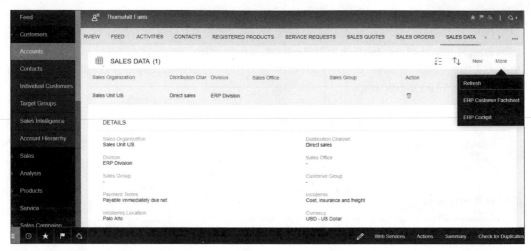

Figure 14.17 Launching the ERP Cockpit

After you choose the **ERP Cockpit** link from SAP Sales Cloud, the transaction from SAP ERP is available to edit, as shown in Figure 14.18. Here you can make the required changes in the transaction.

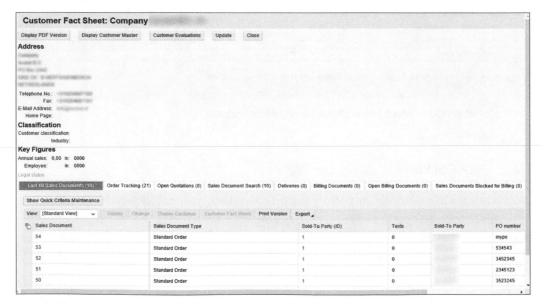

Figure 14.18 Viewing SAP ERP Transactions through the ERP Cockpit

To enable the ERP Cockpit, you need to enable the mashup by updating the URL via **ADMINISTRATOR • Mash up Authoring**. Then, search for "ERP Account Cockpit" (**SM00105**), as shown in Figure 14.19.

URL MASHUP OVERVIEW: ERP ACCOUNT COCKPIT

Status: **Active**   Mashup Category: **Productivity & Tools**   Port Binding: Mashup ID: **SM00105**   Mashup Name: **ERP Account Cockpit**

| Close | Copy |

General Information

			Administrative Information	
Mashup Category:	Productivity & Tools		Created By:	SAP
Port Binding:			Created On:	23/12/2014 09:59
Mashup ID:	SM00105		Changed By:	K8T4UX1J0H7
Mashup Name:	ERP Account Cockpit		Changed On:	18/02/2016 13:37
Description:	Open ERP account cockpit			
*Status:	◉ Active ○ Inactive			

URL Information

URL:	http:// /sap/bc/webdynpro/sap/cfs_application Edit URL Preview
HTTP Method:	GET
Window Features:	☐

| Add | Remove |

URL Parameter	Constant	Parameter Binding	Mandatory
CUSTOMER			☐
sap-language	EN		☐
applid	O2C-CUSTOMER_COCKPIT		☐
salesorg			☐
channel			☐
division			☐
sap-wd-configid	CUSTOMER_COCKPIT_POWL1		☐

Figure 14.19 Enabling Mashup

Then you need to update the URL to connect to the SAP ERP system. To identify the URL from the SAP ERP system, log in to SAP ERP and execute Transaction SICF. After this setup is done, you can launch the ERP Cockpit from the SAP Cloud for Customer account to quickly edit transactions in SAP ERP.

The configuration for the ERP Cockpit is fast and easy. SAP ERP provides a standard customer cockpit that can be personalized by the user. Further customization of the ERP Cockpit is also possible but requires custom coding on the customer cockpit functionality in SAP ERP.

In the SAP ERP system, go to Transaction SFW5, and activate business function SD_01.

Start Transaction SICF in SAP ERP by entering "CFS_APPLICATION" in the **ServiceName** field and pressing ⌊F8⌋. When you right-click on the screen and select **Test Service**, a web browser opens with a URL. Copy this URL to Notepad, and use it in the mashup authoring.

In the next section, we'll review the ERP Customer Factsheet.

14.3   ERP Customer Factsheet

To launch the ERP Cockpit to edit SAP ERP transactions, you need a special setup as covered in the previous section. However, there is another way of launching customer information from SAP ERP or SAP CRM without a special setup through the ERP Customer Factsheet. The ERP Customer Factsheet allows you to get a holistic view of account information from SAP ERP or SAP CRM from SAP Cloud for Customer. You don't need a virtual private network (VPN) connection or any special setup to view the ERP Customer Factsheet in SAP Cloud for Customer from SAP ERP or SAP CRM.

Figure 14.20 shows the ERP Customer Factsheet launched from SAP Sales Cloud.

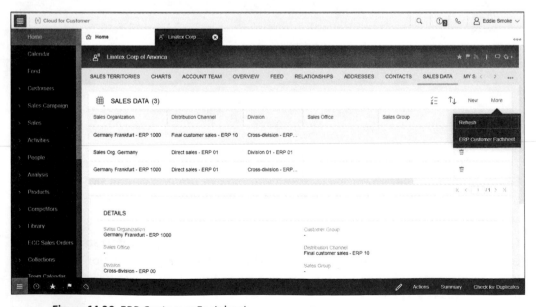

Figure 14.20 ERP Customer Factsheet

When you select the **ERP Customer Factsheet** link, you're prompted to select the customer information such as **Customer Number** and **Sales Area Data** (**Sales Organization**, **Distribution Channel**, and **Division**), as shown in Figure 14.21.

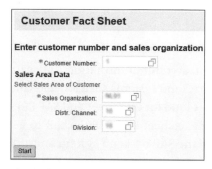

Figure 14.21 Selecting Customer Information to Display the ERP Customer Factsheet

After you select the customer details, click **Start**, and the ERP Customer Factsheet is displayed (see Figure 14.22).

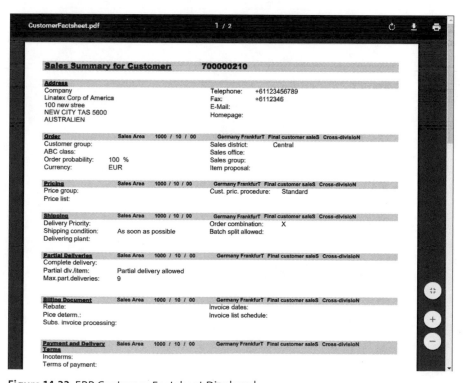

Figure 14.22 ERP Customer Factsheet Displayed

The only difference in the ERP Customer Factsheet is that you can't edit any information here. If you need to make edits to SAP ERP transactions, then you need to use the ERP Cockpit.

14.4   Summary

In this chapter, you've learned how to augment account information and gain account intelligence with additional details from backend systems such SAP ERP and SAP CRM. Out-of-the-box integration between SAP Cloud for Customer and SAP ERP/ SAP CRM allows you to launch the ERP Customer Factsheet and ERP Cockpit to get complete visibility into account information from the SAP backend system and also make edits to SAP ERP transactions directly from SAP Sales Cloud.

In the next chapter, you'll learn about sales reports and dashboards available in SAP Cloud for Customer.

Chapter 15

Sales Reports and Dashboards

SAP Cloud for Customer provides integrated analytics based on real-time data to help you monitor the books of your business and make informed decisions. You can use standard and custom reports along with interactive dashboards for sales analytics as covered in this chapter.

The reporting functionality in SAP Cloud for Customer is consistent throughout all the reports for SAP Sales Cloud. It offers extensive functionality that allows you to edit existing report views; define various selection criteria; and add, move, and remove fields and key figures as needed. The out-of-the-box analytics features are integrated in the solution to support and monitor business processes, helping business users make informed decisions with real-time data. Unlike other data warehouse solutions, there is no persistency in a separate business warehouse layer. You're reporting on live application data. It's worth noting that analytics data in SAP Cloud for Customer is also access context sensitive. It enables data sources to be associated with access contexts to ensure that data is directed to users who are allowed to view the data. There are primarily four types of analytics features: standard reports (predelivered with the solution), custom reports that you create, interactive dashboards that you assemble, and key performance indicator (KPI) tiles that you monitor on the home page.

In this chapter, we'll cover the standard out-of-the-box reports in SAP Cloud for Customer, custom reports, and interactive dashboards.

15.1 Standard Reports

SAP Cloud for Customer provides hundreds of sales-related standard reports that you can use to meet your business reporting requirements for sales reps and sales managers. To view these standard reports, you can navigate to **Analysis** and then choose the **Reports** work center, as shown in Figure 15.1. This list includes standard reports for accounts, activities, leads, opportunities, campaigns, and so on. You can review these reports and identify those that are best suited to your unique business requirements.

Figure 15.1 Standard Reports Delivered with SAP Cloud for Customer

You can filter the reports based on report category or favorite reports. You can also use the free-text search for the reports by typing keywords in the **Search** field, as shown in Figure 15.2. As shown in Figure 15.2 you can also click the flag or star (favorite) icons next to the specific reports or open the report in Microsoft Excel through the **Actions** menu.

To open a report, click on the **Report Name** hyperlink, and the **Reports** screen opens, as shown in Figure 15.3, for **Opportunity Pipeline Report**. In the **Selection** area on the right side of the screen, you can make the appropriate selections (some are required and some optional) based on what you want to report on.

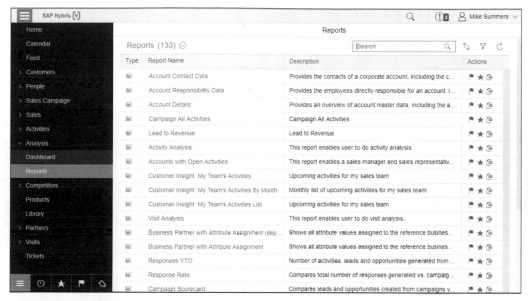

Figure 15.2 Ability to Search for Reports

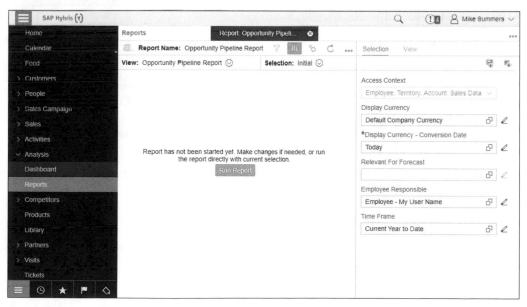

Figure 15.3 Report Selection Screen

After adding selection parameters, click **Run Report**, and the report is displayed, as shown in Figure 15.4.

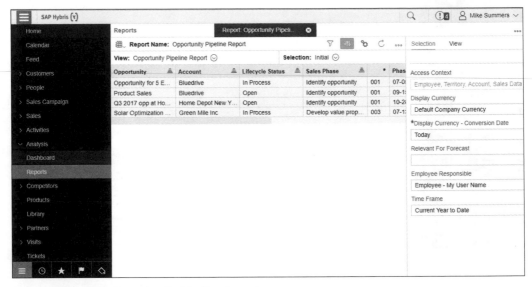

Figure 15.4 Opportunity Pipeline Report

The report can be viewed in various output formats, such as table, bar, pie, or heat map, by selecting the corresponding view, as shown in Figure 15.5.

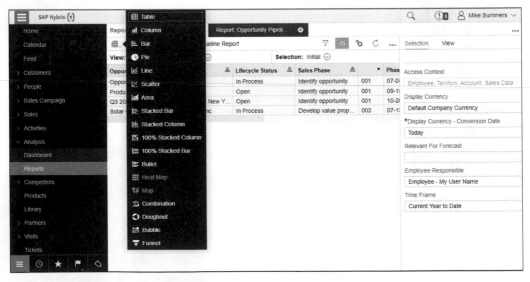

Figure 15.5 Changing the Report Format

For example, if you choose **Column** chart instead of **Table**, then the report is displayed in the chart format, as shown in Figure 15.6. You can hover over the chart to see the chart values.

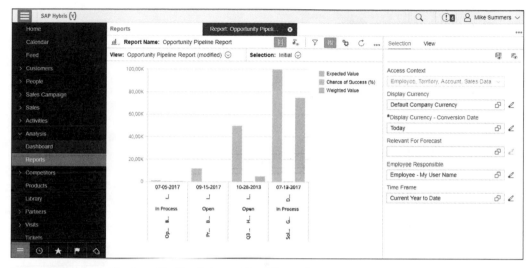

Figure 15.6 Report Displayed in the Column Chart Format

On the right side of the screen, you can select **View** to add or remove fields from report rows and columns. You can also arrange those fields within the report by moving fields up or down, as shown in Figure 15.7.

Figure 15.7 View to Update Row and Column Fields

To add new fields to a row or column per your requirements, click on the **+** icon next to **Row Fields** or **Column Fields**, and a list of available fields for selection for views appears, as shown in Figure 15.8. Select the desired fields from this list, and click **OK** to add the fields to your report view.

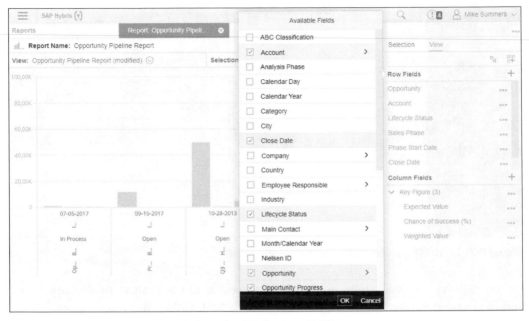

Figure 15.8 Available Fields for Selection for Row Fields

To remove fields in the view or move fields around in the report, click on the three dots next to the fields. The following options will appear regarding field movement: **Move Up**, **Move Down**, **Remove**, **Move the Field from Row to Column,** and **Move the Field from Column to Row** (if a field is allowed for both row and column).

If a field isn't available as part of the report, you can make it available using the **Add Fields** icon under **View**. You can specify that this new field needs to be available **In Report**, **In Selection**, or **As Hierarchy** (see Figure 15.9). After making selections for the fields, click **OK,** and the fields are added to the report or selection screen as selected.

As mentioned earlier, you can open these reports in Microsoft Excel (you need SAP Cloud for Customer Add-In for Microsoft Excel) to perform advanced analysis on the report. You can create or save views, filter, drill down, and set characteristics and key figure properties using the sidebar menu. In Excel, you can also save public or private workbooks and change variable values as needed. You can use the report data in Excel functions, such as pivot tables, for further analysis of data available in the report. The SAP Cloud for Customer add-in for Microsoft Excel allows you to add multiple reports in one workbook. You can use this feature to compare data across repots.

Figure 15.9 Option to Add Fields: In Report, In Selection, and As Hierarchy

Let's review some of the key features of standard reports delivered with SAP Cloud for Customer:

- End users can easily personalize and maintain their own views and selections without needing any help from IT. It's key for business users to analyze their data and take timely actions as needed.
- Data in reports can be viewed in different charts and tables per user preference. You can easily drill down into reports to view details on specific sections, as well as zoom in on charts to change the scale and view data closely.
- In reports, you can maintain chart and table settings and also maintain field-specific settings, such as sorting, scaling, ID and description display, and result rows (subtotals and totals).
- You can mark your own favorite reports.

- You can print reports, send reports via email, or export reports to Excel for further analysis.
- The Excel add-in enables users to work on Excel while still connecting to real-time data in SAP Cloud for Customer. Data from reports inserted in Excel can be referenced, mapped, and saved as part of a document. By logging into SAP Cloud for Customer from Excel, data can be refreshed to include any subsequent activity recorded in SAP Cloud for Customer.
- You can modify a report to perform ad hoc analysis and save your changes as a new view of the report.
- You can highlight your data using exceptions; for example, missed targets can be shown in red.
- You can maintain conditions, such as show the top 10 opportunities.
- Data in reports can be shown in hierarchies.
- You can pass filters and navigate from one report to the other.

15.2   Custom Reports

If standard reports can't meet your reporting requirements, you can create custom reports by using the extensive and flexible business analytics features. You can easily create custom reports by using the guided procedures available in SAP Cloud for Customer. You can control the visibility of those reports by assigning specific business roles or work centers as needed. If you've defined custom fields in your SAP Cloud for Customer solution and want to include those fields in a report, you can add them to data sources or reports. In addition, you can join or combine heterogeneous data sources—your own or those delivered with the solution—as well as create custom calculated measures and comparison metrics. To create any custom report, you need following specific processes:

- **Data sources**
  When you start the process of creating a report using the Report Wizard, the first step is to select a data source. SAP Cloud for Customer ships with several predefined data sources. If needed, you can also create and edit your own data sources to suit your business requirements and use those data sources for your reporting purposes. To create your data sources, you combine or join data sources to merge data into a new data source. You can also create a cloud data source by importing

outside information; for example, you could import outside temperature data and then correlate it with your sales volume or profitability.

- **Key figures**

  Key figures are data items with numeric values that have an associated unit of measure or currency, such as a pipeline value or quantity of products. You can define the data appearing in key figures by setting up restricted or calculated key figures. A restricted key figure is restricted to a specific characteristic value and is often created for comparison metrics. However, a calculated key figure is determined using calculation rules or formulas. You can create a calculated key figure from existing key figures in the selected data source.

  For example, if you choose an existing figure (e.g., revenue), restrict it to last year in the United States, and then run the report, you can see the total revenue compared to last year's US total revenue. To find the incremental revenue per day invested in a sales cycle of an opportunity worth $250,000 with the sales cycle starting on November 1st and ending on December 15th, you create a calculation to divide the total revenue of $250,000 by 45 days in the time period.

- **Characteristics**

  Characteristics are alphanumeric, numeric, or text values. Examples of characteristics are product ID, opportunity status, and account ID. You select characteristics for restricted key figures, such as accounts, opportunities, countries, or industries. You set properties to define additional behavior for specific characteristics such as **Display Settings** to define how the characteristic appears and is used in the report, **Value Selections** to add restrictions to the characteristic values that appear in the report, and **Hierarchy Settings** to define how any hierarchical data associated with the characteristic is used in the report. For example, you can set properties to display the customer characteristic by location.

- **Report assignment**

  To make the reports available to users, you assign the reports to specific work centers and business roles. A report must be assigned to a work center to be available to users. You assign a report to a work center when you create or edit a report. If you've enabled the assignment of reports to roles (in the **Administrator Analytics • Settings** fine-tuning activity), then you can also assign reports to business roles. This assignment of reports by role restricts which users can view the reports on the assigned work center.

- **Views**

  Views enable you to set up one or more variations on which key figures and characteristics appear in the report and the type of chart that appears for the report. After you assign a report to a work center, you can select the view that appears in the end user reports list. You create a view by choosing key figures and characteristics for columns and rows in a table, and then selecting a chart type to best represent that data. When you create a view, you can also define conditions and exceptions by key figures that alter how data is presented based on rules and thresholds. For conditions, you create a condition to limit the data shown to that which fits the defined rules. For exceptions, you set a threshold beyond which the data display is altered to show an alert indicator.

To create a custom report, log in as administrator, and follow the navigation path **Administrator • Business Analytics**, as shown in Figure 15.10. You must be in the HTML5 user interface (UI) to create custom reports under the administrator login.

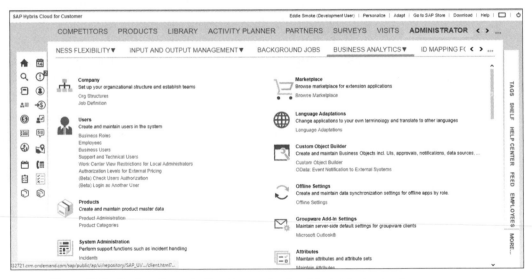

Figure 15.10 Custom Reports Creation under the Administrator Login

If you click on **BUSINESS ANALYTICS**, you'll see the options to **Design Reports, Design Data Sources**, and **Design Key Figures**. To create a new custom report, click on **Design Reports** to open the **DESIGN AND ASSIGN REPORTS** screen, as shown in Figure 15.11.

To create a new report, click on **New** and then **Report**. A wizard screen appears to create a new report, as shown in Figure 15.12.

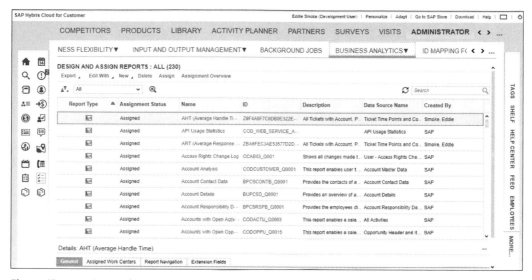

Figure 15.11 Design and Assign Reports Screen

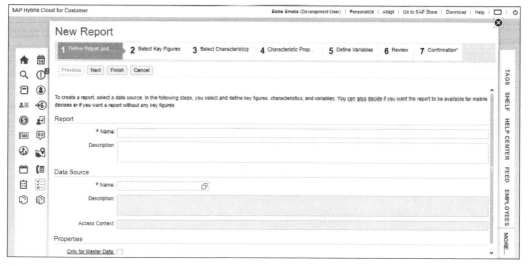

Figure 15.12 Wizard to Create a New Report

On this screen, enter the **Name** and **Description** of this report, and then select the data source under **Data Source** from the available values. After entering these values, click **Next** to go to the second step of the wizard: **Select Key Figures**. As shown in Figure 15.13, click on **Deselect All** to uncheck all the key figures, and then you can select the key figures needed for your report.

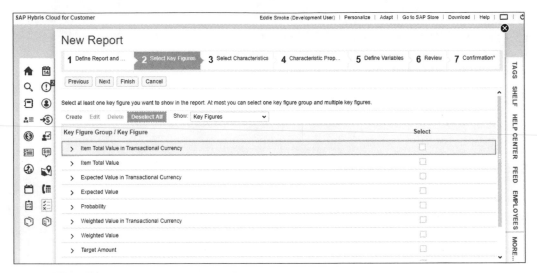

Figure 15.13 Key Figures Selection for a Report

After selecting the key figures, click **Next** again, and go through the subsequent steps to select **Characteristics**, **Characteristics Properties**, **Define Variables**, **Review**, and finally **Confirmation** to finish the report creation process. Depending on your business reporting requirements, you can create your own custom reports by selecting appropriate key figures, characteristics, characteristics properties, and so on via the report creation wizard explained earlier.

15.3   Dashboards

SAP Cloud for Customer delivers several interactive dashboards that provide you with a big picture of your data in real time. You can zoom in by selecting the chart element or by selecting specific characteristics and applying filters. These dashboards are easy to configure and consume, and they provide in-place interactivity and drill-down. Dashboards allow you to do advanced analysis on iPads with a single setup for iPad and browser, and, more importantly, you can create and publish them by using an easy, guided wizard. Dashboards provide a quick view of transactions and also allow you to open the transactions. Figure 15.14 shows an example of dashboards on a user's home page.

Figure 15.14 Dashboards on the Home Page

Figure 15.15 shows an example of dashboards for users to see the team's performance from one screen such as **Forecast Category**, **Key Products**, **My Team Details**, and **My Team's Attainment**.

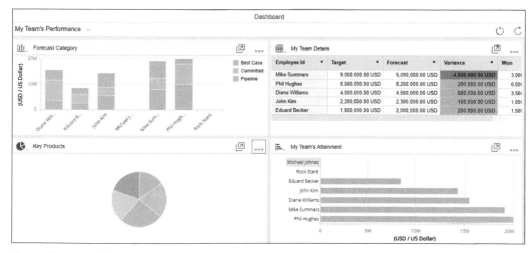

Figure 15.15 Dashboard Examples

These dashboards provide interactivity and drilldown capabilities with an easy-to-use guided wizard to create and publish dashboards. The dashboards can be designed under the administrator login. You log in to SAPUI5 using administrator credentials, and choose **ADMINISTRATOR • GENERAL SETTINGS • Interactive Dashboards**, as shown in Figure 15.16.

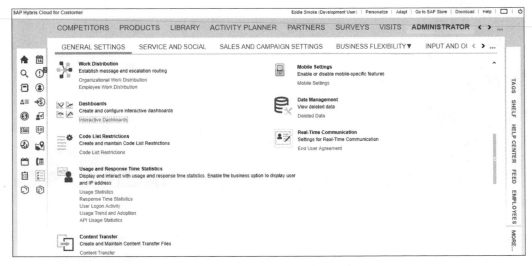

Figure 15.16 Create and Configure Interactive Dashboards

When you click on **Interactive Dashboards**, you can see all the dashboards available to execute, change, or create new, as shown in Figure 15.17.

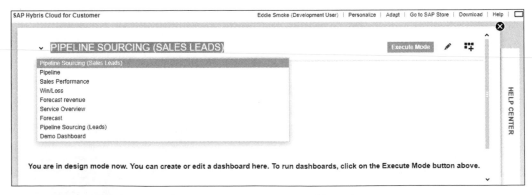

Figure 15.17 Execute, Change, or Create a New Dashboard

If you click on **Execute Mode**, the selected dashboards from the dropdown will be displayed, as shown in Figure 15.18. Figure 15.19 shows a sales overview dashboard with multiple chart types, including a pie chart, bar chart, and line chart.

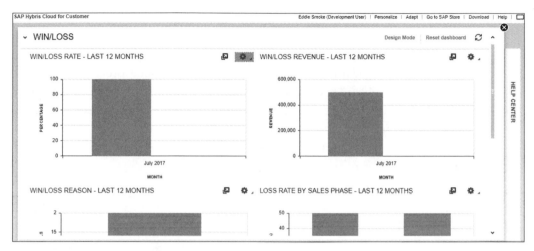

Figure 15.18 Win/Loss Dashboards

Figure 15.19 Sales Overview Dashboards

Before you create a new dashboard, you need to decide which reports you want to include as charts, as well as how you want the charts to respond when the user selects the data element in a linked chart.

To create a new dashboard, follow these steps:

1. Switch to design mode by clicking on **Design Mode** (refer to Figure 15.19), and then click on the **+** button (add new dashboard). The **Create New Dashboard** screen wizard appears, as shown in Figure 15.20. This six-step guided process starts with entering the dashboard name and description and option to publish. By default, a dashboard is published as soon as it's created. However, you can keep it in draft mode until you've finalized it by keeping the **Publish** checkbox unchecked in Figure 15.20. After entering the **Dashboard Name** and **Description** in this step, click **Next**.

Figure 15.20 Creating a New Dashboard

2. In step **2 Sources**, select the sources per your dashboard requirement, as shown in Figure 15.21. Here you select the reports to include as charts or tables on the dashboard. Use the search box to find a specific report.

3. After selecting sources in this step, click **Next** to go to step **3 Variants**. If more than one variant exists for the selected reports, you must select which variant to use on the dashboard. To view exceptions defined on key figures of a report on the dashboard, select a report variant for which you've already defined exceptions for key figures.

4. Click **Next** to go to step **4 Layout**, as shown in Figure 15.22. Here you can define the layout by arranging the reports on the dashboard. On this screen, you can drag the available report from the right side and drop it on the grid per your dashboard

layout requirement. You can use the arrow signs to expand the dashboard to adjacent grids horizontally or vertically.

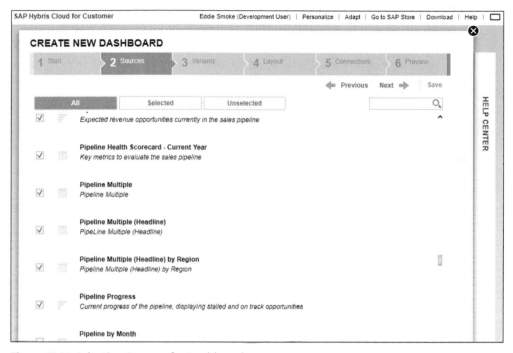

Figure 15.21 Selecting Sources for Dashboard

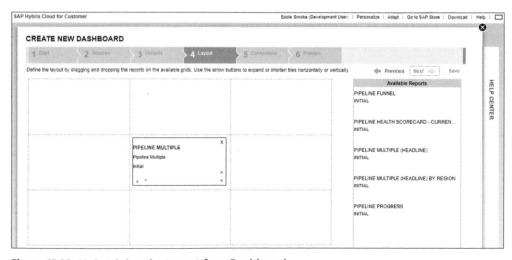

Figure 15.22 Maintaining the Layout for a Dashboard

5. After all the available reports have been placed on the grids, click **Next** to go to step **5 Connections**, as shown in Figure 15.23. Connections are how you set up the interactions between tiles. If you choose **Auto Mapping**, the connection will be made according to the default mapping between two reports. You can also manually select a **Source** and a **Target**. You can also remove connections. The connections you define in this step determine how the charts will interact when a user selects a characteristic in one chart.

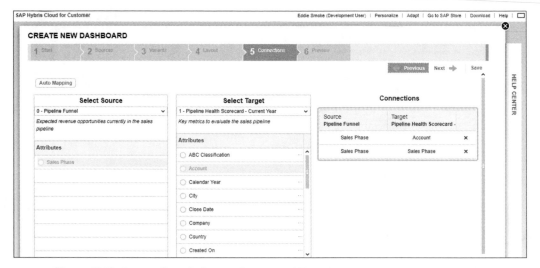

Figure 15.23 Connections between Source and Target

6. Click **Next** to go to step **6 Preview** to see your new dashboard, as shown in Figure 15.24. This screen shows how the dashboard will appear in the browser.

7. Click **Save** to save the newly created dashboard. Once saved, your new dashboard will be available to select from the menu on the **Dashboard** tab.

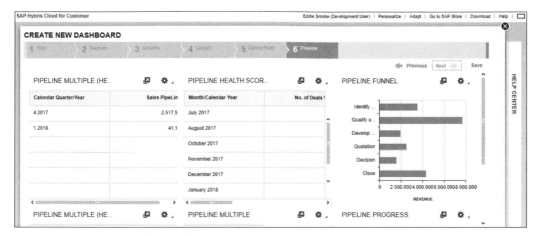

Figure 15.24 Preview of the Newly Designed Dashboard

15.4   Summary

In this chapter, you learned about the reports and dashboard capabilities available in SAP Cloud for Customer. Standard out-of-the-box reports are available for accounts, contacts, leads, activities, opportunities, sales pipelines, and so on. If the standard reports don't meet your business reporting requirements, you can create your own custom reports through a wizard process. In addition to standard and custom reports, you can also create interactive dashboards through a wizard process. In next chapter, you'll learn about integrating SAP Cloud for Customer with external systems such as SAP Customer Relationship Management (SAP CRM), SAP ERP, and Microsoft Outlook.

15

Chapter 16

Integration

SAP Cloud for Customer capabilities can be leveraged and extended with standard integration contents with on-premise SAP ERP/SAP S/4HANA or SAP CRM and with cloud solutions from SAP and third parties.

Most organizations have complex on-premise landscapes. As customers adopt cloud solutions, integration across the boundaries of cloud and on premise is a must to prevent application silos and enable real-time, end-to-end business process integration. In this chapter, you'll learn about the integration options available with SAP Cloud for Customer. We'll specifically cover the SAP Cloud for Customer integration with SAP ERP, SAP Customer Relationship Management (SAP CRM), and SAP Business Warehouse (SAP BW). We'll also cover the integration with Microsoft Outlook and Lotus Notes.

Note that for your integration with the backend system, we've discussed SAP ERP in this chapter; however, the same integration applies to SAP S/4HANA as well. SAP S/4HANA and SAP ERP are interchangeably used in this book. In addition, there are prepackaged integrations available between SAP Sales Cloud and other SAP C/4HANA applications such as SAP Marketing Cloud and SAP Commerce Cloud. Apart from integration with on-premise solutions, we'll cover integration with third-party cloud solutions as well. We'll also review how to extend these integration scenarios.

16.1 Introduction to SAP Cloud for Customer Integration

SAP's cloud integration strategy is based on one of the three options, that is, SAP Cloud Platform Integration, prepackaged integration flows (iFlows) to be leveraged with SAP Process Integration (SAP PI), and open application programming interfaces (APIs) and deployment choices, as follows:

- **SAP Cloud Platform Integration**
  This cloud-based integration technology from SAP enables real-time data and process integration. It also offers prepackaged iFlows with centralized monitoring and administration capability. It includes prebuilt adapters and also has lower cost of change over time. SAP Cloud Platform Integration can be used to integrate SAP Cloud for Customer with SAP on-premise applications such as SAP ERP, SAP CRM, and SAP BW; third-party on-premise systems, and cloud solutions such as SAP Marketing Cloud, as shown in Figure 16.1.

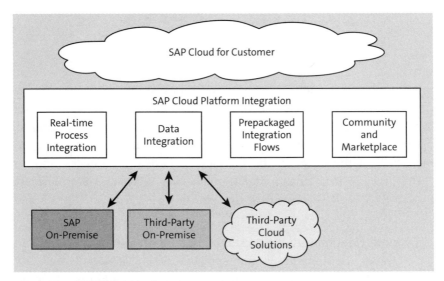

Figure 16.1 SAP Cloud Platform Integration

- **Prepackaged iFlows**
  SAP provides standard integration content as iFlows to integrate SAP Cloud for Customer with on-premise and other cloud solutions. iFlows contain predefined mappings with more than 100 fields, several defined functions, and logical and technical routing rules. These iFlows can be run on SAP Cloud Platform Integration and SAP PI.

- **Open APIs and deployment choice**
  SAP Cloud for Customer offers a rich set of public SOAP web services and OData APIs to provide flexibility for deploying integrations on premise or in the cloud. These open APIs can be used by customers and partners with SAP or third-party platforms.

With the background on these three integration strategies, the next sections will review how to integrate SAP Cloud for Customer with SAP ERP, SAP CRM, and SAP BW.

SAP Cloud for Customer requires either SAP Cloud Platform Integration or SAP PI. Customers have the choice to deploy integrations on premise or in the cloud. SAP Cloud for Customer provides prepackaged integration content for SAP Cloud Platform Integration and SAP PI, as shown in Figure 16.2. You can do direct integration as well as third-party integration between SAP Cloud for Customer and other systems, but for that, you need to do all the mapping yourself. You won't be able to leverage the prepackaged integration provided by SAP as with SAP Cloud Platform Integration and SAP PI.

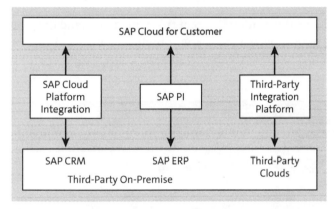

Figure 16.2 Integration Options for SAP Cloud for Customer

Both SAP Cloud Platform Integration and SAP PI have a minimal on-premise footprint because they require only add-ons for integration and leverage existing APIs. Integration contents are portable between SAP PI and SAP Cloud Platform Integration. It's much easier to extend these integrations. You can easily extend mapping instead of new development in on-premise systems. Let's evaluate why you would choose one integration option over another, as follows:

- **SAP Cloud Platform Integration**
  SAP on-premise applications run the core of your business and can be very complex to support your business requirements. Hybrid cloud landscapes are required to drive end-to-end processing. SAP Cloud Platform Integration enables SAP's deep integration expertise in the cloud. SAP Cloud Platform Integration ensures your hybrid scenarios and cloud-to-cloud integration scenarios are integrated via

cloud middleware where SAP ensures the middleware is maintained, upgraded, and ready for execution. SAP Cloud Platform Integration enables you to extend the SAP prepackaged integration to meet your specific requirements.

- **SAP PI**

  SAP PI is on-premise middleware. If you purchased the SAP Business Suite, you may already have license rights to SAP PI. There is no additional software license charge for SAP PI when integrating SAP cloud applications to SAP on-premise. SAP Process Orchestration (SAP PO) is a new release from SAP. SAP PO combines SAP PI with SAP Business Rules Management and SAP Business Process Management. Customers must purchase SAP PO because it's not included with the SAP ERP license. SAP Cloud for Customer integration supports SAP PO and SAP PI.

While choosing an integration platform, it's important that you understand the pros and cons of various options. In the following tables, we provide the pros and cons of SAP Cloud Platform Integration (Table 16.1), SAP PI (Table 16.2), and third-party integration (Table 16.3).

Pros	Cons
■ Leverage SAP-provided prepackaged integration content. ■ Leverage Web UI for configuration of standard scenarios. ■ Runtime in the cloud is maintained by SAP. ■ No installation, patches, or upgrades are required by customer. ■ Options are available to use SAP, SAP Partner, or your own skills for integration configuration.	■ Adapters are limited to SOAP, SFTP, IDoc, XML, SAP SuccessFactors, and more in development.

Table 16.1 SAP Cloud Platform Integration: Pros and Cons

Pros	Cons
■ Leverage SAP-provided prepackaged integration content. ■ Leverage existing SAP PI implementation and skilled resources.	■ Cloud-to-cloud integration requires trip OP for mapping and routing. ■ Customer must upgrade, apply patches, and maintain SAP PI.

Table 16.2 SAP PI: Pros and Cons

Pros	Cons
■ Reuse existing middleware where you have expertise. ■ Some partners (Boomi, MuleSoft) have the cloud for customer connectors.	■ SAP-provided prepackaged integration content can't be leveraged. ■ Deep domain knowledge of the A2X services is required, as well as knowledge of the on-premise interfaces. ■ It must be built and maintained completely on your own.

Table 16.3 Third-Party Middleware: Pros and Cons

16.2   Integrating with SAP ERP

Integration of SAP Cloud for Customer with SAP ERP can be achieved through SAP Cloud Platform Integration or SAP PI. In the following sections, we'll provide an overview of what integration with SAP ERP looks like, then discuss two of the most important tasks: creating communication systems and maintaining communication arrangements.

16.2.1   Overview

This integration between SAP Cloud for Customer and SAP ERP exchanges both master data and transaction data, and most of the communications between SAP Cloud for Customer and external systems are bidirectional. Figure 16.3 shows what master data is exchanged between the SAP Cloud for Customer and SAP ERP systems.

The integration between SAP ERP and SAP Sales Cloud allows real-time integration of master data such as accounts, prospects, contacts, and products, including the option to block prospects back to SAP ERP. Through this integration, you also replicate key master data such as currency conversion rates, employee hierarchy, customer hierarchy, and sales hierarchy. Before you replicate this master data, there are tools to transfer initial business configuration, such as accounts groups, document types, and customer classifications, from SAP ERP to SAP Sales Cloud.

Similar to master data, prepackaged integration with SAP ERP allows the replication of transaction data between SAP Cloud for Customer and SAP ERP, as shown in Figure 16.4.

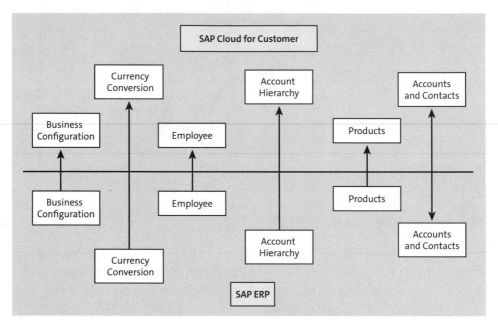

Figure 16.3 Master Data Integration between SAP ERP and SAP Sales Cloud

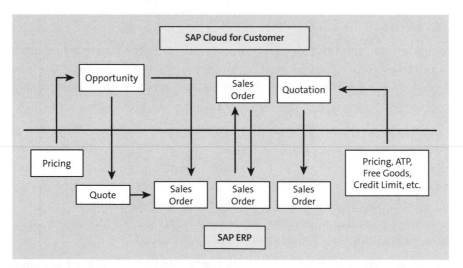

Figure 16.4 Transactional Data Integration between SAP Cloud for Customer and SAP ERP

Through this integration, sales orders created in SAP Cloud for Customer can be replicated to SAP ERP, and SAP ERP orders can be replicated to SAP Cloud for Customer bidirectionally. It allows real-time integration of transaction data such as pricing, document creation, available to promise (ATP), free goods, and credit limit checks. Pricing provides real-time calls to SAP ERP Sales and Distribution (SD). Pricing integration supports the full pricing flexibility of SAP ERP SD in SAP Cloud for Customer. Figure 16.5 shows how quotes created in SAP Cloud for Customer can be priced from pricing data maintained in SAP ERP pricing procedures.

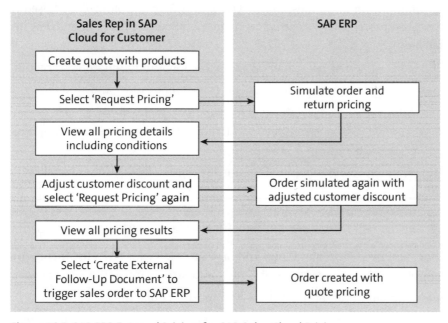

Figure 16.5 SAP ERP External Pricing for SAP Sales Cloud Pricing

With SAP Cloud for Customer and SAP ERP integration, you can launch the ERP Customer Factsheet to get a holistic view of accounts and prospects from SAP Cloud for Customer without the need for a virtual private network (VPN) connection. You can also launch the ERP Customer Cockpit from the **Account** screen in SAP Cloud for Customer to quickly edit transactions in SAP ERP. Through this integration, you can enable sales order integration between SAP ERP and SAP Cloud for Customer and create lean sales orders in SAP Cloud for Customer to replicate to SAP ERP sales orders. You can create new sales orders, maintain header data, add products, and modify the list of involved parties in a sales order.

In the sales order, you can also simulate pricing from SAP ERP and transfer the updated price to SAP ERP. You can also transfer sales orders from SAP ERP to SAP Cloud for Customer, as well as transfer various sales order statuses, such as external reference ID, document type, list of involved parties, and products (including price and quantities) to SAP Cloud for Customer.

For you to leverage this prepackaged integration between SAP Cloud for Customer and SAP ERP, there are minimum requirements for SAP ERP 6.0 such as Enhancement Pack 0 (EHP 0) and Support Package 15 (SP 15). For some business requirements, there are additional prerequisites such as EHP 2, EHP 3, or EHP 4. You're advised to check the latest prerequisites at *http://help.sap.com*. Some of those perquisites are identified here:

- EHP 2 is required to view sales order details in the opportunity, quote, and account.
- EHP 3 is required to view sales quote details in the opportunity and account.
- EHP 4 is required to view print delivery of deliveries and invoices.
- EHP 4 is required to view print preview (PDF) of sales documents in the opportunity, quote, and account.
- Adobe Document Server is required for previewing an ERP Customer Factsheet in PDF format.
- Exchange rate for currencies requires one of the following: SAP ERP 6.0 EHP 2, SP 13; SAP ERP 6.0 EHP 3, SP 12; SAP ERP 6.0 EHP 4, SP 14; or SAP ERP 6.0 EHP 5, SP 11.

In addition, you need SAP Sales Cloud add-on CODEPRINT for SAP ERP. It contains important objects that are used for SAP Cloud for Customer integration as follows:

- Business Configuration Sets (BC Sets) with important Customizing entries
- Remote interfaces needed for SAP Sales Cloud integration but not available with the core SAP ERP **Area** menu in SAP ERP Customizing
- Report to automatically create connectivity settings in SAP ERP
- Reports for data replication of certain objects (e.g., sales organization structure)
- Access role for technical inbound user in SAP ERP
- Pricing web services

Although you need the required integration setting in SAP Cloud for Customer, SAP ERP, and middleware (SAP Cloud Platform Integration), we'll only cover the procedure to make necessary changes in SAP Cloud for Customer. The integration settings on SAP ERP and middleware are outside the scope of this book.

To enable this integration, follow these steps:

1. Choose **Business Configuration • Implementation Projects**.
2. Select the implementation project entitled **First Implementation**.
3. In the **Project Overview: First Implementation** screen that appears, choose **Edit Project Scope**.
4. The **Edit Project Scope: First Implementation** screen appears. Under the **Country** tab, choose **Type of Business**, and then select **Next**.
5. On the **Implementation Focus** tab, select **Next**.
6. On the **Scoping** tab, expand the **Communication and Information Exchange** scoping element and then **Integration with External Applications and Solutions**, and select the **Integration with SAP ERP** checkbox, as shown in Figure 16.6.

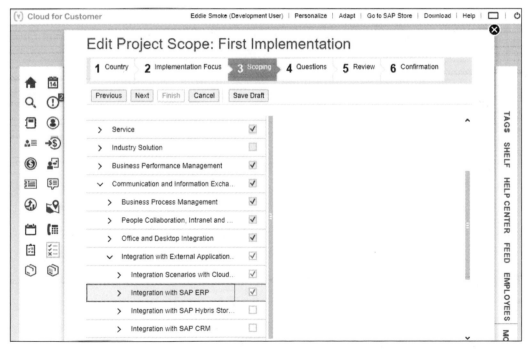

Figure 16.6 Scoping for SAP ERP Integration with SAP Sales Cloud

7. Choose **Save Draft**.

8. Close the **Edit Project Scope: First Implementation** screen.

After you've updated the scoping for SAP ERP integration in your SAP Sales Cloud, you need to configure the connections through the steps described in the following sections.

16.2.2   Create Communication Systems

In the **Communication Systems** view, you can create and edit communication systems to exchange business documents electronically. A communication system represents an external system that is used for application integration. Communication systems can be, for example, external time recording or master data systems. Before you can use a communication system in an application integration scenario, you need to create a communication arrangement.

To access this view, follow these steps:

1. Choose **ADMINISTRATOR • GENERAL SETTINGS**. Under **Integration**, click on **Communication Systems**, as shown in Figure 16.7.

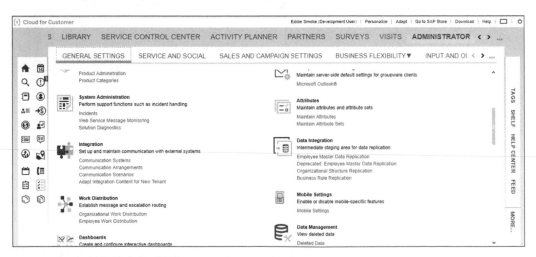

Figure 16.7 Link for Setting Up a Communication System

2. When you click on **Communication Systems**, you're presented with the **Communication Systems: All Communication Systems** screen, as shown in Figure 16.8.

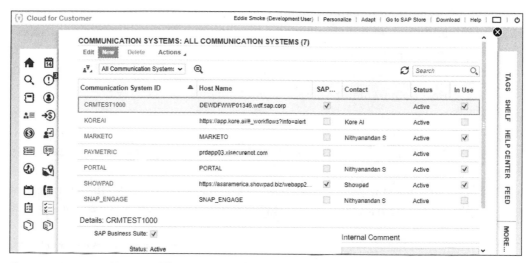

Figure 16.8 Screen Showing All Communication Systems

3. Click on **New** to go to the **New Communication System** screen, as shown in Figure 16.9.

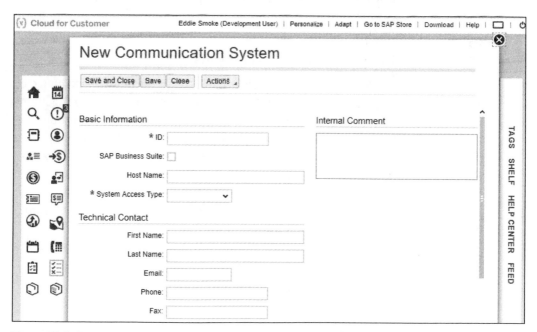

Figure 16.9 Screen to Enter New Communication System Details

4. In the **Basic Information** section, enter the details of the communication systems as follows:
   - **ID**: Enter a unique ID for the communication system.
   - **SAP Business Suite**: Because you're integrating with SAP ERP, select this checkbox.
   - **Host Name**: Enter the host name for the communication system.
   - **System Access Type**: Choose the correct communication method for your communication system.
   - **Technical Contact**: In this section, enter the details of the communication systems contact.
   - **System Instances**: In this section, click on **Add Row**, and enter the ID of the business system as defined in the System Landscape Directory (SLD), for example, PRD_123.
5. When you've entered all the details for the new communication system, click on **Save**.
6. Under **Actions**, select **Set to Active** to activate your communication system. If the status changes to **Active**, the configuration is ready to be used.

Now that you've set up the communication system, you need to maintain communication arrangement.

16.2.3   Maintain Communication Arrangements

Communication arrangements help you configure the electronic data exchange between the solution and a communication partner. Communication arrangements can be set up for multiple business documents and communication methods. The solution provides communication scenarios for inbound and outbound communication that you can use to create communication arrangements. Inbound communication defines how business documents are received from a communication partner, whereas outbound communication defines how business documents are sent to a communication partner. The communication arrangements support communication types of business-to-business (B2B) to define electronic data exchange with a business partner, and they support application integration where the communication type defines an electronic data exchange with a communication system.

To create communication arrangements, follow these steps:

1. Go to **ADMINISTRATOR • GENERAL SETTINGS**.
2. Under **Integration**, click on **Communication Arrangements** to go to the **COMMUNICATION ARRANGEMENTS: ALL COMMUNICATION ARRANGEMENTS** screen, as shown in Figure 16.10.

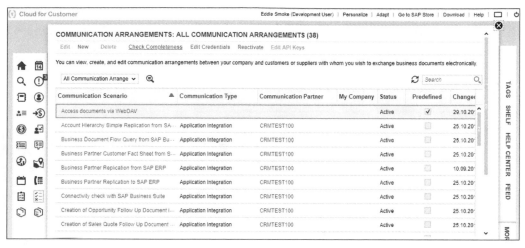

Figure 16.10 Communication Arrangements

3. Click on **New** to access a guided activity on the **New Communication Arrangement** screen, as shown in Figure 16.11.

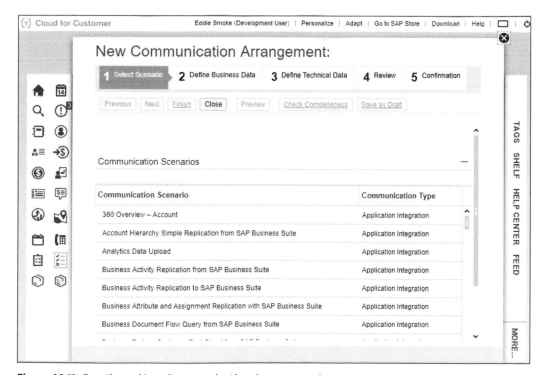

Figure 16.11 Creating a New Communication Arrangement

4. This screen shows the list of **Communication Scenarios**. Select the communication scenario you want to create the communication arrangement for. For example, if you're setting up the communication arrangement for business partner replication with SAP ERP, then select **Business Partner Replication to SAP ERP**, and choose **Next** to go to the next step, **Define Business Data**, as shown in Figure 16.12.

Figure 16.12 Maintaining Business Data for the Communication Arrangement

5. Maintain the system instance ID of the system you're creating the arrangement for. If a communication arrangement contains a service interface that supports code list mapping, the **Code List Mapping** field is displayed. In this field, choose the relevant code list mapping group for the communication scenario that you're using.

6. Click **Next** to go to the **Define Technical Data** screen and define the technical settings for inbound and outbound communication (see Figure 16.13).

7. Select the **Communication Method** you want to use for the communication arrangement.

8. If you use inbound communication, select the **Application Protocol** and **Authentication Method** in the **Inbound Communication: Basic Settings** section.

9. In the **User ID** field, click **Edit Credentials**. Depending on the chosen authentication method, you need to define the credentials of the communication user.

10. Click **Next** to go to the **Review** step to review your settings.

11. Click **Next** again to go to the **Confirmation** step and finally save the changes to complete the settings for communication arrangements.

In the next section, we'll review the integration steps for SAP CRM.

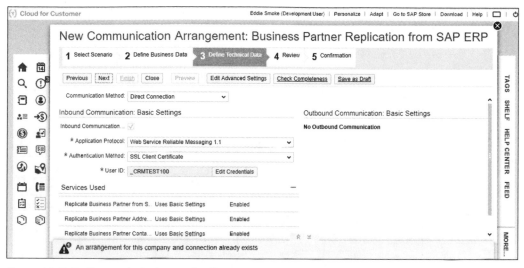

Figure 16.13 Define Technical Data for the Communication Arrangement

16.3   Integrating with SAP CRM

Similar to SAP ERP, integration between SAP CRM and SAP Cloud for Customer provides multiple integration points for master data and transaction data. The real-time master data synchronization provides unidirectional replication from SAP CRM to SAP Sales Cloud for products, sales organizations, marketing attribute definitions, employees, and territory assignments.

For accounts and contacts, a bidirectional synchronization option is available with SAP CRM. For transactions replication, integration with SAP CRM provides real-time opportunity synchronization with attachments, real-time lead synchronization, and real-time quote to sales order synchronization, including pricing. Figure 16.14 shows the replication of master data between SAP CRM and SAP Cloud for Customer. It allows real-time integration of master data such as accounts, prospects, competitors, contacts, account hierarchy, territory assignment, products, employees, and social media profiles.

The integration of marketing attributes, definitions, and assignments of marketing attributes to customers is only from SAP CRM to SAP Cloud for Customer. Marketing attributes are defined only in SAP CRM. The integration of the definition of marketing attributes is unidirectional from SAP CRM to SAP Cloud for Customer. Marketing

16

421

attribute values have bidirectional integration between SAP CRM and SAP Cloud for Customer.

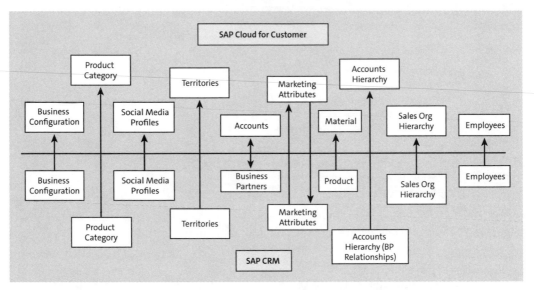

Figure 16.14 Master Data Replication between SAP CRM and SAP Cloud for Customer

Similar to master data, real-time integration of transactional data allows campaign headers, leads, opportunities, and activities replication between SAP Sales Cloud and SAP CRM, as shown in Figure 16.15. Attachments to activities, leads, and opportunities are replicated bidirectionally between SAP Sales Cloud and SAP CRM.

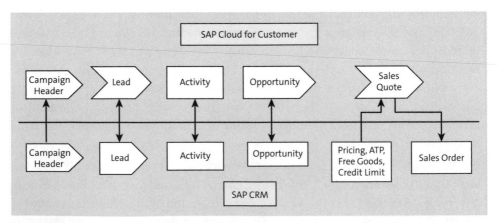

Figure 16.15 Real-Time Transaction Integration between SAP Cloud for Customer and SAP CRM

Transaction integration also supports real-time calls from SAP Cloud for Customer quotes to SAP CRM for pricing the items. When a sales order is created in SAP CRM from a sales quote, SAP CRM takes over the items and prices from the SAP Cloud for Customer quote, as shown in Figure 16.16.

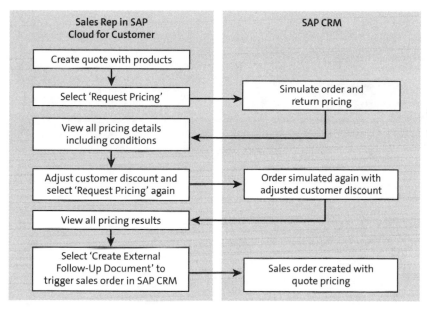

Figure 16.16 SAP CRM External Pricing for a SAP Cloud for Customer Quote

To leverage prepackaged integration content, you need a minimum SAP CRM 7.0 EHP 0, SP 6. In addition, you need SAP Cloud for Customer add-on CRMPCD01700. For social media integration, you need SAP CRM EHP 3.

To enable this integration, follow these steps:

1. Choose **Business Configuration • Implementation Projects**.

2. Select the implementation project entitled **First Implementation**. The **Project Overview: First Implementation** screen appears.

3. Choose **Edit Project Scope**.

4. When the **Edit Project Scope: First Implementation** screen appears, select **Next** under **Country** and **Type of Business**.

5. Under **Implementation Focus**, select **Next**.

6. On the scoping screen, expand the **Communication and Information Exchange** scoping element and **Integration with External Applications and Solutions**, and then select the **Integration with SAP CRM** checkbox, as shown in Figure 16.17.

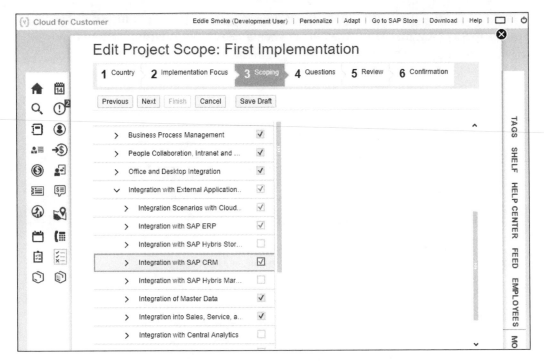

Figure 16.17 Configuring Integration with SAP CRM

7. Choose **Save Draft**.

8. Close the **Edit Project Scope: First Implementation** screen.

After including SAP CRM integration in the scope, you need to configure the connection between SAP Sales Cloud and SAP CRM. The steps for setting up connections on SAP Sales Cloud are exactly the same as explained in Section 16.2, such as creating communication systems and maintaining communication arrangements.

In addition, you need integration settings on the SAP CRM side and middleware, which are outside the scope of this book.

16.4   Integrating with SAP Business Warehouse

Integration with SAP BW allows report integration and HTML mash-up in SAP Cloud for Customer. With SAP BW integration, data can be replicated bidirectionally between SAP Cloud for Customer and SAP BW, as shown in Figure 16.18.

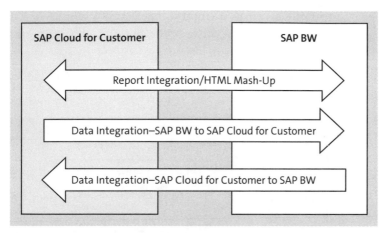

Figure 16.18 Report and Data Integration between SAP Cloud for Customer and SAP BW

Using HTML mash-up, you can create dashboards in SAP Cloud for Customer with SAP BW information combined with information from SAP Cloud for Customer. For data transfer from SAP Cloud for Customer to SAP BW, data sources in SAP Cloud for Customer are exposed via the Operational Data Provider (ODP) services that are consumed by SAP BW, as shown in Figure 16.19.

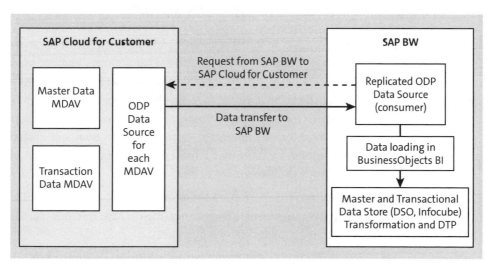

Figure 16.19 Data Integration from SAP Cloud for Customer to SAP BW

To enable these types of integrations, you need a minimum of SAP BW 7.3/SP 8 or SAP BW 7.4. In addition, with this type of integration, only the full upload is supported with the possibility for some selection criteria.

In the next scenario, let's review the data integration from SAP BW to SAP Cloud for Customer, as shown in Figure 16.20.

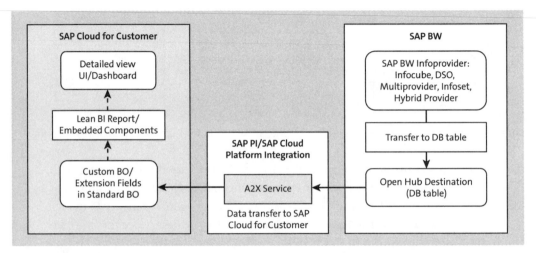

Figure 16.20 Data Transfer from SAP BW to SAP Cloud for Customer

Using this type of integration data in SAP BusinessObjects BI, InfoProviders can be transferred to an Open Hub Destination. In SAP Cloud for Customer, a custom business object table is created to store the data, and its associated web service (A2X) is generated. From SAP BW, a call can be initiated to the web service via a Z program or SAP PI, and data can be pushed from the Open Hub Destination into the custom business objects table in SAP Cloud for Customer. The data in custom business objects can be exposed in the SAP Cloud for Customer UI as embedded tables or as native reports.

In the third integration option, that is, report integration/HTML mash-up in SAP Cloud for Customer, a SAP BW query can be consumed in an HTML web template in BEx Web Application Designer 3.X, as shown in Figure 16.21.

To derive context specific data from SAP BW, the query will have the **Account ID** as a variable parameter. It's important that mapping information regarding account IDs/product IDs be maintained in SAP Cloud for Customer or SAP BW to map the SAP Cloud for Customer account ID with the account ID in SAP ERP or SAP BW.

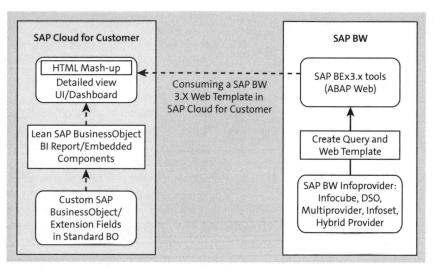

Figure 16.21 Report Integration and HTML Mash-Up in SAP Cloud for Customer

There are trade-offs between these approaches of integration between SAP Cloud for Customer and SAP BW. Depending on your business requirements, you can decide if data transfer or mash integration will meet your specific scenarios. For reference, we provide the pros and cons of these approaches in Table 16.4 and Table 16.5.

Pros	Cons
■ Reuse existing reports in SAP Business-Objects BI ■ SAP BW data authorizations setup honored ■ Real-time data access from SAP BW ■ Equivalent to launching a SAP BW report independently on the web, that is,, no additional impact on SAP Cloud for Customer or SAP BW performance ■ Low effort and investment ■ No continuous maintenance needed ■ No impact on SAP Cloud for Customer for modification in the reporting data model ■ Supported in iPad	■ Potential network latency impact ■ Consideration of mash-up use outside of corporate network ■ No offline access available

Table 16.4 Mash-Up Approach: Pros and Cons

Pros	Cons
■ Supported in iPad ■ No network latency because data is stored in cloud ■ Usage of native SAP Cloud for Customer reporting	■ Re-implement authorization model in SAP Cloud for Customer ■ No real-time reporting from SAP BW, data transferred from SAP BW to SAP Cloud for Customer in batch ■ Requires higher implementation effort because you need to develop new objects and reports in SAP Cloud for Customer and data transfer programs to call the web service to transfer data from SAP BW ■ Needs monitoring and error handling during data transfer ■ Performance impact on load of larger volume of data ■ Modifications to the reports data model need replicated to SAP Cloud for Customer with changes to the business objects and the web service

Table 16.5 Data Transfer Approach: Pros and Cons

Before we end this section, let's review the steps for integrating SAP Sales Cloud with SAP BW. First, you need to make sure that you meet the prerequisites (SAP BW 7.3, SP8 or above) and have authorization to use Transaction STRUST in the SAP BW system.

Next, you need to enable SAP BW integration in the scope of your project by choosing **Business Configuration • Implementation Projects • Edit Project Scope**. Then, click **Next**. Choose the **Scoping** tab. Then select **Communication and Information Exchange • Integration with External Application • Integration with Central Analytics**, as shown in Figure 16.22.

After that, click on **Next**, and select the question for SAP BW integration, and click **Next** to review and finally confirm the scope to save your changes. After updating the scope, you need to repeat the steps for creating communication systems and communication arrangements for establishing a connection with SAP BW, as outlined in previous sections for SAP ERP and SAP CRM.

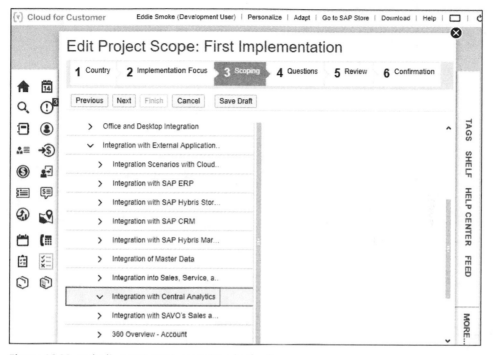

Figure 16.22 Including SAP BW Integration in the Scope

16.5   Integrating with Microsoft Outlook

SAP Cloud for Customer allows both client-side and server-side integration with Microsoft Outlook. In the following sections, we will look at how to set up the connection between Microsoft Outlook and SAP Cloud for Customer and then provide an overview of how to use this connection.

16.5.1   Set Up

To integrate with Microsoft Outlook, follow these steps:

1. Download the **Add-In for Microsoft Outlook** from the **DOWNLOADS** section in SAP Cloud for Customer, as shown in Figure 16.23.

2. When you click on **Download**, the *SAP_SOD_Outlook_Addin.exe* file is downloaded to your local machine. Double click on this file and the add-in for Microsoft Outlook will start installing on your machine, as shown in Figure 16.24.

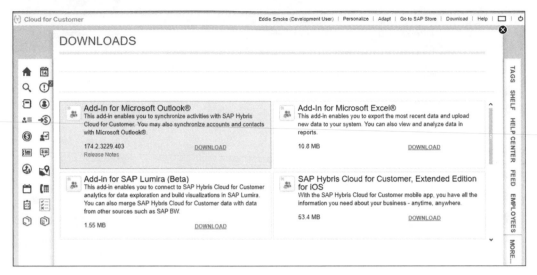

Figure 16.23 Download Add-In for Microsoft Outlook

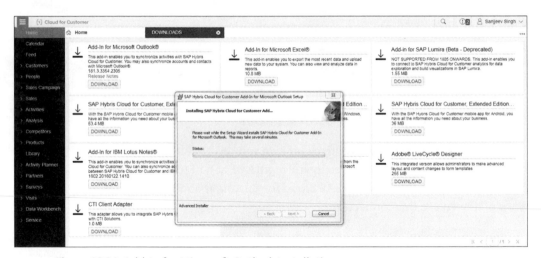

Figure 16.24 Add-In for Microsoft Outlook Installation

> **Note**
>
> As of SAP Sales Cloud release 1802, you need the Microsoft Outlook 2010 client on your local machine for this add-in to work.

3. After installation is complete, you will be prompted with the installation confirmation message shown in Figure 16.25.

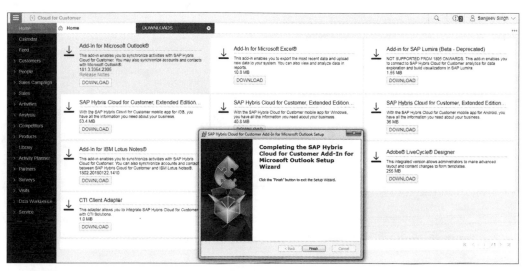

Figure 16.25 Outlook Add-In Installation Confirmation Message

4. Following the installation, open your local Microsoft Outlook and you will be presented with the option to login to the SAP Sales Cloud system. For the integration between SAP Sales Cloud and Microsoft Outlook to work, you must login to SAP Sales Cloud from Outlook. To do so, click on **Log On** (see Figure 16.26) and you will be presented with a pop up screen.

5. Enter the necessary information about your SAP Sales Cloud tenant, including your SAP Sales Cloud system access URL in the **SAP System URL** field and your **User Name** and **Password** (this will be your SAP Sales Cloud user name and password, not your Microsoft Outlook user name and password). In addition you can enable the checkboxes **Remember my user name and password** and **Automatic Logon** so that every time you start Microsoft Outlook you are automatically logged in to SAP Sales Cloud.

6. After you've entered this information, click **Log On**. Once you have done so, you'll be able to see the feeds and contacts from SAP Sales Cloud in Microsoft Outlook, as shown in Figure 16.27.

16

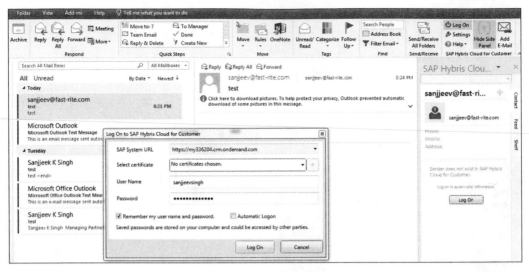

Figure 16.26 Providing Login Details for the SAP Sales Cloud Connection with Microsoft Outlook

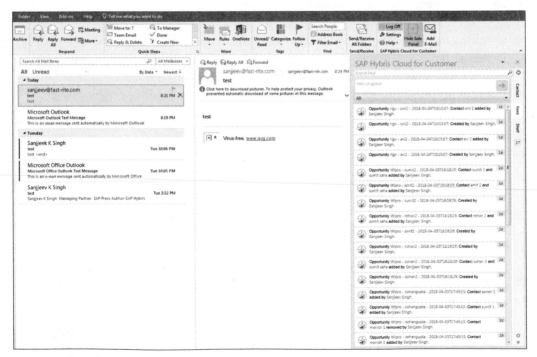

Figure 16.27 Example of Feeds from SAP Sales Cloud in Microsoft Outlook

16.5.2   Functionality

To add an email from Microsoft Outlook to SAP Sales Cloud, select the email in the Microsoft Outlook email panel and then click the **Add E-Mail** icon and you will be presented with the **Add E-Mail** pop-up screen shown in Figure 16.28.

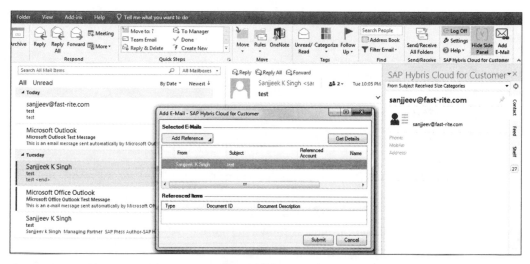

Figure 16.28 Adding E-Mail from Microsoft Outlook to SAP Sales Cloud

Here you can click on **Add Reference** to select which objects (an account, activity, lead, opportunity, etc.) you want to attach this email to. After you select the reference, click **Submit** and the email will be added to SAP Sales Cloud.

The Microsoft Outlook add-in provides allows you some customizable settings to dictate how contacts, accounts, activities, and opportunities are handled between SAP Sales Cloud and Microsoft Outlook. To enable this control, click on **Settings** and you will be presented with the screen in Figure 16.29. Here you have option to keep contacts in sync between SAP Sales Cloud and Microsoft Outlook by enabling the **Keep Contacts Synchronized** check box. The second checkbox will make it so that the system only downloads those contacts from SAP Sales Cloud to Microsoft Outlook with whom you have a valid relationship in SAP Sales Cloud. The **Always Copy Contacts** check box makes it so that you automatically copy any contact from SAP Sales Cloud to Microsoft Outlook (in the SAP Sales Cloud in Microsoft Outlook).

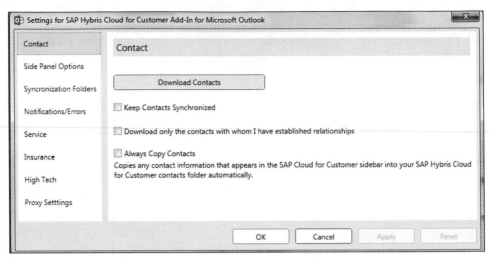

Figure 16.29 Settings for Contacts Sync between SAP Sales Cloud and Microsoft Outlook

In addition to contacts synchronization, you can enable the side panel options by clicking on **Side Panel Options**, as shown in Figure 16.30.

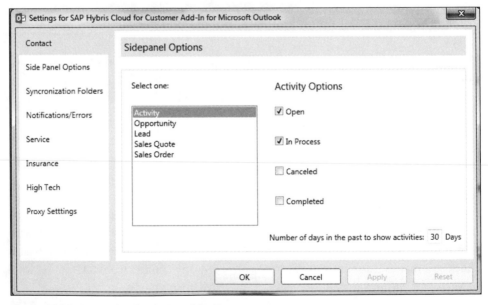

Figure 16.30 Example of Side Panel Options

Here you can control if you want activities, opportunities, leads, opportunities, sales quotes, and sales orders to be displayed in the Microsoft Outlook side panel for SAP Sales Cloud. You can also control what statuses they should have (**Open**, **In Process**, **Cancelled**, or **Completed**) in order to be displayed. In addition you can also control how old (number of days in the past) these transactions can be and still be displayed in the side panel.

In addition to what shows in the side panel, you can also control the synchronization folders. To do so, click on **Synchronization Folders** on the left side and you will be navigated to the screen shown in Figure 16.31.

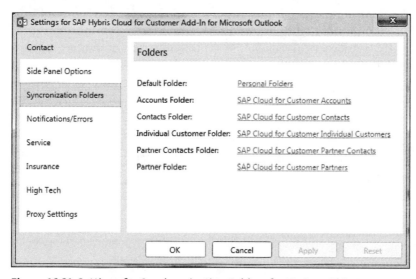

Figure 16.31 Settings for Synchronization Folders for Various Objects

The links for various default synchronization folders are shown in Figure 16.31. Objects such as accounts, contacts, and partners are synchronized between SAP Sales Cloud and these local Microsoft Outlook folders.

For client side, integration is user specific at the client outlook level; however, for server-side integration, it's between SAP Cloud for Customer and Microsoft Exchange Server. With Outlook integration, you can synchronize accounts, contacts, individual customers, tasks, appointments and visits, and emails. Although you need to download the add-in for Microsoft Outlook for the client side, server-side integration doesn't require any add-in.

In addition, with client-side integration, you need to sync your Outlook client with SAP Cloud for Customer, but this isn't necessary for server-side integration, because it's automatic. Let's review a quick comparison of these two integration approaches for Outlook in Table 16.6.

Functionality	Server-Side Integration	Client-Side Integration
Supported groupware systems	Office 365 Microsoft Exchange 2010 or more	Microsoft Outlook 2010, 2013, or 2016
Supported objects and scenarios	Accounts Contacts Individual customers Tasks Activities Visits Attach emails to SAP objects	Accounts Contacts Individual customers Tasks Activities Visits Attach emails to SAP objects
Synchronization filters	Configurable with sync profiles	Fixed (My Queries)
Attachments support	Yes	Yes
Synchronization	Auto-sync in the background Server based synchronization	Manual sync and auto sync at fixed intervals Client-based synchronization
Deployment	No client footprint or deployment required Centralized deployment for Outlook add-in possible	Client-based Outlook add-in installation on end-user machines Centralized deployment via third-party tools possible

Table 16.6 Comparison between Server-Side and Client-Side Integration for Microsoft Outlook

16.6   Integrating with Lotus Notes

Similar to Microsoft Outlook, you can download the **Add-In for IBM Lotus Notes**, as shown in Figure 16.32, and install on your local machine to integrate with SAP Cloud for Customer.

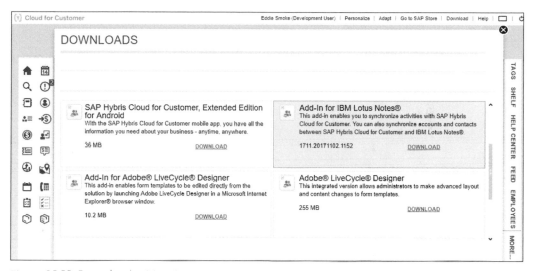

Figure 16.32 Download Add-in for IBM Lotus Notes

After installing the add-in, launch the Lotus Notes add-in component, and you'll be prompted to enter the details of your SAP Cloud for Customer tenant and login information. Your setup will complete after you enter your login details. After setup is complete, synchronization of objects starts automatically. Account information, opportunities, and leads information from SAP Cloud for Customer can be viewed in Lotus Notes. Appointments, tasks, or emails have a bidirectional sync between SAP Cloud for Customer and Lotus Notes.

16.7   Summary

In this chapter, you learned that SAP Cloud for Customer can be integrated with on-premise as well as cloud applications through SAP Cloud Platform Integration, SAP PI, or open APIs. We evaluated these integration options, including their pros and cons. We also covered the integration details for SAP ERP, SAP CRM, and SAP BW with SAP Cloud for Customer. In the next chapter, you'll learn about data migration and replication with SAP Cloud for Customer.

Chapter 17

Data Migration and Replication

Data migration and replication is the process of transferring data between different systems. SAP Cloud for Customer provides various templates to easily migrate data from your legacy system to SAP Cloud for Customer.

Data migration is a critical path item for every project. Without successfully transferring data from legacy applications to SAP Cloud for Customer, you're exposed to unnecessary risk, such as decreased end-user productivity due to bad data or incorrect information and mishandling of open transactions, impacting your business operations. The data migration process involves many steps such as data cleansing, source data extraction, migration template population, test migration, and verification.

In this chapter, you'll learn about configuring data integration with SAP Cloud for Customer and how to mass upload and maintain data. We'll review some specific examples of migrating employees, products, account hierarchies, and territories data to SAP Cloud for Customer.

17.1 Configuring Data Migration and Maintenance

SAP Cloud for Customer provides standard templates for data migration. Before you start your data migration activities, you need to check and update your business configuration. Log in to your SAP Cloud for Customer tenant in the HTML5 user interface (UI) with the administrator role, and navigate to **Business Configuration • Implementation Projects • Open Activity List**, select the **Prepare** tab, choose **All Activities** from the dropdown list, and then click on the **Prepare for Data Migration** link, as shown in Figure 17.1.

Figure 17.1 Prepare Activity for Data Migration

The **Prepare for Data Migration** screen appears, as shown in Figure 17.2.

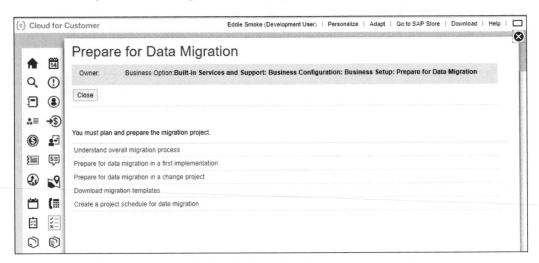

Figure 17.2 Preparation Activities for Data Migration

The five links on this screen related to preparation for data migration are explained in the following sections.

17.1.1   Understand Overall Migration Process

Clicking on the first link, **Understand overall migration process**, provides documentation for the data migration process in SAP Cloud for Customer. This link connects you to the SAP Help page related to data migration.

Here you can see the suggested activities related to data migration for each phase of your SAP Sales Cloud implementation. Let's review some of those activities for each project:

- **Prepare phase**
  In this phase of the project, you perform the following activities:
  - Set up user accounts for migration administrators, and assign the **Business Configuration** work center, including the **Data Migration** view, to each migration administrator.
  - Create a project schedule for data migration using the **Data Migration Scope and Planning Template**.
  - Download migration templates. All legacy data you want to migrate with tool support must be filled in the migration templates.

  We'll review these activities in more detail later in this chapter.

- **Fine-tune phase**
  In this phase, you extract data from your legacy system and fill it into your migration templates.

- **Integrate and extend phase**
  In this phase, you perform the major tasks of migration activities. Each migration activity here is a starting point for tool-supported migration to the SAP Cloud for Customer tenant. In the migration tool, you perform the following activities:
  - Upload your data-filled migration template. During the upload process, the system checks for the formal consistency of the source file.
  - System validates the source file. This step enables you to verify whether the migration template is filled in correctly.
  - After the validation process, the system converts the source values to solution values. During this step, the system automatically proposes new target values based on the business configuration of your solution.
  - The data import process is simulated to allow you to correct any issues before data is actually written to the solution.
  - Finally, the legacy data imports into your SAP Cloud for Customer tenant.

17

You can check the imported data for quality and integrity. This is normally performed during the integration and acceptance test cycles.

- **Migration phases and system environments**
  During the implementation project, you can perform the described steps in two different environments as follows:

  - **Test system**
    The first system provided by SAP is the SAP Cloud for Customer test system. In the test system, you can start fine-tuning your business processes and execute the first business process tests. Here you perform early data migration tests to familiarize yourself with the migration templates and the overall migration process. For example, you can migrate small sample files and use the results to improve data extraction from your legacy system. After that, you can test the migration process with a complete set of data. The goal of the migration tests in the test system is to elaborate the right settings for successful migration. After you complete migration in the test system, you can test your business processes using the migrated data. After you've completed your migration tests, you can download the value conversion from the migration tool for reuse in the production system.

  - **Final migration in the production system**
    You can download the value conversion (the one you downloaded from your migration test system) to import your complete set of data into your production system. Follow your cutover plan (per your project) to import the data into your SAP Cloud for Customer solution. It's recommended that you request a restore point before starting your migration so you can restore your data to the status before data migration.

17.1.2   Prepare for Data Migration in a First Implementation

The second link on the **Prepare for Data Migration** screen shown earlier in Figure 17.2 is related to data migration preparation for the first implementation. When you're implementing SAP Cloud for Customer for the first time, you follow these steps for the data migration. However, if you're already live with SAP Cloud for Customer, and you need to perform any data migration, you'll create a change project, which is covered in the next section. For the first implementation, click on **Prepare for data migration in a first implementation** to open a SAP Help library page for configuration. Following are the three preparation-related activities for data migration:

- **Setting up the migration project**
  Data migration requires the user to have full authorization to import data into various business areas. It provides each member of the migration project with an additional temporary service agent user. In the **Application and User Management** work center, assign the **Business Configuration** and **Data Migration** work centers to these users. Note that when the migration project is complete, you must block the service agent users in the **Application and User Management** work center to guarantee segregation of duties.

- **Downloading the migration templates**
  All data you want to migrate with tool support must be entered in the migration templates. You need to download the required migration templates in the **Prepare for Data Migration** activity. After downloading the template, familiarize yourself with your migration templates and the sheets for each template. For each migration test, create a small sample file by filling in a few records of the template. You can use this sample file to get started with the migration tool.

- **Creating a migration schedule**
  In the **Prepare for Data Migration** activity, under **Create a Project Schedule for Data Migration**, you can download the **Data Migration Scope and Planning Template** to set up a personal migration project plan. You can adjust the template according to your own situation, resources, and data quality, and then you can integrate it into your overall project plan.

17.1.3   Prepare for Data Migration in a Change Project

When you click on the third link, **Prepare for data migration in a change project** (refer to Figure 17.2), it opens an SAP Help library page for configuration. The purpose of this activity is to plan data migration in a change project. It's only required in change projects that include more complex migration. The required preparation tasks for migration in a change project are as follows:

- **Define migration mode: add new records or enhance existing records**
  There are two possibilities to migrate data in a change project. Migrate new records that aren't in the system yet, for example, new prospects, and enhance existing records (select fields in the existing records). For the new records, you can upload and process the filled migration template to the migration tool without special restrictions. When enhancing the existing records, you can add data for certain views or tabs, for example, adding sales data to existing customers. While

uploading this data from filled templates, you click **Properties**, and set the migration mode in advanced options to enhance already existing records. Note that only certain fields in the existing records are allowed in the mode to be updated. You can't overwrite existing customer names by this type of data migration.

- **Plan migration project**
  You've seen in the previous section that data migration requires user to have full authorization to import data into various business areas. User authorizations need to be maintained for team members working on data migration exactly as mentioned in the data migration activity in a first implementation.

- **Fill migration templates**
  All data you want to migrate with tool support must be entered in the migration templates. First, download the required templates, and then enter the related source data into the migration templates just as it's documented in the templates. Always use the templates from the current tenant of SAP Cloud for Customer you're planning the data migration for. For migrating new records, enter the related source data into the migration templates. For each migration object, you must separate new records from records that are to be enhanced in two different migration templates for the same migration object.

  To enhance existing records with additional data, enter the enhancement data in the migration template downloaded from the current system. Copy the existing IDs, such as account IDs, from your current system. To do this, access the relevant work center in your SAP Cloud for Customer system, and filter for all the records you want to enhance, for example, by using the available reports. Don't change the existing IDs. In the downloaded template, don't use the **General** sheet, **Addresses** sheet, **Notes** sheet, **Attachments** sheet, or **Internal Comments** field.

- **Migrate data using the migration tool**
  The new records can be easily migrated by following the upload process from templates populated with new records. For enhancing existing records, you set the migration mode to enhance already existing records before starting the upload process, as mentioned in the previous section for data migration in a first implementation.

17.1.4   Download Migration Templates

The fourth link in the **Prepare for Data Migration** screen is to download migration templates, as shown earlier in Figure 17.2. When you click on the **Download migration**

templates link, you're taken to the **Download Migration Templates** screen, as shown in Figure 17.3.

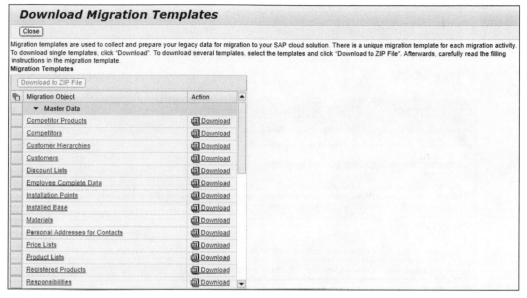

Figure 17.3 List of Data Migration Templates

SAP Cloud for Customer provides standard data migration templates for customers, customer hierarchies, materials, price lists, activities, leads, opportunities, quotes, organizational units, and so on. Depending on your data migration requirements you can select and download these templates individually. If you need to download more than one template, select those templates (by holding the Shift key), and then download to a ZIP file by clicking on **Download to ZIP File** link.

For this example, if you click on the **Customers Template** download link, the template will be downloaded to your machine, as shown in Figure 17.4.

The data migration template is in XML spreadsheet format. It provides instructions on filling in the template, and it's organized with the following tabs: **Introductions**, **General, Addresses, Contact Hours, Contacts, Contacts – Personal Addresses**, and **Direct Responsibility**. You should carefully read the instructions provided before entering data in the template. It's recommended to import data based on a hierarchy. Certain master data uploads need to be in sequence. For example, you must upload the products before you can upload the pricing data for the products. The recommended data import order in SAP Sales Cloud is as follows:

1. Job functions
2. Organizational structure
3. Employee
4. Product category hierarchy
5. Materials
6. Price lists

7. Customer
8. Territory hierarchy
9. Account territory mapping
10. Leads
11. Opportunities

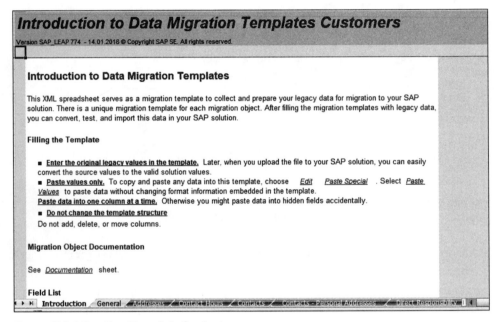

Figure 17.4 Migration Template for Customers

17.1.5   Create a Project Schedule for Data Migration

When you click the last link, **Create a project schedule for data migration**, the **Data Migration Scope and Planning** template in Microsoft Excel format is downloaded to your machine, as shown in Figure 17.5.

The **Read me** tab in the **Data Migration Scope and Planning** template contains instructions about the template, which much be carefully reviewed. The second tab, **DMScopePlanning**, contains data migration scope planning activities, as shown in Figure 17.6.

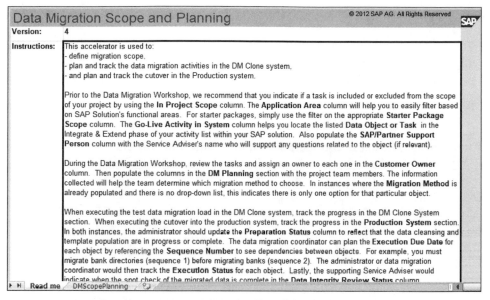

Figure 17.5 Data Migration Scope and Planning Template

Data Migration Scope and Planning

In Project Scope	CRM	PSP	FIN	Application Area	Go-Live Activity in System	Data Object or Task	Sequence Number	Customer Owner	SAP/Partner Support Person	Priority
		Yes	Yes	FIN	Bank Directories	Bank Directories	1			
		Yes	Yes	FIN	Tax Authorities	Tax Authorities	1			
				HRM	Tax Authorities for Payroll	Tax Authorities for Payroll	1			
		Yes	Yes	Foundation	Product Category Hierarchy	Product Category Hierarchy	1			
				SCM	Quality Code Catalogs	Quality Code Catalogs	1			
				SCM	Multi-Level Forecasting	Forecasting Groups	1			
				SCM	Planning Groups	Planning Groups	1			
				SCM	Storage Groups	Storage Groups	1			
				SCM	Production Groups	Production Groups	1			
				SCM	Transport Zones	Transport Zones	1			
				SCM	Locations	Locations	1			
		Yes	Yes	FIN	Set of Books	Set of Books	1			
	Yes	Yes	Yes	HRM	Job Definitions	Job Definitions	1			
				HRM	Reusable Work Schedules	Reusable Work Schedules (Time Models)	1			
				HRM	Create and Maintain Payroll Periods	Create and Maintain Payroll Periods	1			
				SCM	Migration of Engineering Change Orders	Engineering Change Orders	1			
				HRM	Compensation Components Other Providers	Compensation Components	1			
				FIN	Overhead Distribution between Cost Centers	Overhead Distribution between Cost Centers	1			
				SCM	Resource Operating Profile	Resource Operating Profiles	1			

Figure 17.6 Data Migration Scope and Planning Activities

This template can act as a starting point for you to prepare your data migration plan and align with your overall project plan.

After you've populated the data migration template with legacy data, you'll start the data upload process as explained in the next section.

17.2   Uploading Data

Uploading data to SAP Cloud for Customer is much easier and simplified with data migration templates. Before you start the upload process, you must have downloaded the required data migration template as explained in the previous section.

To start the data upload, follow these steps:

1. Log in to SAP Cloud for Customer in the HTML5 UI under the administrator role, navigate to **Business Configuration • Implementation Projects • Open Activity List**, choose the **Integrate and Extend** tab, and select **All Activities** from the dropdown, as shown in Figure 17.7.

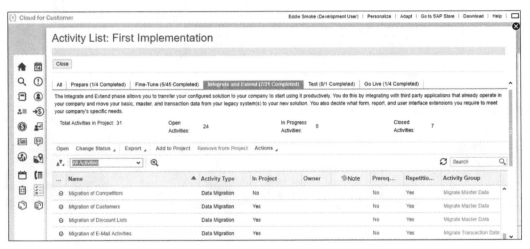

Figure 17.7 Upload Related Data Migration Activities

2. As shown in Figure 17.7, there are individual links for each data upload process. To see the steps for the customer upload process, click on the **Migration of Customers** link. The **Migration of Customers** screen appears.

3. Here you see the **Read about Migration of Customer Data** link, and you can migrate customers using the migration tool. Just like the previous section, you can click on **Read about Migration of Customer Data** to go to the page in the SAP Help library that provides instructions about uploading customer data using templates such as prerequisites and tasks related to migration of customers to SAP Sales Cloud. All business partners share one common number range in the SAP solution. During migration of business partners, such as customers or suppliers, the system

checks whether the IDs already exist. Duplicate IDs are listed in the migration log file. Check the log file, and assign new IDs if necessary.

If you plan to use extension fields in the work center views that are associated with this migration object, you should create the extension fields before you migrate any data for this object. When you upload a source file to the migration tool, the migration tool automatically checks whether additional extension fields have been added to the corresponding work center views. If so, you can add them to your source file and decide whether you want to enter any legacy data in the new columns. The steps for data migration include uploading source data to the migration staging area. Then, using the migration tool, you can migrate data to SAP Sales Cloud.

4. Click on the **Migrate Customers Using the Migration Tool** link to go to the **Migrate Customers** screen, as shown in Figure 17.8.

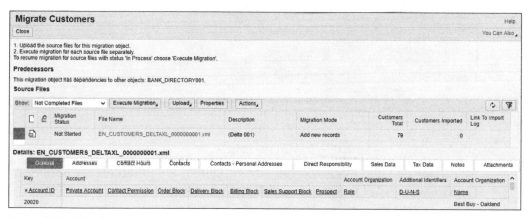

Figure 17.8 Initiating Customer Migration or Upload Activities

5. Under **Execute Migration**, you have options to **Execute Migration Step by Step** or **Execute Data Import Immediately**. It's recommended that you select the **Execute Migration Step by Step** option, at least on the first iteration of the upload, to make sure that you're able to identify and resolve the errors sooner.

6. If you select **Execute Migration Step by Step**, you're taken to a guided five-step process: **1 Validate File**, **2 Convert Values**, **3 Simulate Import**, **4 Execute Import**, and **5 Confirmation** (see Figure 17.9). Click **Next** at each step, and the system will walk you through the import process.

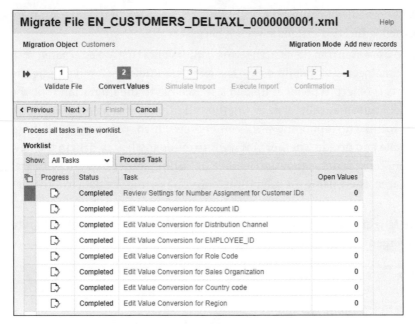

Figure 17.9 Guided Step-by-Step Import Process

For uploading, you can either upload the populated template or a text file. The challenge with using a text file is that mapping becomes very difficult. The template gives you a ready-to-use format to upload the data.

By clicking on **Upload** shown previously in Figure 17.8, you can see the options for **Data from Migration Template** and **Data from Text File**.

17.3   Maintaining Mass Data

In the previous section, we covered how to upload data into SAP Cloud for Customer using standard templates delivered out of the box. If you need to update existing data in SAP Cloud for Customer with new values, then you can leverage the mass data maintenance functionality. Using this allows you to select the exact data you want to update in the system. The mass data maintenance process has basically three processes: you export the data, make your changes, and import the updated data back in.

To carry off mass maintenance, you need to log in to SAP Cloud for Customer in HTML UI under the administrator login and then navigate to **Mass Data Maintenance**, as shown in Figure 17.10.

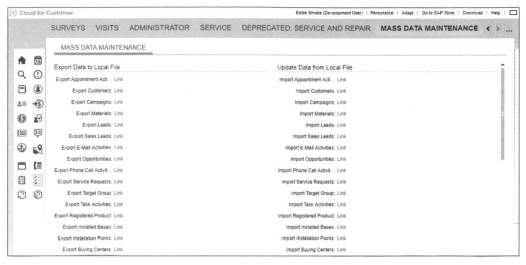

Figure 17.10 Mass Data Maintenance

On the left side of the **MASS DATA MAINTENANCE** screen, export links are provided for various data objects such as appointments, customers, leads, and materials. In the first step, depending on what object you want to mass update, you select the link and export data locally to your machine. For example, if you want to mass update customers, click on the **Link** for **Export Customers** in Figure 17.10, and you're taken to the **Export of Customers** selection screen, as shown in Figure 17.11. On this screen, you can select the filters to identify exactly which customers you need to mass update. You can enable additional filters by clicking on **Additional Fields**, as shown in Figure 17.11.

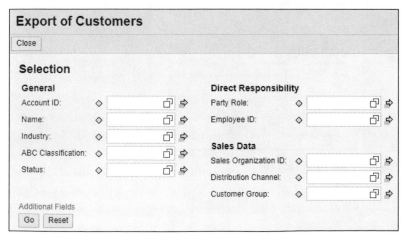

Figure 17.11 Selection Parameters for Export of Customers

After you've selected the filters, click **Go**, and the system generates the export file that can be downloaded as a CSV file (see Figure 17.12).

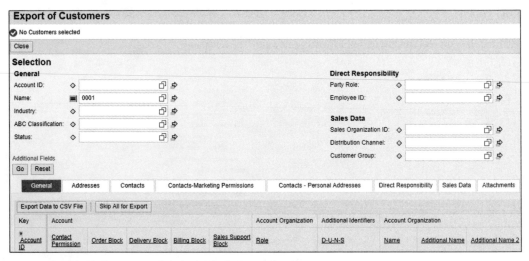

Figure 17.12 Export File Available for Download

In the downloaded CSV file, you can mass update the fields you want to update. In the last step, you need to upload the updated CSV file to the system. To do so, click on the corresponding **Link** for **Update Data from Local File**. In this example, we're mass updating customers, so click the **Link** for **Import Customers**. When you click on this link, the **Upload Data from Text file** popup appears, as shown in Figure 17.13.

Figure 17.13 Uploading Data from Text File

In the **Source File** field, click on **Choose File** to select the local updated file, and then select **Upload** to begin the mass data update process. During the upload process, if there are any data inconsistencies, an error message appears with the erroneous record indicator so that you can update the data and restart the upload process. At the end of update process, you'll be notified with a successful update message if no errors occurred.

17.4 Migrating Employee Data

Migrating employee data to SAP Cloud for Customer shows little difference from migrating accounts and products. In fact, the process for migrating employee data, organizational structure data, and business role data is the same. To start the employee data migration process, log in to SAP Sales Cloud HTML5 UI under administrator access, and then navigate to **ADMINISTRATOR** • **GENERAL SETTINGS** • **Data Integration**, as shown in Figure 17.14.

Figure 17.14 Navigation for Employee Data Migration

There are links for **Employee Master Data Replication**, **Organizational Structure Replication**, and **Business Role Replication**. For employee data migration, click on the **Employee Master Data Replication** link to go to the **EMPLOYEE REPLICATION REQUEST** screen, as shown in Figure 17.15.

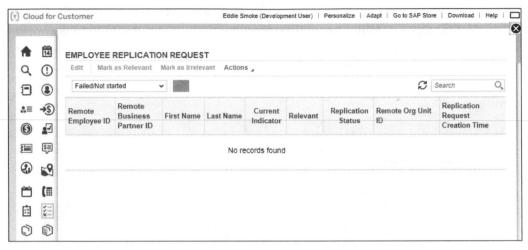

Figure 17.15 Starting the Employee Migration Process

From this screen, click on **Actions**, and select **Upload Complete Data**. The **Migrate Employee Complete Data** screen appears, as shown in Figure 17.16.

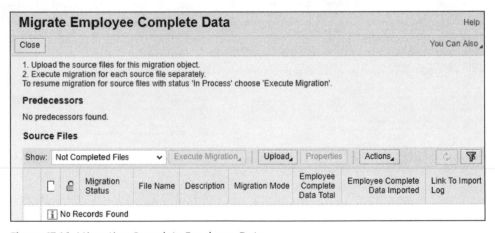

Figure 17.16 Migrating Complete Employee Data

On this screen, you have the option to select and upload the source data from the migration template or from the text file. To select one of these data format options, click on **Upload** (refer to Figure 17.16 and select either **Upload Data from Migration Template** or **Upload Data from Text File**. After selecting the upload file, click on **Actions • Create** to start the migration process. During the data migration process, if there are any inconsistencies in data, you'll receive an error message. After the employee data is successfully migrated, you'll receive a confirmation message.

17.5   Migrating Products

Similar to the previous data migration procedures, you log in to SAP Cloud for Customer HTML5 UI under administrator access and navigate to **Business Configuration • Implementation Projects • Open Activity List**, choose the **Integrate and Extend** tab, and click on **Migration of Materials**, as shown in Figure 17.17.

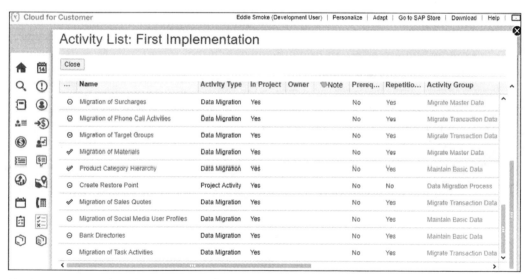

Figure 17.17 Navigation for Migration of Materials

When you click on **Migration of Materials**, you're taken to the **Migration of Materials** link. Similar to previous migrations, you see the link for documentation (**Read about migration of materials**) and **Migrate materials using the migration tool**, as shown in Figure 17.18.

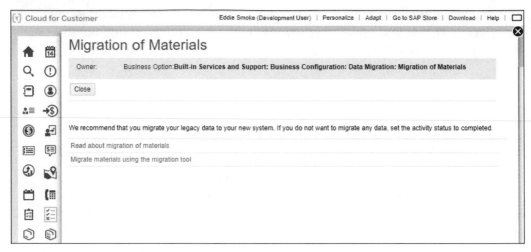

Figure 17.18 Migration of Materials Screen

Click on **Migrate materials using the migration tool** to go to the **Migrate Materials** screen shown in Figure 17.19.

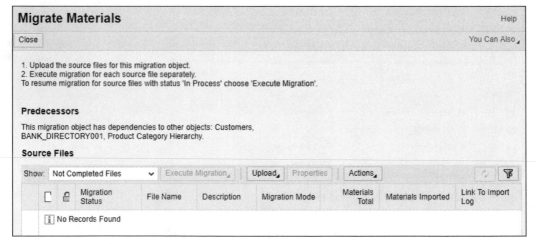

Figure 17.19 Uploading the Source File for Materials Data Migration

The next steps from here are the same as those covered in previous sections. You select the source file either from the materials migration template or a text file and then start the migration process.

17.6   Migrating Account Hierarchies

Similar to migration of materials, for account hierarchy migration, choose **Business Configuration • Implementation Projects • Open Activity List**, select the **Integrate and Extend** tab, and then choose **Migration of Account Hierarchy**, as shown in Figure 17.20.

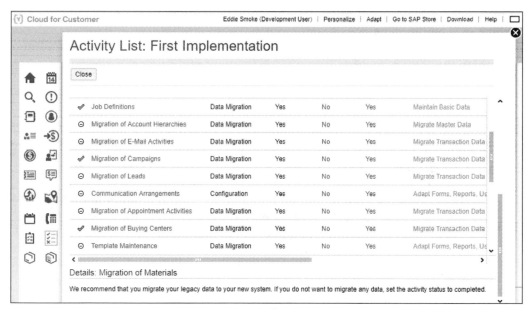

Figure 17.20 Link for Migration of Account Hierarchy

The **Migration of Account Hierarchies** screen appears, as shown in Figure 17.21. The first two links on this screen are related to documentation. You should review these SAP Help links before starting your account hierarchy migration exercise.

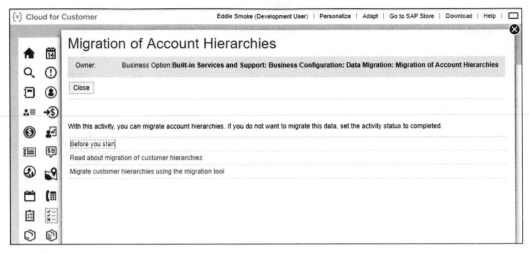

Figure 17.21 Migration of Account Hierarchy

The actual steps for migration of account hierarchies from templates are the same as those for migration of accounts and products.

17.7   Uploading Territories

Territory hierarchies can be uploaded through an Excel spreadsheet by the administrator. To do this, navigate to **ADMINISTRATOR**, choose the **SALES AND CAMPAIGN SETTINGS**, and click on **Territories**, as shown in Figure 17.22.

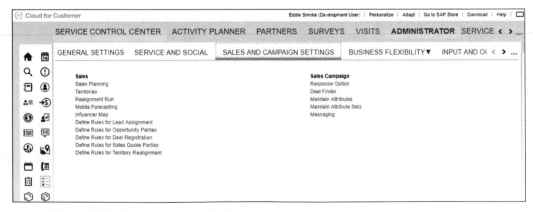

Figure 17.22 Link to Navigate Territories

The **Territories** screen appears, as shown in Figure 17.23.

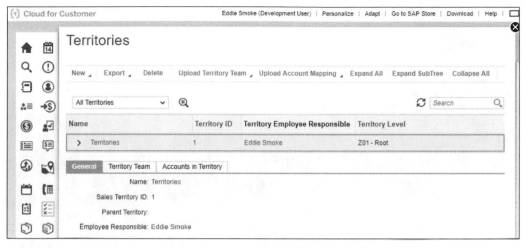

Figure 17.23 Uploading the Territory Hierarchy, Team, and Account Mapping

Here you can upload the territory hierarchy, territory team, and account territory mapping from Excel. Click on **New • Territories from Microsoft Excel** to upload the territory hierarchy. To upload the territory team, click on **Upload Territory Team • Upload Territory Team**. Finally, to upload the account territory mapping, click on **Upload Account Mapping • Upload Account Territory Mapping**.

17.8   Data Workbench

SAP Sales Cloud allows you to export, import, and update data directly from the responsive user interface (RUI), as shown in Figure 17.24. In the following subsections, we'll review these capabilities available under the **Data Workbench** work center.

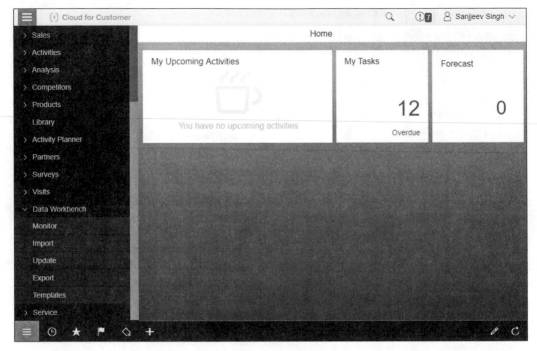

Figure 17.24 Data Workbench Work Center in RUI

17.8.1   Import

To import data in SAP Sales Cloud, click on **Data Workbench • Import**, and the **Import** screen appears, as shown in Figure 17.25. Here you have three options: **Composite Business Objects**, **Individual Objects**, and **Attachments**. The **Composite Business Objects** option allows you to import two objects such as an account and contact persons. As the name suggests, the **Individual Objects** option allows you to import only one object at a time, such as an account or contact. With the **Attachments** option, you can upload attachments to accounts, contacts, appointments, and so on.

The best approach for data import is to download the metadata for the object you're trying to upload, populate the metadata with your own data, and then execute the import process. For example, if you want to upload account and contact, you select the **Composite Business Objects** radio button and then choose **Account Contact Persons** from the list. The **Download Metadata** link is shown in Figure 17.26.

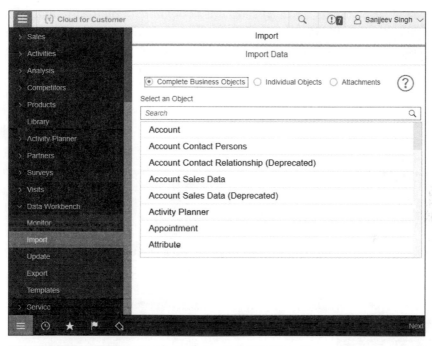

Figure 17.25 Importing Data through the Data Workbench

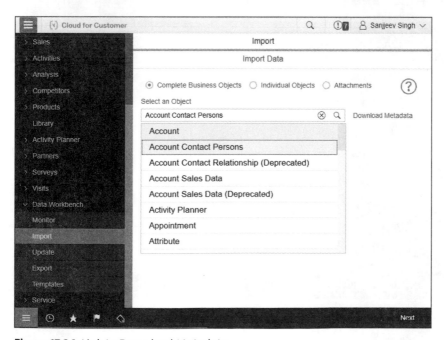

Figure 17.26 Link to Download Metadata

Click on **Download Metadata**, and a ZIP file named *CorporateAccountHasContactPerson.zip* is downloaded to your local machine. This ZIP file contains three folders: *CodeList*, *FieldDefinition*, and *Templates*, as shown in Figure 17.27. You can reference the field definitions of the metadata and then populate the template file with the data that you want to upload.

Figure 17.27 Metadata Containing Three Folders

After preparing your upload data in the template, click **Next** (refer to Figure 17.26), and the **Upload zip file** screen appears, as shown in Figure 17.28.

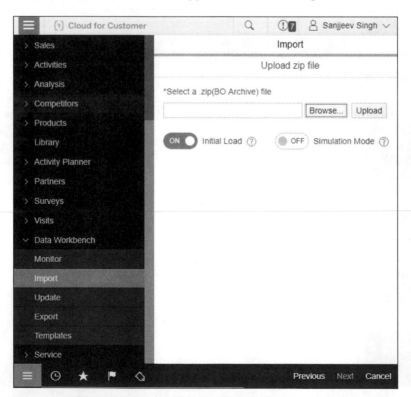

Figure 17.28 Option to Upload the File with Data

On this screen, you can select **Initial Load ON/OFF**. This tells you whether your data is in an initial load to the system or in a delta load. Depending on what kind of data you're uploading, you can select the **Simulation Mode ON/OFF**. Before you actually perform the upload process, it's recommended that you simulate the process so that you can proactively identify any data inconsistency issues during the upload process. After making these settings, select **Browse**, select the file from your local machine that you're planning to upload, and click **Upload**. You'll receive a confirmation system message that records have been successfully uploaded to the system. Following the same process, you can upload individual objects and attachments by selecting those options.

17.8.2 Export

The export functionality allows you to export data from SAP Sales Cloud to your local machine. The export process is fairly straightforward as compared to the import process. To start an export process, click on **Data Workbench • Export**, and the **Export** screen appears, as shown in Figure 17.29.

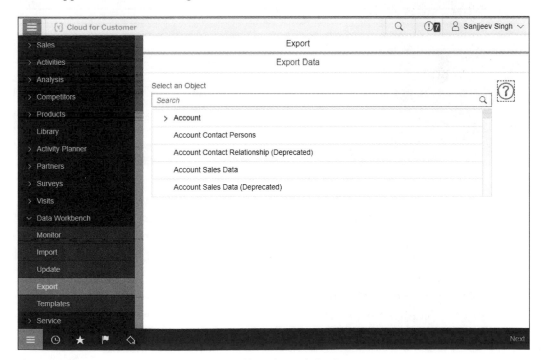

Figure 17.29 Export Screen in the Data Workbench Work Center

On this screen, you select the object you want to export. For example, if you want to download appointments from SAP Sales Cloud, you select **Appointment**, and filters are provided to help you further select the data set you want to export, as shown in Figure 17.30.

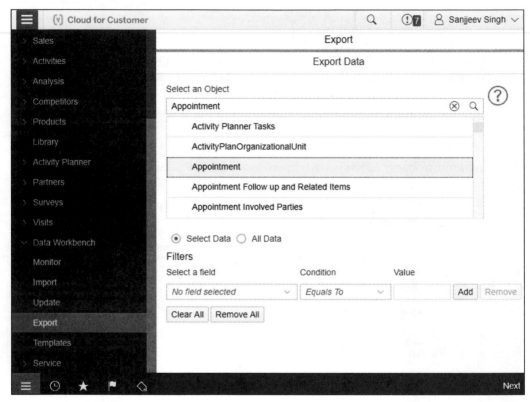

Figure 17.30 Filters to Further Select the Data Export

You can select **All Data** to export all the appointments from the system. However, you can also select filters such as fields matching certain operators. For example, you can select the filter to export appointments for IDs greater than or equal to 100, and then select **Add**, as shown in Figure 17.31.

After adding the appropriate filters, click **Next** to go to the **Review** screen, as shown in Figure 17.32. After reviewing your selection for export, click on **Export Data**, and you'll see the export success message (see Figure 17.33).

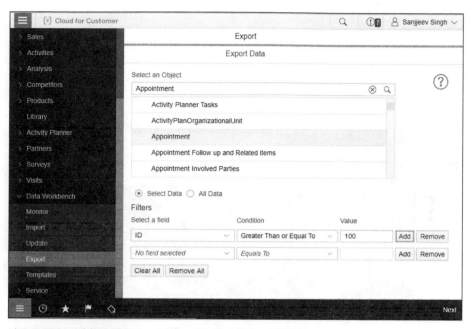

Figure 17.31 Adding an Export Filter for Appointment IDs

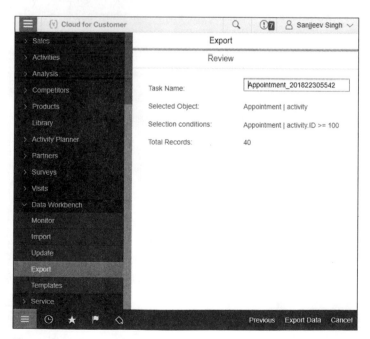

Figure 17.32 Reviewing an Export

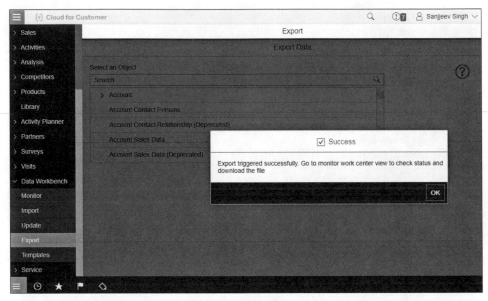

Figure 17.33 Successful Export Message

The message confirms that the export was triggered successfully. To see the status, choose **Data Workbench • Monitor**, and you'll see the export as your task (see Figure 17.34).

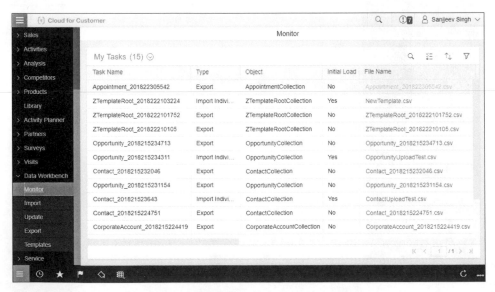

Figure 17.34 Monitor Displaying the Export Task for Appointment

If you scroll to the right on this screen, you'll see the status of your export as **In Process** or **Finished**. When you see the status as **Finished**, you can click on the file name to download it to your machine.

17.8.3   Update

The **Update** process under **Data Workbench** allows you to update data in SAP Sales Cloud from your local machine. Select **Data Workbench • Update**, and the **Update** screen appears, as shown in Figure 17.35.

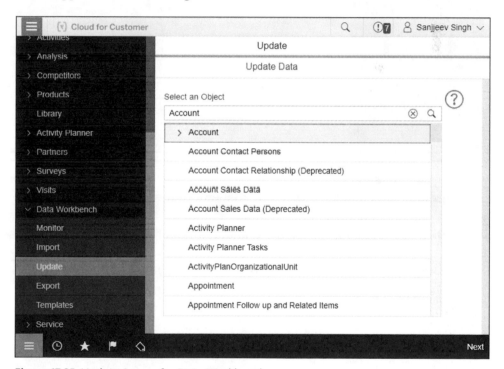

Figure 17.35 Update Screen for Data Workbench

Depending on the data object you want to update, you select the appropriate object from this list, and click **Next**. The screen to select the file to upload for updating appears, as shown in Figure 17.36.

On this screen, you can select the **Update Mode** as **Ignore Blank Values** or **Update Blank Values from Your Data**. As pointed our earlier, it's recommended to select the switch **ON** for **Simulation Mode**, so that the update is simulated first for any potential error or inconsistency. You can select **Browse** to pick the file from your local machine with data to update and then click **Upload**.

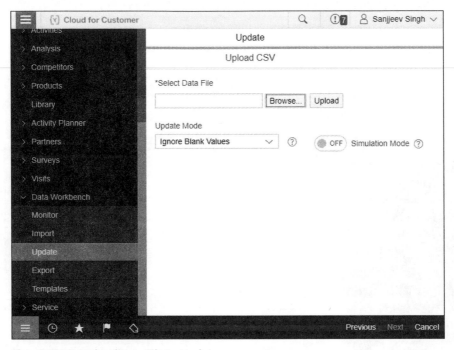

Figure 17.36 Uploading a File to Update

As you've seen, the **Data Workbench** work center is a very powerful functionality in SAP Sales Cloud for exporting, importing, and updating business data in your system.

17.9   Summary

In this chapter, you've learned that by using standard data migration templates available in SAP Cloud for Customer, you can easily mass upload and mass update accounts, products, account hierarchies, territories, and employees as needed. The key is to identify the right template for data migration, download and populate the template with the data to be uploaded or updated, and then run the step-by-step upload process available in SAP Cloud for Customer. In the next chapter, you'll learn about the personalization and extension capabilities available in SAP Cloud for Customer.

Chapter 18
Personalization and Extensions

SAP Cloud for Customer provides personalization options for individual users and administrators to modify their own view of screens to tailor the system to the way they use it on a regular basis.

In this last chapter, we'll cover some unique capabilities regarding personalization and extensions. SAP Cloud for Customer provides several features that enable you to customize fields, screen layouts, output forms, custom objects, and so on. To begin, we'll review the personalization and user interface (UI) adaptation capabilities available to application end users as well as administrators, including adapting the layout per your company logo and branding. We'll provide step-by-step instructions on how to add new fields, how to change attributes of fields (e.g., mandatory or optional), and how to hide fields.

We'll also cover how to add extension fields and change page layouts per your requirements. It's important to understand the code list restrictions so that you know how to limit certain dropdown values for specific fields in the master data and transaction data. We'll review step-by-step instructions on how to use code list restriction capabilities. You'll also learn how to create custom objects, master templates, and form templates.

18

18.1 End-User Personalization

When you implement the SAP Sales Cloud solution, your administrator will define the way your system is displayed. However, personalization is all about making the application suitable to individual user needs as far as the UI is concerned. For example, as an end user, you might want to add your own background image, use drag and drop to easily move screen sections to another location on the screen, set regional time settings, select whether to display additional onscreen explanatory text, manage password and texts, and so on. To extend your personalization experience further, you might want to add or change labels, make mashups, create or change default queries, and more. SAP Cloud for Customer allows you to make all these personalization settings specific to individual users.

The key for personalization settings is that changes on screens take effect immediately. You can go ahead and accomplish your daily activities without having to restart the system. You can always roll back your changes by going to default settings. It's important to note that before an end user can make personalization settings, the administrator needs to enable the personalization option for end users. This option is available by choosing **Adapt • Company Settings • General**, as shown in Figure 18.1. On this screen, if you enable the **Disable User Personalization Features** checkbox, the end user's personalization option won't be available to anyone except the administrator.

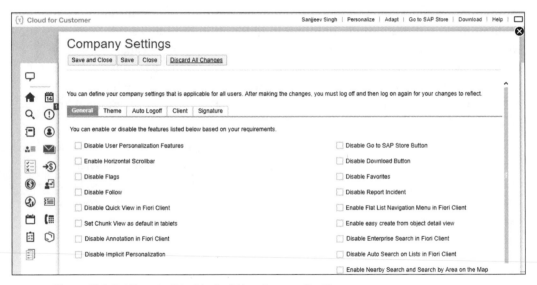

Figure 18.1 Settings to Disable End User Personalization

Under **Personalization**, you can personalize your preferences, system settings, navigation settings, content, and screen layout settings. To personalize your system settings, choose **Personalize • My Settings**, and you're taken to the **My Settings** screen, as shown in Figure 18.2. On this screen, you can change the **Regional Settings** and set your preferred **Date Format**, **Decimal Notation**, **Time Zone**, **Time Format**, **Language**, **Onscreen Help**, and **Accessibility**.

Onscreen explanatory texts consist of text boxes that are shown at the top of a screen or screen section, as well as short help texts that are displayed when you move the cursor over an underlined field. In addition, you can activate country-specific online help content to view content that is specific to your country in the Help Center. On the **Accessibility** tab, you can enable **Support Screen Readers** to read UI texts and mouseover texts in all screens.

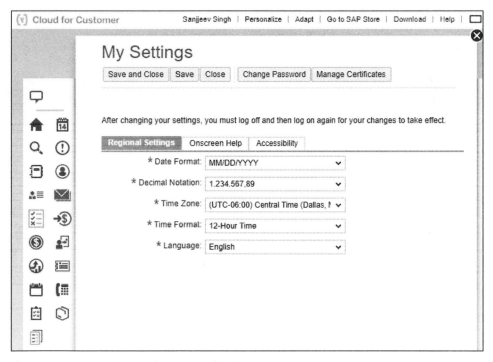

Figure 18.2 My Settings under Personalization

Next, you can use personalization settings to change your background image. Choose **Personalize • My Background Image** to go to the **Shell Personalization** screen, as shown in Figure 18.3. Here you can upload a new background image.

One of the key advantages of personalization is that you can add/hide the field labels on various screens. To do this, you follow the navigation **Personalize • Start Personalization** and screen you're on, is enabled for personalization as shown in Figure 18.4.

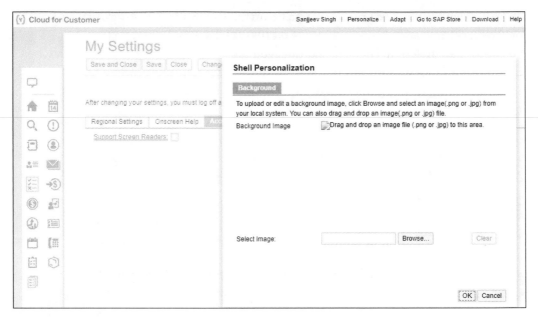

Figure 18.3 Personalization Option to Change Background Image

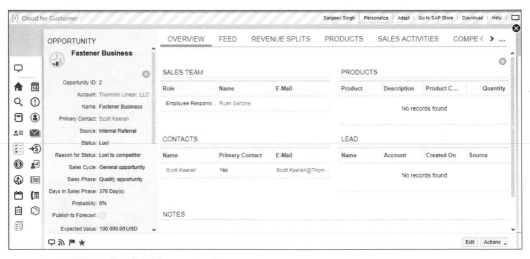

Figure 18.4 Personalizing a Screen

On the personalization **OVERVIEW** screen, you can hover your mouse anywhere on the screen and see options to **Hide Element**, **Add Field**, and **Add Mash Up**. You can also drag and drop screen elements to personalize the screens the way you want. After you complete the personalization, choose **Personalization • End Personalization**, and click on **End Personalization** to exit out of personalization mode.

18.2   Adapting User Interfaces

User adaptation refers to a set of tools administrators can use to add or modify fields, change master screen layouts, assign screen layouts to specific roles, restrict drop-down list values, and modify output forms. You can also migrate adaptation changes from one system to another system, such as a test tenant to a production tenant. The screen adaptation feature allows for changes to fields and screens that appear to all users of SAP Cloud for Customer. This is an extremely important feature if critical business data needs to be captured so that it shows on all user screens.

Unlike personalization, adaptations are done by administrators not end users. As a key differentiator, personalization is for individual users, and adaptation is for a wider user group. As an administrator, you can customize and extend your solution using a variety of tools available in SAP Cloud for Customer. Through UI adaptation, you can add extension fields, create custom objects, change and assign page layouts, and define code list restrictions.

In the following section, we'll review some of the adaptation capabilities available in SAP Cloud for Customer.

18.2.1   Adding Company-Specific Help

The Help Center in SAP Cloud for Customer contains the solution-specific help documentation delivered by SAP. However, as an administrator, you can add company-specific documentation in any work set, for example, process descriptions or general business rules. You can also add a file to all screens within the system as long as you've prepared your document in Microsoft Office format or as a PDF file. To add company-specific help, follow these steps:

1. Navigate to the screen where you want to add a document.
2. Open the **Help Center**. You can add your document to this screen or to all the screens in the system, as shown in Figure 18.5.
3. To add a screen-specific document, click on **Edit Company-Specific Content**. However, if you want to add a document to all the screens, click on **Edit Company-Specific Content for all Screens**.

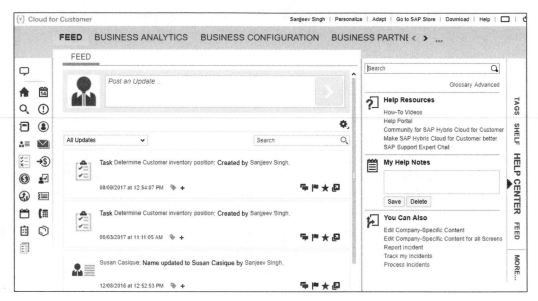

Figure 18.5 Adding Company-Specific Content

4. In both cases, you get a dialog window to select the document or link, as shown in Figure 18.6. On this screen, select the document you want to add, and then click **Save**.

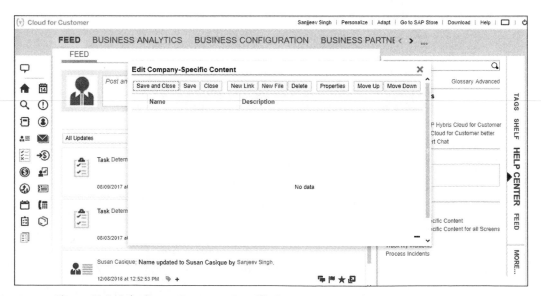

Figure 18.6 Selecting a Company-Specific Document or Link

18.2.2   Adapting a User Interface for Your Company

When you implement SAP Cloud for Customer, it's important that the solution follows company-wide brand consistency. You need to update the UI by adding logos, changing colors and images, and selecting a theme that best fits your company's logo and colors. To adapt the UI for your company, follow these steps:

1. Set the default client. As covered in previous chapters, you can use SAP Cloud for Customer under three different UIs: Microsoft Silverlight, HTML5, and SAP Fiori (or responsive user interface [RUI]).

2. As an administrator, you can set a default UI or client for your users. Choose **Adapt • Company Settings • Client**, as shown in Figure 18.7.

3. From the **Preferred Client** dropdown, select **Fiori Client**, **HTML**, or **Silverlight**. The selected client will be the default client for users.

Figure 18.7 Setting the Preferred Client for Users

4. Similar to the client, you can select the theme, as shown in Figure 18.8. Select either the **Skyline** theme or **Gold Reflection** theme. If you're using HTML5 as your preferred client, then you can only select **Skyline** as your theme.

Figure 18.8 Changing Themes

To add your company logo to SAP Sales Cloud for consistent branding, follow these steps:

1. Log in to HTML5 UI as administrator, click on **Adapt**, and choose **Adapt • Edit Master Layout**, as shown in Figure 18.9.

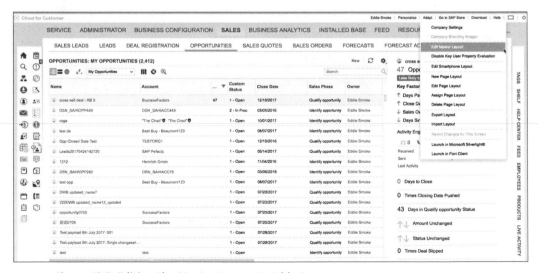

Figure 18.9 Editing the Master Layout to Add a Logo

2. Click on **Adapt** and then **Company Branding Images**, as shown in Figure 18.10, and you're taken to the **Shell Personalization** screen, as shown in Figure 18.11.

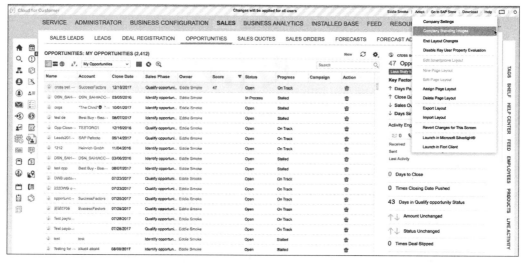

Figure 18.10 Selecting Company Branding Images

Figure 18.11 Browsing for the Logo Image from the Local Machine

3. On the **Shell Personalization** screen, click to the **Logo** tab, and add the logo image file from your local machine via drag and drop or **Browse** and select, as shown in Figure 18.12.

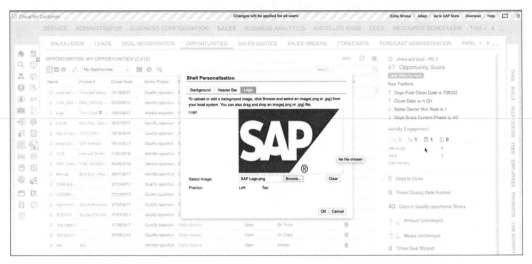

Figure 18.12 Adding a Logo to the Shell Personalization

4. After you've selected your company image logo, click **OK** to see that your company image has been added to the screen on the top-left corner, as shown in Figure 18.13.

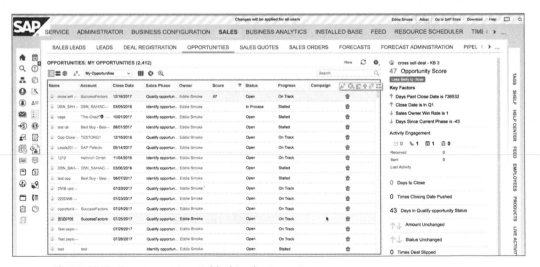

Figure 18.13 Company Logo Added to the Layout

18.2.3   Migrating Adaptation Changes

The adaptation setup from one SAP Cloud for Customer tenant can be easily migrated to another system to avoid any duplicate setup effort. Newly created page layouts, code list restrictions, page layout assignments, other adaptation changes, and so on can be easily migrated between tenants. You can download and upload these adaptation changes in XML format. To begin, follow these steps:

1. To export the layout, choose **Adapt • Export Layout,** and the **Select Page Layout** screen appears, as shown in Figure 18.14.

2. On this screen, select from the **Page Layout** dropdown, and click **OK** to download the layout to your local machine. It's important that you first download the master layout before downloading the individual page layouts.

3. In the new SAP Cloud for Customer tenant, choose **Adapt • Import Layout** to import the layout exported from the other tenant previously. While importing the layout, it's important that you first import the master layout and then the individual page layout.

Figure 18.14 Selecting a Page Layout to Export in XML Format

18.2.4   Working with Validations

You can define validations to generate custom messages for users. These messages can be error messages, warning messages, or simply information messages. To enable these validations, you must define the rule conditions based on the available fields in the UI model. To begin, follow these steps:

1. To define the validation, navigate to the screen where you want to define a validation, and then choose **Adapt • Edit Master Layout**, as shown in Figure 18.15. At the top of the screen, you can see the system message that changes made to the master layout will be applied to all the users.

Figure 18.15 Creating Validations for Opportunities

2. On this screen, hover over mouse on any field to see the options to **Add Field**, **Change Label**, and **Hide Element**.

3. In addition, you can change the property for a field in the master layout, such as make a field **Read Only**, **Visible**, or **Mandatory**, as shown in Figure 18.16.

4. You can also enhance the property by applying rules on the fields by clicking on **Rule**, as shown in Figure 18.16.

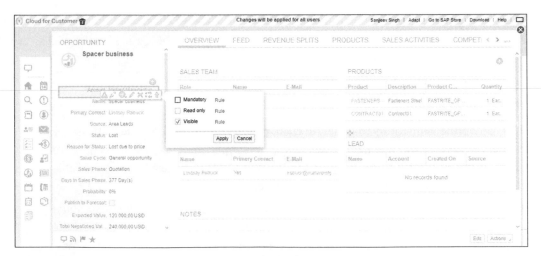

Figure 18.16 Options to Change Properties in the Master Layout

5. To add validation on a field, click on the validation sign, and the **Validations** popup appears to add a validation, as shown in Figure 18.17.

Figure 18.17 Adding a Validation

6. To create a new validation, click on **New**, and the **Model Validation Screen** appears, as shown in Figure 18.18. Here you can add the **Validation Name**, **Event** (on save), and **Severity (Error, Warning, Information)**. On the **Messages** tab, you can maintain messages text in the language of your choice. On the **Editor** tab, you can define the rules for validation as needed.

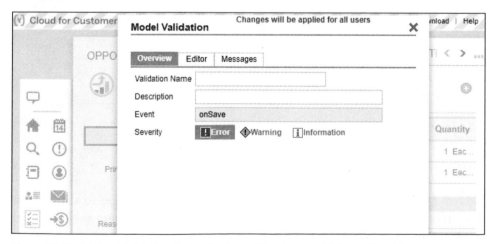

Figure 18.18 Adding Validation Rules for Error, Warning, and Information Messages

18.3   Extension Fields

The extension fields are additional fields that administrators can add to a SAP Cloud for Customer system. Administrators can create extension fields for a screen that has been enabled for extension fields. The field can then be added to other screens, form templates, analytical data sources and reports, and so on. When you first create an extension field, you navigate to a screen on which you want it to appear and add it to a section of the screen. Each screen section is based on an underlying business context. The business context typically corresponds to part of a business document or other object, for example, the header data of a sales order. The business context is used to determine which other screens, form templates, analytical data sources and reports, enterprise search categories, and extension scenarios that the field can be added to.

You can create extension fields using the **Adapt** function. To create a custom field, navigate to the screen where you want to add a new field, and then choose **Adapt •
Edit Master Layout**. At the top of the screen, the message **Changes will be applied for all users** is displayed, as shown in Figure 18.19.

Figure 18.19 Editing a Master Layout for an Opportunity

Adaptation mode allows you, as an administrator, to make changes to a screen and then try out your changes before publishing them and making them available to all users. In adaptation mode, place your cursor over the screen element where you want to add an extension field, and click on the **+** button (**Add Fields**). When the

Additional Fields dialog box appears, select **Add Fields • Additional Fields**. In the extension field dialog box, the system displays the business context to which you've chosen to add the field. You can follow the intuitive icons to enter a label, and select the field type, default value, and so on. After making all the entries for the new field per your business requirements, click **Save**, and your new field is created.

After you've created an extension field, you can define more properties such as whether a field should be mandatory or read only. You can also modify the field and its usage in other areas of the solution such as form templates, data sources for reporting, and enterprise search.

If you want to remove the changes you've made as an administrator for all the users on the current screen, you can discard the changes and revert back to the original screen.

18.4   Page Layout

By editing the master layout, you can make changes to the page layout for users. You can create a specialized page layout and assign it to specific business roles. In a new page layout, you can easily add mashups, fields, tabs, and tables; organize queries; and hide items on the screen. To create a new page layout, follow these steps:

1. Navigate to **Adapt • New Page Layout**, and the **New Page Layout** dialog box appears. Enter a page **Name** and **Description**, as shown in Figure 18.20.

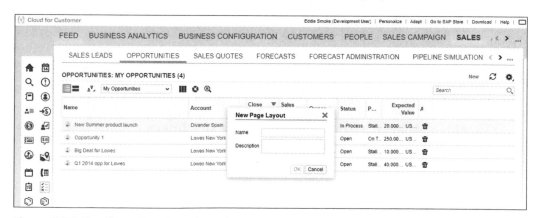

Figure 18.20 Creating a New Page Layout

2. Make the changes you need in the new page layout.

3. After you're done making changes, finish the new layout by choosing **Adapt • End Layout Changes**.

4. After you've created the new page layout, you can assign it to roles or instances by choosing **Adapt • Assign Page Layout**, as shown in Figure 18.21.

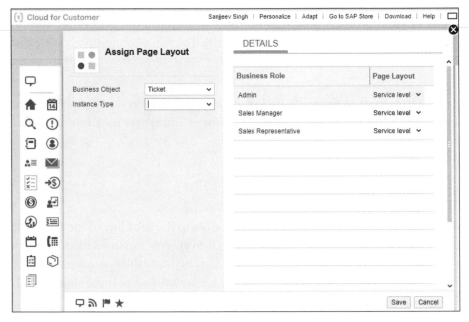

Figure 18.21 Assigning Page Layouts to a Business Role

5. As shown in Figure 18.21, select the **Business Object** (**Ticket**) for the layouts you want to assign. If you haven't made any changes to the business object, you won't see any here under business objects. Based on the business object selected, the system generates a list of **Instance Types** and **Business Roles** you can assign the new page layout to.

6. After assigning the layout, save the changes, and the new layout will be immediately available for those business roles and instances.

18.5   Code Lists Restrictions

Code lists are nothing but the lists of dropdown values for specific fields in business objects. SAP Cloud for Customer allows you to restrict the values available from a dropdown list by creating and maintaining code list restrictions for different business roles. You can restrict those values based on a control field, a business role, or a combination of both. To enable code list restrictions, follow these steps:

1. Log in under the administrator role, and choose **Administrator • General Settings • Code List Restrictions**, as shown in Figure 18.22.

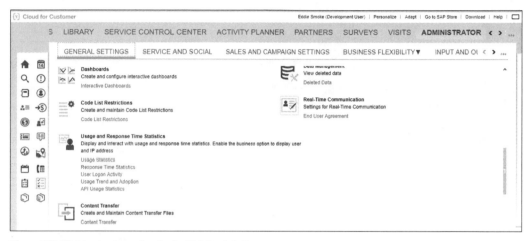

Figure 18.22 Navigation for Code List Restrictions

2. Click on **Code List Restrictions**, and the system displays a list of current code list restrictions in your system.

3. To create a new code list restriction, click on **New**, and you're prompted to enter the details shown in Figure 18.23.

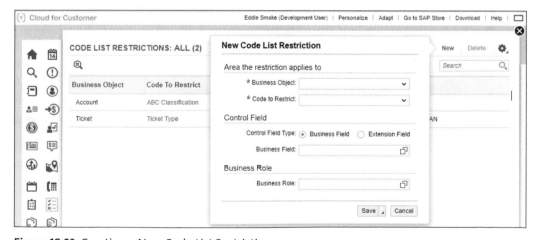

Figure 18.23 Creating a New Code List Restriction

4. Select the **Business Object** from the dropdown depending on the code list restriction you're trying to create. For example, if you're trying to create a code list restriction for **Ticket**, you select **Ticket** from the **Business Object** dropdown, and the **Code to Restrict** field dropdown is enabled. The codes you select from to restrict for **Ticket** are **Priority**, **Processing**, **Status**, and **Ticket Type**, as shown in Figure 18.24.

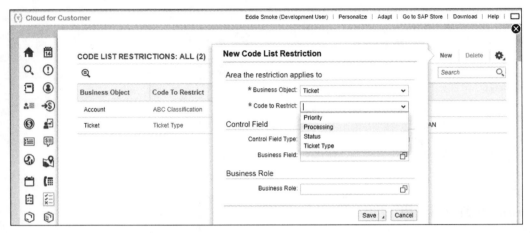

Figure 18.24 Codes to Restrict for Ticket

5. Select **Priority** under **Code to Restrict**, and then select **Escalation** in **Business Field**. If you want the restriction to be valid for only certain business roles, then you can select those business roles in the **Business Role** field.

6. After maintaining the values, select **Save and Open** to open the **Code List Restriction** screen, as shown in Figure 18.25.

7. Here you can edit the values and disable the dropdown values you don't want to see for **Ticket Priority**. You can also select the default values for the priority by going to the **DEFAULT VALUES** tab, as shown in Figure 18.25.

After you've saved your entries, you'll see that the dropdown values have been restricted based on the settings you just made.

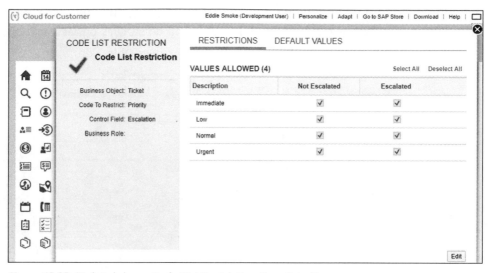

Figure 18.25 Maintaining a Code List Restriction for a Priority

18.6   Custom Forms

SAP Cloud for Customer provides a form template to define the content and layout for all business documents that can be output from the system. You can use master templates to create a standardized document header, footer, and sender address. Both form templates and master templates can be customized to meet your specific business requirements. SAP Cloud for Customer enables you to create custom forms using an easy form editor and Adobe LiveCycle Designer.

For most of the simple business requirements, the easy form editor should be sufficient, but for more complex editing requirements, you need experience in Adobe LiveCycle Designer. It's important to note that requirements for custom forms must be identified early in the project to allow enough time for development and avoid any project delays. If the requirement comes late in the project, it will likely cause project delays. Understanding and communicating the associated cost for this development is also important. Before development begins, detailed requirements must be gathered and agreed upon with business stakeholders before passing those to the development team.

To create a form template, log in under the administrator role, and choose **Administrator • Business Flexibility**. Here you can maintain the master template and form

18

template. Before you create a form template, you need to maintain the master template with your company logo and email disclaimer. To do so, click on **Master Template Maintenance**, as shown in Figure 18.26.

Figure 18.26 Master Template Maintenance under Business Flexibility

Standard SAP Cloud for Customer delivers the **Office Master Template** and **Form Master Template** options, as shown in Figure 18.26. Select **Form Master Template**, and the default template becomes available for you, as shown in Figure 18.27.

Figure 18.27 Default Form Master Template

Select the default **Form Master Template**, and then select **Edit**. The **Form and E-Mail Master Template: Default Form Master Template** screen appears, as shown in Figure 18.28. Here you can upload your company logo and align the logo per the given options. In addition, you can maintain the email disclaimer language and select **Save and Close** to have your own master form template.

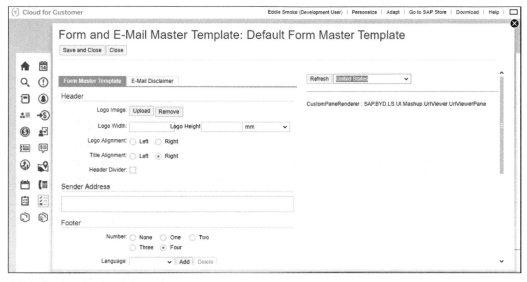

Figure 18.28 Form and E-Mail Master Template Screen

After that, you can modify your form template by going to **Administrator • Business Flexibility • Form Template Maintenance**. Here you select the form you need from the active forms, as shown in Figure 18.29.

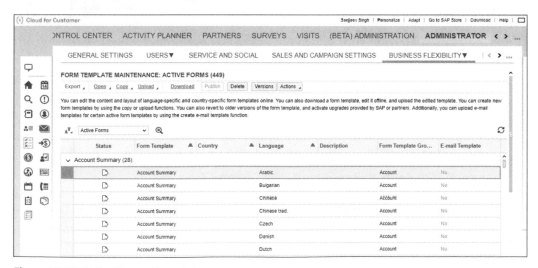

Figure 18.29 Active Forms Template

You can download the form, make updates, and then upload the form. You can even open the form in Adobe LiveCycle Designer by choosing **Open • Adobe LiveCycle Designer** to make necessary changes in the form. After making changes in the form, select **Save** and **Publish** to activate your form.

18.7   Custom Business Objects

SAP Cloud for Customer allows you to create and define custom business objects per your business requirements. This creates a customer-specific solution called KeyUser-Solution in the SAP Cloud Applications Studio. You always create customer business objects in the test tenant first. After it's tested and working as expected, you download and then upload to the production tenant. To create a custom business object, follow these steps:

1. Navigate to **Administrator • General Settings • Custom Object Builder**, as shown in Figure 18.30.

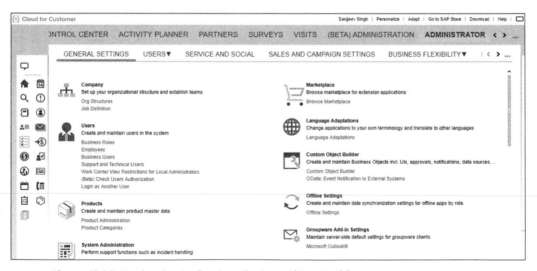

Figure 18.30 Navigation to Create a Custom Object Builder

2. Click on **Custom Object Builder** to open the **Custom Object Builder** screen. Here you can click on **New** to create a new custom object, as shown in Figure 18.31.

3. Enter the **Name** of the new custom object that uses only alphanumeric values but doesn't start with a digit. You can also use capital letters, but the system doesn't allow you to use spaces or other special characters.

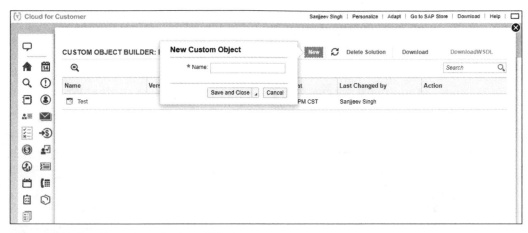

Figure 18.31 Creating a New Custom Object

4. After entering the name of the custom object, select **Save and Close** to see the newly created custom object in the list.

5. After creating the custom object, you need to open it to add fields and additional attributes for your custom object. Click the link for the custom object, and select **Add** under **Fields** to add new fields for the custom object, as shown in Figure 18.32.

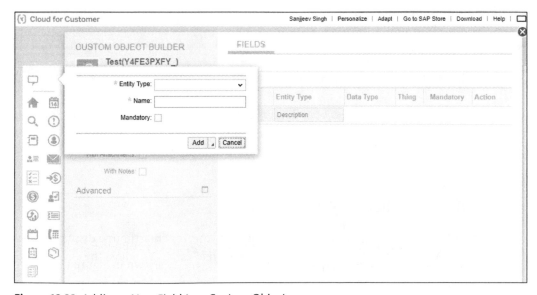

Figure 18.32 Adding a New Field to a Custom Object

6. For a new field, select a value from the **Entity Type** dropdown such as **Amount**, **Code**, **Date**, **Description**, **List**, or **Quantity**. In addition, name your field, and, if needed, make it a mandatory field for your custom object.

7. After entering all the details for the field, select **Add**. You can use advanced options to make additional settings for your object such as **Assign to other Work Center**, **With authorization**, **With Multiple Nodes**, and **With Actions**, as shown in Figure 18.33.

Figure 18.33 Setting Advanced Options for a Custom Object

You can repeat this process of adding fields to include all the needed fields for your custom object and then save and publish. You've now successfully created a custom object.

18.8   Smartphone Layout

In SAP Sales Cloud, you can adjust the master layout for smartphone display so that the contents can be optimized for smaller screen real estate. To adjust the smartphone layout, choose **Adapt • Edit Smartphone Layout**, and you'll be navigated to the smartphone layout, as shown in Figure 18.34.

Figure 18.34 Editing the Smartphone Layout

To change the layout, select the element you want to remove from smartphone displays, choose **Change Properties**, and then deselect the visible control. When you're finished with your changes, choose **Adapt** and **End Smartphone Changes**. There is no additional assignment step required. Anytime the relevant screen is opened on a smartphone, the new optimized layout is displayed. When logging on from a smartphone, the smartphone layout supersedes any page layouts.

For example, let's say you've modified the page layout for the **SALES TERRITORIES** tab on an account screen by adding or removing a section. When users assigned this layout log on their smartphones, the changes still apply. Then you modify the smartphone layout to hide sales territories. Now, when users who are assigned that page layout log on with their smartphones, they won't see the **SALES TERRITORIES** tab; they will still see the modified layout when they log on with any other device though.

18.9   Adjusting Sections within Item Details

Within the item details, you can rearrange sections and adjust their column and row spans. You can adjust the master layout for an item details screen so that the sections within a tab are arranged in the order you like. You can also manage the white space by adjusting the column and row spans individual sections use. For example, on the **OVERVIEW** tab of an account, you can select the **Account Team** section and drag it to the top left. The other sections are pushed down or moved over. Now if you remove the section to the right of **Account Team**, you'll be left with an empty space; so you can adjust the **Account Team** section to span two columns rather than one. Select the section to change. Choose **Change Properties**, set the column and row spans, and apply your changes.

You can change the item details by choosing **Adapt • Edit Master Layout** and then opening the object you want to change the item layout for. For example, if you want to update the item details for addresses in a customer account, you open the account details and hover the mouse over **ADDRESSES**, as shown in Figure 18.35. **Add Validation**, **Change Properties**, **Reset to Default**, **Hide Element**, **Paste**, and **Select Parent** options are available for the **ADDRESSES** element.

Figure 18.35 Updating Item Details for Addresses

If you need to add a new item element, click on the **+** button, as shown in Figure 18.36.

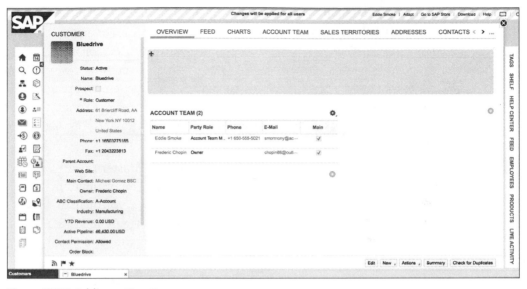

Figure 18.36 Adding a New Item

Within the item details, you can add columns and rows as needed. Figure 18.37 shows details for an **ACCOUNT TEAM** item. Hover the mouse over the item, and click on **Change Properties** to open the popup in which you can select **Column Span** and **Row Span**.

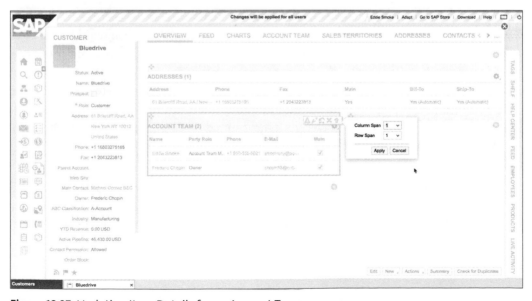

Figure 18.37 Updating Item Details for an Account Team

After you select the **Column Span** and **Row Span**, click **Apply** to see the changes applied to the **ACCOUNT TEAM**, as shown in Figure 18.38.

Figure 18.38 Item Details Updated through Adjustments

18.10   Summary

In this chapter, you learned about the powerful personalization and extension capabilities available in SAP Cloud for Customer that allow you to enhance end-user experience as well as meet new business requirements for custom fields and custom objects. You saw that with administrator access, you can create master templates and page layouts applicable for all users, as well as enable end users to personalize their experience to create the page layout most suited to their interaction with the application. Adaptation capabilities available in SAP Cloud for Customer are very intuitive and self-explanatory.

We hope you're able to take advantage of the features and key capabilities covered in this book to successfully implement and support your SAP Sales Cloud solution.

Appendix A
Machine Learning in SAP Sales Cloud

This book would be incomplete without a discussion of the machine learning capabilities added to SAP Sales Cloud starting with release number 1711. *Machine learning* is the process of searching for patterns in data sets. The goal of machine learning is to make predictions using these patterns. Though the machine learning concept was first introduced in 1959, the practical application of machine learning is a recent event, due to the following reasons:

- Data
  Large sets of data (structured, unstructured, and streaming) are created across applications (in cloud, on-premise, and third-party). It is now easier to find patterns by analyzing these data sources via machine learning algorithms.

- Computing power
  With massive improvements in hardware performance and computational power, it is now much easier to process and analyze huge amounts of data.

- Algorithms
  Access to a wide variety of best-in-class supervised and deep learning algorithms further enable us to define enterprise machine learning models.

Machine learning and artificial intelligence are redefining the landscape of enterprise computing and end user experience. SAP is extending its SAP Leonardo solution to SAP Sales Cloud to enable businesses to transform how they engage with customers, innovate how they do business, and simplify their front office landscape. SAP Sales Cloud is embedded with machine learning capabilities, which help better leverage customer information, analyze behaviors, and interactions as well as structured and unstructured data to transform front office scenarios into truly intelligent experiences for business users and end customers.

Enabling machine learning in any enterprise application involves three steps: input, machine learning, and output (as shown in Figure A.1).

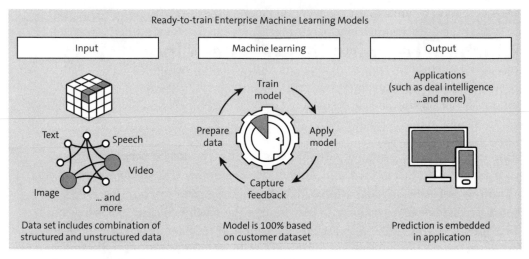

Figure A.1 Example of Machine Learning Model

In the first step, structured and unstructured datasets (text, speech, video, images, and etc.) are fed through the machine learning model. In the second step, we leverage machine learning through an interactive closed loop process (such as prepare date, train model, apply model, and capture feedback). The model is 100% based on customer dataset. The output from the model application can be embedded in various end user scenarios and enterprise applications like SAP Sales Cloud.

SAP Leonardo Machine Learning provides the foundation and tools used to enable artificial intelligence and machine learning into SAP applications. With this background in machine learning, let's review the machine learning scenarios included in SAP Sales Cloud at the time of publication: deal intelligence, lead intelligence, and account intelligence.

A.1   Deal Intelligence

It is estimated that only 40% of forecasted opportunities actually close. High volumes of low propensity opportunities mostly inflate pipelines for most sales managers. *Deal scoring* leverages machine learning scoring algorithms to help sales managers focus on opportunities with the highest probability of closure and to deprioritize ones with high risk. It improves win rates and helps sales managers achieve quota targets by focusing on deals with high likelihood to close. You may accelerate sales execution by understanding key influencer signals for each stage of a deal and then aligning the sales team's efforts on highly scored deals with this information. Using machine learning scoring algorithms, sales managers can better prioritize their most important opportunities. Opportunity diagnostic features such as opportunity score, activity score, deal status, key risks, and others enable sales managers to evaluate what's going on with each opportunity.

A.2   Lead Intelligence

Lead intelligence helps businesses search external data sources to create tailored list of prospects. Lead scoring focuses on the leads with the highest propensity of becoming customers. SAP C/4HANA predictive lead scoring will be a shared predictive service based on data from both SAP Marketing Cloud and SAP Sales Cloud. Customers can benefit a single common lead score across marketing and sales funnels instead of having separate models that are siloed that don't look at the full spectrum. Customers don't have to wait to implement both solutions to make use of the predictive lead scoring capabilities. They can start even if they have either set of data–be it marketing leads or sales leads.

A.3   Account Intelligence

With *account intelligence*, you can gauge the health of your accounts and use insights to engage in account-based selling and nurturing. Use scoring generated from hundreds of internal and external data sources to improve conversion rates and focus on top-of-the-funnel prioritization. Account insights help to target business-to-business accounts with the highest propensity to buy/close while maximizing lifetime value. Lead contact scoring alone does not give full picture of an account. We don't get the real-time intent and engagement metrics at an account-level just from lead intelligence. Account intelligence offers better account-based targeting that's consistent with account planning as it provides a 360-degree-view of account both from internal and external data sources. This helps us achieve improved customer lifetime value and satisfaction.

Machine learning is one of the key areas where more and more capabilities will be added to SAP Sales Cloud in future releases.

Appendix B
The Authors

Sanjjeev K. Singh is a managing partner at ASAR America, Inc. and a former SAP America client partner. For the past 17 years he has helped customers implement SAP Cloud for Customer, SAP Commerce Cloud, SAP CRM and SAP ERP Sales and Distribution. He has been involved in many large scale SAP implementation projects. He is extremely passionate about helping customers develop their roadmap and implement customer engagement solutions using the SAP C/4HANA product portfolio. In his current role, he leads the SAP C/4HANA practice at ASAR America Inc., a SAP C/4HANA services partner.

Karan Sood is a key driver of innovation and is the head of product management and user experience for SAP Sales Cloud and SAP Service Cloud. He is a business and technology executive in the software industry with more than two decades of experience in the CRM space. He has held global leadership positions in product management and strategy, business development, solution management, consulting, and general management for CRM software solutions. He has an extensive track record of exploring emerging technologies and launching new disruptive products from the ground up and making them commercially successful. Karan holds a bachelor's degree in electronics engineering, a master's degree in business administration, and completed an executive program on artificial intelligence from the MIT Sloan School of Management.

Index

Interested in reading more?

Please visit our website for all new book
and e-book releases from SAP PRESS.

www.sap-press.com